The Cambridge Companion to
Modern Indian Culture

India is changing at a rapid pace as it continues to move from its
colonial past to its globalized future. This *Companion* offers a
framework for understanding that change, and how modern cultural
forms have emerged out of very different histories and traditions.
The book provides accounts of literature, theatre, film, modern and
popular art, music, television and food; it also explores in detail social
divisions, customs, communications and daily life. In a series of
engaging, erudite and occasionally moving essays, the contributors,
drawn from a variety of disciplines, examine not merely what
constitutes modern Indian culture, but also just how wide-ranging are
the cultures that persist in the regions of India. This volume will help
the reader to understand the continuities and fissures within Indian
culture and some of the conflicts arising from them. Throughout,
what comes to the fore is the extraordinary richness and diversity of
modern Indian culture.

Vasudha Dalmia is Professor of Hindi and Modern South Asian Studies
at the University of California, Berkeley.

Rashmi Sadana is a writer and researcher based in Delhi. She was
previously Visiting Assistant Professor in the Department of
Humanities and Social Sciences at the Indian Institute of Technology,
Delhi.

The Cambridge Companion to
Modern Indian Culture

Edited by
VASUDHA DALMIA
and
RASHMI SADANA

CAMBRIDGE
UNIVERSITY PRESS

CAMBRIDGE UNIVERSITY PRESS
Cambridge, New York, Melbourne, Madrid, Cape Town,
Singapore, São Paulo, Delhi, Mexico City

Cambridge University Press
The Edinburgh Building, Cambridge CB2 8RU, UK

Published in the United States of America by
Cambridge University Press, New York

www.cambridge.org
Information on this title: www.cambridge.org/9780521736183

First published 2012

Printed in the United Kingdom at the University Press, Cambridge

A catalogue record for this publication is available from the British Library

Library of Congress Cataloging-in-Publication Data

The Cambridge companion to modern Indian culture / edited by Vasudha Dalmia and
Rashmi Sadana.
    p.   cm. – (Cambridge companions to culture)
   Includes bibliographical references and index.
   ISBN 978-0-521-51625-9 (Hardback) – ISBN 978-0-521-73618-3 (Paperback)
1. India–Civilization–1765–1947.   2. India–Civilization–1947–   3. India–Intellectual life.
4. India–Social conditions.   5. Social change–India.   6. Regionalism–India.
I. Dalmia, Vasudha, 1947–   II. Sadana, Rashmi, 1969–
   DS423.C27 2012
   954.05–dc23
                                                                                    2011042623

ISBN 978-0-521-51625-9 Hardback
ISBN 978-0-521-73618-3 Paperback

Contents

Illustrations

Maps

Contributors

AMITA BAVISKAR, Institute of Economic Growth, Delhi

STUART BLACKBURN, School of Oriental and African Studies, University of London

SUPRIYA CHAUDHURI, Jadavpur University, Kolkata

VASUDHA DALMIA, University of California, Berkeley

DEBJANI GANGULY, Center for Cross Cultural Research, Australian National University, Canberra

ANN GRODZINS GOLD, Syracuse University, New York

AMRITA IBRAHIM, Johns Hopkins University

CHRISTOPHE JAFFRELOT, Centre d'étude et de recherches internationales (CERI); Sciences Po/Centre national de la recherche scientifique (CNRS)

KAJRI JAIN, University of Toronto

SONAL KHULLAR, University of Washington, Seattle

RASHMI SADANA, independent scholar

SMRITI SRINIVAS, University of California, Davis

RAVI VASUDEVAN, Centre for the Study of Developing Societies, Delhi

AMANDA WEIDMAN, Bryn Mawr College

Chronology

The Brahmanical tradition and the Vedic period

The Brahmanical tradition dates from the Vedic period (roughly 1500 to 600 BCE), when the sacred Hindu texts known as the *Vedas* were first composed. This period becomes a critical reference point for many Indian modernists, revivalists and nationalists in the nineteenth and twentieth centuries who, in the face of British colonialism, hark back to 'tradition' in order to help define a modern India. Despite the coeval influences of Buddhism, Jainism, *bhakti* devotional traditions, and later, of Islam and Sufi traditions, Indian 'tradition' in the modern period is almost exclusively focused on Hindu texts and mythologies dating from the Vedic period.

3000–1500 BCE	Period when the Indus Valley civilization, one of the world's oldest, arose and flourished.
second millenium BCE	The so-called Aryan migrations occur – that is, migrations into the Indian subcontinent of people speaking an Indo-European language.
1500–1200 BCE	The *Rig Veda*, or first book of the *Vedas*, is composed.
900–500 BCE	The later *Vedas*, the *Brahmanas* and the early *Upanishads* are composed.
500 BCE – 500 ACE	Hindu law books (e.g., *The Laws of Manu*) and epics (e.g., the *Ramayana* and the *Mahabharata*, of which the *Bhagavad-Gita* is a part) are composed, and the six orthodox systems of philosophy are developed.

| 326 BCE | Alexander leads incursions across the Punjab until his army faces stiff opposition, followed by his retreat and withdrawal from India in 324 BCE. |
| 268–233 BCE | Height of the Maurya empire under the reign of Ashoka. A propagator of Buddhist-inspired morality, Ashoka is known for having accepted the principle of non-violence and denouncing caste. |

Classical and medieval India

320–647	Reign of successive emperors of the Gupta dynasty. The Gupta age is known for both its religious and social tolerance and its renewal of Brahmanical orthodoxy. It is also a period of great literary, scientific and cultural production. The poet Kalidasa writes the play *Shakuntala* and poem *Meghaduta* in this period; the cave paintings of Ajanta in western India come from this period, as does the calculation of the value of 'pi' (3.141) by the mathematician and philosopher Aryabhatta.
405–11	The Chinese scholar Fa-Hsien travels to India and writes of the Buddhist culture that he finds there.
Sixth century	Development by Shaivite (the Nayanars) and Vaishnavite (the Alwars) saints in Tamil Nadu of *bhakti* worship, which calls Brahmanism into question and celebrates the direct communion of devotee and God; rise of the Pallavas in South India.
Sixth to Seventh centuries	Rise of multiple kingdoms including Harsha of Kanauj (606–47) and Pulakeshin II of Badami (609–42).
711	Arabs conquer Sind.
mid eighth century	Founding of the Rashtrakuta dynasty; overthrow of Chalukyas.
871–907	Aditya I defeats the Pallavas, founds the Chola dynasty.

985–1016	Rajarajachola founds the Chola empire of South India. The Cholas further economic and cultural exchange between southern India and south-east Asia.
999–1026	Mahmūd of Ghazni raids palaces and temples in north-western India, in large part to finance his imperial ambitions in Central Asia.
1017	The Islamic scholar Alberuni is sent by the Sultan Mahmud of Persia to India to learn about 'the Hindus'. He stays in India for thirteen years and writes *Tarikh al-Hind* ('History of India'), which is part travelogue, part discussion of Hindu belief systems and ways of life.
1206–1526	The period of the Delhi Sultanate, when political power became centralized under a series of Muslim rulers, most of whom were Turkish.
c. 1250	Sun Temple of Konorak in Orissa.
1293	Marco Polo in South India.
1346–1565	Vijayanagara, Hindu kingdom of South India.
1469	Birth of Guru Nānak, founder of Sikhism.
1498	Vasco de Gama in Calicut.
1510	The Portuguese conquer Goa.

The Mughal Empire and the English East India Company

Indian modernity is often correlated with the arrival of the British and the cultural and economic changes that ensued during the colonial period; however, the dates in this subsection will suggest that modernity is a process with no fixed start date. European colonization developed in fits and starts, and the decline of Mughal sovereignty was also gradual.

1526	The Mughal Empire is founded when Babur, a descendant of Timur (or Tamerlane), defeats Ibrahim Lodi, the last Delhi Sultan, at the battle of Panipat.
1600	Queen Elizabeth I grants a charter to the English East India Company for trade with the East Indies.
1605	Accession of Jahangir to the Mughal throne.
1619	The English East India Company obtains permission from Emperor Jahangir to trade in India.

1628	Accession of Shah Jahan to the Mughal throne. Builds the Taj Mahal in Agra and the Red Fort in Delhi during his reign.
1639	Madras is founded, as Fort St George, by the English East India Company.
1651	Foundation of the English East India Company's first factory, at Hugli in Bengal.
1657	Shah Jahan falls ill and a fraternal struggle for succession to the Mughal throne begins.
1658	Aurangzeb, third son of Shah Jahan, imprisons his father, takes the throne.
1668	Bombay is ceded to the English East India Company.
1690	Calcutta is founded by the English East India Company.
1707	Death of Aurangzeb, which marks the beginning of the decline of the Mughal Empire.
eighteenth century	During this period Mughal power becomes decentralized, and Hindu and Muslim revenue farmers as well as Hindu and Jain merchants and bankers gain in economic power. The Mughal emperor is still recognized as the legitimate ruler of India, and Muslim civil servants and Hindu scribes skilled in Persian are still the mainstays of administrative structures, but political power shifts from the centre towards regional rulers, small potentates and even Hindu rajas of local villages.
1757	The English East India Company defeats Nawab Siraj-ud-daula of Bengal at the battle of Plassey. The British take political control of Bengal.
1765	The right to collect revenue (*diwani*) in Bengal is ceded to the British.
1770	Bengal famine; one-third of the population dies.
1799	Final defeat and death of Tipu Sultan, who as the ruler of Mysore Kingdom fought multiple incursions by the English East India Company.
1793	The Permanent Settlement gives *zamindars* (landholders) private property rights and holds them responsible for collecting revenue from *raiyats* (peasant cultivators) in perpetuity and remitting those revenues to the colonial state.

Nineteenth-century social and religious reform

Major themes of this period are British colonial governance in India, the rise of English-speaking Indian intellectuals in Bengal, the influence and importance of Brahmanism, Muslim and Hindu identity formation, and the changing role and position of women.

1803	The British take Delhi after repelling fierce resistance from the Marathas – warriors from dominant peasant castes whose power and influence had spread since the seventeenth century over much of the Deccan region of western and central India. The British gain political dominion over Gujarat (in western India), aided by their alliance with Hindu merchants.
1813	The British Parliament lifts a ban on allowing Christian missionaries into India. Entry is permitted under a new system of licensing.
1815–30	Rammohun Roy emerges as a key figure in social reform movements and religious controversies in Calcutta. Many will come to consider him the 'father of modern India'.
1818	The British overthrow the Marathas and assert their dominance over western and central India.
1829	*Sati*, widow immolation on the funeral pyre of the husband, is officially abolished by the colonial government in India. Brahmo Sabha is founded by Rammohun Roy as a group devoted to theism and universality.
1833	Britain outlaws slavery, infanticide and human sacrifice in India. Rammohun Roy dies in Bristol, England.
1835	Thomas B. Macaulay presents his 'Minute on Indian Education' to Lord William Bentinck, Governor-General of India. The British colonial government subsequently introduces English education for Indians, and English replaces Persian as the language of the British colonial higher administration in India, marking the defeat of the Orientalists by the Anglicists.
1843	Brahmo Samaj is founded by Debendranath Tagore, who institutionalizes the ideology of Hindu reform started by

	Rammohun Roy's Brahmo Sahba. Vedanta is accepted as the authentic scriptural source of Hinduism.
1853	The first railway and telegraph are established in India.
1857	On the night of 10 May, Indian soldiers of the XI Native Cavalry based in Meerut rise up after having witnessed their fellow soldiers being taken away in chains for refusing to load their rifles with cartridges rumoured to be greased with pork and beef fat. This anti-British campaign, which comes to be called the Mutiny or Rebellion of 1857, spreads across India and lasts for over a year, causing much bloodshed. The British quell the rebellion in 1858. The Emperor, Bahadur Shah II, is exiled to Burma, and his sons and grandson are killed by a British military officer, exterminating the Mughal line.
1858	In response to the 1857 uprising, the British Crown abolishes the English East India Company and assumes direct rule, appointing a Viceroy of India.
1859	Syed Ahmad Khan publishes 'Asbab-e-baghawat-e-Hind' ('Causes of the Revolt'); it is translated into English in 1873. This document catapults Khan on to centre stage in public debates about religious and social reforms as he speaks for Muslims in India.
1868	Rassundari Debi, a Bengali woman, completes her autobiography, *Amar Jiban* ('My Life'), the first work of its kind. An expanded version is issued in 1897.
1875	Swami Dayananda founds the Arya Samaj, a Hindu religious reform movement calling for rejection of ritual and idolatry and a return to purity and simplicity through adherence to the *Vedas*.
1877	Syed Ahmad Khan founds the Mohammedan Anglo-Oriental College at Aligarh, later known as the Aligarh Muslim University, to foster the education of Muslims in particular.
	Queen Victoria proclaims herself Empress of India.
1885	The Indian National Congress is founded in Bombay, with the intention of creating a dialogue with the British colonial government and gaining more rights for Indians under colonial laws.
1888–91	Mohandas K. Gandhi studies law in London.

| 1893 | Swami Vivekananda receives great acclaim at the World Parliament of Religions held in Chicago, at which he represents Hinduism. |
| 1893–1914 | Gandhi works in South Africa as a lawyer and activist for the rights of Indians there. He employs ideas of *satyagraha* (non-violent protest) for the first time. |

Twentieth-century nationalist movement

Major themes of this period include the rise of competing Indian nationalisms, the anti-colonial struggle, Hindu nationalism, the Muslim Question and the call for a separate Muslim state, independence from Britain and the Partition of 1947.

1905	Bengal is partitioned by the British into two new presidencies, one of which has a Muslim majority. In protest, Indians begin to boycott British-made cloth and other imported goods, launching the *swadeshi* ('one's own country') movement.
1906	The Muslim League is founded, with the purpose of protecting the political rights of Muslims.
1907	The Indian National Congress is split between moderates, who believe in constitutional principles and seek reform, and extremists, who favour active opposition to British rule, including the boycott of British goods and services, and in some cases, violence.
1908	Gandhi's *Hind Swaraj* ('Indian Home Rule') is published.
1909	The British institute the Morley-Minto Reforms, which increase Indian membership on advisory legislative councils and introduce a separate electorate for Muslims.
1911	The Bengal Partition is revoked by the British.
1911	Hindu Mahasabha, a Hindu nationalist party critical of the secular Indian National Congress, founded.
1912	The capital of British colonial India is moved from Calcutta to Delhi.
1913	Rabindranath Tagore is awarded the Nobel Prize in literature.
1913	Dadasaheb Phalke's *Raja Harishchandra*, India's first silent film, is shown commercially.

1919	The Rowlatt Acts (or the Anarchical and Revolutionary Crimes Act) are instituted in February by the British colonial government (based on a 1918 report by Justice S. A. T. Rowlatt). It allows for Indians suspected of sedition to be imprisoned without trial and is seen as an affront to Indian civil liberties. It fuels widespread protest.
1919	The Amritsar Massacre is committed on 13 April, when General Reginald Dwyer orders British and Gurkha soldiers to open fire on a mass gathering of Indians in Jallianwala Bagh, an enclosed park in Amritsar, killing 379 men, women and children, and injuring 1,200.
	The anti-British Khilafat Movement is launched by Indian Muslims in support of the Turkish Sultan and Caliph, spiritual leader of the world Muslim community, whose position is threatened by the dissolution of the Ottoman Empire by Britain and its allies. In an attempt to forge unity between Hindus and Muslims in India, Gandhi strongly supports the Khilafat Movement.
	Gandhi leads an India-wide protest against the Rowlatt Acts.
1924	The Khilafat Movement ends as the Muslim Caliphate in Turkey is abolished.
1928	Hindu nationalist ideologue Vinayak Damodar Sarvarkar (1883–1966) publishes *Hindutva: Who is a Hindu.*
1930	Muhammad Iqbal (1873–1938) gives the Presidential Address at the All-India Muslim League session in Allahabad. Working towards a federalist solution to the communal problem, he emphasizes the need for specifically Muslim interests to be part of the political sphere in order for Muslims to reap the benefits of their numerical majorities in certain Indian provinces.
1930	Gandhi's 'Salt March' (12 March–5 April). Along with seventy-eight followers from the Sabarmati Ashram and many more who join along the way, Gandhi marches 241 miles to Dandi, where he breaks the law by picking up a natural lump of salt at the sea shore. Gandhi gains worldwide fame after this event, with photos appearing in *Life* magazine, among other publications.
1931	India's first sound film, *Alam Ara*, in Hindi-Urdu is released.

1932	Iqbal delivers a second Presidential Address to the Muslim League.
1935	The Government of India Act is passed, providing for limited home rule, with continued British control over foreign policy and defence.
1940	The Lahore Resolution, calling for a separate Muslim state, is ratified by the Muslim League. It is inspired by the Presidential Address to the League session in Lahore delivered by M. A. Jinnah (1876–1948).
1942	The 'Quit India' Movement is launched by the Indian National Congress, advocating mass civil disobedience and an immediate end to British rule in India. Britain outlaws the Congress.
1943	The Bengal Famine causes the death of over 3 million people.
1945	Britain concedes the necessity of granting Indian independence and advocates formation of an interim government.
1946	General elections are held, and the Congress Party and Muslim League emerge as dominant parties. Attempts to form an interim government fail. Muslim–Hindu violence breaks out.

Partition, Independence and beyond

1947	In June, the Congress Party and Muslim League agree to the partition of India. In July, the British Parliament passes the Indian Independence Act, providing for two independent dominions to be created, to be known as India and Pakistan. Pakistan gains independence on 14 August, with M. A. Jinnah as the nation's Governor-General. India gains independence on 15 August, with Jawaharlal Nehru as the nation's first Prime Minister. On 29 August Dalit leader B. R. Ambedkar becomes chair of the newly set up Drafting Committee of the Constitution of India.
1948	Gandhi is assassinated by a Hindu extremist in Delhi.

Jinnah dies.

Ceylon gains full independence from the British.

India and Pakistan go to war over disputed territory in Kashmir.

1949   The Awami League is established to campaign for East Pakistan's autonomy from West Pakistan.

1950   The Indian Constitution goes into effect.

1951   Ambedkar establishes Milind College in Aurangabad, deliberately choosing one of the most impoverished and neglected areas of Marathi-speaking western India.

1952   India's first general election is held.

1955   Bandung Conference of 'non-aligned' Afro-Asian states.

1956   Indian states are reorganized along linguistic lines.

On 14 October Ambedkar, along with many other low-caste Hindus, converts to Buddhism in a massive ceremony in Nagpur.

1958   General Muhammed Ayub Khan takes power in Pakistan.

1961   The Dowry Prohibition Act is passed, authorizing penalties for demanding, giving or accepting dowry.

1962   India and China go to war over a border dispute in the remote area of Aksai Chin; India is defeated.

1964   Nehru dies.

1965   War breaks out once again between Pakistan and India over Kashmir.

1966–76   The Green Revolution in agricultural techniques commences, which over the next decade greatly increases India's food production.

1966   Indira Gandhi, daughter of Jawaharlal Nehru, becomes Prime Minister of India.

1970   The Awami League, under Sheikh Mujibur Rahman, wins an overwhelming election victory in East Pakistan. The government in West Pakistan refuses to recognize the results, leading to rioting.

1971   East Pakistan secedes from Pakistan and declares itself the new, independent nation of Bangladesh. India goes to war with Pakistan to help the Bangladeshi cause.

1974   The National Committee on the Status of Women in India publishes its report, highlighting women's work

	and the invisibility of most women's contributions to household incomes.
1975–77	'Emergency' is declared by Prime Minister Indira Gandhi after she is found guilty of illegal campaign practices. Democratic rights are suspended and leaders of the political opposition are jailed.
1977	Indira Gandhi and the Congress Party lose elections. A Janata Party coalition leads India. General Mohammad Zia ul-Haq takes power in Pakistan.
1980	The Congress Party wins elections and once again Indira Gandhi becomes Prime Minister.
1981	Salman Rushdie's *Midnight's Children* is published and wins the Booker Prize.
1983	The Indian Penal Code is amended, with the aim of better addressing 'dowry deaths' and domestic violence; the Criminal Laws Amendment Act, section 498A, makes cruelty to a wife a cognizable offence (that is, police are obliged to take action once a complaint has been registered) that is also non-bailable.
1984	Indira Gandhi is assassinated by her Sikh bodyguards in retaliation for having launched Operation Blue Star, the storming of the Golden Temple in Amritsar. Her assassination ignites riots all over Delhi in which thousands of Sikhs are targeted and killed. Her son, Rajiv Gandhi, becomes Prime Minister. In December, a gas leak at a Union Carbide pesticides plant in Bhopal kills thousands immediately, and many more subsequently die or are left disabled.
1985	The court case of Shah Bano, a Muslim woman and mother of five whose husband refused to pay her maintenance after divorcing her, sparks intense national debates over the merits of women's rights (seen as being protected by a uniform civil code) versus minority rights (as followed in 'personal laws' set by each religious group within the Indian polis).
1987	On 4 September Roop Kanwar, a convent-educated 17-year-old Rajput widow, commits *sati* (she immolates herself on her husband's funeral pyre), launching a series

of national debates and protests regarding women's rights.

1990   In August the Mandal Commission issues its report recommending that 50 per cent of government jobs and education be reserved to the castes officially classified as 'backward'. In response, there are several riots and self-immolations by middle- and upper-middle-class students in many cities, who fear they will lose employment and educational opportunities soon to be reserved for others.

1991   Reforms are instituted in India leading to economic liberalization, the intensification of consumer culture and a new prominence of the ill-defined but ever-expanding middle class.

1991   Rajiv Gandhi is assassinated by a suicide bomber sympathetic to the Sri Lankan separatist group, the Liberation Tigers of Tamil Eelam (LTTE).

1992   On 6 December, Babri Masjid (Babur Mosque) in Ayodhya is demolished by Hindu nationalist volunteers (*kar sevaks*) bent on clearing the way for the construction of a Hindu temple on the site of the mosque, which they believe is the sacred birthplace of Lord Ram.

1992   The government of India sets up a National Commission for Women (following the National Commission for Women in India Act No. 20, 1990) to review the constitutional and legal safeguards for women and recommend remedial legislative measures, facilitate redress of grievances and advise the government on all policy matters affecting women.

1993   A third of all seats in village councils (*panchayats*) are reserved for women.

1997   Arundhati Roy's *The God of Small Things* is published and wins the Booker Prize.

1998   On 11 May India begins a series of five nuclear tests at the Pokhran test site in Rajasthan.

1999   A third of all seats in state legislatures and the Parliament are reserved for women.

2002   From February to June riots erupt in the state of Gujarat between Hindus and Muslims after the Godhra train incident, leading to a massacre of Muslims.

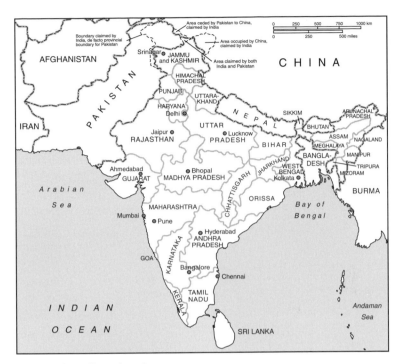

Map 1 The Indian subcontinent.

RASHMI SADANA AND VASUDHA DALMIA

Introduction

On 25 February 2008 a group of student activists, accompanied by a camera crew, charged into the office of the head of the history department at Delhi University demanding that a particular text be removed from the syllabus of an undergraduate course on ancient Indian history. The activists belonged to the Akhil Bharatiya Vidyarthi Parishad (ABVP), part of a larger Hindu-nationalist group of organizations known as the Sangh Parivar. The text in question was A. K. Ramanujan's 'Three Hundred *Ramayanas*: Five Examples and Three Thoughts on Translation', an essay that documents the array of tellings of Valmiki's great Sanskrit epic, *The Ramayana*. By detailing five of these alternative *Ramayanas*, the essay brings to life different interpretations of characters and alternative narratives of the epic itself. Ramanujan (1929–93) was a translator, poet and scholar who for many years taught at the University of Chicago. In the essay in question, he writes with genuine reverence of how the 'number of *Ramayanas* and the range of their influence in South and Southeast Asia over the past twenty-five hundred years or more are astonishing'. He goes on to list the numerous languages in which the Rama story can be found, including Balinese, Bengali, Cambodian, Chinese, Gujarati, Javanese, Kannada, Kashmiri, Laotian, Malaysian, Marathi, Oriya, Prakrit, Sanskrit, Sinhalese, Tamil, Telugu, Thai and Tibetan –

> Through the centuries, some of these languages have hosted more than one telling of the Rama story. Sanskrit alone contains some twenty-five or more tellings belonging to various narrative genres (epics, *kavyas* or ornate poetic compositions, *puranas* or old mythological stories, and so forth). If we add plays, dance-dramas, and other performances, in both the classical and folk traditions, the number of Ramayanas grows even larger. To these must be

added sculpture and bas-reliefs, mask plays,
puppet plays and shadow plays. . .
   In these versions the story is told differently from one of the earliest
and most prestigious of them all: Valmiki's Sanskrit *Ramanyana*.[1]

The ABVP activists, in various retellings of that day at Delhi University, were said to have vandalized the department head's office and roughed up the head of department himself. They objected vehemently to the documentation of other *Ramayanas*, arguing that it was an insult to Hindu gods and goddesses. There was one cultural tradition and story, and any other would tarnish the Hindu cultural tradition and identity, they said. The essay was 'offensive to the beliefs of millions of Hindus', one activist proclaimed. Another likened the other tellings of the epic to nasty rumours. It was clear that the activists thought that students at Delhi University should not be reading about the existence of these other *Ramayanas*, even if, gathered together, they are far more numerous and, arguably, influential than Valmiki's *Ramayana*.

Students from the afflicted history department, some faculty members and many others from the university joined in a march the following day to protest what had happened. Hundreds chanted slogans such as 'Campus Chor Do' ('Leave the Campus Alone'), held signs denouncing the ABVP's actions and called for the campus to be 'a free and democratic space', open to the discussion of all ideas. At the end of the march, a professor from the history department addressed the crowd, pointing out that the article in question was in fact arguing just how popular Valmiki's *Ramayana* was since it is a text that has been adapted by so many Indians and others, thereby suggesting Ramanujan's essay was about the spread of Hindu culture rather than an insult to it. The crux of the debate then was about the nature of culture itself, its boundaries and definitions. Are there many incarnations, and hence, interpretations of a cultural tradition, and if there are, does this dilute or diminish people's identities?

In the following days, the ABVP installed a tent at the main gate of Delhi University. People walked by and sometimes went into the tent to discuss what had happened. In the end, the ABVP found itself in the minority; its view was unacceptable to the campus majority. Nevertheless, the issue re-surfaced in October 2011 when the Academic Council of Delhi University, against the advice of the history department, decided to remove Ramanujan's essay from the BA history course syllabus. Ramanujan's essay meanwhile was sent around on numerous email lists, and links to the article were prominent on several blogs. Columnists and bloggers shared their experiences growing up with one alternative version of the *Ramayana* or another from one end of India to the other. *Outlook*, an Indian weekly news magazine in English, reprinted part of the essay. The discourse grew. And the divide between 'secularists', or 'pseudo-secularists' (as their detractors call them), and those who believe they are defending Hindu culture and identity by patrolling its religious and literary borders, arguably remained unchanged. Controversies such as this one occur often, especially over films, but also over literature and other cultural forms. They are part and parcel of India's 'culture wars'. And they have become part of the grammar of political debate, rallying points for parties and groups. The secularists are often but not always the English-language educated, living in 'the metros', as the large Indian cities of Delhi, Mumbai, Chennai, Bangalore, Hyderabad and Kolkata are called. They are seen to be arrogant and out of touch with the concerns of the majority of Indians, but they often wield the reins of cultural influence and power.

This story offers an entrée into the question of not merely what constitutes modern Indian culture, but how overwhelming a task it is to try and represent even a small fraction of the plethora of cultural forms and variants that have occurred in the geographical space – with its numerous regional specificities – of the modern national entity known as India. This India was an idea, a 'wager' as Sunil Khilnani calls it, put forth by the Indian nationalist elite: 'For all its magnificent antiquity, and historical depth, contemporary India is unequivocally a creation of the modern world. The fundamental agencies and ideas of modernity – European colonial expansion, the state, nationalism, democracy, economic development – all have shaped it.'[2]

In our reading and rendering of 'modern Indian culture', we have had to make a number of demarcations, first in regard to focusing on the *modern* Indian nation-state, which before the 1947 partitioning of the Indian subcontinent into the nation-states of India and Pakistan, was a bigger geographic and cultural entity, mostly under British colonial rule. Thus, with regard to the period before partition we deal with the Indian subcontinent at large and after partition with the Indian nation-state. And even of the Indian nation-state, we cover only sections. What emerges in this volume in terms of regional specificity, then, is less by design and more by the area of focus of the particular set of scholars who responded to our invitation to participate in this volume.

If the first demarcation is about space, the second, not surprisingly, is about time. Many scholars see the 1757 Battle of Plassey as the beginning of British rule in India, yet most of the cultural formations we consider emerge from the early nineteenth century onwards. In fact, there are many transitions from the Mughal period to the beginnings of British commercial, political and cultural influence from the late eighteenth century on (first through the English East India Company and then in the form of direct Crown rule after the 1857–8 uprising), spanning at least three centuries. Thus the beginnings of what we see as modernity can be set yet further back in time, well into the late fifteenth and sixteenth centuries; nevertheless the colonial encounter clearly hastened the process already underway, leading to the polarization we know today as 'modernity' and its apparent opposite, 'tradition'. As many of the cultural productions discussed in this volume show, modernity and tradition create and reinforce each other. Ranajit Guha captures the dynamic nature of their interaction in 'Dominance without Hegemony and its Historiography', his classic essay which includes a discussion of the interplay of what he sees as three cultural idioms.[3] One of these idioms derives from the metropolitan political culture of the colonizer, in this case, typically British; the second derives from the pre-colonial tradition of the colonized, that is, from the Indian. Since, as Guha has convincingly shown, colonial rule never achieved absolute hegemony, the indigenous Indian idiom always retained more than a measure of autonomy. The two idioms overlapped, crossed or subverted each other, in order to flow and coalesce in the third idiom, which was the modern Indian. This third idiom could be a replica neither of the Western nor of the ancient Indian it so often invoked. Instead, the constituent elements formed a new compound, 'a new and original entity'.[4] The third idiom as it emerged in a given context often carried signs of struggle and unresolved tensions.

This notion of the third idiom allows us to break down the tradition/modern polarity, and see it not only as a distinction between the indigenous and the alien, but also as part of the self-representation of those who sought to depict their tradition as being defiantly resistant to change. It further allows us to understand those who sought to transcend tradition altogether. The three idioms themselves are to be regarded as heuristic devices rather than rigidly demarcated entities, since there was incessant change and exchange between the first two idioms at all times.

The third set of demarcations we had to make for this volume concerns the cultural formations included in our selection. We do not claim to offer a comprehensive or even partial survey of the various elements and forms that might constitute modern Indian culture. What we do aim to offer, in each chapter and in the way the chapters relate to one another, is a historical understanding of what different strands of modernity have come to signify, and how various cultural forms have been taken up and become harbingers of those modern strands. Our goal in the essays that follow, then, is to provide an entry point into topics in modern Indian culture from a variety of perspectives and approaches, and in doing so, to focus on the analysis of parts rather than surveys of wholes. Some authors use a case-study approach, others survey a particular time period, while still others offer a combination of overview and the analysis of particular cultural productions in more detail.

Some of the stories we want to tell have to do with the ways in which political power translated into cultural power under British rule, and the cultural tensions that arose in emergent Indian modernities from the nineteenth century onwards, sometimes formulated in terms of seemingly simple questions regarding what was 'ours' and what was 'theirs'. We have been interested not only in how these questions became more pressing during the nationalist movement, but also why they have remained acute even after Indian independence. For the search for 'Indian' idioms has persisted, whether in regional or national contexts, through popular, folk and urban formations, and with or without the involvement of the state.

In the first part of the book, 'Cultural contexts', each contributor provides the backdrop for a topic central to modern Indian life: caste politics, tribal identity, the changing village, the relationship between agrarian change and the cultures of food, and new forms of religiosity in the changing urban landscape. In the broadest sense, this section aims to deal with the experience of modernity; how modern ideas and practices become constitutive of politics and social life; specifically how people live and think about themselves in the so-called peripheries as much as in the centres. One could argue that the most relevant divide in India today is the one between urban and rural livelihoods and perspectives, and yet they are also continually intersecting. This topic was explored in the popular Hindi film, *Peepli Live* (2010), which in the context of farmer suicides gives a satirical portrait of how English and Hindi television journalists exploit rural Indians. Tellingly, the film is not about the causes of poverty, but rather the political shenanigans of our media age, where a farmer's potential suicide turns into a spectacle.

To start off, Ann Gold offers a *longue durée* perspective on village life from her years of fieldwork in Rajasthan in order to understand how modern goods and technologies intersect with rural ways of life. At stake here, as she shows, are people's values and ethics; the biggest conflict may not in fact be an urban–rural, but rather an inter-generational one.

Part of the imagination of the rural is the 'tribe' or 'tribal'. A good 8 per cent of India's population consists of tribal groups, scattered over various parts of the subcontinent, but found most densely concentrated in central India and in the north-east. Stuart Blackburn's chapter shows how, when faced with the pressure to accede to dominant cultural forms, language and religion can be utilized in order to express identity in the ongoing tussle with modernity. Meanwhile, Amita Baviskar shows just how interlinked the urban and rural are through her discussion of food production, distribution and changing eating habits of the rural as well as urban consuming classes.

Peripheries exist not only out there, but right in the heart of the metropolis. Smriti Srinivas's chapter on urban change in Bangalore highlights changing forms and sites for religious worship for newly marginalized groups co-existing with the globalized world of charismatic guru figures such as Sai Baba. We are reminded of the fact that 'Hinduism' is composed of sects and strains, and how religious practice and organization is not static but changes to adapt to new environments. Finally, Christophe Jaffrelot traces the nature of modern caste identities by focusing upon low-caste social movements from the nineteenth century to the present. This political history is vital to understanding the emergence of Dalit politics in contemporary India and the cultural form of the 'life history' as analysed by Debjani Ganguly later in the volume. These disparate contexts – not exhaustive but representative – become the larger backdrop for a range of cultural forms. The larger question in each chapter in Part I is about social mobility and the nature of change itself; what are the mechanisms, political and cultural, by which this might occur for the most disadvantaged in society?

The second part of the book considers specific forms of cultural production: literature, art, theatre, music, film and television. The section begins with three chapters on literature and in particular the novel, in an effort to offer diachronic as well as synchronic depth. The Bengali intelligentsia of the second half of the nineteenth century pioneered the novel as the new genre to register and herald social and cultural change. Supriya Chaudhuri's detailed narrative of modern

Bengali literature – Bankim, Tagore, Sharat, among others – documents the modernist enterprise with its touchstones of gender, class and nation formation from the nineteenth century onwards. In a parallel narrative on the English language, Rashmi Sadana shows how it goes from being a marginal presence and vexed symbol of colonial modernity to becoming central to the articulation of urban elite experience and India's entry on to the world stage of literature. English has become not only the subcontinent's window to the world but also, more controversially, its face to the world. And yet, the story of English in India is also becoming increasingly reflective of larger trends within the country, as evidenced in Sadana's discussion of the popularity of Chetan Bhagat. Debjani Ganguly's chapter, focusing on three Dalit life-writing narratives from three different regions of the subcontinent, offers insight into one of the most dynamic literary landscapes of modern India, as Dalits seek to wrest power from the dominant media and literary establishments to represent the violence and suffering of their existence themselves.

In another juxtaposition, the chapters by Sonal Khullar and Kajri Jain take up elite and popular manifestations of art. By focusing on the work of three major modern artists, Khullar shows how each one of them identified a national tradition that could serve as the ground of modernism, and indeed, a post-colonial identity in twentieth-century India, whether by taking recourse to the wall paintings of Ajanta and the miniature painting of the Rajput and Mughal courts, the crafts practices and performing arts of the subcontinent, or the visual forms and print culture of the bazaar. Their engagements with cultural production associated with pre-colonial, folk or marginal practices and life-worlds would become the hallmark of modernism in twentieth-century India. As Jain shows, from the late nineteenth century onwards, new technologies from the West introduced mass reproduction and commodification, known today as calendar or bazaar art, allowing images to become more mobile and thus circulate in an arena delinked from the territorial and symbolic control of temples and courts. These newly commercialized images then became available to the various projects of identity formation that came to characterize Indian modernity – projects of nation, region, sect, caste and language, as well as the political and ideological projects of not only the nascent nation-state but also of a resurgent Hindu nationalism. The ruthless adaptation of 'Western' and the locally prevalent Indian by popular mass media, guided entirely by the uses to which they could be put, stands in sharp contrast to the almost painful awareness of 'ours' and 'theirs' as it found expression in elite art forms.

A similar impulse drove the theatre makers of modern India, from at least the 1940s on, to search for the 'folk' idiom in theatre as a mark of the traditions specific to the Indian subcontinent. Vasudha Dalmia's chapter traces the process over the last century, showing how the cultural and social impulse which propelled playwrights and directors as well as cultural policy makers could veer off into widely divergent political directions, into the left as in the 1940s and again in the 1970s, as much as into the radical right wing in the 1980s and 1990s, as successive Hindu-nationalist governments occupied the seat of power at the centre.

Being 'Indian' could impose restrictions as much as open up new avenues for the newly articulated 'classical' arts of India. Amanda Weidman's chapter focuses on south India and the discourses that emerged around classical and film music from the 1940s to the 1960s, with their competing notions of authenticity. Weidman examines how the genre called Karnatic classical music crystallized through the standardization of repertoire and concert format, and how it was disseminated through All India Radio. Not surprisingly, classical music was widely regarded as an authentically Indian realm, while film music came to be seen as hybrid, illegitimate and imitative of the West. Film music, however, would also come to be valued positively as a kind of music that could keep pace with and represent India as a modern nation.

Rather than try and offer a survey of the massive film industry in India, the chapter on cinema in our volume seeks to provide an entry point into the particular kind of spectacle that is the Bombay film and its particular mode of addressing spectators. As Ravi Vasudevan points out, all of India's cinemas were involved in constructing a certain abstraction of national identity, not only the pan-Indian one, but also regional constructions of national identity. Bombay crystallized as the key centre for the production of film at the precise moment that the new state came into existence, so its construction of the national narrative carried a particular force. Vasudevan focuses on issues that resonate with many other chapters in the volume – how the ideology of the 'traditional' is constituted in cinematic narration; the function of cinematic techniques of subjectivity in the construction of narrative space; and finally, how the overall representational field of the popular film system addresses the spectator.

Our volume concludes with a chapter by Amrita Ibrahim on reality television and the creation of a fictional wedding in a 2009 series about a starlet transformed into a demure bride. The show becomes a voyeuristic fantasy of the great Indian wedding as it encapsulates the unresolved tension between the traditional demeanour of the bride in an extended family and the demands of a modernized television audience. Private television production has come to be constituted, as all other forms discussed in this volume, by a process of citation from familiar genres and cultural artefacts, drawing on motifs from much-loved Hindi films, soap operas and narratives around marriage and family. The key to the show discussed by Ibrahim lay in turning a controversial, overtly sexual, Hindi film star into a respectable and decent bride-to-be, making her 'marriage' a family affair, suitable for all ages.

Cultural struggles, tensions and sometimes wars – on numerous predictable and some not so predictable fronts – are ongoing in modern India. We hope that this volume will help the reader understand multiple facets of culture in India and some of the conflicts arising from them.

Notes

1 A. K. Ramanujan, 'Three Hundred *Ramayanas*: Five Examples and Three Thoughts on Translation', in Paula Richman (ed.), *Many Ramayanas: The Diversity of a Narrative Tradition in South Asia* (Berkeley: University of California Press, 1991), pp. 24–5.
2 Sunil Khilnani, *The Idea of India* (London: Penguin, 1998), p. 5.
3 Ranajit Guha, 'Dominance without Hegemony and its Historiography', *Subaltern Studies*, ed. Ranajit Guha, vol. vi (New Delhi: Oxford University Press, 1989).
4 *Ibid.*, p. 271.

Part I

Cultural contexts

1
———

Scenes of rural change

A large majority of India's population – 72 per cent according to the 2001 census – live at least partially rural lives and derive a significant portion of their income from agriculture. Some village residents migrate seasonally or occasionally for urban employment, and significant numbers of village households have family members already located, permanently or temporarily, in urban areas. Rural-to-urban migration trends are ongoing, but demographic shifts have not been as dramatically rapid as some had predicted.[1] While global flows and urban cultures seem to epitomize the twenty-first century, rural life remains of vital significance to understanding Indian modernity.[2] Tremendous changes have continuously affected India's rural spaces from the agrarian revolutions of the 1960s to the communications revolutions of the present. These changes permeate every aspect of life from domestic relations to cropping patterns; entertainment choices to employment opportunities; social and gender hierarchies to political formations. Government development projects as well as a multitude of non-governmental organizations concerned with improving agricultural productivity, primary education, adult literacy, health care, gender equity and environmental sustainability – to mention only a few major foci of ongoing interventions – are at work modernizing rural India.[3]

To survey all such manifestations of change, or to outline comprehensively the concrete, quantifiable elements of rural modernity is not possible in one chapter. Here, drawing on ethnographic fieldwork, I focus on people's perceptions of and responses to change as they experience it. Specifically, I aim to highlight the ways that residents of one small region in central Rajasthan have described to me transformations which they understand to be both material and moral. This focus on the experiential is not only about livelihoods and corporal existence, but also internal dispositions and interpersonal relationships. Other research from other regions, to which I shall occasionally refer, corroborates as widespread many if not all of these reactions to, and assessments of, change. If rural Rajasthanis view the connected forces of modernity as overwhelming – as a sweeping flood or an irresistible wind – they also see themselves moving with the currents, neither drowning nor blown away but surely transported. It is these perceptions of dynamic change that I seek to explore.[4]

At this chapter's core and heart are transcribed texts of interviews conducted in 1997, 2003 and 2007. During these fieldwork periods, often with the assistance of Bhoju Ram Gujar, a government school headmaster with whom I have worked closely since 1980, I sought out people mostly in their mid forties or older who had experienced tremendous change and vividly remembered living under very different conditions. Through these interviews we were able to elicit articulate contrasts between past and present. In 2007 we also asked some younger people about the impact of new communications technologies on their lives.

Modernity in the village and the village in modernity

Modernity has many dimensions: from modes of production to modes of thought. In rural South Asia, modernity may be located in systematized agricultural practices or in socio-economic conditions, including the availability of new objects of desire: consumer goods and the power to purchase them. Modernity is also calibrated to morality and to emotions, affecting not just what people have in their homes or pockets but in their souls and hearts. Modernity is about things such as telephones and tractors, but it is also about feelings such as conjugal love, charity, ambition, jealousy. All such aspects of change are complexly interconnected.

About a quarter-century ago, envisioning what might constitute a 'new theory of modernization', Milton Singer offered suggestions still curiously timely today. Two key elements Singer proposed are particularly germane to this chapter. Singer's propositions also help us come to terms with Indian sociologist Satish Deshpande's more recent question, 'Why has the conceptual pursuit of modernization been so debilitating?'[5] Singer considered that a new theory would necessarily 'go beyond the "traditional versus modern" dichotomy'.[6] Singer's approach would 'look at the process of modernization as envisaged by those engaged in it, in their cultural categories, world view, and value system, as well as in the objective evidence of behavior'.[7] Recent ethnographic projects focused on rural development and more recently globalization have provided rich descriptions of the diverse ways modernization is perceived and understood by those experiencing it.[8] These shifts have also been the subject of evocative literary representations.

Many studies of change in rural areas begin sensibly enough with a focus on objects: those novel, visible, tangible trappings that signal a new era. M. N. Srinivas noted in his 1962 essay on changing values in what was *already* modernizing village India, that, 'The desire for gadgetry is fast becoming a feature of all sections of Indian society including the poor in rural areas.'[9] In the early 1980s, when I first worked in a Rajasthani village, many women there had watches tattooed around their wrists. Women, whose working days and ritual lives were closely connected to biological and seasonal rhythms, had little need to check the time; they liked the look of watches. Yet many yearned for functional timepieces, offering to pay me cash to purchase and bring back for them working watches from America.

Two decades later, when studying goddess shrines, I encountered displays of multiple wall and table clocks that had been offered to gorgeously adorned stone goddesses. Keeping time was no more the point at goddess shrines than on village women's tattooed wrists, for no one bothered to change the batteries of clock offerings. Yet tattooed watches and clock offerings are linked as objects of desire, recalling the 'desire for gadgetry' noted by Srinivas as a sign of modernity – in this case, a desired modernity in which deities participate.

More than watches or clocks, big machines – tractors, pumps and generators – may appear to have the greatest material and psychological impact on people's lives. Such technologies transform agricultural practices and are also symbolically weighted. In the mid twentieth century, the progressive Indian English writer, Mulk Raj Anand, portrayed the advent of such 'monstrosities' in several stories about village life. In one of these stories, 'The Tractor and the Corn Goddess', the narrator describes a group of awestruck farmers as they confront a tractor for the first time: 'the peasants gathered from all sides, chased the tractor, some shouting, some just staring, some whispering to each other, all aghast with wonder or fear at this new monstrosity which had appeared in their lives and which threatened to do something to them, they knew not what'.[10] Literary merit aside, this description says more about urban views of villagers and rural life than about rural realities.

As noted earlier, village people sometimes represent modernity's forceful assault on their lives as an irresistible wind or a river in full flood. Such metaphors certainly imply a sense of surrender to the new, a sense of lack of choice. But this is not the same as paralysis or ignorance. I would characterize rural people's reactions to the many-faceted changes in their worlds as sifting, selecting and above all continuously, self-consciously, appraising both what is gained and what is lost. They often simultaneously embrace opportunities for altered lives – in the realms of technology, education, consumer goods – while critiquing and at times resisting associated social and cultural consequences.

The social sciences have long been preoccupied with the transformation from (moral) subsistence economy to (amoral) market economy and its associations with the transformation from need to desire or longing.[11] Intertwined material and moral changes form the core of modernity, as is clearly articulated by Rajasthani villagers. In interviews from the 1990s, for example, a number of older people with whom I spoke pointed neither to watches nor to tractors as emblems of change, but to soap. The use of soap is a marker of change, close to the body, transforming the body's odours. To bathe with soap was to be modern, long before the arrival of TV and mobile phones. If not readily affordable, it was at least more affordable than watches. And not everyone embraced it.

A carpenter I talked with in 1993 spoke of soap as a costly thing inviting jealousy and planting seeds of discord among neighbours. 'People are envious of one another … Like, we see that he washes with soap, he washes his clothes with soap, and we feel envy, and try to do the same. But you have money and I don't, so I get even poorer [from spending money on soap].'[12] A feisty old widow, however, told me with characteristic vehemence, 'I don't like using soap, the same way I don't like poison for food.'[13]

These two statements reveal the potential polarities of desire and revulsion for the trappings of modernity and convey something of the intense affect surrounding them.[14] To follow D. P. Gaonkar, modernity is 'an attitude of questioning the present', and it is through 'creative adaptation' that people make themselves modern and 'give themselves an identity and a destiny'.[15]

Lightweight times: appraisals of the present in and around Ghatiyali

What I know about the experience of rural modernity is based on nearly three decades of intermittent research as a cultural anthropologist in one small area of Rajasthan. Ghatiyali village, where most of my field-work was based, is located near the centre of Rajasthan in the geograph-ical region known, after its major river, as the Banas Basin. In the years preceding India's Independence and Rajasthan's slightly later incorporation into the new Indian republic, Ghatiyali was part of a twenty-seven-village kingdom named after its capital, Sawar. While Sawar had at one time been attached to the pre-eminent princely state of Mewar, by the early twentieth century it had come under direct British rule from Ajmer. People here have memories of the double rule and double taxation of local kings and remote colonizers and have a heart-felt appreciation for present-day economic conditions.[16]

The Banas Basin supports a mixed agricultural–pastoral economy. Ghatiyali is a large and diverse village with over twenty-five *jatis* or caste communities, spanning the Hindu social hierarchy and including Muslims and Jains. Farming, gardening and herding are primary occu-pations for the majority of village residents. Though subject to periodic drought followed by bursts of out-migration (as in all of Rajasthan), in good monsoon years Ghatiyali is a relatively prosperous place – as the gradual transformation of its houses from mud to stone and its shrines from open-air platforms to domed temples amply testifies.

In 1993 and 1997 Bhoju and I gathered oral histories of environ-mental change in which discourses of morality were embedded. It was then that we started to ask questions about the past versus the present, querying the difference between *u taim* (that time) and *ajkal* (nowadays). From responses to these questions rural views of modernity emerged.[17] In 2003 a different research project specifically targeted transform-ations in agricultural praxis surrounding seeds, but conversations about seed-saving also often played out as contrasts between then and now. That same year, I undertook comparative work in Karnataka, research which has provided contrasting material. In 2007 we interviewed people in and around the rural market town of Jahazpur (twenty-eight kilometres down country roads from Ghatiyali with a population of approximately 20,000). We posed the same broad questions about the past and the present but also included specific enquiries about mobile phones.

In an era of rapidly accelerating change, our interviews dating from more than one fieldwork period themselves reveal some subtle shifts. However, by and large the late twentieth-century critique of the present remains recognizable in the twenty-first century. Most of the people Bhoju and I interviewed were men and women from the middle-caste farming communities – Gujar, Mali, Lodha. But our interlocutors also included Brahmins, artisans, leather workers and others. While I found general agreement on the nature of present circumstances among adults, responses to these circumstances could vary considerably according to age, gender, community and source of livelihood. But all, without exception, ascribed moral deterioration to the present, seeing it as a time of declining religion, virtue, community (aspects of *dharma*) as well as love (*prem*). With these declines came a corresponding ascent of egotism.[18] Problematic moral behaviours include a decline in courteous behaviour and respect within families; less neighbourliness; less sense of community; more violence perpetuated by humans against other living beings, both human and non-human. Desire itself has increased, and this leads to vexed moralities in multiple ways and at multiple levels.[19] A number of people interviewed describe the present as *kamzor* (weak) or *halki*, literally 'lightweight', but implying inferior, trashy or shallow.

The same people have already, and by and large willingly, adapted and adjusted to much that has been transformed or is transforming, from clothing styles to agricultural technology to entertainment. I did not encounter a single individual without a strong view that these changes are not only all-encompassing but irreversible. Where I observed partial change, village residents would speak of total revolution. For example, persons frequently stated, 'Nobody ploughs with oxen any more.' This is not true even today, yet many were proclaiming it so in 1993. There are indeed far fewer oxen than there once were, and more tractors. Villagers' blanket statements suggest that they perceive change as total and anticipate, before the fact, that previous modes of existence have become obsolete.

Open-ended interview strategies are not easily moulded according to linear logics. In citing passages from especially evocative conversations, I do not necessarily present changes chronologically. Nonetheless, if tea and soap were among the first inroads of a global market economy, mobile phones are evidently the latest. One long interview from 1997 features a herder woman's take on changing times. Mangi Mali was probably in her mid sixties at the time we spoke with her. We encountered her in the company of a group of child herders whose work she loosely supervised. She jokingly called herself their '*Mar-sa*', the local word for schoolteacher (from the British 'Master'). Mangi spoke volubly about women's work in the old times:

> We knew that when the rooster crowed it was time to get up and grind five kilograms of flour, milk the animals, pile up the cow dung, roll the bread, and make the vegetables. And then we would tie our children on our backs and go to the fields to do irrigation work.
> [*Agricultural work varies considerably with the seasons; Mangi chooses for her generic account of women's work in the old days a task notorious as the most backbreaking of all labour required of women in the fields.*]
>   In the evening we would put the rope and the leather water buckets on our heads and bring them home.
> [*I interrupted to ask why, and the explanation was 'fear of thieves'. On reflection, this offers one small but perhaps telling contradiction to the golden vision of the good old days that she proceeds to present.*]
>   Then we would put down the child and tie up the animals, milk them, cook dinner, feed the children, eat our own meals and it would be midnight.
>   We didn't even know about tea. If we were cold we would make *karhi* [thickened, spiced buttermilk] from barley flour and drinking that would make us feel well. But these days, until afternoon comes, we are waiting for our tea.
> [*In other words, anticipating it eagerly as I admit I always did myself. Mangi opposes store-bought tea to karhi which is made from buttermilk, the by-product of churning creamy yogurt to make clarified butter or ghee. Buttermilk itself is symbolic of old times, of hospitality, and of an explicitly non-market economy. I was told many times, especially by Gujars, that it was totally improper, sinful in fact, ever to sell buttermilk. On the contrary, neighbours could freely ask one another for it. In recent years, though, I have heard sharp criticism of some people who continue to request free buttermilk.*]
>   In the old days women did so much work and still they were very healthy but today's women do no work and still they are weak. They are weak because they drink tap water and eat electrically milled flour. Women used to eat barley bread; first they pounded it with the pestle, and then they ground it and ate it. That's why they were so strong. Also, they drank well water. In the old days, mostly they ate barley, and white wheat.
> [*Mangi seamlessly moves to a description of ritual.*]

> After harvesting they used to thresh the grain with oxen and
> everyone would gather and wait for an auspicious time, and then they
> would do *puja* and light incense. They would take some grain and
> make a circle around the big pile, and then they would wait for
> the jackals to howl and then they would start winnowing; it used
> to take one or one-and-a-half months.
> [*The howling of jackals had the power to override any astrological obstacle,
> a convenience for farmers in the days when wildlife were plentiful.*[20]]

Bhoju asked, 'But today do people look for an auspicious time?' Mangi
answered:

> No! not at all. Today they get a tractor and 'slap-bang let's go!' ...
> This is why the times are so weak (*jamana kamjor*). Today people don't
> have as much love; if you are eating and I am sitting here hungry
> I will not ask, 'Have you eaten or not?' I will eat and leave.
>   But it used to be that we would all sit together and eat together
> and help each other, it used to be that way, but not today!
>   People used to be more satisfied but today they are not satisfied,
> and so they will fight and quarrel over any matter; that is the kind of
> times (*jamana*) that have come. The times have become lightweight
> (*halka*), and people are weak (*log kamjor*).
> [*In Mangi's discourse adjectives seem readily transposable between people and
> conditions that both reflect and causally constitute one another.*]
>   People have started drinking a lot of liquor, and because of
> drinking they fight, and that's another reason there is no love ...
> There used to be love between your family [*addressing Bhoju*] and the
> Malis; our fields are next to each other and we used to call each other
> on festival days, but today there is no memory, no one remembers one
> another ... It used to be people would consult each other, take each
> other's opinions and then work together, but today people don't
> even like to look at one another.
>   One reason is that the population has increased too much, and so
> there isn't so much love.

Bhoju asked, 'Besides that, why is rain less these days?' Mangi answered
without hesitation, 'Sin has spread over human hearts' (*manako ke dil
mem pap cha gaya*).

Mangi shares with others of her generation a sense of an increase in
sinful behaviour, and its relation to climate change on the one hand
and loss of community on the other. Tea, a colonial legacy that has
penetrated society and altered the rhythms and bodily cravings of a

working day, is a common token of these changes; it was, I suspect, along with soap, one of the first widely desired necessities of life that had to be obtained from outside, with cash. Modern times – unsavoury and light-weight – are directly linked to drought conditions and the displeasure of the gods. Mangi's perspective shows multiple dimensions in the moral ecology of change. I turn now to flavour as another indicator.

Winter is brinjal season, and talk about modern brinjal's lack of tastiness carried with it a subtle but perceptible moral evaluation. I had many conversations in January 2003 about two species of brinjal, one readily visible and one largely invisible. The latter scarce item is 'deshi' brinjal, literally 'of the land'; implying local and indigenous. Deshi brinjals are whitish in colour, and the vine on which they grow has annoying thorns on it, but everyone with whom I spoke asserted this variety to be the most delicious. Yet the widely prevalent species nowadays is called 'disko': it is small, shapely, perfectly purple, its stem free of unpleasant prickles, but people say it lacks taste. Disko is not only easier to cultivate but also sells better.

Barji Mali, a gardener woman, was among several people who told us, 'There used to be local brinjal (deshi bangan). We used to grow it, but now we have modern (adhunik) brinjal, called "disko." Now, disko is available.' Shambhu Nath, an educated villager in his forties who has worked with me on and off over the years, immediately chimed in to emphasize a contrast in flavour: 'The local brinjal was tasty, but it had prickles on it. It was really delicious, but the disko has no flavour. Even today, the local is available in the market but it costs more than disko.' He then gave an elaborate recipe for what he said was the best way to cook deshi – stuffed with spices after roasting. Nostalgia for the tasty past is invested in the white variety which has shifted from staple to luxury, and is now presumably cultivated by a few for sale to the well-to-do in town markets rather than village lanes.

This contrast between the pervasive, modern shiny, purple, attractive disko and the indigenous variety – white, prickly, flavourful but no longer consumed – captures much about nostalgia for a past that people do not necessarily strive to reclaim. Pleasures such as the taste of white brinjal, roasted and spiced as Shambhu recalled it, are missed but deemed irretrievable.

I am struck by an obvious symbolism in the disko/deshi contrast and the psychology of loss it evokes. Tasteless modernity is perfectly embodied in the shiny purple tasteless brinjal, named after an emblem of urban amorality – disco dancing. The word *disko* had entered village language in the 1980s, long before television was widespread. Women's songs contrasted the allure of mixed gender dancing, referred to as 'disko', with the traditional Rajasthani women's dances performed solo, with fully veiled faces, and in gender-segregated company. In writing on women's songs, I observed elsewhere that, 'Uneducated females married to educated boys fear their husbands will go astray in the world of modern transportation and foreign "dancing" . . . the Westernized "disco" scene of which villagers are aware from media images.'[21]

As many scholars of memory have told us, the past is readily evoked by flavours and other sensory modalities including scent, sound and touch.[22] The irrevocable loss of a particular taste experience – whether it is comforting barley gruel or delectable white brinjal – stands for much larger losses. Indigenous varieties of grain, also no longer cultivated, trigger highly emotional responses.[23] Yet, those who repeatedly lament the cherished tastes of yesteryears seem oddly willing to allow them to vanish from their lives. In this region, awareness of species loss has not translated into any organized protest against the marketing of commercially produced seeds, or even any strong urge to save old plant varieties.

In other rural regions, more influenced by urban markets and environmental activists, however, such campaigns are effectively at work. For example, in targeted areas near the south Indian city of Bangalore – famous for its information technology companies, call centres and generally accelerating prosperity – multiple NGOs have raised consciousness about biodiversity issues and the use of indigenous seeds versus commercial agricultural products. In January 2003 I visited several seed banks in rural Karnataka, just a few hours from thriving Bangalore, and I met men and women farmers who were excited and enthusiastic about the many kinds of native seeds they were saving and swapping. They spoke about *bij jatras* (seed pilgrimages) and *bij melas* (seed fairs), activities that involve, respectively, gathering seed varieties from village to village, and creating opportunities for exchange of indigenous grain and vegetable varieties. In general, from brief interviews (either with English-speaking farmers accustomed to visitors, or through an interpreter of Kannada to English), what I gathered was a fervent commitment to return to traditional seeds and the practices, both practical and ritual, associated with them. All the farmers I met in Karnataka, however, had been influenced by environmental activists associated with the Green Foundation, the organization which had facilitated my visit.[24]

Back in Rajasthan in February 2003, Barji Mali spoke about the convenience of commercial seeds in spite of her critique of the flavour of '*disko*' brinjal:

> Now we get them all: white radish, spinach, we get them all from the bazaar; small, big, they are all available whether you need a little or a lot. They sell them with a picture on the packet, on each bag; and from that you know what kind of seed it is; we could produce them ourselves if we wanted to, but we don't need to worry because we know we can get them in the bazaar. Whatever we need we can get them and nothing is mixed with them.

Thus, as an accomplished and successful produce-gardener, she lauded the modern convenience of commercial seed packets even if, earlier in the same interview, she had expressed preference for the flavour of a local variety. These changes from home-saved to market-purchased seeds have had far-reaching gendered consequences as well as consequences for biodiversity. Women's work is reduced, and Barji appears to appreciate this in spite of some negative ramifications for the evaluation of women's contributions to agriculture and gardening.

Ladu Lodha, a farmer in Ghatiyali famous for his agricultural skills and dedication, along with his political wisdom as a respected member of the village council, described for us clearly in 2003 the implications for gendered work in the change from saved seeds to purchased seeds:

> Women would protect them [seeds]. They would mix them with ashes and store them so bugs could not attack them. That's why they mixed them with ashes. But nowadays the government has sent pills, medicines to use instead ...
>
> [In the old days] women did it. When it began to rain [and was time to plant], they would say, 'This is chickpea, this is lentil', and so they would give advice: 'Put this here and plant this here.' They would have collected all the seeds for one season's crops. But today, direct from the bag, no mixing with ash, no work of women protecting; there is no work left for women.
>
> Cucumber, watermelon, summer squash, green beans, bottle-gourd, white gourd-melon ... all kinds of seeds: now they all come from the store. But in the past women stored all the seeds at home; and before the rainy season, they would gather them all; if they were missing any they would collect them from their

neighbours. Women were the ones who kept seeds, formerly.
Now every seed comes in a bag!

The change in seed source from home to market also means less reliance on a community, on helpful neighbours. When I asked, 'So you think the modern way is good?' Ladu immediately responded, 'Yes it is good, there is no difficulty.'

The important role women once played, which involved selecting seeds while crops were still standing, gathering, storing and protecting those seeds in the home, and bringing them to the fields for planting the next season, has now more or less disappeared without fanfare. Activists, meanwhile, deplore such transformations. Vandana Shiva's influential writings, for example, strongly valorize the time-honoured associations between women and seeds.[25] But in Ghatiyali neither men nor women seem bothered by the switch to commercial products. This contrasts with many of the other changes that, as I have shown, village people code as morally negative.

Farmers' evaluations of modern times and things are never blanket judgments, nor are they always congruent with urban activist views of ideal village traditions. In October 2009 India's regulatory authority for transgenic crops gave an 'in-principle approval for the commercial cultivation of Bt Brinjal' which – if cleared by the environment minister – would be the first 'genetically modified edible item' legalized for commercial cultivation.[26] Controversy continues to swirl around this decision and it appears that, as with packaged seeds, at least some farmers are more eager for change than are urban activists.

Conversations about mobile phones in spring and summer of 2007 in Rajasthan offer a final and revealing example of ambivalent attitudes towards modern technological incursions. I present here a series of responses extracted from four interviews with men ranging in age from their early thirties to mid sixties.

Ram Svarup Chipa, at age 65, is a full-time farmer who lives in Jahazpur town. He offered me a purely negative assessment of mobile technology on moral grounds:

> The mobile spoils much. I think it is misused. We used to sit and talk with one another, but now talking costs money. Today's women want to be independent, and so do the children. The boys and girls are out of control: they meet outside – I'm sorry, Madam, forgive me, but it is true. Our culture is changing, all things are changing, and it is all harmful, nothing about it is good.

This man, although a town resident, made his living solely as a farmer. He sees no good whatsoever in the new technologies around him. However, others belonging to younger generations, with whom Bhoju spoke, found value as well as moral disorder in the impact of new media and communication opportunities.

A 34-year-old Meena man, also an agriculturalist, noted some benefits of mobile phones, but elaborated far more on their damaging impact, together with the impact of television:

> There is nothing so wonderful [about mobiles]. Well, if I have any emergency, the mobile is very convenient. But today's new generation have all been spoiled because of this mobile. Thanks to the mobile, boys and girls are able to get into mischief. There are more crimes because of both mobile and TV ... TV and mobile are spoiling our culture, the biggest responsibility lies with TV and mobile – because of these, social ills are spreading in our society. In the old times, when there was no TV and no mobile, our children couldn't make contact – well, maybe sometimes at a fair or a funeral feast – but now: how easily they can make contact due to mobiles! They decide everything on the mobile: where to go, which way to go, which bus. Before there was no method of communication, and no transportation but now there are taxis, there are buses, running every twenty minutes in every direction!

An image of the terrifying ease with which younger people are now able to plan and execute elopements strikes fear in the hearts of many parents. But this speaker did not fail to acknowledge at the outset the assistance mobile communication indisputably affords, and so do many others.

A similarly ambivalent vision gripped a Muslim teacher from Maganpura, a small and remote village far from the main roads:

> When the mobile came, it was like a big revolution [*kranti*] for our society ... As many good uses as there are, there is even more misuse. If we look in our village, we see the benefits and the harms. Boys and girls meet with each other, they run off, they take the money from the house, and they are running. In the past, before mobiles, if they went to one another's houses you would see them but now they can plan and nobody sees them and that is worse. They can set the time, location, all those things, and their parents won't know. This is the worst thing for villages. One will say, 'I am going to Indore', and one says, 'I am going somewhere else', and no one knows where they are *really* going.

He thus articulates not only the opportunity for youth to communicate, but the insidious ease with which they can now deceive their parents.

Bhoju asked another teacher at Maganpura school, also in his thirties, about the impact of mobile phones. His response was somewhat rambling, and included an acknowledgment of usefulness, but he concluded with the spectre of inter-caste elopement:

> And inter-caste connections [that is, elopements] are all arranged with mobiles. In the past, there was only one chance to meet – at festivals and social functions. But now they can make contact anywhere. The mobile is bad for all these things: love-and-affection, good behaviour, they are all finished.

While there is no doubt that twenty-first-century gadgetry is considerably more intrusive than were wristwatches, it is notable that the 'bad behaviour' of the young and the decline of valued social bonds were also prominent themes in earlier critiques of modernity. In terms of popular assessments of change, it appears that the exact nature of specific, innovative objects may matter less than the values they have come to represent.

Conclusion

Cultural performances offer additional responses to rural change, and in concluding I present just one example. Women's songs often comment creatively on new aspects of domesticity, putting unsettled feelings to the tune of traditional melodies.[27] In 2007 I asked my Gujar friends if they knew any songs about telephones. What I was looking for in truth were songs about how mobile communications had made an impact on human relationships, especially romantic relationships – as I had heard so much about this phenomenon. However, what I recorded from young women in their late teens and early twenties was a sweet song imagining telephones put to religious use:

> Install telephones in all the temples,
> Then through those phones
> we'll hear the sound of hymns.
> Come, come to me, my dearest husband,
> we'll hear the sound of hymns.[28]

These lyrics reflect an emotional configuration uniting two themes I have observed in Rajasthani women's songs for three decades, expressing two separate yearnings of young married women whose movements are restricted in their in-laws' homes. A woman longs for her husband's company and she longs for the freedom, often denied to her by strict in-laws, to participate in pilgrimage and temple worship. Besides the telephone, the only thing new about this song is that it unites both kinds of longing, usually confined to separate genres (songs about gods and songs about feelings).

I recorded this along with many other devotional songs at a gathering of Gujar women belonging to two generations at a home where there were three unmarried, school-going daughters (ages 14–20). The educated girls, easily distinguished from married teens of the same age by their dress and behaviour, joined in for only a few songs, including the telephone song. For chunks of the evening they retreated beyond the edge of the circle of singers, to pore over homework in the dim light while their married peers quite happily went on singing. The school-going girls did not leave the courtyard but remained in the company of the others, even if outside the circle.

Modernity in multiple manifestations is omnipresent in rural settings. Elements of change (educated girls, imported technologies) may be analytically isolated as new. But in everyday life these are inevitably experienced and incorporated through pre-existing lenses and practices that we might call tradition, with the understanding that tradition itself is always evolving. Especially striking to me in modernity's tale as envisaged in village Rajasthan, a tale reflecting deep rural sensibilities, are the causal juxtapositions in which inner and outer worlds – morality and climate change; human relationships and the foods sustaining human life; souls and bodies; hearts and machines – are so very closely linked. These interpenetrating causalities invite contemplation as relevant to present circumstances for all of us.

Notes

1 Rakesh Mohan, 'Urbanization in India: Patterns and Emerging Policy Issues', in Sujata Patel and Kushal Deb (eds.), *Urban Studies* (New Delhi: Oxford University Press, 2006), pp. 59–80.
2 For the receding of the rural, see Ashis Nandy, *An Ambiguous Journey to the City: The Village and Other Ruins of the Self in the Indian Imagination* (New Delhi: Oxford University Press, 2001); for cogent arguments to keep villages in view, see Diane Mines and Nicolas Yazgi (eds.), *Village Matters: Relocating Villages in the Contemporary Anthropology of India* (Delhi: Oxford University Press, 2010).

3 Two recent panoramic works on changing rural India squarely focused on development and globalization respectively are Barbara Harriss-White and S. Janakarajan (eds.), *Rural India Facing the 21st Century: Essays on Long Term Village Change and Recent Development Policy* (London: Anthem Press, 2004) and G. Bhaskar and A. V. Reddy Vinayak (eds.), *Rural Transformation in India: The Impact of Globalisation* (New Delhi: New Century Publications, 2005).

4 For wind, see Sally Steindorf, 'Walking Against the Wind: Negotiating Television and Modernity in Rural Rajasthan', unpublished Ph.D. dissertation, Department of Anthropology, Syracuse University, 2007. For floods, see Ann Grodzins Gold, 'New Light in the House: Schooling Girls in Rural North India', in D. P. Mines and S. Lamb (eds.), *Everyday Life in South Asia* (Bloomington: Indiana University Press, 2002), p. 89.

5 Satish Deshpande, 'Modernization', in Veena Das (ed.), *The Oxford India Companion to Sociology and Social Anthropology*, vol. 1 (New Delhi: Oxford University Press, 2003), p. 76.

6 Milton Singer, *When a Great Tradition Modernizes* (New York: Praeger, 1972), p. 384.

7 *Ibid.*

8 See for example, Dia Mohan Da Costa, *Development Dramas: Reimagining Rural Political Action in Postcolonial Eastern India* (New Delhi: Routledge, 2009); Akhil Gupta, *Postcolonial Developments: Agriculture in the Making of Modern India* (Durham, NC: Duke University Press, 1998); A. R. Vasavi, *Harbingers of Rain: Land and Life in South India* (New Delhi: Oxford University Press, 1999); Susan S. Wadley, 'The Village in 1998', in *Behind Mud Walls: Seventy-five Years in a North Indian Village* (Berkeley: University of California Press, 2000), pp. 319–38.

9 M. N. Srinivas, *On Living in a Revolution and Other Essays* (New Delhi: Oxford University Press, 1992), p. 112.

10 Mulk Raj Anand, *Selected Short Stories of Mulk Raj Anand*, ed. M. K. Naik (New Delhi: Arnold-Heinemann, 1977), p. 187.

11 See Ronald J. Herring, 'Contesting the "Great Transformation": Local Struggles with the Market in South India', in James C. Scott and Nina Bhatt (eds.), *Agrarian Studies: Synthetic Work at the Cutting Edge* (New Haven: Yale University Press, 2001), pp. 235–63; see also J. Parry and M. Bloch (eds.), *Money and the Morality of Exchange* (Cambridge University Press, 1989); Marshall Sahlins, *Culture in Practice: Selected Essays* (New York: Zone Books, 2000), pp. 527–83.

12 Ann Grodzins Gold, 'Sin and Rain: Moral Ecology in Rural North India', in Lance Nelson (ed.), *Purifying the Earthly Body of God: Religion and Ecology in Hindu India* (Albany: State University of New York Press, 1998), pp. 165–95.

13 Ann Grodzins Gold and Bhoju Ram Gujar, *In the Time of Trees and Sorrows: Nature, Power, and Memory in Rajasthan* (Durham, NC: Duke University Press, 2002), p. 195.

14 See Da Costa, *Development Dramas*, for a brilliant discussion of encounters with a similarly complex appraisal she encountered in rural Bengal on the subject of bio-medicine versus traditional methods for healing snake bites.

15 Dilip Parameshwar Gaonkar, 'On Alternative Modernities', in Dilip Parameshwar Gaonkar (ed.), *Alternative Modernities* (Durham, NC: Duke University Press, 2001), pp. 13, 18.

16 Gold and Gujar, *In the Time.*

17 *Ibid.*, pp. 277–323.

18 Ann Grodzins Gold, 'Love's Cup, Love's Thorn, Love's End: The Language of *Prem* in Ghatiyali', in Francesca Orsini (ed.), *Love in South Asia: A Cultural History* (Cambridge University Press, 2006), pp. 303–30.

19 Ann Grodzins Gold, 'Tasteless Profits and Vexed Moralities: Assessments of the Present in Rural Rajasthan', *Journal of the Royal Anthropological Institute* 15 (2009), pp. 365–85.

20 Ann Grodzins Gold, 'Abandoned Rituals: Knowledge, Time, and Rhetorics of Modernity in Rural India', in N. K. Singhi and Rajendra Joshi (eds.), *Religion, Ritual and Royalty* (Jaipur: Rawat Publications, 1999), 262–75.

21 Gold, 'New Light', pp. 89–90.

22 C. N. Seremetakis, *The Senses Still: Perception and Memory as Material Culture in Modernity* (University of Chicago Press, 1996); David E. Sutton, *Remembrance of Repasts: An Anthropology of Food and Memory* (London: Berg Publications, 2001).

23 Gold, 'Tasteless Profits and Vexed Moralities'.

24 See Vanaja Ramprasad, Krishna Prasad and Gowri Gopinath, 'The Synergy of Culture and Spirituality Enhances Biodiversity', in B. Haverkort and W. Hiemstra (eds.), *Food for Thought: Ancient Visions and New Experiments of Rural People* (London: Zed Books, 1999), pp. 71–86.

25 See Vandana Shiva, 'Seed Satyagraha: A Movement for Farmers' Rights and Freedoms in a World of Intellectual Property Rights, Globalized Agriculture and Biotechnology', in B. Tokar (ed.), *Redesigning Life: The Worldwide Challenge to Genetic Engineering* (London: Zed Books, 2001), pp. 351–60.

26 *Indian Express*. 'Govt panel clears Bt Brinjal for entry as first GM food.' www.indianexpress.com/news/govt-panel-clears-bt-brinjal-for-entry-as-first-gm-food/ 529241/ (accessed 20 November 2009).

27 Ann Grodzins Gold, '*Khyal*: Changed Yearnings in Rajasthani Women's Songs', *Manushi* 95 (1996), pp. 13–21.

28 Song recorded at Bali Gujar's house, July 2007.

2
_____

The formation of tribal identities

The economic and political position of tribal populations in modern India is not unusual. It is familiar enough from what we know of similarly marginalized peoples in other parts of the world. What is perhaps less obvious is how tribes in India utilize language and religion to express their identity in the ongoing encounter with modernity.

Tribal populations

Tribes constitute only about 8 per cent of India's total population, and they are unevenly distributed (1 per cent of Tamil Nadu but 95 per cent of Mizoram is tribal, for instance). These roughly ninety million people are largely concentrated in two regions: the central and eastern hills of Chhattisgarh, Orissa and Madhya Pradesh; and the mountainous states in the north-east. Sizeable populations also live in Rajasthan, Gujarat and Jharkhand. Among these approximately 500 tribal groups, the variety of social practices, cosmologies, rituals and material culture is staggering. And the ethnographic record is still far from complete.

Such heterogeneity is not easily categorized, and we have known for a long time that the term 'tribe' is imprecise. For some anthropologists, the salient criterion in defining a population as a 'tribe' is its type of political authority, while for others it is social organization, descent system or religious belief; and many definitions ultimately rely on a specious spectrum stretching from simplicity to complexity. Confusion arises, in part, because the concept of 'tribe' is inseparable from modernity. As a convenient shorthand for pre-industrial societies, it helped to define, by contrast, the new world of rational, wage-earning citizens.

Even today 'tribal' is often used to describe an undesirable form of politics considered the opposite of enlightened debate.

Although the term first gained widespread acceptance in the ethnography of north America and Australia, it passed quickly into early nineteenth-century accounts of India. The paperwork empire of British colonialism soon generated a number of variants, such as 'hill tribes', 'forest tribes' and 'frontier tribes.' During the twentieth century, these terms based on habitat gave way to others implying historical precedence: 'Aboriginal', *'Adivasi'* ('first-inhabitant') and 'indigenous people'.

In the context of modern India, however, a tribe is best described not by these criteria but rather by its position vis-à-vis the state, and dominant cultural practices and ideologies.[1] Again, the considerable variation in size and location of India's tribes produces different histories of contact with outsiders. The Santals and Bhils, for example, who number in the millions but are surrounded by mainstream groups, have fared differently than the few hundred Handuri and Mra, who live in isolated mountain valleys in the Himalayas. In their relation to state power and powerful neighbours, however, these otherwise dissimilar groups share commonalities.

In modern times, contact between tribe and the state has been characterized by conflict, exploitation and expropriation. In most of the north-east, for instance, the authorities conducted a low-level yet almost continuous war with tribes from the 1830s to the 1950s; and hostilities have not ceased in some areas. In other parts of India, dominant mainstream populations frequently played a role, especially when intimidation, taxation and manipulation of the law proved sufficient to wrest control of rights to the land.

Even when these forms of expropriation were ineffective, the more benign forces of assimilation – cultural borrowing, intermarriage, language shift and religious conversion and keeping up with the Kumars – took their toll. As a result, more than one tribe, such as the Chutiya (in Assam), have disappeared. Outside the north-east, armed conflict is today uncommon, and overall tribes are more integrated into the mosaic of Indian civilization. Still, the past has left unhealed wounds.

Much of this description applies also to low-status caste groups, whose eating, drinking and ritual practices, like those of most tribes, are considered unclean by mainstream populations. Tribes, however, are further marginalized in that they typically remain outside even local networks of hierarchy. No tribe plays a significant role in any sphere of India's public life, from politics to entertainment to sport. In summary, tribes in India are politically and economically marginalized, set apart by culture and religion, and often geographically isolated. Most are also stigmatized by the language they speak.

Tribal languages

India has more than a hundred different tribal languages, mostly Tibeto-Burman but also Dravidian, Austro-Asiatic, Indo-Aryan and Daic. Of these, only two (Santali and Bodo) are included among the nation's twenty-three official languages.[2] In 2003, as part of political settlements in Assam and eastern India, these two tribal languages were added to the Eighth Schedule of the Indian Constitution. The status of tribal languages at the state level is similar. A total of twenty-seven languages are sanctioned for official government use in the various states: those at the central level, plus Khasi and Garo (in Meghalaya), Kokborok (in Tripura) and Mizo (in Mizoram).[3] Behind state recognition of these tribal languages stand decades of political struggle and sporadic violence.

Even at the state level, tribal languages wield less political clout than the official languages. Those latter languages determined the reorganization of states in the 1950s, but since then all new states (Meghalaya, Arunachal Pradesh, Tripura, Mizoram, Nagaland, Manipur, Jharkhand, Chhattisgarh, Uttarakhand) have been based on ethnicity. The same is true of the demands for future states (Bodoland, Gorkhaland). A tribal language is too weak a platform for a state to stand upon.

In socio-linguistic terms, too, tribal languages lack power. Most are endangered, several are near extinction, and some (such as Tolcha, Paite, Sengmai and Rangkas) are no longer spoken. Only half of the tribal population in India speaks a tribal language as their first language. Although bi- and tri-lingualism is the norm across the country, tribal languages are rarely one of those second or third languages.[4] Speaking a tribal language is not just different; it is also low status.

Arunachal Pradesh

The situation in Arunachal Pradesh, the focus of this chapter, is somewhat different. The proportion of the tribal population who speak a tribal language in the state far exceeds the Indian average of 50 per cent.

If mother-tongue retention is high, however, marginalization is extreme. This is largely because Arunachal Pradesh, tucked into the north-east corner, is the most geographically isolated state in India. It sticks out so far east, beyond the central landmass, that some maps of India show the region in a separate inset. A few maps fail to show it altogether.

Restrictions on access to the state imposed in the 1870s remain in place. The 'Inner Line' of 1873, the state's southern boundary with Assam, separates it from the rest of the nation. Indian citizens require a permit (easily acquired) to enter, and they are prohibited by law from owning land or a business or standing for elected office in Arunachal Pradesh. The state remained off limits to foreigners until the end of the 1990s, when they were permitted to visit only for short periods of time and at considerable expense, although these conditions have recently been relaxed. As a result of geography and legislation (as well as official indifference), tribal groups in the state own most of the land and control local politics. The bulk of the state's budget comes from Delhi, however, and hydro-electric projects, national party politics and the security agencies have begun to undermine that control.

Just over one million people live in the state, of whom one-quarter are Indians from the plains. The tribal population consists of about thirty-five different ethnic groups, speaking about twenty-five languages, all but one of which are Tibeto-Burman. None, however, is an official language of the state. The state government chose English as its official language, although Hindi is equally popular in government, education and the public sphere. Assamese, which was the medium of instruction at primary level and the contact language with the rest of India, is still used in some contexts but is now a distant third to Hindi and English.

The state government pays lip service to the development of tribal languages, and a few NGOs have attempted to introduce schoolbooks at the primary level. None of these projects, however, has seen much success. According to long-standing central government policy, tribal languages should be used in schools as the 'third language', after either Hindi or English and the regional language. This has not occurred in Arunachal Pradesh. A 2006 report from the central government's commission on linguistic minorities was candid:

> As in the previous years, this year also, Arunachal Pradesh has said that no language has been recognized as a minority language . . . Earlier also attention of the Government has been drawn to this but it

> does not appear that attention has been paid to it ... [I]t has been said that students of the classes VI to VIII are being taught third language. Five languages of the State viz. Adi, Apatani, Bhoti, Khampti and Nishi, which are spoken by the principal tribes have been adopted as the third language ... The State Government will have to be requested once again that they should pay more attention to the development of the tribal languages.[5]

Although candid, the report was both inaccurate and misleading. Bhoti is not spoken in the state, and while a few tribal languages may have been 'adopted' as the third language, none is actually used in the classroom.

Tribal languages in Arunachal Pradesh lack not only state support but also a script. Scripts derived from Tibetan or Burmese writing are used in some contexts by tribes practising forms of Buddhism. A few animist tribes in the centre of the state have invented scripts. In addition, romanization of tribal languages, begun in the early decades of the twentieth century, has recently gained new impetus in promoting religious movements in the region. One tribe has also produced its own dictionary, translating romanized local words into English. These acts of reinventing language and religion are key elements in the expression of tribal identity, not only in contemporary India but also over the past 150 years. That process is illustrated by looking at one tribe in central Arunachal Pradesh.

Apatanis

Apatanis are a tribe of about 35,000, who live in a small but fertile valley equidistant from the high Himalayas and the Brahmaputra River. They practise a sophisticated method of wet-rice agriculture, tend bamboo groves and small gardens, and seldom hunt for food. Known as shrewd traders, comparatively well educated and cohesive as a group, Apatanis have a fairly clear and positive sense of themselves. They are the only tribe in the central region whose ethnonym is also their autonym. Regular contact with the world beyond neighbouring tribes, however, began half a century ago and has now shaken that confidence.

Disputed dictionary

In July 2001, more than one hundred copies of a newly published Apatani–English dictionary were burned in protest in the burial ground near Hapoli, the administrative centre of the Apatani valley. Smaller numbers of copies were similarly destroyed in other places around the valley. Although two other Apatani dictionaries had appeared earlier, this was the first compiled by Apatanis for Apatanis. Produced by computer, and with some knowledge of lexicography, the dictionary was anticipated with pride. On printing, however, it stimulated fierce opposition and its own destruction.

Controversy centred on the definitions of the two clan groups in Apatani society: *gyutii* and *gyuci*. *Gyuci* clans (about 25 per cent of the total population) are considered lower status, have owned fewer resources and have held little local authority. Traditional village councilmen, the government-imposed *guanboras* and elected officials have overwhelmingly come from the higher-status *gyutii* clans. However, in recent years, with the advent of a cash economy and education, this correlation between social, economic and political status is breaking down. Today many *gyuci* families are well-off and have been elected to local administrative posts. Still, the divide between these two groups continues to run down the centre of Apatani life. Marriage between them is rare (perhaps 5 per cent), and *gyuci* shamans are not permitted to conduct certain rituals during public festivals.

Oral tradition explains the inferior status of *gyuci* as the reversal of an original moral superiority. Two stories, both told by a *gyuci* man, are representative:[6]

Story 1

There were two brothers. Kojin was the older, and Pusan was the younger. One day they went to the forest. When Pusan was injured by a sharp piece of bamboo, Kojin carried him on his back. Pusan said, 'Since you are carrying me, you are my servant.' Kojin accepted this, even though he was the older brother. This is how Kojin became the ancestor of the *gyuci* and Pusan the ancestor of the *gyutii*.

Story 2

Two plants grew wild in the jungle, one was *kempu* [white banana] and the other was *kelang* [red banana]. It's said that Kojin was honest and sincere, and that Pusan was not. In any case, while in the forest one day, Kojin picked the *kempu* plant and Pusan picked the *kelang* plant. Pusan quickly realized the *kempu* was more valuable, so he tricked his older brother by saying, 'Kojin, those leaves you have are no good. You'd better throw them away.' Kojin believed him and threw them away. Pusan picked them up and gave Kojin the worthless *kelang* leaves. From then on, the person with the *kempu* plant has been the dominant one.

In the first story, the older brother lost status and became *gyuci* because he showed affection for his younger brother. In the second story, the younger brother comes out on top because he cheats his honest, older brother. In other words, today's low-status clans believe that their ancestor had seniority and a superior character.

Gyutii clans, on the other hand, account for the current difference in another way; not as oral narrative (as above) but as an episode of local history. They claim that many *gyuci* assimilated into Apatani society from neighbouring tribes as slaves and servants. While this assimilation did occur (just as today some Nepalese and Assamese servant girls assimilate), it appears not to have been restricted to *gyuci* clans alone and not to have represented a large section of any clan. Historical truth aside, what matters is that the *gyutii* clans explain the current contrast in status as a continuation, and not a reversal, of an original difference in social ranking.

When they produced their dictionary, the *gyutii* editors endorsed this view with the following definitions: '*gyuchie* n, "people of lower caste", *gyuttii* n, "people of upper caste".'[7] An earlier Apatani–English–Hindi dictionary, compiled by an Indian linguist and published in south India, used similar definitions but is more or less unknown in the valley.[8] The disputed dictionary, by contrast, was published by the Apatani Cultural and Literary Society.

Several objections arose when the dictionary appeared. For instance, some people complained that it left out ritual words and variants of words in village dialects. What enraged *gyuci* clans, however, was the equation of themselves with low Hindu castes. That is what they attempted to destroy by burning the books: not just the ascription of low status, but the identification as caste.

After the burning, many *gyuci* demanded that the dictionary be reissued with an apology and new definitions. They wanted themselves to be defined as 'the group descended from Kojin' and *gyutii* to be defined as 'the group descended from Pusan'. They demanded that their claim to an original moral superiority, as expressed in oral tradition, be given the authority of a printed book.

Initially, the *gyutii* man who had compiled the dictionary responded to these events with the threat of a lawsuit for destruction of property. Later, he accepted the demand for a public apology, but other *gyutii* refused to negotiate with the book-burners. When someone suggested that a *mithun* be given to the offended party, this traditional act of reconciliation was rejected by most *gyutii*. The anger died down, but the controversy simmered, factions emerged, associations formed and resolutions were adopted. In summer 2004, as state-wide elections approached, *gyuci* groups invited the entire Apatani population to a reconciliation meeting, and *gyutii* groups countered with a call for their own meeting. The next day the District Commissioner published a formal announcement from his office in Hapoli that prohibited the movement of anyone outside their house. Then he organized a reconciliation meeting in the valley, which was followed by another in the Chief Minister's office in the state capital. With his support, an agreement was reached, including a public apology and a promise to revise the definitions in a second printing and not to sell the original dictionary.

When a second edition of the dictionary was published in October 2004, by a second group of *gyutii*, it contained definitions even more offensive than the first. In it, *gyutii* are defined as 'patrician class ... aristocrats'; and *gyuci* are said to have three sub-groups: 'original', 'slave' and 'immigrant slave'. The political fall-out was immediate. In the elections a few weeks later, the *gyutii* incumbent Member of the State Legislative Assembly (and a Minister) was unable to distance himself from the conservative *gyutii* who had published the first and second editions of the dictionary. His opponent in the election was also a *gyutii*, but he had publicly agreed with those who wanted reconciliation. As a result, the challenger gained most of the *gyuci* vote and won the election. The controversy was eventually resolved in July 2008, when a third edition was released at a large public event. These editors conceded that the first two editions were in error and defined the two social groups as descendants of Kojin and Pusan, the two brothers in the oral stories.

This dictionary dispute among Apatanis reveals a contradiction in movements to protect tribal culture and identity. The foreword to the first edition explains that it was compiled

> at a time [when] modernity is taking heavy toll on oral literature of
> Apatanis, which had hitherto been handed down from generation to

generation orally, deserved critical review and constructive suggestions. The Apatani Cultural and Literary Society which was established to arrest this type of dwindling trend is working effortlessly for standardisation of Apatani script, preservation, promotion and popularisation of our cultural values and social system.[9]

Intended to preserve traditional culture, the dictionary instead illustrates the power of print to disrupt oral tradition. Before it appeared, two competing explanations of the clan groups circulated, but they were both oral. After the dictionary, one of those explanations had the added authority of print. And a dictionary, as an arbiter of language, commands more authority than most printed books.

All dictionaries search for equivalences, but a bilingual one must find them in another language. This double translation in the Apatani–English dictionary widened the normal gap between speech and print, removing the definitions further from the compensatory flexibility of oral tradition, in which inconsistent accounts can circulate side by side. In our case, the compilers of the first two editions chose a Portuguese-derived English word (caste), used by colonial writers to describe Indian society, to stand for social divisions among caste-less Tibeto-Burman speakers in the eastern Himalayas.

Behind the disputed definitions lie the lineaments of Apatani cultural identity. Apatanis define themselves (*tanii*) in opposition to two groups: neighbouring tribes known collectively as *misan*; and non-tribal outsiders called *halyang*. The *halyang* are principally the Assamese and the British, and by extension all Indians and foreigners with whom Apatanis had limited interaction until the 1950s. Apatanis draw a firm line, conceptually and in practice, between themselves and these powerful outsiders from the plains. To be considered a low-caste Indian is unpleasant to any Apatani, including the roughly 15–20 per cent who are Christian. To have your social group defined in your own dictionary as low caste is offensive.

Invented script

Lacking their own script, educated Apatanis use both devanagari and roman, which came to the Brahmaputra valley in the fifth and early nineteenth centuries, respectively. Not having a script is nothing unusual: two-thirds of the world's approximately 6,000 languages have no indigenous script, and many writing systems were invented or adapted during the past 200 years. But this is no comfort to the unscripted people who live on the margins of powerful states built on textual traditions, such as India and China. For them, illiteracy is a source of humiliation. For those of us familiar with the long literary histories of Indian languages, including the dynamic exchange between orality and writing, this lack of a script is difficult to imagine.

I was therefore unprepared for my first trip to the Apatani valley in December 1999. Sitting on the back porch of a bamboo house, sipping warm rice-beer on an icy cold morning, I explained to my hosts (through an interpreter) that I was interested in oral stories. 'We know just the person you want,' they said, and sent for a local storyteller. Mudan Donny arrived a few minutes later, wrapped in a large, dark, smoke-blackened coat. Over the next several years, this imaginative and energetic man in his thirties would fill dozens of my audio-cassettes with stories – he was, as my hosts said, the best storyteller in the valley. When he climbed on to the porch that day, however, Mudan Donny carried a large notebook. He wasn't interested in telling stories. Instead, he wanted to show me the script he had invented.

Opening the notebook, he proudly pointed to three neatly written columns of letters and explained them while a friend translated. There were fifty-six symbols, including long and short vowels, aspirate and non-aspirate consonants, with phonic equivalents in both English and Hindi. All this had been revealed to him in a dream on 15 May 1988, when he wrote it down.

He had devised three separate scripts, one for each stage of a linguistic evolution. The 'ancient' writing became 'middle' writing (which he also called *nyibu agung*, the shaman's ritual speech), which finally turned into 'modern'. The first looked like a confection of Tibetan and Chinese with diacritical marks; the second was an adaptation of Assamese devanagari; and the modern was the roman script used to write Apatani today. Although he couldn't speak an English sentence, Donny had an eclectic smattering of the language – in fact, almost everything about him was idiosyncratic, including his own concoction of a religion from elements of Hinduism, Christianity and local practices. His invented script, like his 'religion', remains a private obsession, with no public recognition or usage.

Donny's is not the only invented script. In Arunachal Pradesh alone, at least five others have been created since the 1980s. None has had

much public acceptance, although one is supported by the state government because it has been devised for all the tribal languages in the
central region. Despite such high-profile endorsement, however, this
script is more a symbol of cultural preservation than a practical solution
to endangered languages. Although it is available on the Internet and
sometimes occupies half a page in a small, English-language weekly
newspaper, it is not used in schools.

This invented script, moreover, reveals a paradox in many attempts
to preserve tribal culture. It is called *tani lipi*, an artificial combination
of a local Tibeto-Burman word and an Indic word. *Tani* refers to Abo
Tani, the mythic ancestor of these tribes who defines their identity.
They are the 'Tani' group of tribes, and their languages form the 'Tani'
branch of the Tibeto-Burman family. The Apatani autonym (*tanii*) is
another form of the same word. *Lipi* ('script/writing'), however, is an
Indo-Aryan root. Even this promotion of tribal identity, it seems, cannot
escape the literary culture in which it is marginalized.

Invented scripts have played and still play an important role in tribal
identity movements throughout India. In the 1930s, a 'secret' and
unknown writing was used by a Naga woman to lead her followers in
a millenarian movement against British colonialism. Similarly, a rediscovered Meithei script is central to the revival of pre-Vaishnava cultural
identity in today's Manipur valley. Other scripts were invented as a part
of revitalization movements among tribes in eastern and central India,
largely in the late nineteenth and early twentieth centuries. 'The process
of discovery of the scripts', as K. S. Singh wrote, 'will go on as long as
the search for a new identity is on ... A script, whether revealed (Ho),
invented (Santal), or recovered (Meitei) is an essential complement to a
language, which is indispensable to cultural identity.'[10]

After Independence, the North-East Frontier Agency (1954–72) and
its tribal advisor, Verrier Elwin, supported the development of new
scripts for tribal languages in what is now Arunachal Pradesh.[11] Some
politicians, however, feared this would splinter an already fragile nation
and argued that only a national script would integrate tribes into the
new state. In 1962, Prime Minister Jawaharlal Nehru called for devanagari to be adopted for all tribal languages in the north-east, an idea
that one leading politician welcomed because it would 'put a stop to the
concerted effort of devising new scripts for hundred different dialects
[*sic*]' in the northeast.[12] Devanagari and roman were adopted, but
invented scripts still possess the mystique to express tribal identity.

Lost writing

Invented scripts, however, are only half the story. In local eyes, many are not 'invented' but rediscovered. In Donny's case, his identification of a 'modern' script with roman and a 'middle' script with a regional variant of devanagari reflects the influence of those scripts in the Apatani valley. His unidentifiable, ancient script, however, is a lost script. The story of lost writing, which is told by many tribal populations in north-east India (and elsewhere in the eastern Himalayas), is another expression of tribal identity.

The politics of scripts is a recurring theme in modern Indian history, including the Urdu/Hindi, Bengali/Assamese, Tulu/Malayalam controversies and the many scripts for Konkani. Legends about lost texts are also numerous: the Vedas are lost in Sanskrit and Tamil traditions, and oral epics disappear in Telugu. The loss of writing, however, is a different kind of deprivation. It is the absence of the technology that produces the cultural capital possessed by dominant populations.

The Apatani explanation of how they lost writing is not a separate narrative. Instead, it is embedded in a ritual text that describes the migration of their ancestors across mountains and rivers to their present location. Here is an edited, prose translation of the relevant episode:

> During the long journey, Apatanis and other tribes were travelling with the *halyang* [non-tribal outsiders]. They came to a wide river, got into one big boat and began to row across. During the crossing, the *halyang* kept their papers between their teeth, but the Apatanis and other tribals kept them under their arms. When the boat rocked and everyone put out their arms to steady it, the Apatanis and other tribals lost their papers. Since then Apatanis have had no writing, while the Assamese have writing because they held their papers with their teeth.[13]

As with many other accounts of lost writing, this Apatani version is a compensatory narrative. It explains contemporary illiteracy as the consequence of a past accident.

Being unscripted in a nation of scripts is at the core of tribal identity in India. Lacking a script, however, does not mean that tribal populations are illiterate. In fact, literacy rates (according to the 2001 Census) in most of the states in the north-east exceed the 65 per cent in India as a whole: 88 per cent in Mizoram, 74 per cent in Tripura, 68 per cent in Manipur, 67 per cent in Nagaland, 63 per cent in Meghalaya and

55 per cent in Arunachal Pradesh. What these figures indicate, however, is the ability to read and write in Hindi, English, Bengali or Assamese, not in tribal languages. Speakers of tribal languages are illiterate in their mother tongues.

Apatanis are reported to have 71 per cent literacy. Most people under 30 can read and write Hindi, and many have that proficiency in English. Some educated men over 50 are literate only in Assamese, which was the medium of instruction in primary schools when education was first introduced to the Apatani valley (and throughout the North-East Frontier Agency) in the 1950s. English, first used only at secondary level, became the language of education for all levels in 1972, when Arunachal Pradesh became a Union Territory. In practice, however, most teachers in government schools use Hindi, and only private schools teach in English. In state schools in the Apatani valley, Apatani is heard in conversation, and outside the classroom, but rarely as part of a lesson after primary school. The state government has supported the publication of school books in romanized Apatani, but these brightly coloured pamphlets are not popular with teachers or students. No local script, neither Donny's fanciful invention nor the *tani lipi* developed for all the languages in the central region, is anywhere to be seen. With few exceptions (notably Santali), this is true for tribal languages throughout India.

Religion

Romanized Apatani, on the other hand, is more and more visible, especially in the contested field of religion. Apatanis, like other tribal populations in central Arunachal Pradesh, practise a form of shamanism in which animal sacrifice, divination and ritual chanting are used to contact 'spirits'. Apatanis recognize more than a hundred different spirits (*wi*), who have few anthropomorphic traits, although some are known as 'wise', 'brave' or 'harmful'. Shamans contact these spirits in order to increase prosperity, cure illness or ward off potential danger. Danger lies mainly in crossing boundaries, in trespassing on the spirits' territory, during transit to and from the land of the dead, in the ghosts who are not peacefully settled there and in the return of the dead to the living. This Apatani system of beliefs and rituals shows no influence of the Hinduism widespread in Assam and little of the Tibetan Buddhism practised elsewhere in Arunachal Pradesh.

Compared to its penetration elsewhere in the north-east, Christianity came late to the interior of Arunachal Pradesh and the Apatani valley. Missionary efforts based in Assam from the mid nineteenth century targeted tribes south of the Brahmaputra, which led American Baptists, Welsh Presbyterians and English Anglicans into the Naga Hills, Garo Hills, Mizo Hills and Manipur Valley. Tribal populations in central Arunachal Pradesh probably first encountered the new religion as students at Roman Catholic schools on the north side of the river. Tribal students began to attend these and other Christian schools in the 1930s, but missionary activity came to the region only in the 1970s. Alarmed at the rapid spread of the new ritual system, local people burned dozens of churches and hundreds of Christian homes. In 1979, the State Legislative Assembly passed the Freedom of Indigenous Faith Act, which outlawed 'forced' conversion.

Christianity arrived among Apatanis at the same time, but the valley remained peaceful. A bamboo hut was built for a Roman Catholic priest who periodically came up from Assam to hold Mass. Another hut was erected for the handful of local Baptists. Both, however, were carefully located on the outskirts of the administrative centre and away from the villages. When huts were put up near villages, they were knocked down by angry protesters. By 2000, a large Baptist and a large Roman Catholic church stood side by side, on the spot where the bamboo huts once stood. They and three smaller Protestant churches serve the roughly 5,000 Christians in the valley. Still, no church has yet appeared inside an Apatani village, where outsiders are also prohibited from owning a house or land. In 2003, however, a bamboo 'church' was allowed to stand close to a village, and now there are two more.

Approximately 15–20 per cent of Apatanis are Christian, mostly Baptist but also Roman Catholic. Roman Catholics, who are generally educated and reasonably well-off, produce Apatani translations of prayers, hymns and some scriptures, although no one has attempted a full translation of the Bible. They also compose new Christian songs, which are printed in romanized Apatani and distributed among themselves.

Protestant converts, mostly Baptists but also Evangelicals and Pentecostals, make up about four-fifths of Apatani Christians. They are visited by enthusiastic preachers from Nagaland, Mizoram and south India, who distribute printed pamphlets, mostly about Christ's life and teachings, in romanized Apatani and English. These pamphlets are convenient targets for protest. In 2004, for example, hundreds of copies of a glossy tract, with lurid images of Satan and Hell blazing on the cover, were handed out to nearly every house in the valley. The text inside attacked local shamanistic religion, condemning specific practices as 'evil' and 'harmful'. Many people were incensed, some burned the tracts and others demanded a ban on Christian propaganda within 300 metres of Apatani ritual structures.

Hinduism (and Sikhism) arrived with the Indian army, which set up a major compound in the valley after the Chinese invasion in 1962. Two small temples inside the compound were joined in the late 1980s by a larger one built, amid public protest, on a hill in the administrative centre. Well-funded Hindu organizations (Vivekananda Kendra Vidyalaya, Vishwa Hindu Parishad, Ramakrishna Mission) run independent (and well-respected) schools in the valley. They also promote Hinduism through publications, mostly in Hindi but also in English and romanized Apatani. One line of argument attempts to persuade animist Apatanis that they are crypto-Hindus: 'You worship the Sun, just as we ancient Hindus did and still do.' To some Apatanis, this subtle Hindu propaganda is more dangerous than the blundering efforts of Christianity.

Local opposition to the advance of Christianity (and to a lesser extent Hinduism) has taken the form of a reinvented religion. The Donyi-Polo ('Sun–Moon') movement began in the 1970s among tribes to the east of the Apatani valley and is now growing in popularity throughout the central region. While Apatanis were initially reluctant to embrace this counterweight to outside religions, they are now joining in small but significant numbers. The first Donyi-Polo hall in the valley was built in 2004, and several more have appeared since.

Like most revitilization movements, including those among tribes elsewhere in India, Donyi-Polo is an eclectic mixture of Christian, Hindu and local practices. Some elements are borrowed, some revised and some entirely new. In one Apatani village, for instance, a few dozen people gather in a purpose-built hall on Sunday mornings; led by a woman, they sing songs, printed in romanized Apatani and dedicated to Donyi-Polo. The hymns sung by the congregation are scrupulously composed in Apatani, employing not just conversational speech but the ritual language used by shamans when chanting.

Other printed pamphlets, some in English, some in romanized Apatani, present the principles of the newly systematized faith and explain its philosophy. Where once a set of practices and ideas varied from clan to clan, and village to village, now a supreme deity (Donyi-Polo) reigns over a uniform and formalized theology. This is Donyi-Polo-ism, with the all-important suffix. It may be an odd concoction, but to many it is preferable to 'Other', the label under which animist tribes in Arunachal Pradesh were classified in the 2001 Census.

Conclusion

Colonialism came late to the Apatani valley, only at the very end of the nineteenth century, and even a semi-permanent government presence was not established there until the 1940s. Since then Apatani lives have been transformed. Unlike many tribes elsewhere in India (but like most in Arunachal Pradesh), Apatanis still retain ownership of their land and control of local politics. However, their economic and political systems have been displaced by a cash economy and state-party politics. And their material culture has been sidelined by goods brought up from the plains and sold in the bazaar. The shaman's shawl, once hand-woven from wool traded over the high Himalayas and dyed with colours extracted from local plants and tree bark, is now woven with synthetic fibres and cotton, coloured with chemical dyes and manufactured in the Punjab. A man's red cane belt and loin cloth have been discarded in favour of short pants and now trousers. Women's facial tattoos and wooden nose plugs have given way to lipstick and eyeliner.

But perhaps it is misleading to measure tradition and modernity by changes in objects and adornments. Apatanis themselves seem to place more value on what they do, on practices rather than objects. Women may wear skirts woven by other tribes, but they are still Apatani because they carry baskets of rice to a bride's granary when the harvest is over. Men may wear shoes, but they will have few doubts about who they are as long as they lead the large ox-like animals to sacrifice during the winter feasts. A shaman, wrapped in his new shawl of synthetic fibres and chemical dyes, and wearing rubber boots (it is cold in January at 5 a.m. and 5,000 feet), will still feel himself a traditional ritual specialist because he chants for twelve hours.

This is what we might call the ritualization of identity. With other traditional aspects of social life displaced or transformed, Apatanis are concentrating more and more of their self-image in ritual practices. Throughout central Arunachal Pradesh, tribes in this largely animist but increasingly Christian region have fashioned a single ceremony as a public display of collective identity. A minor agricultural ritual, which used to be celebrated by individual families, on different days, in separate locations, sometimes a day's walk apart, is now orchestrated by local leaders into an annual celebration by the entire tribe on a single day and largely in one place.

Several factors lie behind this centralization and ritualization of tribal identity in central Arunachal Pradesh, but none is more influential than the recently arrived religions. Before regular contact with the *halyang* outsiders began in the 1950s, Apatanis did not know they had a 'religion'. Until the bamboo huts, the temple and then the churches appeared, they thought of themselves as members of their tribe, clan and village (and probably gender). Now they have another box to tick; not only the self-defined Christians but also the supporters of Donyi-Polo. Even for the majority of Apatanis, who do not embrace either new religion, the concept of religious identity is firmly fixed.

This history of the formation of tribal identity is specific to the Apatani valley. Its key elements and general dynamics, however, are typical of tribal movements across India, past and present. The basic tools of this identity-making are new religions and new language technologies. Pride is the primary motivation.

Invented scripts, lost writing and a local dictionary are three separate but similar attempts to establish equivalence with the more powerful languages of the nation-state. The story of lost writing is an assertion of parity in the past: Apatanis are illiterate not because they never had writing but because writing slipped away from them while crossing a river. An invented script is the recovery of that highly valued technology: while Donny's scripts have no purchase among Apatanis, his three-phase scheme authenticates unknown Apatani scripts as predecessors and thus equivalents of roman. The Apatani dictionary also claims parity, through translation. This is what a dictionary does – it declares equivalences between two languages. Printed in neat columns, romanized Apatani words claim the same semantic and grammatical status as English words.

When we recall the incongruous admixture of elements in the Donyi-Polo movement, and the curious compound of the invented script *tani lipi*, we see the paradox of tribal identity in contemporary India. The project of preservation relies on technologies and concepts – scripts, print, lexicography, 'identity' and 'religion' – borrowed from the outsiders, whose growing influence the project wishes to arrest. This disjunction between ends and means is unmistakable in a poster seen throughout the Apatani valley. It reads, in English, 'Preserve your indigenous faith to save your identity.'

Standing on the geographical and cultural edge of the nation, the tribal people of Arunachal Pradesh can see where they are placed. Nearly everyone wants to occupy a more central position, within or at least alongside dominant practices and ideologies. Participation in economic or political terms is possible only for a few, and most turn to religion or language, over which they have more control. Some people try to assimilate by acquiring a mainstream manner of praying or speaking. Others wish to remain distinct but at the same time to stand on a more or less even footing with the rest of the country. One step towards that parity is a reinvented religion, with congregational singing from printed hymns, that can line up alongside other religions.

Another strategy is to reinvent your language. Language is central to Apatanis' sense of themselves: no one else speaks in exactly the same way. It is also free and easily acquired. It does, however, need improvements, such as a script and a dictionary. Speaking Apatani, or even writing or printing it, will not get you very far. But knowing that yours is a proper language, like the others, is a source of pride. Self-esteem among tribes has been in short supply for some time, and it is becoming less and less visible through the glass and steel of today's India.

Notes

1 See André Béteille, 'The Concept of Tribe with Special Reference to India', in *Society and Politics in India* (London, Athlone Press, 1991 (1986)), pp. 57–78.

2 This number includes English, the 'associate official language'.

3 This total does not include Sikkim, which has four official languages: Bhotia, Lepcha, Limbu and English.

4 E. Annamalai, 'Linguistic Dominance and Cultural Dominance: a Study of Tribal Bilingualism in India', in D. P. Pattanayak (ed.), *Multilingualism in India* (Clevedon: Multilingual Matters, 1990), pp. 29–30.

5 42nd Report, National Commissioner Linguistic Minorities, July 2003 to June 2004. www.nclm.nic.in.

6 These stories were told to me by Tage Diibo in 2002.

7 Apatani orthography has not been standardized.

8 These definitions – '*gyuci* n, low class (among Apatani)' and '*gyutu* n, higher class (among Apatani)' – are found in P. T. Abraham, *Apatani–English–Hindi Dictionary* (Mysore: Central Institute of Indian Languages), 1987.

9 Habung Donyi, *Apatani Dictionary*, 1st edn (Naharlagun, Mamkee, 2001).

10 K. S. Singh, *Tribal Society in India: An Anthropo-historical Perspective* (New Delhi, Manohar, 1985), p. 287.

11 See Ramachandra Guha, *Savaging the Civilized. Verrier Elwin, his Tribals, & India* (University of Chicago Press, 1999).

12 G. S. Ghuyre, *The Scheduled Tribes of India*, 3rd edn (London: Transaction Books, 1980 (1963)), p. 331.

13 Stuart Blackburn, *Himalayan Tribal Tales: Oral Tradition and Culture in the Apatani Valley* (Leiden, Brill, 2008), p. 116.

3

Food and agriculture

Introduction

In essence, food is a way of fulfilling a biological need – nutrition – within an ecologically and culturally defined context. At the same time, it is a way of expressing one's sense of self – individually and collectively – in relation to the past, present and future. Concerns about authenticity and belonging, taste and distinction, health and safety converge when food is at issue, as do embodied feelings like comfort, pleasure, craving and deprivation. This constellation of ideas and emotions makes food a particularly rich site for exploring the diverse ways in which Indians construct cultural identities at the cusp of imagined traditions and desired modernities. This chapter explores these processes of social formation – cultural being and becoming – by relating them to shifts in the modes of producing and consuming food. It attempts to analyse some of these shifts through a selective discussion of changing food practices in post-Independence India. It locates these changes in the context of the political economy of agriculture since the Green Revolution of the late 1960s and 1970s, a programme that radically reconfigured how and which foods are cultivated and consumed. The chapter goes on to delineate the widening circuits of food as a commodity form within the home and outside, spanned by the growth of processed foods and the practice of 'eating out'. And it examines the multiple meanings that food conveys for different social groups by drawing upon three ethnographic vignettes from western India.

The sociological and anthropological literature on food in India can be broadly classified into three streams. Of these the oldest is the

Indological, one which draws upon Hindu (and occasionally Buddhist) texts to analyse religious prescriptions around preparing, exchanging and consuming food. This stream of analysis has focused on the core organizational principle of caste society – the opposition between purity and pollution – which determines how particular social groups relate to each other around food and marriage.[1] The emphasis on hierarchy is supplemented by attention to the ritual calendar of fasting and feasting and its correspondence to the cycle of the seasons, as well as to the epistemological continuities between food and medicine.[2] The second stream is more historical, primarily concentrating on the colonial encounter and the assimilation of New World crops such as potatoes, tomatoes and chillies, and culinary items such as crystallized sugar and tea, into Indian diets.[3] Even more attention is paid to the reverse flow of spices and opium, along with other cash crops such as indigo and cotton, from colonial India to Europe, and its influence upon European lifestyles.[4] The third stream, which overlaps with the growing body of popular fiction and memoirs about food,[5] examines food practices among diasporic Indians, descendants of indentured labourers in the Caribbean and white-collar immigrants in north America, and principally examines how food becomes a way of preserving cultural memories and identities.[6] While significant in themselves, these streams of literature shed little light on contemporary food practices in India, especially the differences across classes and between rural and urban parts of the country, something which this chapter attempts to do.

Village India: on the road to urban lifestyles

Kadmal village lies in the Nimar plains along the river Narmada in western Madhya Pradesh. Its alluvial lands produce papaya and bananas, wheat and cotton, crops that make their way through the bustling town nearby to more distant markets. Shobharam Patel owns ten acres of irrigated land in the village that he farms with his family. They belong to the locally dominant Patidar caste and are regarded as being well-off. Their comfortable circumstances are reflected in the food they eat. Their day begins with sweet milky tea, boiled on a gas stove and slurped quickly out of saucers by Kamla and Guddi, Shobharam's wife and sixteen-year-old daughter, who must then busy themselves with cleaning out the byre of their two buffaloes and one cow while

Shobharam and his son Mohan go off to the fields. The midday meal consists of *tuvar dal* (lentils) and wheat *rotis* (unleavened flat bread), which Kamla prepares alone since Guddi is menstruating and cannot enter the kitchen. In the afternoon, their next-door neighbour Sunita drops in with her infant son and toddler daughter. Sunita has had trouble producing breast-milk, so the child is on formula, heavily diluted with water to make the expensive tins last longer. On this winter afternoon, Shobharam has brought in a sheaf of tender chickpea stalks fresh from the fields which the women peel and eat as they watch a serial on television. The little girl has her own snack, her hand groping around the shiny foil packet for the last bits of spicy rice-flour sticks as she gazes at the screen. Meanwhile Shobharam goes off to the row of shops along the road for a shave, followed by a leisurely halt at the *chai* (tea) shop, reading the newspaper and trading rounds of 'cut-*chai*' – half-glasses that are easy on the pocket – with his fellow men. In the evening, as Shobharam sits down to eat maize rotis, brinjal curry and *karhi* (chickpea and yoghurt broth), he enquires about his son's absence. When Kamla tells him that Mohan has gone into town with his friends, he grunts, thinking to himself that the boys will probably end up in one of the 'hotels' that abut the bus-stand, splurging money on meat and perhaps even liquor, items that are strictly forbidden in their house.

A generation ago, a family like Shobharam's would have eaten the same food at home but would have processed and cooked it rather differently. Food used to be cooked on an open hearth that was fired by dried cotton stalks and cow-dung cakes. Maize was the staple and wheat a luxury, but all grain was ground into flour at home by the women before the advent of electricity in the village. Salt, chillies and coriander seeds were the only everyday condiments, with oil and spices used sparingly and on special occasions. Tea was offered only to guests and it was sweetened with jaggery, not sugar. Milk was rarely drunk as such, but set into curds for making ghee and *chhaachh* (buttermilk). A few seasonal vegetables like brinjals and broad beans were available only immediately after the monsoons and, even then, were not bought and sold but exchanged between neighbours and relatives. Ready-made and packaged snacks were unknown in the village; for women and children, fresh chilli *pakoras* (fritters with chickpea flour batter) were the sole and much-looked-for treat during visits to the weekly market in town. Infants were breast-fed as a rule; if the mother could not feed the child, another lactating woman, usually from within the family, would. And for all people of the Patidar caste, including men, eating meat and drinking liquor were taboo, unimaginable violations of their community's *dharma* (righteous conduct, moral duty).

While food practices in India have always been differentiated by region, religion, caste, class, age and gender, these aspects have undergone a wide set of shifts in the last thirty years. The expansion of irrigated agriculture that occurred with the Green Revolution resulted in sharp increases in the production of wheat and rice. The subsidized spread of these cereals across the country through the Public Distribution System edged out dry-land grains like maize, *ragi* (finger millet), *jowar* (sorghum) and *bajra* (pearl millet) from local diets. The rise in wheat and rice production was underwritten by massive state investment in agricultural infrastructure including marketing which, by the 1980s, had yielded a dense network of trade linking rural farms with the rest of the country. These changes also facilitated the movement of off-season fresh produce from distant parts of the country to consumers in the cities. Government-supported horticultural and dairy cooperatives were able to purchase capital-intensive inputs such as cold storage units and chilling plants that, along with faster transportation, were central to the White Revolution which, by 1988, had made India the largest producer of milk in the world. Ten years later, meat and poultry production also began to rise swiftly with the expansion of concentrated feeding operations on factory farms, and by 2008, the per capita consumption of chicken – the fastest-growing animal protein in India – had doubled from 1998. Indians now not only eat more chicken, but also beef (cow and buffalo), goat and pig. According to National Sample Survey data, in 2007, 42 per cent of Indians described themselves as vegetarians who do not eat eggs, fish or meat. However, this group has been steadily diminishing over the last two decades as many households that were 'strict vegetarians' have begun to cook eggs at home, and a number have gone on to include poultry and meat in their culinary repertoire. In the last decade, this move away from vegetarianism has been four times faster in rural areas.

The shift towards agricultural produce that fetches higher prices in the market – wheat, rice, sugar cane, vegetables and fruit, dairy, poultry and meat – has not only changed the food that people eat but also the environment that they inhabit. Intensive cultivation and transportation have now become the norm, requiring larger injections of fossil fuels, water and synthetic chemicals. In several regions of the country, this form of food provisioning is no longer ecologically and economically sustainable; polluted and depleted water and soil have created a crisis in the countryside that directly affects farmers' lives and livelihoods. The most extreme manifestation of this crisis is the spate of suicides among farmers in agro-ecological settings as disparate as Punjab, Kerala and central Maharashtra and Karnataka. The ecological transformation of agriculture also includes new risks for more dispersed populations, animal as well as human. The new monocultures of crops and animals are highly susceptible to pests and diseases; epidemics like the avian flu that compelled the culling of millions of chickens in concentrated poultry factories reflect the changed vulnerabilities of crops as well as the people who grow and eat them. The increased use of pharmaceuticals such as antibiotics and growth hormones in animal husbandry and horticulture brings an entirely new meaning to the Ayurvedic notion of food as medicine. For instance, the hormone oxytocin which is used to induce labour in pregnant women is also injected into cows and buffaloes to raise milk yields and into vegetables to increase their size. Since the use of oxytocin induces uterine contractions that are painful, milch cattle are given diclofenac, a powerful painkiller, now known to be responsible for the mass extinction of vultures in the subcontinent due to feeding on cattle carcasses containing this drug. The use of these chemicals is intrinsic to the logic of the new technologies of industrialized agricultural production that seek economies of scale and speed in order to maximize profits. In the absence of effective food safety standards, factory and farm-owners are able to place profitability over health. Thus, while the consumption of higher-value foods may suggest that some Indians are eating better than ever, its impact on the environment and on health – that of plants, animals and humans – is proving to be more deleterious than ever.

New products and processes

Changes in government policy with economic liberalization in the 1990s resulted in significant foreign investment in agriculture and food processing. While limited in scale, the entry of multinational firms such as Pepsi that entered into direct contracts with farmers for purchasing tomatoes for ketchup and potatoes for chips, brought horticulture into prominence, with better-off farmers taking to speciality crops – exotic vegetables and fruit such as bell pepper and baby corn, asparagus and artichoke, strawberries and kiwi – for sale in the affluent neighbourhoods and restaurants of big cities. Reduced import duties and restrictions introduced new commodities to metropolitan grocery shelves, with New Zealand apples, Turkish pasta and Thai curry pastes figuring among the items to enter Indian homes. To make up the shortfall in the production of pulses and oilseeds – the two essential food groups whose cultivation was neglected by the Green Revolution – the government began to import lentils from Myanmar and palm oil from Malaysia to distribute through the Public Distribution System. The volume of agricultural produce imported into and exported from India's ports reflects the pervasive presence of these global food commodity chains that touch the lives of not only the elite but also the poor. At the same time, Indian corporate firms have begun to purchase land in Africa in order to supply agricultural products and other primary goods to the 'mother country'. These new resource flows, reminiscent of colonialism, signal the emergence of India and China as the world's most populous nations whose growing prosperity fuels domestic appetites at the expense of food for more needy people elsewhere.

While reconfigured regulatory regimes and new institutional arrangements have played a major role in changing food availability, simultaneous innovations in packaging technology have also been crucial. The biggest breakthrough for producers of FMCG (fast-moving consumer goods such as snacks) was the development of metallized polymer films that replaced the more expensive aluminium foil packaging and proved to be equally airtight and eye-catching. This technology makes it possible to sell small sachets of processed foods such as corn crisps and instant coffee, as well as masticants such as *pan masala* and chewing tobacco, at low prices to customers who cannot afford to buy large volumes at one go. These bright metallic-coloured packages are now ubiquitous in urban and rural shops and, being non-biodegradable, contribute substantially to the solid waste burden of the country.

The consumers for these new food commodities thus include not only the burgeoning middle classes to whom has flowed the lion's share of the gains from economic growth, but also the working classes who can now, in a modest way, enjoy some of the same pleasures as the class above them. In a nation still defined by sharp economic and social disparities, this convergence of consumption styles – similarities in form if not always in substance or quality – is celebrated in the media through numerous television advertisements that resonate with the aspirations of subaltern classes for upward mobility.

The proliferation of packaged foods extends not only across classes but also the urban–rural continuum. The association of these foods with modernity – signalled not only by the packaging but also by advertising campaigns that stress convenience and hygiene while also appealing to the premium placed on instant gratification in the present – has created new demands among rural social groups for whom consuming products such as potato chips and instant noodles would have been previously unthinkable. At the same time, however, the preference for processed foods can also be seen within a traditional matrix of food values where refined foods rich in fat and sugar are associated with affluence. Their consumption thus speaks not only to the desire to be modern but also appeals to a long-standing sensibility which regards fried and sweet foods as luxuries. Although the nutritional content of most packaged foods is generally inferior to that which is local and freshly cooked, these foods are steadily becoming a larger part of Indian diets, as is the case around the world. The rise of obesity, diabetes and heart diseases among affluent Indians, especially children, is directly attributable to lifestyles where processed foods rich in refined sugars and fats have come to dominate the palate.

The growing demand for processed foods also stems from demographic and occupational shifts in the Indian population. Increasing urbanization means that fewer people have a direct connection to agriculture and must rely on purchasing food that might earlier have been home-grown. The size and layout of most urban homes militate against tasks that require large open spaces: food processing activities that were previously performed at home such as washing and drying grain, making *papad* (lentil crisps) or preserving vegetables and fruit, are now no longer possible. The decline of the joint family and the fact that many more women work outside the home have also made it more difficult to undertake collective, labour-intensive activities around food preparation. At the same time, even full-time home-makers have given up the practice of preparing *papad* and pickles at home even though they may have the time to do so. There are adequate substitutes available in the market and shifts in the relative importance attached to different domestic responsibilities means that tasks such as supervising children's studies now command greater priority. However, food processed outside the home is being sourced not only from big-brand industrial manufacturers, but also from small cottage industries and family firms that supply within a smaller geographical and social radius. It is commonplace in Bombay and Pune, for instance, to order the flour for *thalipeeth* (multi-grain savoury bread) or the thick curds for *shrikhand* (a sweet) or ready-made delicacies like *puran poli* (thin lentil-stuffed bread) and *karanji* (a fried sweetmeat stuffed with coconut and dried fruits) from a local housewife, just as households in Chennai and Madurai can now get prepared *dosa* (rice-lentil crepes) batter and *sambar* (lentil and vegetable curry) powder from a local shop. These practices point to the parallel rise in the professionalization of home-based cooking that caters to urban demands for traditional food.

Eating out

The cultural effects of urbanization include the rapidly growing trend of eating meals and snacks outside the home. In his informative essay 'Dining Out in Bombay',[7] Frank Conlon distinguishes between the utilitarian and discretionary aspects of eating out. For many of the male industrial workers who migrated into Bombay in the early twentieth century and lived in shared tenements, separated from their families, 'eating out' was a compulsion and not a choice. Conlon describes the proliferation of *khanavals* (eating houses) that supplied the cuisine appropriate to their patrons' regional and caste affiliations and that enabled migrants to maintain rules about eating food cooked by, and in the company of, those of one's caste or higher. Such community-specific eating houses were earlier to be found in pilgrimage and trade centres that attracted a diverse clientele. Their spread into other cities was facilitated by the new modes of work and living generated by the growing educational, industrial and service sectors. While caste-related rules of commensality continued to govern where one ate outside the home, they were harder to follow for those with tighter budgets. If one could not completely control *where* one ate, the strategy was to regulate *what* one ate. When confronted with hotels whose caste affiliation was uncertain, many Hindus resorted to the practice of eating *pakka* food – which carried less threat of being polluted because it was fried. For those at the very bottom of the food chain – rickshaw pullers and porters who live on the street and must eat the cheapest meals – the rules of commensality were perforce relaxed in the search for affordable food. Yet, despite poverty, deep-seated cultural notions about what food is acceptable still prevail. Homeless and low-caste Hindu migrants to the city are unlikely to report eating buffalo meat, just as poor Muslims will not eat pork, even though these are the least expensive available sources of animal protein.

For those increasing 'number of Indians with sufficient discretionary income to indulge in the habit of dining out not from necessity but from opportunity, and for display',[8] hotels and restaurants are places for experimenting with new forms of sociality where caste-based proscriptions are a diminishing concern. For vegetarians, the first encounters with meat and fish are often in a restaurant, in the company of friends. Several Brahmin and Bania informants describe how they came to relish the taste of forbidden flesh – mutton *biryani* (rice with meat) or burger, butter chicken and *seekh kabab* (minced meat roasted on skewers) – eaten clandestinely away from home. In homes where the non-vegetarian proclivities of some family members – usually male – are known and tolerated, the practice of eating out together allows people to order the food that suits their individual dietary preferences, without violating the sanctity of the vegetarian domestic space. The popularity of 'multi-cuisine' restaurants that generally serve Punjabi, Chinese and Western items along with the ethnic cuisine of the region where they are located attests to the importance of catering to the simultaneous desires for the familiar and the exotic, the adventurous and the safe, emanating from the palates of different members within the same family.

If the idea of eating out for pleasure was once confined to the Westernized elite or restricted to the occasional enjoyment of street foods, generally snacks, it has now become far more widespread. While fears about caste pollution have faded, equally enduring middle-class concerns about 'hygiene' and 'cleanliness' – terms which have lost their connotation of being euphemisms for 'low-caste' or of uncertain social provenance, and are now used to refer only to bacterial and not social contamination – do not seem to deter people from eating out more frequently at a range of establishments. Along with eating out, the practice of 'ordering in' has also become ubiquitous. While it may be an occasional indulgence for households with stay-at-home women for whom it is a change and 'a break from the monotony of home-cooked food',[9] it is a frequent resort of young professionals and students who are unable to cook because they lack the time and skill. With economic liberalization there is more disposable income to be spent on consumption, especially among the upper strata. For these sections, and the youth among them in particular, drinking and eating out is now regarded not as a choice but as a defining marker of identity and status. Patronizing cafés, restaurants and pubs has become the norm for contemporary sociality among young adults and adolescents, for bonding with friends and lovers and signalling belonging in a desired social world.

The 'opening up' of the Indian economy with liberalized trade and other policies has also ushered in greater familiarity with tastes and lifestyles across the globe and has increased the cultural premium associated with cosmopolitanism. Being seen to appreciate a variety of cuisines has become a contemporary marker of connoisseurship whereas, in the past, virtuosity lay in mastering the codes of one's own cuisine at home. At the same time, the incremental accretions of regional and international cuisines in Delhi – burgers and ice cream that initially catered to American soldiers posted in the city during the Second World War and subsequently indigenized; 'Mughlai' food that accompanied Punjabi refugees after Partition; Udupi 'tiffin' or snacks that followed South Indian settlers as they took up jobs in the burgeoning bureaucracy; 'Chinese' noodles and, later, *momos* (stuffed dumplings) that were introduced by Tibetan settlers – have over time led to a fusion such that many foods once considered 'foreign' no longer seem alien or requiring the effort of cultivating one's palate. Restaurants, even international chains, are more than willing to meet customers halfway on the road to adaptation: not only do McDonald's Indian outlets sell their signature 'Big Mac' – rechristened Maharaja Mac – without beef, they have no red meat on their *desi* menu.

The elite, however, tend to reject the hybrid forms that have emerged as international and regional cuisines have been domesticated by dominant Indian preferences. *Paneer dosa* and *gobhi* Manchurian, for instance – are charged with being inauthentic and debased. With increased exposure to metropolitan settings such as London, New York and Singapore and their proliferation of ethnic eateries, upper-class metropolitan consumers have created a demand for restaurants devoted to specialized cuisines, with Italian and Thai being the most popular. Since the 1990s, regional cuisines from within India have also managed to break through the stranglehold of Punjabi/Mughlai cooking to much critical acclaim. The flourishing restaurant scene in Indian cities is fostered by the rise of the 'foodie' – a recently coined term of self-identification that encompasses current ideas of cosmopolitan connoisseurship in a manner different from existing appellations like 'gourmand'. A foodie not only cultivates his or her palate but enjoys educating others as well. This trend is best-illustrated in the restaurant reviews that are now a regular feature of newspapers as well as city-specific magazines such as *TimeOut*: rather than being critical evaluations of quality, the reviews are primarily pedagogical in tone – informing readers about different kinds of cheeses or lettuces, how wine glasses should be held or sushi eaten. This mode of aspirational education, which is presented as a device for democratizing elite forms of cultural knowledge, often ends up re-confirming the superiority of the foodie pedagogue, underlining social distinctions rather than obliterating them. This culture of cosmopolitan food appreciation not only marks the phenomenon of eating out but has also begun to influence the practices of cooking and eating within the home.

At home, in the world

The Marathi cookbook *Ruchira* was first published in 1970 and has since sold more than 125,000 copies. Without ever mentioning the term 'Brahmin', the caste identity of its author and primary readership is clearly signalled by the (vegetarian) repertoire it covers. The pictures that punctuate its twenty-ninth revised edition[10] offer a glimpse of the ideal domestic spaces for cooking and dining among upper-caste Maharashtrians, and capture a social world in the process of transition. The cover photograph, for instance, shows a nuclear family eating a meal. The husband and two young children (a girl and a boy) are seated at a dining table instead of on the floor as would have been the case in previous generations. The woman, however, is not sitting and eating with them; in conformity with older norms, she is shown standing and serving them. She is smiling at her husband, whose expression suggests that he has just complimented her on the food. The food before them is an incongruous assortment of *puris* (fried puffed bread), a wet vegetable or *dal* preparation, *pulao* (rice with vegetables), a salad – an elaborate arrangement of lettuce, cucumber and tomato slices on a plate – and three kinds of sweets, quite different from the items and spatial arrangement of the traditional Marathi *thali* (plate). Food is served in and eaten on melamine dishes, as distinct from the more traditional metal utensils that were considered to be an essential part of a woman's wealth.

Another photograph depicts the ideal kitchen, once again straddling both traditional and modern styles and functions. A refrigerator and a mixer-blender are prominently displayed, as is a *soop* (winnowing fan) and a heavy cast-iron mortar and pestle. An array of gleaming metal containers lines the shelves alongside a row of recycled Bournvita glass jars. There is a gas cylinder, pressure cooker, cups, saucers and plastic flowers in a vase placed on the fridge. One is left to imagine the carved, canopied wooden stand on the opposite wall from where the icons of the household deities preside over this sacred space. This compact, neatly equipped kitchen exemplifies the virtues of organization and hygiene that the modern woman must embody in her practices, especially now that there is less time, space and labour available to carry out the food preparation tasks that still remain her primary responsibility.

The ideal kitchen that *Ruchira* depicts strikes a familiar chord with the cookbook's women readers. A generation ago, when Shubhada Deshpande was a young bride, she lived in a household in Pune that included, besides her bank officer husband and two-year-old son, her parents-in-law and an unmarried brother-in-law who was studying engineering. Every day at dawn, she and her mother-in-law would squat on the floor to scrape coconuts on a *whili* (curved cutting and scraping blade) and to churn cream from yogurt. The shredded coconut would then be ground into chutney on a stone slab. Now that Deshpande is in her sixties and lives alone with her retired husband, she still makes coconut chutney but in an electric blender. Instead of churning butter, she buys it ready-made, often serving it on toast for breakfast, a practice that her mother-in-law would have frowned upon as a lazy short-cut, vastly inferior to the cooked *pohe* (flattened rice) or *saanja* (savoury semolina porridge) that she still makes occasionally. When relatives visit, she is likely to prepare the more elaborate fare as a gesture of being properly hospitable by taking the trouble to cook something 'special'; but, even in this respect, the far more labour-intensive meals of her mother-in-law's days, with different dishes being cooked to suit the ritual requirements and dietary preferences of differ-ent generations and genders, are now only a distant memory. There is a tinge of nostalgia in Deshpande's reminiscences about the labour that went into the lavish meals orchestrated by her mother-in-law: 'We would start working in the kitchen before dawn. There was an endless stream of chores to be done, one after the other, non-stop. But we did things properly in those days. Now it's easier: we take short-cuts;

we buy ready-made things from the market. How can it be the same? The quality has gone down.'[11]

Perhaps the biggest physical change for Deshpande, and for most other middle-class women, is that the kitchen has moved up from the ground to a waist-high counter top. Old tools like the coconut scraper have been redesigned – they can be used on kitchen counters and require less muscular effort. When exchanging recipes or cooking techniques, Deshpande and her female relatives and friends often discuss the new appliances that they see in each other's homes or advertised on television. Acquiring a hand-held blender, electric chopper or sandwich-maker that costs a few hundred or a couple of thousand rupees is not only regarded as a necessary convenience but as an affordable way of indulging the periodic urge for novelty. These electric-powered gadgets and appliances are not treated on a par with other kitchen equipment. The *bai* (domestic worker) who comes to wash Deshpande's dishes and do initial preparations such as chopping vegetables is not allowed to use or clean the plastic and glass equipment; it is assumed that an 'uneducated' woman who is a 'servant' will damage the appliance due to her carelessness or ignorance.

Each new electrical appliance makes an incremental change in the kitchen, but these are small shifts compared to the arrival of refrigerators into middle-class urban homes in the 1960s, the new technology radically transforming food processing and storage. Deshpande recalls how before the coming of the refrigerator, all cooked food had to be consumed or given away at the end of the day:

> Everything was eaten fresh. We would manage the quantities so
> that nothing was wasted, though sometimes this meant that a dish
> I really liked would be finished by the time we women sat down to eat
> after serving everybody else! Day-old food was considered stale and
> spoiled. And now look, my daughter-in-law takes leftovers out of
> the fridge after two days even, heats them in the microwave and
> serves! It might be convenient, but it's not healthy.[12]

The other big change that started when Deshpande's son became a teenager, and accelerated once her mother-in-law passed away, was her increasing experimentation with cooking new dishes outside the Maharashtrian Brahmin repertoire. In the 1980s, she baked a sponge cake for the first time – without eggs and in a pressure cooker. She subsequently acquired a round table-top oven and, mainly in response to her son's demands but also the admiration of her peers and their children, started to bake regularly, even using the eggs that were once forbidden in their household. A separate bowl was set aside for egg-related operations. Once ready-made pizza base and cheese became available in the local grocery store, Deshpande began making pizza at home. After her in-laws were no longer alive, a light meal of soup and pizza would often end the day for the whole family, a menu that was unthinkable even in the early 1990s. Similar transformations have occurred in middle-class urban kitchens across the country. Exposure to different cuisines through the practice of eating out has fuelled a strong trend towards preparing the same dishes at home, with greater control over the ingredients and at a cheaper price. Condiments such as soya and chilli sauces became available for home use in retail-size bottles in the 1980s, reflecting the growing popularity of cooking 'chow mein' and 'chilli chicken' in metropolitan households. Subsequent additions to kitchen shelves include packaged soup and curry powders and pastes, pasta and pizza toppings. Children's tastes have been decisive in terms of encouraging the consumption of non-traditional food that is purchased in semi- or fully processed form.

If children have acted as cultural brokers within the household – along with the grocer and vegetable vendor outside in the local market – they have been vigorously supported by the print and television media. Women's magazines, where recipes are a regular feature, and cookbooks such as the series by Tarla Dalal, which has sold over four million copies in multiple Indian languages, are now supplemented by television shows of which the most popular – and longest running at seventeen years – is Sanjeev Kapoor's *Khana Khazana* ('Food Treasure'). Kapoor is now a celebrity with a chain of restaurants, books and product endorsements to his credit, but his initial success rested on his presentation of recipes from the various regions of India and, less often, Europe and the rest of Asia, modified to suit middle-class Indian palates and kitchens. Adapting diverse ingredients and cooking techniques to bring them within the reach of home-makers who are committed to work hard at cultivating their culinary skills, Kapoor provides instructions for hosting birthday parties, looking after special nutritional needs during pregnancy, recreating the cuisines of the former royal families, and helpful tips such as the ideal way to flambé a dish. The appeal of his television show lies in how fluently it translates potentially alien cuisines into terms and techniques with which viewers can feel comfortable, even as it encourages them to be more adventurous and expand their culinary repertoire.

Kapoor's *Khana Khazana* reaches a receptive audience for whom the parameters of being a good cook have shifted significantly. No longer is virtuosity in the kitchen based upon the mastery of a classic caste- and region-specific cuisine; versatility is now crucial. A good cook is one who regularly attempts to make new dishes and serve a variety of foods from different cultural traditions. At the same time, as *grihani* or guardian of the sacred hearth, a Hindu woman must still protect the sanctity of the kitchen, by ensuring that while the boundaries of acceptable food practices are stretched, they are not broken. The same applies for Muslim women. In some cases, women have dealt with the changes in food practices within their domestic spaces and among members of their family by personally taking on stricter food prohibitions. In urban Bengal, for instance, more and more middle-class Hindu women claim not to eat meat, a proscription that was traditionally confined to widows and regarded as a sign of inauspiciousness.[13] The new vegetarianism among married women denotes a counter-current of austerity and abstinence in an era of consumerism, usually expressed through a bio-medical discourse of nutrition and hygiene. Even though the notions of purity and pollution that earlier shaped social interactions around food have faded from public spaces, they remain alive – and perhaps have even been strengthened – within the middle-class home that now includes the world.

Food from below

For Indians across the country, food is not only a source of nutrition, it is medicine, a mode of worship and a marker of social relations. Yet, for those at the very bottom of the social pyramid, the sheer dearth of nourishing food makes its cultural meanings that much more tenuous. Clinical signs of chronic under-nutrition are visible in 33 per cent of India's population. UNICEF reports that 47 per cent of all Indian children under five years are underweight or severely underweight, indicating the presence of chronic malnourishment, the high incidence of which among children is an indicator of poor maternal health and nutrition as well. The figure is higher for girls, for children in rural areas and among Scheduled Castes and Scheduled Tribes. While there have been notable strides in improving children's access to nutritious food through state welfare programmes such as the *anganwadis* (day care centres) and the school midday meals, a recent review by the World Bank observes that these schemes do not address a fundamental issue, namely, parents' inability to provide adequate food at home. With economic liberalization, the Public Distribution System which provided basic food provisions and cooking fuel at subsidized rates to all citizens was downsized into a 'targeted' programme, focusing only on low-income groups but in a manner that excluded many needy people. The incidence of under-nutrition is especially acute in Bihar, Uttar Pradesh, Madhya Pradesh, Rajasthan, Maharashtra and Orissa, and is closely linked to poverty and the lack of assets and incomes that allow people to grow or buy food.

Khodamba village lies in the mountain ridges that flank the Narmada River's flow along the south-western border of Madhya Pradesh and Maharashtra. Its population of Bhil adivasis (members of Scheduled Tribes) cultivates small patches of hill land that they plant with maize, *jowar* and *bajra*, three kinds of pulses, groundnut and sesame, small millets and hill rice, chillies, pumpkin and beans in an intricate mosaic of mixed cropping. Most households own draught bullocks, the occasional cow, several goats and hens. They also fish in the river in the summer months but do not catch much. The forest is more forthcoming: each season yields different fruit and vegetables, besides other useful produce. In Vanjaria's house, the availability of food ebbs and flows with the seasons and from year to year. The monsoons are the worst. That's when the children die, when the stored stock of grain from the previous year runs out, prices rise and the money earned from migrant work in the summer no longer suffices. Meanwhile, there is the hard labour of ploughing, planting and weeding to be done, far harder to accomplish on an empty stomach. Vanjaria's wife Kandli will coarsely grind a fistful of corn kernels, boil them into a soup that's fermented overnight to make *raabdi* – a filling meal, though nowhere as nutritious as *jowar roti* and *dal* spiked with chillies and salt which they manage to eat during the post-monsoon months. If the harvest has been good that year – and the rains tend to fail every third or fourth year – Vanjaria's family will stay in the village through the year, cooking the occasional chicken to provide hospitality to visiting relatives, and sacrificing a goat once every year or so to propitiate their gods and ancestors, or to celebrate a marriage. These ritual occasions culminate in major feasts, where fiery goat curry is eaten with *roti* or *jowar ghaat* (sorghum meal), washed down with liquor from *mahua* flowers collected from the forest. These are considered to be good times, when the stock of food in the granary will last for several months and when the crop of pulses and oilseeds yields enough to be sold for some cash.

When the rains fail, Vanjaria, his wife and their four children – including one still feeding at Kandli's breast – migrate around the time of Diwali to the irrigated areas of Gujarat to earn a living. They go with a tin canister full of flour that Kandli has ground for days ahead; food is expensive at their worksite and every rupee earned must be stretched to the utmost. They work in cotton and tobacco fields, sometimes picking vegetables, sometimes cutting sugar cane – earning thirty to forty rupees a day, living in a shack which offers some shelter and safety for their meagre belongings – bedding, the tin canister, clay griddle, battered aluminium saucepan and plates, and the sickle that serves as an all-purpose knife. They are surrounded by prosperity – the village shops by the roadside are bursting with all manner of colourful packets – but they must suppress their desires. The children, in particular, look longingly at the goods on offer but that remain beyond their means. In their own village, Khodamba, they could go into the forest and find delicious titbits like *tendu* fruit, amla, green mango or *ber* (berries); there is nothing to be gleaned or gathered in *this* setting where everything costs money. When Vanjaria gets his family's weekly wages, his purchases include some tea dust and sugar for Kandli, *bidis* (country cigarettes) for himself and a packet of cheap glucose biscuits for the children – small indulgences that they can ill afford. In the chilly morning, Kandli brews the tea and gives a plateful each to her children huddled around the hearth, who concentrate silently as they drink the dark, sugary liquid. They will not get a hot meal till the end of the day.

Notes

1 R. S. Khare (ed.), *The Eternal Food: Gastronomic Ideas and Experiences of Hindus and Buddhists* (Albany: State University of New York Press, 1992); R. S. Khare and M. S. A. Rao (eds.), *Food, Society and Culture: Aspects in South Asian Food Systems* (Durham, NC: Carolina Academic Press, 1986).

2 Francis Zimmerman, *The Jungle and the Aroma of Meats: An Ecological Theme in Hindu Medicine* (Berkeley: University of California Press, 1987).

3 K. T. Achaya, *Indian Food: A Historical Companion* (New Delhi: Oxford University Press, 1994); K. T. Achaya, *A Historical Dictionary of Indian Food* (New Delhi: Oxford University

Press, 1998); Elizabeth Collingham, *Curry: A Tale of Cooks and Conquerors* (New York: Oxford University Press, 2006).

4 Sidney W. Mintz, *Sweetness and Power: The Place of Sugar in Modern History* (New York: Penguin Books, 1986).

5 Chitrita Banerji, *Feeding the Gods: Memories of Food and Culture in Bengal* (Calcutta: Seagull Books, 2006); Anita Desai, *Fasting, Feasting* (London: Chatto and Windus, 1999); Nilanjana S. Roy, *A Matter of Taste: The Penguin Book of Indian Writings on Food* (New Delhi: Penguin Books, 2004).

6 Uma Narayan, 'Eating Cultures: Incorporation, Identity, and Indian Food', *Social Identities* 1:1 (1995), pp. 63–86; Jennifer B. Saunders, '"I Don't Eat Meat": Discourse on Food among Transnational Hindus', *Contributions to Indian Sociology* 41:2 (2007), pp. 203–33.

7 Frank F. Conlon, 'Dining Out in Bombay', in Carol A. Breckenridge (ed.), *Consuming Modernity: Public Culture in Contemporary India* (New Delhi: Oxford University Press, 1996), pp. 90–127.

8 *Ibid.*, p. 106.

9 Interview with Shubhada Deshpande, 8 October 2007.

10 Kamlabai Ogle, *Ruchira* (29th revised edn) (Pune: Mehta Publishing House, 1994).

11 Interview with Shubhada Deshpande, 11 October 2007.

12 *Ibid.*

13 Henrike Donner, 'New Vegetarianism: Food, Gender and Neo-Liberal Regimes in Bengali Middle-Class Families', *South Asia: Journal of South Asian Studies* n.s. 31:1 (2008), pp. 143–69.

4

Urban forms of religious practice

Driving in eastern Bangalore beyond the Intermediate Ring Road, I pass a roadside temple dedicated to Shiva and his holy family; it is guarding the entrance to the old village from which Marathahalli Road, the local name for Airport Road in this area, derives its name. While the road has become more congested, and the village has been incorporated into the city, the temple has nevertheless been embellished over the last three decades, most recently with a new coat of paint and a patio marking its perimeter. Further down Airport Road's intersection with the Outer Ring Road near Brookefields, a banner advertises the ritual consecration of a large new temple dedicated to Shirdi Sai Baba, a relatively modern holy figure. Indian cityscapes have long made space for the celebration of 'the sacred' or 'the religious' in a wide array of forms, and public life itself is interlaced with religiosity in at least three significant ways.

First, there has been a proliferation of new temples, religious buildings and altars of various scales and genealogies. These include fixed ones such as roadside temples, vernacular shrines in market places, taxi stands, exterior walls of homes, or within the courtyards of apartment complexes. In urban Goa, wayside shrines alter the centuries-old religion of Goan Hindus and Catholics by allowing devotees to worship saints and deities outside what might have been their own parochial religious associations.[1] On a grander spatial scale, there is also the model of 'the religious campus'. These are elaborate constructions around a particular guru or leader, such as Auroville (inspired by Sri Aurobindo and the Mother) in Pondicherry and Tamil Nadu inaugurated in 1968, or the more recent Swaminarayan Akshardham temple complex in New Delhi, inaugurated in 2005.

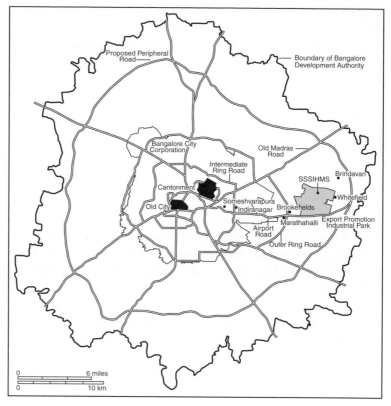

Map 2 Bangalore metropolitan region, 2005.

Some altars are mobile and are found on the dashboards of public and private buses and auto-rickshaws and, like fixed shrines or temples, may consist of a range of old and new deities, icons and images. In Bangalore one regularly encounters Hanuman, Shani, the Infant Jesus, the Quran, Gayatri or Om Shakti. Commenting on the growing popularity of Hanuman in cities in particular, Philip Lutgendorf writes that Hanuman's complex iconographic and textual history (including Shaiva, Vaishnava and Shakta traditions), his reputation as a go-between/in-between figure, and his connection with healing and yogic powers, makes him especially appealing to India's rapidly growing middle classes.[2]

Second, there has been the creation of new rituals or the modification of older ones that accompany the altered cultural and spatial boundaries of the urban landscape. There are religious processions of new deities and images; old processions laying claim to emerging routes, suburbs and other spaces; and other types of ritual movements through the city that attempt to recover and recall older spaces and times. Mattison Mines, for example, describes how the role of mercantile communities, rituals, and temples shifted over the centuries in Madras or Fort St George, founded by the British as a trading post in 1639. In Georgetown, the settlement near the fort, the number of East India Company servants and soldiers was small and Indian traders largely carried out trade and production. The town was divided into the western part, occupied by the Komatis and an eastern part, by the Beeris. The Beeri Chettiar merchants were largely Tamil-speaking Shaivas and their rivals, the Komati Chettiars and Balijas, were Telugu-speaking Vaishnava merchants. In each division, temples associated with one of these communities came to represent their prestige, wealth and status. Today, there is an annual procession of the Kandasami temple from Park Town (considered a 'satellite' area of residence of the Beeri Chettiar community) to the older 'centre' where the community, in fact, no longer has houses, businesses or control over the main community temple.[3] Yet, this procession and others like it, reflect earlier memories of place. Ritualization of the urban fabric may also involve the invention of new festivals and large-scale performances sponsored by neighbourhood associations, local religious collectives and caste-groups; global religious organizations, meanwhile, capitalize on the mobile technologies of acoustic and visual media from cassettes to video, enabling new sensory experience.

Third, gurus and religious leaders with diverse origins, philosophies, organizational capacities and transnational reputations command the devotion of urban constituencies in increasingly important ways. For example, while older religious collectives and religious sites retain their salience in metropolitan areas, the middle classes are developing a fast-growing interest in techniques of the body such as yoga, or meditation taught by new spiritual teachers claiming descent from a variety of older traditions. These include Sri Sri Ravi Shankar and Swami Ramdev. Some of these practices of the body such as yogic breathing have an Indian cultural background but have been adapted for new social concerns and strata. Others, such as Japanese-origin Reiki, are attributed to teachers or traditions from other world areas. What is also significant is the way in which the built environment of cities has been augmented because of the personal charisma of a master, holy person or saint. While there are several historical examples, there are innumerable recent cases that present novel urban perspectives. The branches of the north Indian Radhasoami movement and its gurus have founded a site called Dayalbagh that includes factories, stores, educational institutions and residences. Most of these sites 'are to be found in suburban or rural locations and are constructed so as to suggest what an ideal Indian village should be; they are urban visions of rural life'.[4] By contrast, Auroville, designed as an ideal township and an experiment in human unity, is a self-conscious exercise in city planning: its central core consists of a peace area, which is surrounded by industrial, cultural and residential zones, both of which are enclosed by a green belt. Its concentric city plan is reminiscent of 'garden city' frameworks that became popular around the world from the early twentieth century onwards.

This chapter dwells on the creative intersection of the Indian urban and the religious. I take as my point of departure two bodies of work: studies of urban India and studies of religion in urban contexts. Usually, studies of urban India focus on one of three historical and ethnographic sites: (1) the city as sacred space (embodied in the temple town of Madurai in south India or Varanasi in north India); (2) the colonial city (such as Calcutta/Kolkata or Madras/Chennai); and (3) the city as a managerial/ developmentalist project (sometimes celebrated in examples such as Chandigarh). Meanwhile, studies of religion in urban locales have tended to revolve around what have become two predictable themes: (1) the city as a secular realm or site for liberal enactments of citizenship and identity, where religion is cast as a failure of the modern/modernizing project; or (2) religious nationalism, communal violence and fundamentalisms. Many of the concerns in this chapter stem from the realization that there has been a theoretical neglect of the myriad religious forms and practices that are embedded in the processes of contemporary Indian urbanization. In 1950, the number of people living in urban areas was 60 million; in 2009, it had increased to over 350 million, one of the most important demographic transitions in recent history. I draw attention, thus, to the fact that there is an urgent need to address how the Indian urban is produced by agents and communities who bring a range of religious imaginations and practices to the city.

This chapter focuses on the city of Bangalore, a metropolitan region approaching a population of about 7 million, in the southern India state of Karnataka. Since the 1990s, Bangalore has sometimes been celebrated as 'India's Silicon Valley', while there has also been a backlash by some locals against the increasingly cosmopolitan character of some areas of the city. Bangalore is an interesting site for an enquiry into urban religiosity precisely because it is *not* a sacred city in the mode of Madurai or Varanasi, and instead has been regarded as exemplifying the secular rationalist model of a Nehruvian industrial and science city. It presents us, therefore, with the opportunity to move the debate forward in new directions, and to develop more subtle analytical lenses and languages for Indian urbanity and religious life. The sections below, which also reflect on the three ways in which public life in urban India is interwoven with the religious, are concerned with two case studies: the Karaga festival and the Sai Baba movement, allowing us to bring the analysis of contemporary religion in India into dialogue with urban studies.[5]

The Karaga festival as an urban mnemonic

Bangalore or 'Bengaluru' is said to have emerged in 1537 through the efforts of a local chieftain, Kempe Gowda I, who established a fort (*kote*) and market-cum-habitation area (*pete*). As in many parts of southern India, the feasibility of an urban complex rested on the construction of artificial water-bodies such as lakes or tanks (*kere*); in the case of the Old City of Bangalore, these included the Sampangi, the Dharmambudi, the Kempambudi and the Siddikatte tanks. The Old City became part of the Wodeyar kingdom of Mysore by the seventeenth century, later falling under the rulership of General Haider Ali in 1766. Haider Ali and his son, Tipu Sultan, engaged in a series of battles with the British East India Company, which finally seized Bangalore in 1799. The Company reinstalled the Wodeyar kings, who allowed the British to set up a civil and military station (the 'Cantonment') north-east of the Old City beyond Sampangi tank (see map). Water-bodies were significant in this new dispensation: the Cantonment was located close to Halsur tank but new ones, including Sankey tank, were also added. By the early twentieth century, the Old City and the Cantonment were separated by a large wooded area, Cubbon Park, and the twin urban complex with a population of about 228,000 persons was interwoven with hundreds of interlocking tanks and several large green spaces created by various authorities.

The popular image of Bangalore as a 'garden city' (linked in significant ways to garden city frameworks in Bangalore's post-Independence planning documents) emerges from these developments but is also linked experientially and spatially to the numerous horticultural gardens found in and around the city. These gardens (*tota*) are tended by personnel from a Backward Caste community called the Tigalas, who are Tamil-speakers established in the Bangalore region through several waves of migration over the centuries. The approximately 250,000 Tigalas today view themselves as 'Vanhikula Kshatriyas' or descendants of 'fiery warriors'. Today, they are no longer connected with martial livelihoods and are largely part of the urban informal economy and factory-sector. They remain famous locally for their customary skills in cultivating vegetables, fruits and flowers in gardens and nurseries, all of which were fed traditionally by canals flowing from the city's tanks and with organic waste from its habitation areas. Although the landscape of the city has been dramatically altered, their association with gardening continues to remind us of a habitat of lakes and gardens that constituted Bangalore's distinctive urban fabric.

Bangalore's largest civic ritual, the Karaga festival (*jatre*) organized by the Tigala community in the first month of the Kannada calendar (usually late March to early April), attracts thousands of people on its final days and defines the religious life of the Old City. The official centre of the festival is the Dharmaraja temple in the south-eastern corner of the Old City, but the rituals mainly focus on the appearance of a cosmic female power, or *shakti*, within the adjacent Sampangi tank area bordering Cubbon Park. The *shakti* is Draupadi (the polyandrous wife of the five Pandava heroes of the pan-Indian *Mahabharata* epic), who manifests herself every year on the thirteenth day of the month in the form of an elaborately decorated red icon called the 'Karaga'. A priest from the Tigala community starts out by carrying the icon at his waist. On the fifteenth day of the month, however, the priest becomes completely identified with the *shakti*, as he dons female wedding clothes and a grand coiffure of jasmine, and carries the Karaga on his head. Tigala 'hero-sons' (*virakumara*), who protect the deity, join the procession that winds through several roads of the Old City on the final full-moon night of the festival, making stops at other goddess and Hanuman temples, a Sufi shrine and junctions of several bazaars. The hero-sons wear swords and wristbands to signify their service to the fiery goddess, their participation in the festival, and the demands made on their diet, physical prowess and sexuality during the event.

Unlike the Sanskrit *Mahabharata* epic, various community narratives – including an oral epic in Tamil and Telugu called the *Karaga Purana* recited after the conclusion of the procession – portray Draupadi's transformation into a fierce cosmic warrior goddess fighting a demon and his blood-offspring. Her hero-sons join her, Draupadi-*shakti*, in her ultimately victorious contest, where she ingests the demon. The unisexual reproductiveness of the goddess, the celibacy of the hero-sons and the martial representations of both, stand in contrast to the increasing impotence of the gardeners in the urban milieu today. They have lost their garden land in the city, even as the tanks and canals that fed it have been choked with industrial waste and metropolitan sewage, or have vanished under public and domestic buildings.

Post-Independence Bangalore has become the sixth largest Indian city, the capital of Karnataka state, a centre for textiles, engineering, electrical and software production. Its population has increased exponentially from 991,000 persons in 1951 to around 6.5 million persons in 2005. One of the shadow narratives of this accelerated development, documented in several government reports and non-governmental agencies' findings, is the decay of the city's hydraulic and garden environment. For instance, after a single Bangalore City Corporation was created incorporating the Old City and the Cantonment in 1949 (see map), the Kanteerava stadium was constructed in the bed of Sampangi tank that had been closely associated with Tigala habitation areas, garden lands and the Karaga festival. As Bangalore's tank and horticultural practices rapidly disappear, the Karaga festival becomes an act of remembering an urban past. Ritual activities and movement, such as when the Karaga priest performs devotions for sacred images at nine different sites across the city (including the Dharmaraja temple, three tanks, two large wells and a saltwater pond), retrieve the public memory of Bangalore's water and green spaces. Today, only one of these water bodies exists, and that too, only barely; the garden cover is considerably depleted, and the emergence of Draupadi as *shakti* occurs in a small hall overshadowed by the Kanteerava sports complex that had been built for the 1997 National Games held in the city. Because the 'fluids' of the city have been depleted or gone dry and no circulation occurs, the Karaga priest has to create a virtual flow through ritual movement in order to cool the heated bodies of the hero-sons and the goddess.

This kinetic device of remembering pasts, which is premised on a protocol of enactment and embodiment, has implications for the present: political mobilization emerges on the ground of ritual activity or kinship ties created through origin myths. The Karaga festival has become a basis over time for alliances between different communities engaged in factory or informal sector occupations in Bangalore. These allied communities, mostly Backward Caste groups, also possess fiery warrior ancestors and temples dedicated to Draupadi. They also participate in the Old City Karaga procession, or sponsor other Karaga-type festivals. Further, as metropolitan Bangalore ingests or extends into villages and towns on its periphery (for example, Devanahalli, which is now the site of Bangalore International Airport), Karaga festivals in these sites also become part of a cycle of urban and suburban performance. There is political mobilization by different groups aiming for visibility in the legislature or job reservations, but also continuing campaigns for the protection of gardens and water-bodies in metropolitan Bangalore. The Karaga festival, therefore, is located in a discursive arena occupied by the state, businesses and different classes, all of which are engaged in struggles over urban pasts and futures, planning and public space.

Sacralizing the Export Promotion Industrial Park

Prashanti Nilayam (located in Puttaparthi, Andhra Pradesh) is a famous sacred township in southern India centred on the charismatic guru Sathya Sai Baba (1926–2011), who stands at the apex of a religious movement commanding several million devotees globally, including urban middle-class professionals, scientists, doctors, teachers, businessmen and public sector employees. The Sri Sathya Sai Organization, with over 11,000 official centres of devotion worldwide, has made significant interventions in education, health care, provision of social utilities and disaster response carried out through service (*seva*) activities and financial donations by a transnational network of devotees. Sathya Sai Baba's residence over several decades in Puttaparthi has not only led to the growth of Puttaparthi from a small village with a population of 3,471 in 1961 to 11,340 in 2001, but the urbanized and urbanizing population of the proximate area also grew from 7,182 in 1961 to 25,672 in 2001, a growth rate of 257 per cent over four decades. Although the hermitage area and its connected buildings are located in what was once purely a rural location, this is not a model of rural self-sufficiency, but a vision of the ideal polis. This vision is not restricted to the hermitage area of Prashanti Nilayam but includes hospitals, stadiums, a music college, a planetarium, temples, residences and above all, sites associated with the life and message of Sathya Sai Baba, whether in the village of his childhood, the Chaitanya Jyoti Museum, or the university, Vidyagiri. While there are many types of building styles here, architecture and the built landscape in the hermitage and other sites are not rooted in a 'Hindu' revivalist project but have a rhetorical function, i.e., they give effective expression to ideas central to the Sathya Sai Baba movement. They are meant to provide an arena where practices of the self such as devotional singing (*bhajan*) or service (*seva*) orient devotees towards righteous conduct and to becoming ideal citizens. This city mediates several religious traditions, regional and global, for a highly visible, vocal and central constituency – the pan-Indian and global middle class.

The power of gurus such as Sai Baba also embellishes the material environment of other cities. In metropolitan Bangalore, there are several sites associated with Sai Baba, a name adopted by Sathya Sai Baba in 1940, but historically linked to an older symbolically multivalent figure. In Someshvarapura (see map), for example, there is a modern temple dedicated to Shirdi Sai Baba (d. 1918), who was closely identified with Sufi genealogies and other mendicant orders in the Deccan. According to the testimony of the hagiographical text, *Shri Sai Satcharita*, Sai Baba appeared at Shirdi, a small village in Maharashtra, when he was about sixteen years of age (probably around 1854). Between 1886 and 1908, Shirdi Sai Baba's charisma as a miracle-worker, healer and religious teacher grew, and his popularity among the emerging middle classes in Gujarat and Maharashtra increased; the practice of congregational worship also crystallized during this period. Shirdi Sai Baba had an attack of fever and died in 1918, without having named a spiritual successor. However, tales of his spiritual grace travelled across India and throughout the South Asian diaspora in the form of Hindi films, magazines and calendar art. Apart from the development of Shirdi into an urban site attracting devotees from different religious and class backgrounds, institutions such as the All-India Sai Samaj, founded in 1941 by B. V. Narasimha Iyer (1874–1956) or Narasimha Swami, were also conduits for his charisma. Narasimha Swami founded the Sai Baba temple in Madras in 1952–3, the first such temple to be associated with the All-India Sai Samaj. Like many other Sai Baba temples across urban India, the Bangalore Someshvarapura temple, constructed in 1985, is also affiliated with the All-India Sai Samaj. In this site, as in many All-India Sai Samaj temples, Shirdi Sai Baba is represented largely as a Hindu guru or deity clad in ochre or rich silks, a far cry from the uncoloured, sober garments he probably wore in real life. In this image, his Sufi connections disappear into a zone of amnesia and a new urban mythology is created. This representation sits comfortably with devotees from Someshvarapura (a housing colony established in the 1950s for defence and public sector personnel) or with those who visit from other neighbourhoods and share the same mid-level managerial, professional, commercial and bureaucratic background with Someshvarapura devotees. In their religious imagination, Shirdi Sai Baba becomes a divine figure whose image might be purchased and framed like other deities of the Hindu pantheon, and then supplicated in domestic altars.

Other spaces in Bangalore are identified with Sathya Sai Baba, who is considered an *avatar* or incarnation of Sai and Shirdi Sai Baba by his devotees. Certain symbols used by Shirdi Sai Baba (such as the sacred ash), the festivals celebrated by him, his role as a healer and his attempt to mediate between two or more religious traditions are also part of the repertoire of Sathya Sai Baba. In doing so, he not only absorbed some of the charisma of Shirdi Sai Baba but inserted himself within a genealogy that connects him with other traditions in South Asia, some of which have overseas mobility. Sathya Sai Baba also referred to various 'world' religions, attracting a wide range of devotees within and outside India. With its emphasis on 'human values' such as truth (*satya*), righteousness (*dharma*), peace (*shanti*), love (*prema*) and non-violence (*ahimsa*), the movement has also developed complex interfaces with new religious movements and New Age ideas, as it has sought to globalize since the 1960s. The globalization of the movement spatially and epistemologically is matched by its embedding in several urban locales. As is the case with many religious movements, the city and its expanding boundaries – whether in Bangalore, Atlanta or Nairobi – through new road systems, freeways, electronic pathways, or the formation of suburbs and exurbs, have become important arenas in the Sai Baba tradition for the recruitment of devotees, the creation of architectural edifices (such as community halls, places of worship, hospitals or educational institutions) and expressions of citizenship through service activities.

Sai Darshan temple (inaugurated by Sathya Sai Baba in 1988) is the locus of the Indiranagar *samiti*, an urban unit of the global Sri Sathya Sai

Organization. The *samiti* began in 1973 in the upper-class neighbour-hood of Indiranagar, which had emerged as a planned suburb in eastern Bangalore in the 1960s and 1970s for public sector workers, security personnel and administrators (see map). Sai Darshan is the site of daily and weekly devotions to Sathya Sai Baba, who is represented by a giant photograph beside an empty chair on which Baba sat when he visited the temple. Devotees also study Baba's teachings and undertake service activities such as holding medical camps, giving tuitions for economic-ally disadvantaged school children, and rural outreach work.

Another site is Whitefield (see map), a peri-urban settlement on the eastern edge of the city, famous today as the space of Sathya Sai Baba's second most important hermitage, Brindavan. This was previously an Anglo-Indian exurb known for its numerous nurseries, rose gardens and tanks, and also the site of a small railway station for trains running between Bangalore and Madras. Today, as one travels to Brindavan from central Bangalore, one goes past high-rise apartment blocks and gated communities with expensive stand-alone 'villas', including the famous Florida or California-inspired 'Palm Meadows'. Because this highway runs past the Export Promotion Industrial Park (EPIP) – formerly the village settlement of Pattandur Agrahara – it has become a conduit not only for global business and the high-profile International Technology Park, but also for new suburbs for the corporate sector and the middle classes who seek to produce an urban lifestyle that might well be found beyond the beltway in Atlanta or in the endless sprawl of Silicon Valley.

Brochures from construction companies and housing developers advertise the proximity of new suburban estates to both the EPIP and Sathya Sai Baba's hermitage: 'Looking for a flat in Whitefield?' Alpine developers offer 'Alpine Viva' near the Sai Baba hermitage with two-, three- and four-bedroom apartments. Aashrithaa Properties's 'Cosmo City', 'the modern gated layout designed to suit everyone's budget', 'where happiness grows in your life', highlights the fact that their development is located 1.5 kilometres from the Sai Baba hermitage and 3.5 kilometres from the International Technology Park. While the refashioning of Whitefield into these bedroom communities is related to staggered dislocations from the colonial past and partial relocations in a global present, Sathya Sai Baba's role as a guru with a worldwide following has brought new institutions to the EPIP.

The Sri Sathya Sai Institute of Higher Medical Sciences (SSSIHMS), built on 52.26 acres of land donated by the Government of Karnataka in the EPIP, was inaugurated in 2001. This mega-project, whose work was estimated at costing 640,000,000 Indian rupees, had about 55 doctors and 160 nurses in 2001; a significant amount of work at the facility is carried out by service volunteers of the Sri Sathya Sai Organization (for instance, from the Indiranagar *samiti*) who might clean the hospital, do laundry, assist in the kitchen or engage in counselling patients. The 'spiritualization' of technology and skilled healthcare is immediately visible in the image of Dhanvantri, the divine physician associated with the Indian medical tradition of Ayurveda, who appears in the front garden of the SSSIHMS and in the elevated prayer hall past the main lobby of the building that contains a large picture of Sathya Sai Baba. The SSSIHMS is largely intended for the poor, and all treatment, inpatient and outpatient, is free; it also has diagnostic, pre-operative, post-operative and surgical facilities in cardiology and neurology for the economically disadvantaged, who are its main beneficiaries and come not only from states in southern India but from as far away as Pakistan and Nepal. The rationale for the SSSIHMS is that in the last two decades of Indian economic liberalization, there has been a decline in government spending on healthcare, and tertiary care is increasingly out of reach for large segments of the population; the SSSIHMS is a non-governmental and non-corporate intervention that seeks to provide high-technology and skill-intensive medicine mainly to the underprivileged. Its monumental building looks much like the state capitol in Bangalore and is a decided contrast to its steel and glass neighbours in the Information Technology Park. The status of Bangalore as India's high-technology centre with numerous mega-projects from beltways to the International Airport is paralleled by this transnational religious movement's own utopian monumentality that links globalization and export promotion with the language of healing, human values and holiness.

Conclusion

This chapter makes several claims about the intersections between the Indian urban and the religious. First, my argument is that urban spatiality is mediated and inflected by religious imaginaries and practices that act as a creative bridge between multiple pasts and the openness and uncertainty of civic futures. The Karaga performance's promotion by Backward Castes and the ritual movement through the city allows us to contest ideas of Bangalore solely as India's high-tech city by recollecting – as if to remember or to collect again – other urban histories and spaces within the civic imagination. Similarly, the monumentality of the Sri Sathya Sai Institute of Higher Medical Sciences refracts medical technology, information and export through the filter of spirituality. These mediations of space might be read as critiques of the 'modern' constitution premised on the separation between religion, science and technology, and citizenship. Second, both case studies show that formulations of the urban and citizenship are deeply embedded in ritual, architectural, devotional and somatic practices. These practices enable us, of course, to move beyond the simple opposition of 'the secular' and 'the religious' and to elaborate on the significance of religion as a constitutive force in modern India, but also to argue that there are multiple enactments of Indian urban modernity.

Notes

1 A. Henn, 'Crossroads of Religions: Shrines, Mobility and Urban Space in Goa', *International Journal of Urban and Regional Research* 32:3 (2008), pp. 658–70.
2 P. Lutgendorf, *Hanuman's Tale: The Messages of a Divine Monkey* (New York: Oxford University Press, 2006).
3 M. Mines, *Public Faces, Private Voices. Community and Individuality in South India* (Berkeley: University of California Press, 1994).
4 M. Juergensmeyer, *Radhasoami Reality: The Logic of a Modern Faith* (Princeton University Press, 1991), p. 149.
5 See S. Srinivas, *Landscapes of Urban Memory: The Sacred and the Civic in India's High-Tech City* (Minneapolis: University of Minnesota Press, 2001), and *In the Presence of Sai Baba: Body, City, and Memory in a Global Religious Movement* (Leiden/Boston: Brill and Hyderabad: Orient Longman, 2008).

5

The politics of caste identities

Caste in India has been inextricably linked to the politics of caste from at least the late nineteenth century onwards. Since then, like religion, caste has gone through an identity-building process overdetermined by considerations of power. Like religious identities, caste identities are not 'given' but produced according to social cum political strategies and the contexts – often regional – in which they are evolved. In the following pages, I shall focus on the way lower castes' identities have been shaped and infused with new meanings according to an ethnicization process that was largely due to ideologies of autochthony (indigeneity), electoral politics and public policies such as state programmes of positive discrimination.

The transformation of caste during the British Raj

The caste system relies on hierarchical principles that Bhimrao Ramji Ambedkar (1891–1956) has defined very perceptively in terms of 'graded inequality' (see below): the Brahmins (the *literati* or priestly caste) come first in what is known as the first of the four *varna* (literally meaning 'colour'), whereas the Untouchables (technically *avarna*, or outside of the caste schema) lie at the bottom of the social pyramid, and between these two extremes one can observe a clear-cut social hierarchy: the Kshatriyas (the warrior castes, former rulers and today largely made up of small and big landowners) and the Vaishyas (the merchants and traders) take the second and third positions respectively, but are still upper castes (the 'twice-borns') like the Brahmins, whereas the Shudras (cultivators, herdsmen and artisans) are situated between the twice-borns and the Untouchables. Within each of the *varna*, there are numerous, region-specific occupational and endogamous subdivisions, or sub-castes, which form *jati* (from the word *jana*, to be born), representing a more tangible reality in day-to-day life than the *varna*.

This social hierarchy may be said to form a caste *system* only so far as the dominant – upper-caste – values are regarded by the whole society as providing universal references and role models. Hence the notion of Sanskritization – a word coming from the classical language and cultural knowledge systems associated with Brahmins – that M. N. Srinivas has defined as 'the process in which a "low" Hindu caste, or tribal or other group, changes its customs, ritual, ideology and way of life in the direction of a high, and frequently, "twice-born" caste that is the Brahmins, but also the Kshatriyas or even the Vaishyas.'[1] Low castes may for instance adopt the most prestigious features of the Brahmin diet and therefore become vegetarian. Such a process reflects a special consensus in society, all the groups admitting the values of the upper castes as the most respectable ones. For Srinivas, 'the mobility associated with Sanskritization results only in *positional changes* in the system and does not lead to any *structural change*. That is, a sub-caste moves up above its neighbours and another comes down, but all this takes place in an essentially stable hierarchical order. The system itself does not change.'[2] Indeed, the values sustaining the social system remain the same.

In our analysis of the politics of caste that follows, we will see how the values, and the cultural history from which they emerged – in the so-called system placing Brahmins at the top – were questioned and overturned by various low-caste leaders who had been able to ethnicize caste in the context of a certain democratization process during the British Raj.

From castes to caste associations

The socio-economic and political changes which took place during British colonial rule probably affected castes more directly than at any other time.[3] Modernization implied the making of a new class of functionaries, an industrialization process relying on a new working class, and the development of new means of transportation, such as the railways. These three phenomena transformed castes, which till then were confined to discrete territories, delimited by matrimonial relations, since castes formed endogamous entities.[4] Geographical mobility favoured the territorial extension of the frontiers of caste and the emergence of horizontal solidarities. This mobility not only generated feelings of anomie, but also made the finding of a suitable match for endogamous marriages more complicated, hence the idea to create associations which could link members of the same caste, or more specifically, sub-caste or *jati* group. However, these associations also resulted from the introduction of the census, which from 1871 onwards was a key element in the formation of the colonial state.[5] The census, as devised by the British, did not only enumerate caste groups, but also classified them according to the *varna* system. Caste associations, therefore, also became pressure groups whose aim was to improve their *varna* rank in the census tables. This process was especially prominent among the low castes. Each census provided castes with an opportunity to petition the government for a higher place in the order of precedence and for being recorded under new, Sanskritized names that would make their new *varna* affiliations more plausible.

Caste associations in British India were thus transforming themselves into interest groups, which gradually acquired features of mutual aid structures. They founded schools for the caste's children and co-operative movements. The Rudolphs have underlined the modern character of these caste associations,[6] one which prepared the ground for the ethnicization of caste, whereby ethnic identity was mapped on to that of caste on the basis of a new reading of the origins of the lower castes in terms of autochthony.

The ethnicization of caste through autochthony

This process was partly shaped by European ideas, as propagated by the missionaries and the British schools. Certainly, castes have always been perceived in India as 'kin groups or descent units',[7] but the racial dimension that caste tended to acquire in the nineteenth century derived from European interpretations of Indian society. In 1792, William Jones had deduced from the discovery of the Indo-European linguistic family the notion of a common, original race whose branches had migrated towards Europe and India.[8] This theory was developed during the nineteenth century by many German philologists such as Albrecht Weber, R. Roth, A. Kuhn and J. Möhl, whose books were published in the 1840s to 1850s. Notions of 'Sanskritic race' or 'Vedic people' appear in their writings. These speculations reached India from the late 1850s onwards through Max Müller, who tended to be somewhat more cautious, and J. Muir, who in 1860 published a study on 'The Trans-Himalayan Origin of the Hindus, and their affinity with the western branches of the Aryan race'. In contrast to the 'Aryan Race', British Orientalists identified a 'Dravidian Race' which was largely co-extensive with the lower castes of South India. In 1886, the Governor of Madras Presidency, Mountstuart Elphinstone Grant-Duff, in his address to the graduates of the University of Madras, emphatically declared: 'You are of pure Dravidian race. I should like to see the pre-Sanskrit element amongst you asserting itself rather more.'[9] Gradually, non-Brahminism and Dravidianism coincided and low-caste groups saw themselves as forming an ethnic category. This ethnicization process was also prominent in western India where low-caste leaders appropriated this discourse at a very early stage and invested it with new political meaning.

The making of the Bahujan Samaj in western India: Phule and the Sathyashodhak Samaj

Jyotirao Phule (1827–90) played a pioneering role in the ethnicization of caste. He used the Aryan theory to his own advantage since the fact that upper-caste leaders traced their origin from Aryan conquerors enabled him to argue that they descended from foreigners and that their culture, including the caste system, was alien to India's original people. Phule, therefore, portrayed the Aryans as invaders who had settled in India at a rather late period, who subjugated the first inhabitants of India and subsequently destroyed their civilization. He claimed that the low castes were the descendants of these people.[10]

Phule was the first low-caste leader who avoided the traps of Sanskritization by endowing the low castes with an alternative value system. For the first time, the low castes were presented as ethnic groups that had inherited the legacy of an antiquarian golden age and whose culture was therefore distinct from that of the wider Hindu society; secondly, his efforts in favour of the low castes were not confined to his own *jati*: he wanted to unite the *bahujan samaj* (the masses), and more especially the Shudras and the Atishudras (Untouchables).[11] As early as 1853, for instance, he opened schools for Untouchables. Indeed, he projected himself as the spokesman of the non-Brahmins at large, and kept targeting the Brahmins in strongly worded pamphlets where he presented them as rapacious money-lenders or corrupt priests eager to extort as much as they could from poor and ignorant villagers.[12]

Phule was also the first low-caste political organizer. He remained aloof from the Congress Party, the first all-Indian nationalist party established in 1885, which he regarded as a Brahmin movement.[13] Nationalism, according to him, was an illusion created by upper-caste manipulation to conceal the inner divisions of Indian society.[14] Instead, he founded his own movement, the Sathyashodhak Samaj (Society of Seekers of Truth), in 1873 in order to strengthen the sentiment of unity among the low castes. This organization was able to attract rich peasants as well as agricultural tenants who belonged to very different castes; and in some places, 'the Sathya Shodhak message seemed to have reached even the untouchable'[15] and, on the other extreme of the social grouping of the *bahujan samaj*, the Marathas, including the Jedhe family, from Poona, who realized 'the futility of a purely Maratha politics'.[16] Maratha princes such as the Maharajah of Kolhapur and even before him, the Maharajah of Baroda, strongly approved of Phule's ideological commitments and donated large amounts of money to his movement.[17]

The Dravidians as sons of the soil in southern India

The associations that the lower castes developed in Madras Presidency also emancipated themselves from the Sanskritization ethos through the claim to autochthony.[18] This development was well exemplified by the case of Iyothee Thass, a Pariah (the largest untouchable caste of the province), who argued somewhat like Phule that the lower castes were the proponents of India's oldest civilization, the Dravidian one, whereas the Brahmins descended from foreign invaders.[19] By the late nineteenth century, therefore, the Non-Brahmin Movement claimed that the lower castes were the original inhabitants of India.[20] Gradually, the non-Brahmin South Indian caste associations adopted the suffix 'Adi', meaning 'initial, primordial', in their titles, and mentioned this Dravidian origin too. The Pariah Mahajan Sabha, which had been founded in 1890, became the Adi-Dravida Mahajan Sabha, which, in 1918 appealed to the government to replace the pejorative word 'Pariah' with 'Adi-Dravida'.[21]

The main architect of non-Brahmin Dravidianism was E. V. Ramaswami Naicker, alias Periyar, a religious mendicant who had become completely disillusioned by the Congress and Gandhi.[22] The notion of human dignity was so central to his thinking that after quitting Congress in the mid 1920s, he launched the Self-Respect Movement, whose key word was *Samadharma*, equality. But Periyar regarded it as much a Buddhist as a Western notion.[23] In the same vein as Thass, he presented the lower castes as having descended from the first Buddhists and endowed them with a Dravidian identity. Periyar argued that the Dravidian-Buddhists were ill treated by the Aryan-Hindus because they opposed caste hierarchy.[24]

One of the resolutions of the first Provincial Self-Respect Conference in 1929 concerned the boycotting of Brahmin priests, especially for wedding rituals: Periyar initiated 'Self-Respect weddings' celebrated without the use of such priests. In the late 1920s, the movement had the *Manu Smriti* ('Laws of Manu') burned repeatedly.[25] Periyar's hostility to the caste system was spelled out in terms of a valorization of the sources of Dravidian culture: '[S]amardharma came to stand in for a cultural and civilisational alternative, a social order based on radically different principles from the present, which needed to rest on premises derived from a non-Aryan, non-Sanskritic ethos.'[26]

Thus, Periyar had an explicitly ethnic conception of the low castes' identity. (He compared their situation to that of blacks in South Africa.[27]) And so, the non-Brahmins who all shared a Dravidian identity had to be united. As a result, Periyar advocated the coming together of Christians, Muslims and low-caste Hindus, and, within the latter, of the Untouchables and the Shudras.

The scope and strength of this social coalition must not be exaggerated since old cleavages persisted, such as in western India. In Maharashtra, the Marathas hijacked the Sathyashodak Samaj and marginalized the few Untouchables in the organization. In Madras Presidency, not all the non-Brahmins backed the Self-Respect Movement. There were many Nadars (a set of sub-castes in Tamil Nadu listed as 'Backward Caste') in the Congress ranks, for instance. However, the idea of a common origin, in the non-Brahmin discourses, which from Phule to Periyar relied on the notion of autochthony, helped its leaders to unite low-caste people and mobilize them on behalf of an alternative identity outside the caste system. Caste frontiers had not eroded; on the contrary, they became more rigid. However, they did no longer fit in a social hierarchy; instead, they defined groups in competition on a potentially equal footing. The lower castes who saw themselves as sons of the soil no longer internalized a feeling of inferiority, and instead were proud of their identity harking back to a prestigious antiquity. This ethnicization process has continued in the politicization of caste resulting from the democratization of India, especially since 1947.

The democratization process and the politicization of caste

Before Independence the gradual democratization of the political arena had already accompanied the ethnicization of castes. Locked in an increasingly intense political competition, caste-group leaders attempted to build a majoritarian support base by aggregating all the *jatis* which could fit under one common umbrella. Large categories like 'Dravidians' were most useful in this context. Indeed, the non-Brahmin politicians who founded the Justice Party in 1920 tried to bring together all the lower castes under this common umbrella. They argued: 'The Brahmins differ from the non-Brahmins in caste, manners, customs and interests and even in personal law in some respects. The former are Aryans and the latter are Dravidians and thus they differ in race. In the past the Brahmins have practically monopolised all or almost all the seats in the Local and Imperial Legislative Councils.'[28] During the 1920 election campaign, their leaders requested 'all non-Brahmins in this presidency to immediately organise, combine and carry on an active propaganda so as to ensure the return to the reformed Council of as many non-Brahmins as possible'.[29] This tactic paid off since the Justice Party came first in the elections and was able to form the government with some support from the British. However, the impact of electoral competition on caste identity became much stronger after Independence when universal franchise was introduced and the rivalries between parties therefore intensified.

The political making of castes – the case of the new Kshatriyas in Gujarat

After 1947, caste group leaders adopted new strategies in order to form an electoral majority or to prevent their common enemies from gaining power. Such collective actions resulted in the making of caste federations at the state level – the only relevant one since most *jatis* do not expand beyond the frontiers of one province. Kothari and Maru have analysed caste federations as resulting from the strategy of individual caste associations which tried to shape such coalitions for political reasons:

> The concept of caste federation refers to a grouping together of a number of distinct endogamous groups into a single organisation for common objectives, the realisation of which calls for a pooling together of resources or numbers or both. By and large, the objectives pursued are secular and associational, although the employment of traditional symbols for evoking a sense of solidarity and loyalty towards the new form is not uncommon. The traditional distinctions between the federating groups are on the whole retained, but the search for a new organisational identity and the pursuit of political objectives gradually lead to a shift in group orientations.[30]

This definition was evolved in the course of a study of the caste federation phenomenon in Gujarat where the 'Kshatriyas' exemplified this development. Right from the 1910s the state Rajput leaders had constituted caste associations for promoting education.[31] In the late 1930s, the descendant of one of these leaders, Natvarsingh Solanki, wanted to extend these associations to other castes that he considered to be Kshatriyas.[32] He tried to refashion the social identity of those groups in order to allow others to join hands with the Rajputs and, in this way, to acquire more power.

Gujarat's largest caste group was the Kolis. They had been classified by the British as a 'criminal caste' but they themselves claimed they were Kshatriyas. In this, they imitated the Rajputs in a logic of Sanskritization. Some Koli clans had been able to make matrimonial alliances with Rajputs[33] and/or had established small principalities before the British took over. Yet, they had retained some control over land under the British Raj as landowners or big tenants. Many of them met the necessary conditions for being enfranchised when the British established provincial legislative councils. The right to vote therefore enabled the Kolis to use their main asset, their numbers: in 1931 they represented about 20 per cent of the population, almost twice that of the Patidars (12.16 per cent), the dominant caste and the main rival of the Rajputs, who were only 4.85 per cent of the population. Solanki opened his caste association to the Kolis for this very reason – in order to transform it into a mass organization.

In 1947, the Kutch, Kathiawar, Gujarat Kshatriya Sabha was created at a time when India was becoming a democracy. The term 'Kshatriya' was a useful umbrella under which to bracket the Rajputs and the Kolis together. This *sabha* (association), therefore, is a good example of the way castes with very different ritual status can join hands to defend common interests. In this case, the Kolis and the Rajputs had the same enemies, the Patidars. Certainly, this alliance has been legitimized in the idiom of 'tradition', since its leaders claimed that its components belonged to the same *varna*; but the use of the word 'Kshatriya' was largely tactical, and the original caste identity was seriously diluted. The Rajput leaders of the Kshatriya Sabha emphasized that a Kshatriya was not to be defined by descent but by military values.

Political calculations had deep social implications in the case of the Kshatriyas of Gujarat as several taboos were abolished. Rajputs and Kolis of the Kshatriya Sabha shared meals,[34] and the Kolis elite married their daughters to lower Rajputs (who practised hypergamy anyway), and this process fostered the Rajputization of the upper Kolis. By and large, Kshatriyas tended to form a new caste, born out of political considerations. The use of terms like Koli Kshatriyas and Rajput Kshatriyas certainly show that the merger was far from complete.[35] Yet, important dimensions of the caste system were eroded by the after-effects of what were basically socio-economic and political strategies.

Right from the 1950s, the Kshatriya Sabha tried in exchange for its electoral support for the Congress to obtain the nomination of a number of its members as party candidates. The party was not fully responsive, especially because of some strong opposition from the Patidars, who were very influential in the Congress. The Patidars disapproved of the Kshatriyas' demand for land reform. The Kshatriya Sabha therefore kept its distance from the Congress before the 1962 elections and the party underwent a setback. Instead, the association gave its support to the Swatantra Party (a liberal party), which became the leading opposition party in the state. This situation persuaded the Congress to change its strategy and to nominate a large number of Kshatriya candidates before the 1967 elections. The Kshatriya Sabha then supported the Congress, which gained a more comfortable majority than it had in 1962.[36]

The case of the Kshatriya exemplifies the impact of regime change on the collective identity of caste groups. The democratization process has fostered another form of ethnicization of caste by inciting leaders of a *jati* to join hands to form a new caste endowed with a common, new identity, largely irrespective of the traditional hierarchy and status. Ethnicity, in this case, is not defined by autochthony, but by other cultural characteristics, such as the warrior ethos in the case of the Kshatriyas of Gujarat. While caste federations like the Kshatriyas took shape at the state level, Dalits (formerly known as Untouchables) were the only group to become imbued with a pan-Indian ethnic identity. This achievement is largely due to the fact that they all share one common privilege: reservations.

The Dalits, by-products of politics and policies

The main architect of Dalit politics in India was B. R. Ambedkar. A remarkable sociologist, economist and social reformer, he analysed the caste system before fighting it on behalf of the egalitarian values he had learned from Phule and scholars based in the West while completing doctoral degrees in economics at Columbia University and the London School of Economics and Political Science. He examined the different kinds of social hierarchy in world history and came to distinguish inequality from "graded inequality" which, according to him, was at least twice as dangerous.[37] In industrial societies, the working class could rise up against the bourgeoisie. In the *ancien régime* in France, the Third State was able to rise up against the aristocracy and the King, etc. But the type of inequality that exists in a caste-ridden society is of a different kind because its very logic divides the dominated groups and therefore prevents them from overthrowing the oppressor. Ambedkar wrote:

> In a system of graded inequality, the aggrieved parties are not on a common level. This can happen only when there are only high and low. In a system of graded inequality there are the highest (the Brahmins). Below the highest are the higher (the Kshatriya). Below the higher are those who are high (Vaishya). Below the high are the low (Shudras) and below the low are those who are lower (the Untouchables). All have a grievance against the highest and would like to bring about their downfall. But they will not combine. The higher is anxious to get rid of the highest but does not wish to combine with the high, the low and the lower lest they should reach his level and be his equal. The high wants to overthrow the higher that is above him but does not want to join hands with the low and the lower, lest they should rise to his status and become equal to him in rank. The low is anxious to pull down the highest, the higher and the high but he would not make a common cause with the lower for fear of the lower gaining a higher status and becoming his equal. In the system of graded inequality there is no such class as

completely unprivileged class except the one which is at the base of the social pyramid. The privileges of the rest are graded. Even the low is a privileged class as compared with the lower. Each class being privileged, every class is interested in maintaining the system.[38]

Here Ambedkar exposes one of the most powerful mechanisms of the caste system. However, he does not take his own argument to its logical conclusion, since he considers only the *varnas*, as if they constituted social entities. If that was the case, the highest castes would have been easily marginalized by the Shudras, who represent more than half of the Hindu population, as the British census has shown. As a matter of fact, the mechanisms which he describes here are reproduced at the level of *jati* since every *varna* gets subdivided into multiple *jatis* whose hierarchy rests also on a gradation of status. And Ambedkar was well aware of this phenomenon since he deplored the division of the Untouchables into so many *jatis* which made them, in his opinion, 'a disunited body ... infested with the caste system in which they believe as much as does the high caste Hindu. This caste system among the Untouchables, has given rise to mutual rivalry and to jealousy and it has made common action impossible.'[39] Ambedkar was especially disturbed by the fact that in his own province of Maharashtra neither the Mangs nor the Chambhars supported him because these Untouchable *jatis* looked at him as representing a third group, his own caste, the Mahars.

Drawing on the ideology of ethnicity that his predecessors such as Phule had used, Ambedkar hoped to instil a sense of a common identity among the Untouchables by referring to them as 'Dalits'. The term promoted the idea that Untouchables descended from the 'broken men' ('Dalit' in the Marathi language) who were the original inhabitants of India before the conquest of the country by Aryan invaders. According to Ambedkar, these 'broken men' were early followers of the Buddha soon after he began his teachings in the sixth century BC, and they remained Buddhists when the rest of the society returned to the Hindu fold under the pressure of Brahmins.[40]

Ambedkar thus infused the Dalit with a sense of an indigenous, ethnic identity and a religious affiliation to Buddhism, a religion to which he converted a few weeks before he died in 1956, along with thousands of followers. To sum up: his aim was to instil a new sense of dignity among Dalits in order not only to emancipate them from the caste system but to unite them. However, Dalit unity resulted more from a public policy of positive discrimination that the state started to implement during Ambedkar's lifetime.

Reservations and the making of Dalits

The British initiated a policy of positive discrimination in favour of the Untouchables as early as the late nineteenth century when they realized that this group was so stigmatized that its members would never accede to education otherwise. As early as 1892, schools reserved for them were established.[41] But it turned out that educated Untouchables, though small in number, could not get jobs in relation to their qualifications. As a result, the British, under pressure from Ambedkar, who had been a victim of discrimination on the job market himself, introduced quotas for the Untouchables in the administration. In 1934 the Government decided to reserve 25 per cent of the vacancies in the administration to Muslims and 8.3 per cent to other minorities, including Untouchables, who then represented 12.5 per cent of the population according to the 1931 census. By that time, the Untouchables – who had been known as Depressed Classes till then – were rechristened 'Scheduled Castes', and the list of the *jatis* belonging to this category, which had been established in order to reserve access to the quotas to the relevant beneficiaries, was updated in the relevant 'schedule'. The latter quota was increased to this level – 12.5 per cent – in June 1946, which means that proportionality became the rule.[42] This measure was extended by the first government of independent India and then, since the proportionality principle continued to apply, the quota for the Scheduled Castes was increased to 15 per cent when the 1951 census indicated that this was their share in the population. The same quota was implemented in the educational institutions.

However, most of these quotas remained unfilled, allegedly because of a lack of good candidates, but also because of a lack of good will among those in charge of recruiting them.[43] In fact, the quotas were only filled in the lower categories of the administration, which meant that the Scheduled Castes continued to accomplish some of their traditional tasks, but in uniform! For instance, sweepers hired by the state (at the national or at the local level) come mostly from the untouchable Bhangi caste. This is evident from the following table, which shows the proportion of the Scheduled Castes employees in the Central Government services in 1961 and 1967.

Such discrimination incited the Scheduled Castes, irrespective of their *jati*, to mobilize in order to get their due. A public policy that

Table 1 Class-wise distribution of the Scheduled Castes in the Central Government services (in %)

Class of the Indian administration	1953	1961	1963	1967	1974	1980	1987
Class 1	0.53	1.2	1.78	2.08	3.2	4.95	8.23
Class 2	1.29	2.5	2.98	3.1	4.6	8.54	10.47
Class 3	4.52	7.2	9.24	9.33	10.3	13.44	14.46
Class 4	20.52	17.2	17.15	18.18	18.6	19.46	20.09

Sources: The Commissioner for Scheduled Castes and Scheduled Tribes, *Report – volume 1* (New Delhi: Udyogshala, 1969), cited in S. N. Dubey and Usha Mathur, 'Welfare Programmes for Scheduled Castes. Content and Administration', *Economic and Political Weekly*, 22 January 1972, p. 167 (for 1961 and 1967) and cited in O. Mendelsohn and M. Vicziany, *The Untouchables. Subordination, Poverty and the State in Modern India* (Cambridge University Press, 1998), p. 135 (for all the other years).

made a new social category – the Scheduled Castes – the beneficiary of new privileges became the framework for a new political consciousness, and even a new political culture. This mobilization was strengthened by the fact that there was also a 15 per cent quota of reserved seats for Scheduled Castes in the lower house of Parliament, and these 'SC MPs', as they came to be known, used this Assembly, the Lok Sabha, to demand the full implementation of the law. In addition, Dalits formed political parties to articulate their grievances regarding reservations and other issues.

Towards a Dalit political party?

Ambedkar launched his first political party, the Independent Labour Party, in 1936. As its name suggests, the party was not only meant to appeal to Dalits. Indeed, the Scheduled Castes (as the 'Untouchable' castes were later to be listed and recognized in the Indian Constitution) only appeared under the guise of labourers in the party's 'aims and objectives', and the word 'caste' was only mentioned in the last item of its 1937 election programme: 'The party will also endeavour to prevent the administration from becoming the monopoly of any single caste or community. Consistently with efficiency of administration, the party will endeavour to bring about a fair admixture of all caste [*sic*] and communities in the administration of the Presidency.'[44] The ILP's programme seemed to be at odds with Ambedkar's own caste-centred discourse.[45] Indeed, most of the ILP's candidates were Mahars. There was only one Mang among them. This is one of the reasons why Mahars and Mangs saw Ambedkar as the leader of the Mahars and the ILP as solely representing them.

This contradiction led to the replacement of the ILP by the Scheduled Castes Federation (Dalit Federation in Marathi) in 1942. Ambedkar gave up the idea of broadening his base to encompass the working class and, as the name of the federation suggests, instead put a stress on the need to unify the Scheduled Castes on a pan-Indian scale. Now Scheduled Castes were presented by the party as a minority, much like Muslims. A resolution passed by the SCF Working Committee in September 1944 in Madras explicitly stated that 'the Scheduled Castes are a distinct and separate element in the national life of India and they are a religious minority in a sense far more real than the Sikhs and Muslims can be . . .'[46] Therefore the SCF did not only demand separate electorates but also a separate land. However, the first general elections after independence in 1951–2 were a disaster for the SCF; it could only win two Lok Sabha seats, one in Hyderabad and the other in the Province of Bombay, where Ambedkar himself lost.

Ambedkar then decided to replace the SCF with still another party. Even though it was officially founded in October 1957, ten months after Ambedkar's death, this Republican Party of India had been shaped by him. It returned to the original intention of the ILP, that is to say, not to represent the Scheduled Castes alone, but all the underprivileged. The party platform sought to 'engage itself in organizing the downtrodden masses of India, particularly the Buddhists [mainly Mahar converts], Scheduled Castes, Scheduled Tribes and other Backward Classes'.[47] In the 1960s, the RPI did not do that badly electorally, but it did not succeed in making any significant inroads either and gradually became a marginal player.

The BSP, from Dalit politics to Dalit policies

While the RPI never managed to emerge as the political representative of the Dalit, the Bahujan Samaj Party gained momentum on this very platform in the 1990s. The founder of the BSP, Kanchi Ram, a disciple of Ambedkar's, drew his inspiration from his mentor's reading of Dalit identity. The *bahujan samaj* he claimed he was representing continued to be projected as descending from the pre-Aryan, indigenous inhabitants of India,[48] but like the RPI, the BSP first attracted its supporters from among one *jati*, that of its leaders: the Chamars and more specifically, the Jatavs, a sub-group that had taken shape in the late nineteenth century. Jatavs are Chamars who claim descent from the Yadu race, which, allegedly, entitled them to be known as Kshatriyas.[49] The fact that Jatavs were first prisoners of the logic of Sanskritization is evident from this claim. But Ambedkar made a strong impact on the Jatav movement in the 1940s, so much so that this sub-group of Chamars converted to Buddhism in large numbers and acquired a separate identity – one based on Buddhism and autochthonous pride – that could be used to neutralize the impact of Sanskritization.[50]

By the 1960s, and particularly in the elections of 1962 and 1967, the RPI had such strong support from the Jatavs that the party was more successful in Uttar Pradesh than in Maharashtra. Soon after, however, the party became internally divided, and some of its leaders were co-opted by the Congress Party. Nevertheless, twenty years later, the BSP was able to cash in on the legacy of the RPI in Uttar Pradesh. Founded in 1984 by Kanshi Ram, the BSP became the second largest party – even larger than the BJP – in 1989 and started to grow again in the 1990s. In 1995, Mayawati – a Dalit woman leader and confidant of Kanshi Ram, who was to succeed him after he had a stroke in 2003 – became Chief Minister of Uttar Pradesh. For the first time the largest state of India was governed by a Dalit. She immediately became a source of pride for this community. The core of her support base was then made of Jatavs, but she managed to expand it to other Dalit *jatis* by implementing policies in favour of the Dalits at large.

The Ambedkar Villages Scheme, which had been started by Mayawati's predecessor for allotting special funds for socio-economic development in villages with 50 per cent Scheduled Castes population, was revised in order to include those with more than 30 per cent (and even 22 per cent in certain areas) Scheduled Castes only. Mayawati gave special treatment to the Dalits of these villages since 'all the roads, handpumps, houses, etc., have been largely built in their bastees [neighbourhoods]'.[51]

Six months later, the BSP decided to stand alone in the 1996 Lok Sabha elections. Yet the party doubled its share of valid votes in Uttar Pradesh from about 10 per cent during the 1989, 1991 and 1993 elections to 20.6 per cent. The BSP was especially successful in consolidating the Dalits behind its candidates. Eleven years later, the BSP was able to win an absolute majority in Uttar Pradesh. The

Ambedkar Villages Scheme was revived in a big way under the direct supervision of the Chief Minister, who also implemented the Scheduled Castes and Scheduled Tribes (Prevention of Atrocities) Act (1989) – a law enabling the state to punish the oppressors of the Dalits – in a more drastic way than any of her predecessors had. As a result, in the general elections of 2009, the BSP did not only attract 85 per cent of the Jatavs, but also 64 per cent of the second largest Dalit *jati*, the Pasis, and 61 per cent of the other Dalit *jatis*. As a whole, the non-Jatav Dalit support for the BSP registered an 8 percentage points increase in Uttar Pradesh. This was a new development in a state where non-Jatav Dalit groups used to vote massively for other parties. This qualitative change towards the making of a Dalit political culture resulted from the Dalit politics of the Mayawati government, but also from its policies.[52]

Conclusion

Caste identities have changed a great deal in the course of time. Traditionally, the sense of belonging to one caste relied on occupation and the ranking in the social hierarchy according to one's status. British rule in India prepared the ground for a major transformation. The creation of a modern state, the industrialization process and the modernization of the means of communication, in addition to the development of the census, resulted in the formation of caste associations which came to act as interest groups. But lower castes' identities have also been modified by the way plebeian leaders appropriated the British reading of ethnic divides in India, an interpretation which enabled low-caste groups to claim that they were the sons of the soil whereas the Brahmins descended from Aryan invaders.

In addition, politics and policies made a significant impact on caste identities. Regime change, through the democratization process, led *jati* leaders to join hands through caste federations – and even to merge their caste groups in the case of the Kshatriyas of Gujarat – in order to increase their weight in the new political game responding to the law of numbers. Positive discrimination, a public policy implemented first by the British in favour of the Untouchables, transformed the collective identity of this social category by inciting most of the Dalit *jatis* to get united in order to fight more effectively for common interests, like the filling of quotas in the bureaucracy. In Uttar Pradesh politics and policies had cumulative effects in the making of a Dalit political culture. The BSP attempted to mobilize Dalit voters irrespective of their *jati* to gain power, and once in office they fostered this sense of unity by implementing policies in favour of Dalits only.

Interestingly, the impact of politics and policies has not transformed the political culture of the lower castes to the same extent. Certainly, Shudras mobilized when reservations for the Other Backward Classes – the bureaucratic name for most of the Shudra *jatis* – were at stake, for instance during the Mandal affair of the early 1990s.[53] But the OBC identity could never transcend the *jati* divisions the way the Dalit identity has started to transcend them. This difference, evident from the existence of a 'Dalit literature', for instance, harks back to the specificity of the Untouchable experience that has no equivalent in existential terms. But things may change since the story I have just narrated suggests that caste identities are more malleable than many social scientists used to think until recently.

Notes

1 M. N. Srinivas, *Social Change in Modern India* (New Delhi, Orient Longman, 1995), p. 6.

2 *Ibid.*

3 For a full analysis of the relationship between caste and colonialism, see Nicholas Dirks, *Castes of Mind. Colonialism and the Making of Modern India* (Princeton University Press, 2001).

4 S. Bayly, *The New Cambridge History of India, IV. 3, Caste, Society and Politics in India from the Eighteenth Century to the Modern Age* (Cambridge University Press, 1999), p. 263.

5 A. Appadurai, 'Number in the Colonial Imagination', in A. Appadurai (ed.), *Modernity at Large. Cultural Dimensions of Globalization* (Minneapolis: University of Minnesota Press, 1996), pp. 119 ff.

6 L. I. Rudolph and S. Hoeber Rudolph, 'The Political Role of India's Caste Associations', in I. Wallerstein (ed.), *Social Change: the Colonial Situation* (New York: J. Wiley, 1966), p. 448.

7 Bayly, *The New Cambridge History of India*, p. 10.

8 P. J. Marshall, 'Introduction', in P. J. Marshall (ed.), *The British Discovery of Hinduism in the Eighteenth Century* (Cambridge University Press, 1970), p. 15.

9 Cited in E. F. Irshick, *Politics and Social Conflict in South India. The Non-Brahman Movement, 1916–1929* (Bombay: Oxford University Press, 1969), p. 281.

10 J. Phule, *Collected Works of Mahatma Jotirao Phule. vol. II* (Bombay: Government of Maharashtra, 1991), p. 8.

11 G. Omvedt, 'Jotirao Phule and the Ideology of Social Revolution in India', *Economic and Political Weekly*, 11 September 1971, p. 1974.

12 See 'Priestcraft Exposed', in Phule, *Collected Works of Mahatma Jotirao Phule, vol. II*, p. 67 and 'A Poem about the Crafty, Cunning and Spurious (Religious) Books of the Brahmins (A Contrast between the Comfortable Lives of the Brahmins and the Miserable Lives of the Shudras)', in *Collected Works of Mahatma Jotirao Phule, vol. I* (Bombay: Government of Maharashtra, 1991), p. 81.

13 *Ibid., vol.* II, p. 25.

14 *Ibid., vol.* II, p. 29.

15 M. S. Gore, *Non-Brahman Movement in Maharashtra* (New Delhi: Segment Books, 1989), p. 26.

16 G. Omvedt, 'Non-Brahmans and Nationalists in Poona', *Economic and Political Weekly*, Annual Number (February 1974), p. 207.

17 *Collected Works of Mahatma Jotirao Phule, vol.* II, pp. 81 and 97.

18 For an overview, see, D. Washbrook, 'Development of Caste Organisation in South India, 1880–1925', in C. Baker and D. Washbrook (eds.), *South India: Political Institutions and Political Change* (New Delhi: Macmillan, 1975).

19 Cited in V. Geetha and S. V. Rajadurai, *Towards a Non-Brahmin Millennium. From Iyothee Thass to Periyar* (Calcutta: Samya, 1998), p. 108.

20 M. Ross Barnett, *The Politics of Cultural Nationalism* (Princeton University Press, 1976), pp. 315–16.

21 R. K. Kshirsagar, *Dalit Movement in India and its Leaders* (New Delhi: MD Publications, 1994), p. 72.

22 Mohan Ram, 'Ramaswami Naicker and the Dravidian Movement', *Economic and Political Weekly*, Annual Number (February 1974), p. 219. Periyar organized *satyagrahas* (civil disobedience campaigns) before the Mahadevar temple in Vaikkom, 'which earned him two jail terms and the honorific "Vaikkom Veerar" (Hero of Vaikkom)' title. M. S. S. Pandian, '"Denationalising the Past". Nation in E. V. Ramaswamy's Political Discourse', *Economic and Political Weekly*, 16 October 1993, p. 2282.

23 Ram, 'Ramaswami Naicker', p. 421.

24 Pandian, '"Denationalising" the Past', p. 2284.

25 Irshick, *Politics and Social Conflict in South India*, p. 341.

26 Cited in Geetha and Rajadurai, *Towards a Non-Brahmin Millennium*, p. 352.

27 *Ibid.*, p. 297.

28 *The Humble Memorial of the Non-Brahmins of Madras* (23 April 1920), IOLR, L/P&J/9/14.

29 *Justice* (29 March 1920), IOR, L/P&J/9/14.

30 R. Kothari and R. Maru, 'Federating for Political Interests: the Kshatriyas of Gujarat', in R. Kothari (ed.), *Caste in Indian Politics* (New Delhi: Orient Longman, 1986), p. 72.

31 G. Shah, *Caste Association and Political Process in Gujarat* (Bombay: Popular Prakashan, 1975), p. 33.

32 See M. Weiner, *Party Building in a New Nation. The Indian National Congress* (University of Chicago Press, 1967), p. 97.

33 L. Lobo, 'Koli Kshatriyas of North Gujarat: a Shift from Sanskritised Mobility to Politicised Mobility', *The Eastern Anthropologist* 42:2 (April–June 1989), pp. 176–7.

34 Kothari and Maru, 'Federating for Political Interests', p. 73.

35 Lobo, 'Koli Kshatriyas of North Gujarat', p. 188.

36 G. Shah, *Caste Association*, p. 127.

37 B. R. Ambedkar, 'Revolution and Counter Revolution in Ancient India', in *Dr Babasaheb Ambedkar Writings and Speeches*, vol. III (Bombay: Government of Maharashtra, 1987), p. 320.

38 B. R. Ambedkar, 'Untouchables or The Children of India's Ghetto', in *Dr Babasaheb Ambedkar Writings and Speeches*, vol. V (Bombay: Government of Maharashtra, 1989), pp. 101–2.

39 B. R. Ambedkar, 'Held at Bay', in *Dr Babasaheb Ambedkar Writings and Speeches*, vol. V, p. 266.

40 B. R. Ambedkar, 'The Untouchables', in *Dr Babasaheb Ambedkar Writings and Speeches*, vol. VII (Bombay: Government of Maharashtra, 1990), p. 317.

41 For an overview of the reservation policy of the British, see B. A. V. Sharma, 'Development of Reservation Policy', in B. A. V. Sharma and K. M. Reddy (eds.), *Reservation Policy in India* (New Delhi: Light and Light Publishers, 1982).

42 *Ibid.*, pp. 2–3.

43 M. Galanter, *Competing Equalities – Law and the Backward Classes in India* (New Delhi: Oxford University Press (1984), 1991), p. 94.

44 *Independent Labour Party – Its Formation and its Aims*, reprinted from the *Times of India*, 15 August 1936; Bombay: *Independent Labour Publications* 1 (1937), p. 8, in Ambedkar Papers, National Archives of India, reel 2, file 9.

45 E. Zelliot, *Dr Ambedkar and the Mahar Movement*, Ph.D. dissertation, University of Pennsylvania, 1969, p. 249, and R. I. Duncan, *Levels, the Communication of Programmes, and Sectional Strategies in Indian Politics, with Reference to the Bharatiya Kranti Dal and the Republican Party of India in Uttar Pradesh State and Aligarh District (UP)*, Ph.D. dissertation, University of Sussex, 1979, p. 214.

46 'Political Demands of Scheduled Castes – Resolutions Passed by the Working Committee of the All-India Scheduled Caste Federation', Appendix XI, in B. R. Ambedkar, 'What Congress and Gandhi Have Done to the Untouchables', in *Dr Babasaheb Ambedkar. Writings and Speeches*, vol. IX (Bombay: Government of Maharashtra, 1990), pp. 346–7.

47 Cited in Duncan, *Levels, the Communication of Programmes*, p. 236.

48 'Marching to Awaken the Ambedkarite Masses', *The Oppressed Indian* 5:1 (April 1983), p. 16.

49 O. Lynch, *The Politics of Untouchability – Social Mobility and Social Change in a City of India* (New York: Columbia University Press, 1969), pp. 68–9.

50 *Ibid.*, p. 93.

51 S. Pai, 'Dalit Assertion in UP', *Economic and Political Weekly*, 13 September 1997, p. 2314.

52 For more details, see C. Jaffrelot, 'The BSP in 2009: Still making progess but only as a Dalit party', in Paul Wallace and Ramashray Roy (eds.), *India's 2009 Elections: Coalition Politics, Party Competition and Congress Continuity* (New Delhi: Sage, 2011), pp. 140–66.

53 See C. Jaffrelot, *India's Silent Revolution. The Rise of the Lower Castes in North Indian Politics* (New York: Columbia University Press, 2003).

Part II

Cultural forms

6

The Bengali novel

The Bengali novel originated in the nineteenth century as a product of the colonial encounter, though it drew upon a multiplicity of literary traditions, indigenous as well as foreign. Like its counterpart in Europe, it is linked to the social, domestic and intellectual aspirations of a new bourgeoisie, the spread of print culture, the growth of urban centres and the formation of a middle-class readership hungry for novelty and diversion. But the conditions for its inception and development in colonial Bengal are clearly distinct from those of eighteenth-century Europe, making the novel both witness to and participant in the creation of a distinctly Indian modernity. In its representational function, it records not just the self-imposed compulsions of this process, but its fissures and uncertainties, opening up a space for moral, emotional and intellectual debate. At the same time, it becomes the site for an entirely new set of experiments with literary language and the techniques of representation.

Print, the public sphere and public culture

The coming of print and the consequent opening up of the public sphere is clearly the inaugural moment of this history. The first Bengali typefaces precede the novel by little more than half a century, with the publication of Nathaniel Brassey Halhed's *A Grammar of the Bengal Language* at Hooghly in 1778, using moveable metal type designed by Charles Wilkins. From 1800 onwards, missionary activity at Serampore and the establishment of the College of Fort William make printing in Bengali a necessary part of the colonial project, and contribute to the development of discursive prose through early narratives such as the

Raja Pratapaditya Charitra (1801) composed by Ramram Basu for his students at Fort William. But formal, literary Bengali prose, drawing upon Sanskrit as well as Persian, emerges only a couple of decades later in the polemical essays of Raja Rammohan Roy, who wrote in three languages, vigorously championing religious and social reform in Bengal.

Around the same time, the need for school texts and the birth of a vernacular press initiate new genres of descriptive and topical Bengali prose. Much periodical literature focuses upon the new city of Calcutta and its typical inhabitant, the *babu* (sometimes paired with his wife or mistress, the *bibi*), usually a salaried dependant on colonial rule, who continues to be the butt of satirical attack through the long nineteenth century for his greed, laziness, incompetence, neglect of traditional values, sensuality, ignorance and conceit. The anonymous *Babur Upakhyan* ('The Tale of the Babu'), published in *Samachar Darpan* in 1821 and attributed to Bhabanicharan Bandyopadhyay, and the same writer's *Naba Babu Bilas* ('A Pleasant Tale of the New Babu', 1825, under the pseudonym Pramathanath Sharma) and *Naba Bibi Bilas* ('A Pleasant Tale of the New Bibi', 1831) draw on the traditions both of the satirical sketch or *naksha* (from Persian *naqsa*, design) and the moral tale. The *naksha* remains the preferred form for descriptions of Calcutta, a rapidly changing metropolis offering limitless riches and social mobility to the amazed newcomer, as we find in Bhabanicharan's fragment *Kalikata Kamalalay* ('Calcutta, the Abode of the Goddess of Wealth', published in *Samachar Chandrika*, 1823), and later in Kaliprasanna Sinha's *Hutom Pyanchar Naksha* ('Sketches by Hutom the Owl', 1862), a brilliant series of satiric vignettes of Calcutta life.

While a steady stream of printed books flowed from Serampore and, by the second decade of the century, from the Baptist Mission Press in Calcutta, independent presses were also being set up by Bengali printers both in Calcutta and in other parts of Bengal. Throughout the century, despite the restrictions imposed by Lytton's Vernacular Press Act (1878), literary journals serialized new fiction. From the 1820s to the 1860s, the area of north Calcutta known as *bat-tala* (the banyan tree quarter), the heart of the 'native' town with its centre in Chitpur, had evolved into a great market of cheap print, publishing a range of texts, from the epics and mythological tales to almanacs, medieval devotional poetry, illustrated pamphlets, translations of Arabic and Persian tales, sensational fiction, plays, sketches and erotica. Linguistically, too, this popular print culture reflected considerable diversity, from the Sanskritized prose of upper-caste Hindu intellectuals to racy, abusive and colloquial speech, as well as what

James Long described as 'Musalman-Bengali', notable for its high proportion of Perso-Arabic and Urdu words, found in Muslim religious works and romances such as *Amir-Humza*, *Hatim Tai* and *Yusuf-Zuleikha*. Historians have noted a remarkable increase in the quantity of drama and fiction produced from these presses after mid-century. In addition to older tales like *Kamini Kumar*, *Jiban Tara* and *Bidya Sundar*, the new forms of novel and historical romance were anticipated or accompanied by *bat-tala* fiction such as *Hemlata-Ratikanta* (1847). By the time of the Obscene Publications Act of 1857, an emergent *bhadralok* (gentry) class had begun to voice its anxiety about the spread of *bat-tala* literature.

It is against this simultaneous emergence of a native elite and 'urban folk culture' that we must place the first novel in the Bengali language, *Alaler Gharer Dulal* ('The Spoilt Son of a Rich Family', 1858; serialized in *Masik Patrika*, 1855–7) by Pyarichand Mitra (1814–83), writing under the pseudonym Tekchand Thakur. Its inaugural status was recognized by Bankimchandra Chattopadhyay, the greatest novelist of the nineteenth century, in his account of 'Bengali Literature' (*Calcutta Review*, 1871), but the place thus given to *Alal* depends on complex prior understandings of the novel genre, the use that it might be put to in colonial Bengal and its subsequent history. Despite its claim of precedence, therefore, Hannah Catherine Mullens's *Phulmani o Karunar Bibaran* ('The Story of Phulmani and Karuna', 1852), a moral tale which can be interestingly linked with other Christian literature of its kind (such as the Revd. Lal Bihari De's *Chandramukhi Upakhyan*, 1859), is usually seen as failing to meet the novel's generic requirements. By contrast Pyarichand seems to be fully conscious of the demands of his chosen genre. The social realism of *Alal*, its vivid account of the culture of Calcutta and its village or small-town environs, ending with a description of Benares, lays the foundation for the nineteenth-century novel's commitment to realist representation. At the same time, it draws upon earlier satire directed at the new bourgeoisie, and the traditions of *naksha* and moral fable. A remarkable achievement is Pyarichand's vigorous and colloquial prose style, freeing the language from much of the stiffness and formality of an earlier period.

Genre and representation

The historical circumstances that give birth to *Alal*, however, are by no means the sole determinants of the new form, which draws upon a variety of narrative exemplars. Colonial readers represent a rapidly growing market for books imported from England. Early translations and imitations in several Indian languages attest to the popularity of Shakespeare, Bunyan's *Pilgrim's Progress*, Johnson's *Rasselas* and Goldsmith's *The Vicar of Wakefield*. But by mid-century the market is also flooded with novels and historical romances, not only Scott, Dickens and Disraeli, but also the sensational fiction of G. W. M. Reynolds, widely translated into Bengali, which created a new *rahasya* (mystery) genre with the two series of his *The Mysteries of London* (1844–8) and the four series of *The Mysteries of the Court of London* (1848–56).

For all that the form is derived from Western exemplars, the novel in Bengal is deeply indebted to indigenous narrative and to the affective and tonal registers of classical poetics. In an essay on education ('Lokshiksha', *Bangadarshan*, 1878), Bankimchandra laments the decline in traditions of oral storytelling (*kathakata*), and Rabindranath Thakur (Tagore) speaks of Bankimchandra's own fiction as having replaced 'children's fables' such as the *Gul-e-Bakavali* and *Bijay-Basanta* ('Bankimchandra,' *Sadhana*, 1894). Nevertheless, both learned and popular imaginations are steeped in a rich narrative tradition drawing upon the epics, the Sanskrit *kavyas* and prose fiction such as Banabhatta's seventh-century classic *Kadambari*, retellings of the *Ramayana* and *Mahabharata* in Bengali verse, the *mangal-kavyas* or devotional chronicles such the *Manasa-mangal* and *Chandi-mangal* (as well as Bharatchandra Ray's eighteenth-century *Annada-mangal*), popular collections of tales and legends, such as the *Hitopadesha*, *Betal Panchabimshati*, *Batris Simhasan*, *Arabian Nights*, *Gul-e-Bakavali* and *Tuti Nama,* and classic love stories like *Laila-Majnu*.

However, the 'realism' of the novel clearly offers native writers a unique opportunity for the self-representation of their class and people in a period of rapid transition. Indeed, early novelists in several Indian languages are urged by British officials (such as H. A. D. Phillips in the introduction to his translation of Bankimchandra's *Kapalkundala*, 1885) to serve the needs of colonial ethnography by producing vivid and exact portraits of social types and customs. To some extent this project of representation follows the trajectory of desire, thus confirming Fredric Jameson's assessment of the novel's role in 'what can be called a properly bourgeois cultural revolution – that immense process of transformation whereby populations whose life habits were formed by other, now archaic, modes of production are now reprogrammed for life and work in the new world of market capitalism'. The novel then assumes 'the task of producing as though for the first time the very life world, that very "referent" ... of which the new narrative discourse will then claim to be the "realistic" reflection'.[1] But at the same time, the form is a potent site for fantasy, its narrative materials not always amenable to the claims of reality. Though early historians of the novel in Bengali repeatedly emphasize its commitment both to realism and to a 'republic of letters', romance, that unacknowledged other of realist narrative in both Europe and India, remains one of its most powerful elements. Equally important is the attraction of a moral or allegorical substructure, such as the cautionary tale embedded in *Alal*.

Imagined history

Essential to the project of self-representation is the sense of a shared history, but Bengal, Bankimchandra says categorically, has no history ('Bangalar Itihas' ('The History of Bengal'), *Bangadarshan*, 1874). Faced with the incompatibility of a mythological or legendary past and an evidence-based colonial historiography, nineteenth-century writers are driven either to reconstitute a national history from its fragments, or to imagine it anew. As Sudipta Kaviraj puts it, '[i]n Bengali discourse of the nineteenth century "history" breaks out everywhere'.[2] This may explain the early rise of the historical novel, drawing upon chronicles of past valour, particularly of the Rajputs and the Marathas as related by British historians or antiquarians like James Grant Duff (*The History of the Marathas*, 3 vols., 1826), James Tod (*Annals and Antiquities of Rajasthan*, 2 vols., 1829–32) and Hobart Caunter (*The Romance of History: India*, 3 vols., 1836). But the debt is by no means a simple one. In 1857, the year of the Revolt, the scholar and educationist Bhudeb Mukhopadhyay (1827–94) composed two novellas based on Caunter under the single title *Aitihasik Upanyas* ('Historical Novels'). Almost at the end of the century, after having produced several histories for young readers, he wrote a strange 'alternative' history of India called *Svapnalabdha Bharatbarsher Itihas* ('The History of India Received in a Dream', 1895), where he imagines the course of events if the Marathas had not lost the Third Battle of Panipat and the British had not come to rule the subcontinent. This fictional staging of a past free from the reality of colonial subjection confirms the spirit of Bhudeb's social thought, but goes beyond his critique of Western historiography and its rejection of the Hindu *puranas.* It suggests the possibility not just of an alternative history, but of another way of thinking about history, as an instrument of imaginative release. Kaviraj suggests that 'the fundamental asymmetry between the European and the Bengali made a simple imitation of the European manner of doing history impossible. To discover the truth of historical objects and connections is the ironical privilege of the subaltern.'[3] There is in nineteenth-century Bengal a double turning towards history – as a subject of empirical research on the one hand and as a site of imaginative freedom on the other. While the project of a nation remains central, the difficulty of defining it makes a single national allegory impossible to locate: rather, the historical novel stages a 'theatre of alternatives'.[4] Such a staging is encountered as early as Kylas Chunder Dutt's novella in English, 'A Journal of Forty-Eight Hours of the Year 1945' (*The Calcutta Literary Gazette*, 1835) which imagines future armed uprisings against British rule. But it was in the Bengali of Bankimchandra's *Durgeshnandini* ('The Daughter of the Lord of the Fort', 1865), rather than the English of his first novel *Rajmohan's Wife* (published in the *Indian Field* in 1864) that the historical novel was to take root in India.

Nowhere is the engagement with history more complex than in the fiction of Bankimchandra Chattopadhyay (1838–94). Of his fourteen novels, seven take their materials from history; his third novel, *Mrinalini* (1869), was labelled an *aitihasik upanyas* (historical novel) in the first two editions, though the adjective was removed in the third. But in the preface to the greatly amplified fourth edition of *Rajsimha* (1893; serialized 1878, published 1882), almost at the end of his life, Bankimchandra describes it as his first historical novel (*aitihasik upanyas*), explicitly dismissing the claims of earlier romances like *Durgeshnandini, Chandrashekhar* (1875; serialized 1873–4) and *Sitaram* (1887; serialized 1885–6), which focus on tragic conflicts of love and morality rather than national history. *Rajsimha* seeks to recover a forgotten or obliterated Hindu past, one that must be reclaimed by labour and imagination from the prejudices of Muslim historians and the partialities of Rajput witnesses. The seriousness of this project drives Bankimchandra's developing sense of what a historical novel should contain, and although the plot of *Rajsimha* is based on a single paragraph in Tod and brief references in Robert Orme's *Historical Fragments of the Mogul Empire* (1782) and Niccolao Manucci's *History of the Mogul Dynasty in India* (1826), a number of historical characters do appear in the course of the novel's reconstruction of Rajput heroism. Yet *Durgeshnandini* left more of a mark on the imaginations of contemporary readers, and the controversial *Anandamath* (serialized 1880–2, published 1882), set against the background of the Bengal famine of 1770 and the *sanyasi* rebellion of 1772–3, answered the call of history more directly.

Though Bankimchandra stated explicitly that it should not be read as a historical novel, *Anandamath* describes the activities of a patriotic and disciplined band of Hindu ascetics who call themselves *santans* (children) of the Mother Goddess (identified with the motherland), and who have vowed to continue armed rebellion until she is reinstated in her glory and the *sanatan dharma* (eternal faith) has been established. While the *santans* in the novel fight against the British, they are also bitterly opposed to Muslim rule; at the end of the novel, they are assured by a mystical Physician that the British are destined to govern India and ensure her prosperity. This assurance, coupled with the novel's patently anti-Muslim content, has drawn Bankimchandra's politics into extreme disrepute, and has cast a shadow, too, on the *santans'* song *Vande Mataram* ('I hail the Mother') which inspired nationalists during India's struggle for independence, and has been adopted as the 'national song' of India. There can be no doubt that Bankimchandra's projected nation merges Bengali, Hindu and Indian identities into an indissoluble whole, and that he regarded Muslim rule and Hindu servitude as unmitigated evils. But his treatment of the British is also deeply critical, and the Muslim population of Bengal (particularly its peasantry) is never excluded from his 'national' vision. Further, the complexity of *Anandamath*'s textual politics, as represented by its publishing history, prevents an easy conclusion regarding Bankim's intentions. Yet, in its mystical exaltation of the motherland and the power of its fantasy of courage and sacrifice, *Anandamath*, even if it is not a historical novel, is certainly the work in which Bankimchandra addresses history most directly, and the novel has gone on to exercise a historical function quite independent of its historicity.

Bankimchandra's friend and younger contemporary, Rameshchandra Datta (1848–1909), a distinguished economic historian, said that he had been inspired by him to write his first novel in Bengali, the historical romance *Bangabijeta* ('The Conqueror of Bengal', 1874). Rameshchandra drew upon history again for his subsequent novels, adapting, in *Maharashtra Jiban-prabhat* ('The Dawn of Maharashtra Life', 1878) and *Rajput Jiban-sandhya* ('The Twilight of Rajput Life,' 1879), episodes of Maratha and Rajput history that might give substance to a patriotism deeply invested in the idea of a heroic past. In her novel *Dip-nirban* ('The Dying of the Lamp', 1876), the first in a succession of historical romances, Svarnakumari Debi, sometimes called the first Bengali woman novelist, turned to the history of Prithviraj, the last Hindu king of Delhi. This search for heroes, however, is not without its contradictions. Just a few years after *Durgeshnandini*, Pratapchandra Ghosh (1845–1921) published the first volume of a weighty historical novel, *Bangadhip Parajay* ('The Defeat of the King of Bengal', 1869), dwelling upon the personal flaws that led to the defeat of Pratapaditya (the late sixteenth-century Hindu ruler of Jessore) at the hands of the Mughals. In the second volume, published in 1884, Pratapaditya became a champion of Bengal's independence. The transformation can be traced to the course of nationalist thought in the intervening years; but in a historical romance on the same subject, *Bouthakuranir Hat* (1883), the young Rabindranath Tagore followed the earlier volume's lead, offering a strongly critical view of a figure later glorified by what the historian Jadunath Sarkar described as a 'false provincial patriotism'. Near the end of the century, Mir Mosharraf Hussain's *Bishad-Sindhu* ('The Ocean of Sorrow', 1885–91), narrating the tragic martyrdoms of the Prophet's grandsons at Karbala, opened up the novel in Bengali to the sweep of the Islamic religious epic.

The novel and society

In an essay published in *Prabasi* (1931) Rabindranath Tagore distinguished the social realism of Bankimchandra's novel *Bishabriksha* ('The Poison Tree', 1873) from historical romance, for which he used the term *kahini* (usually translated as 'tale') as contrasted with *akhyan* (chronicle, narrative). While the terminology he was trying to establish (at a time when the choice of the term *upanyas* for 'novel' was still fairly recent) never found favour, Rabindranath's autobiographical account of the breathless anticipation with which instalments of *Bishabriksha* were awaited (as they appeared serially in the journal *Bangadarshan* from its first issue in 1872) memorably evokes an unprecedented literary experience. Bankimchandra's contemporaries, such as the poet Nabinchandra Sen or the anonymous reviewer in the *Calcutta Review* of 1873, felt that it was with this book that Bankim became a novelist, dealing with 'men and women as they are, and life as it is'. *Bishabriksha* deals with an unhappy domestic triangle, a situation of deep psychological complexity which, as contemporary readers were quick to notice, is resolved conservatively through the suicide of the woman who, as a remarried widow, constitutes both an obstacle to the happiness of the household she enters and an offence to traditional morality. Yet the depth and sympathy with which the characters, especially the women, are treated goes beyond conventional moral attitudes. Women in Bankim's fiction are frequently driven by their social vulnerability and marginal status to act in ways that threaten orthodox domestic structures. Yet it is these very actions that drive the engine of plot, and produce his women characters as vivid, singular, intense and struggling figures in whom moral and ideological crises are most fully articulated. This is true of the historical novels as well, several of which (such as *Chandrashekhar* and *Sitaram*) feature turbulent emotional relationships at the centre of their narratives, or adopt women as their heroines, as in *Durgeshnandini*, *Mrinalini* (1869) or *Debi Choudhurani* (1884; serialized 1883). But the only work comparable to *Bishabriksha* in its analysis of social and domestic realities (and as controversial in its treatment of them) is *Krishnakanter Will* (1878; serialized 1875–7). Here again a young widow, a liminal figure hungry for love and social acceptance, sets off a series of moral and emotional crises. The modernity of the novel's plot resides not just in its relevance to contemporary debates surrounding widow remarriage, but in its use of the Victorian device of old Krishnakanta's will, as much an object of family machinations as it is an instrument of manipulative control.

Unique amongst Bankimchandra's novels is *Kapalkundala* (1866), drawn partly from personal experience, partly from his reading of Shakespeare and classical Sanskrit drama. The heroine Kapalkundala, after being brought up in isolation by a fearsome ascetic, saves a young man's life and marries him, but is unable to accept the restrictions of domesticity. The story ends tragically, and its plot is complicated by the addition of a 'historical' strand involving, at a distance, the Mughal court. Though the novel is set in the past, before the advent of British rule, history is not its focus: it is a work of exceptional imaginative intensity concentrated in the figure of its heroine, Kapalkundala, who represents the undomesticated freedom of a nature (*prakriti*) both merciful and terrifying. The novel demonstrates Bankim's mastery of Bengali prose, of rhetorical description drawing on classical Sanskrit poetics and of the many registers of speech ranging from the formal to the colloquial.

It is this extraordinary command, not just of narrative structure, but of a sophisticated and flexible medium of representation that distinguishes Bankimchandra as a novelist. He initiated first-person narration in *Indira* (1893; expanded from *Bangadarshan*, 1872) and multiple narrators in *Rajani* (1877; *Bangadarshan* 1874–5). While human figures, as Shrikumar Bandyopadhyay pointed out, are pushed to one side in the event-filled canvas of his historical novels, his domestic fiction focuses unerringly on the physical and emotional substance of everyday life. Realist description, a technique involving the accumulation of synecdochic detail so as to ground fiction in the 'world', had already been initiated in *Alaler Gharer Dulal*. Bankimchandra's singular achievement was to adapt this technique to the requirements of an affective register so that European realism and *alamkara* (the rhetorical figures of classical Sanskrit poetics) are brought into close proximity, as in the dense semiotic interplay of the description of Suryamukhi's bedroom in *Bishabriksha*. Most of all, his novels serve to articulate the ideological and moral crises as well as the hopes and aspirations of Indians at a critical moment in their history; and they do so with clarity, vigour and ironic intelligence.

If patriotism runs like a somewhat tangled thread through the historical fiction of the nineteenth century, the social fiction of the same period draws upon another element in the project of the nation – reform. Despite his own conservatism, Bankimchandra had focused upon two of the most pressing issues confronting reformers: the condition of widows and the practice of polygamy. Rameshchandra Datta's social novels, *Samsar* ('Family', 1886; serialized in *Prachar*, 1885) and *Samaj* ('Society', 1894; partly serialized in *Sahitya*, 1893–4) directly advocate widow remarriage and inter-caste unions, which, he stated in a letter of 1894, 'unite[s] our divided and enfeebled nation'.[5] The third element in this nationalist project was the choice of a language, a historically critical decision for bilingual writers who had begun in English, like Michael Madhusudan Datta and Bankim himself. Urged by Bankim to choose Bengali as his medium of creative expression, Rameshchandra dedicated *Samsar* to Rammohan, Vidyasagar and Bankimchandra as social reformers, and *Samaj* to Madhusudan, Akshay Kumar Datta and Dinabandhu Mitra as writers who had enriched the Bengali language.

Samsar deals with the fortunes of a poor rural family, compelled by a land dispute to seek shelter in the city of Calcutta. Rameshchandra's experience as an economist and administrator gives substance to the scrupulous realism with which both village community and urban settlements are treated, though here, as in his later book *Samaj*, the narrative resolution is perhaps too simply achieved. Particularly remarkable is Rameshchandra's attempt to reproduce regional speech and accents, especially those of women – an impossible task for Lal Bihari De (Lal Behari Day)'s English novel *Govinda Samanta* (1874; later renamed *Bengal Peasant Life*). But the domestic novel in Bengali had already been memorably attempted, almost simultaneously with Bankimchandra's *Bishabriksha*, in Taraknath Gangopadhyay's *Svarnalata* (1874; serialized from 1872), an immensely popular book that ran into seven editions during the author's lifetime (1843–91). Here, as in Shibnath Shastri's novels *Mejabou* (1880) and *Jugantar* (1895), or Shrishchandra Majumdar's *Phuljani* (1894), one can glimpse the elements of an alternative novelistic tradition free of the dramatic excess of Bankim's fiction, but attempting to treat ordinary life with a sympathy that anticipates Sharatchandra's. *Svarnalata* was widely admired for the integrity of its portrayal of the middle-class family, especially in extended, joint households, and for its realistic depictions both of village society and the crowded metropolis of Calcutta. Shibnath Shastri's fiction engages more directly with reformist issues but draws on similar material. The concerns of the reformers and the mores of the Anglicized bourgeoisie are vigorously satirized in Jogendrachandra Basu's *Model Bhagini* (1888), while Trailokyanath Mukhopadhyay's fantasy, *Kankabati* (1892) blends humour and pathos, dream and reality.

For the women novelists who emerge in the last quarter of the nineteenth century, the field of fiction is also divided between history and society, though domestic life claims more sustained attention. A contender for the title of first Bengali woman novelist is Hemangini, whose *Manorama* may have appeared as early as 1874, though little is known about this writer who composed at least one other novel about a chaste and long-suffering woman, *Pranay-pratima* ('The Image of Love', 1877). Equally obscure are the origins of women writers like Shatadalabashini Debi (*Bijanbala*, 1882; *Bidhaba Bangalalana* ('The Bengali Widow'), 1884) and Basantakumari Mitra (*Ranonmadini*, 1884). But the first woman novelist to achieve independent recognition was Rabindranath Tagore's brilliant and gifted elder sister, Svarnakumari Debi (1855–1932), who wrote a number of historical romances as well as the domestic tragedies *Chhinamukul* ('Torn Blossom', 1879) and *Snehalata* (1892–3), and the 'progressive' love story *Kahake* ('To Whom?', 1898). Svarnakumari's writing has been much criticized for its uneven blend of romantic sentiment, social realism and moral discourse. But as an early feminist brought up in the enlightened Tagore family, she offers incisive critiques not just of conservative, but also of professedly liberal households, and in *Snehalata* she deals with the continued suffering of young women in a period of social transition. By contrast, *Kahake* is more of a wish-fulfilment fantasy, allowing its heroine an ideal resolution of tradition and modernity. More persuasive and naturalistic treatments of domestic life are to be found in the novels of Kusumkumari Raychoudhuri and Sharatkumari Choudhurani, though few writers of the period match Svarnakumari's intellectual range.

New subjectivities

Like his nineteenth-century contemporaries, the poet Rabindranath Tagore (1861–1941) was drawn early to the historical romance, but at the turn of the new century he initiated a number of remarkable experiments with the form of the novel, transforming it into a subtle and responsive vehicle for the representation of individual subjects. In *Chokher Bali* ('Mote in the Eye', 1903; serialized in *Bangadarshan* 1901–2), he turned his attention precisely to that unhappy domestic triangle which Bankim had explored in *Bishabriksha*, but the young widow he places at the heart of his narrative – the desiring, transgressive, 'hungry-hearted' (*kshudita-hridaya*) Binodini – emerges as a far more powerful and complex figure than the relatively passive Kundanandini of Bankim's masterpiece. Nevertheless, Rabindranath never achieved Bankim's mastery of plot, and his next novel, *Noukadubi* ('The Capsized Boat', 1906; serialized in *Bangadarshan* 1903–5) fell back, as he acknowledged, on the chance-ridden, improvised narrative characteristic of serial composition. But *Gora* (1910; part-edition 1909), written in the wake of the *svadeshi* agitation following the first Partition of Bengal (1905), engages in a direct and complex way with the apparently opposed modes of history and allegory. The novel's hero, Gora, is a Mutiny orphan, an Irish child fostered by Bengali parents. Unaware of his origins, he is a fervent, anti-British Hindu patriot. The working-out of the novel's plot casts all exclusive models of nationhood or identity into sharp ironic focus, anticipating Rabindranath's later critique of nationalism and his hostility to myths of racial or religious purity.

The forty-odd years that separate Bankimchandra's major novels from those of Rabindranath had witnessed a transformation of India's political landscape. By the turn of the century, the struggle for political self-determination was well advanced, and in the first decade of the twentieth century, terrorist movements advocating armed rebellion against the British had taken root in Bengal. While many such groups drew inspiration from Bankimchandra's *Anandamath*, the politics of that work in fact had little bearing on the contemporary situation. For Rabindranath, however, it was impossible not to engage with the political identifications and conflicts of his time, though for him these are always inflected by social and moral imperatives. *Ghare Baire* ('At Home and in the World', 1916; serialized in *Sabuj Patra*, 1915–16) is set against the backdrop of the *svadeshi* movement, but on the domestic level it deals with the liberal landowner Nikhilesh's attempt to 'emancipate' his wife Bimala by bringing her into society, where she meets and is overwhelmed by the magnetic personality of his friend Sandip, a fiery nationalist. The novel uses an alternating series of first-person narratives by Bimala, Nikhilesh and Sandip, producing a complex interplay of voices and perspectives. Again, Rabindranath finds himself unable to espouse either an exclusive model of nationhood, or the claim that the end might justify the means. Nikhilesh is gravely injured in an attempt to calm a riot-torn Muslim village, and the intoxicating rhetoric that attracts Bimala to Sandip is seen to be false. But the novel is as much about domestic relationships and the intimate history of a marriage as it is about political action. In his last novel, *Char Adhyay* ('Four Chapters', 1934), written when he was seventy-three years old, Rabindranath returned to his interrogation of the politics of terror, though in a controversial preface to the book, and still more controversial *apologia* (*Prabasi*, 1935), Rabindranath defended his tale of two lovers caught up in revolutionary bloodshed, urging that it be judged on literary merit alone. Writing to the poet Amiya Chakrabarti in the same year, he spoke of the magical charm of poetry with which he had attempted to suffuse the dry air of the novel, drawing attention to its experimental style as well as to its critique of idealist violence.

Rabindranath's intervening novels, the most important being *Chaturanga* ('Quartet', 1916; published as a short-story series in *Sabuj Patra* 1914–15), *Jogajog* ('Relationships', 1929; serialized in *Bichitra* 1927–9) and *Shesher Kabita* ('The Last Poem', 1929; serialized in *Prabasi* 1928–9), do not focus on political action, choosing instead to explore individual lives in the context of a society in rapid transition. The four-part structure of *Chaturanga*, juxtaposing the inter-linked stories of four characters, offers a complex study of human relationships; here, as in *Jogajog*, the major part of the narrative deals with a triangulated relation between two men and a woman, a situation of extreme psychological complexity. But the novels have contrasting plots, the unfinished *Jogajog* being an extended study of bourgeois marriage, exploring the inner life of its heroine Kumudini as well as the mental and material structures of class formation in colonial Bengal. *Shesher Kabita* is a lighter and more parodic work, a novel of ideas rather than of psychological interiority, where Rabindranath pre-empted his critics by mocking his own writing. In all his novels, Rabindranath seeks to open up the form beyond the limitations of nineteenth-century romance and realism and to ask new questions about human subjects and social conditions in prose of astonishing depth and sensitivity.

Sentiment and satire

Yet the most popular Bengali novelist, then as now, was Sharatchandra Chattopadhyay (1876–1938), whose novels of domestic life, with their sharp edge of social satire, reformed public sensibilities in unprecedented ways. Writing a simple, natural prose, he invited sympathy for the sufferings of ordinary people, particularly women. Indeed, he is supposed to have compiled a history of women (*Narir Itihas*) but the manuscript was destroyed by fire; what we do have is the seminal essay *Narir Mulya* ('A Woman's Worth', 1923). Sentiment becomes the defining element in his fiction, functioning as an instrument of moral identification for middle-class readers. Though Sharatchandra's own life was wayward and unsettled, and his heroes wander in search of a living throughout the eastern part of the subcontinent as far as Burma and the Malay Peninsula, he chose for the most part to describe the narrow, socially orthodox domestic settings of rural Bengal. His first novel, *Bardidi* ('Elder Sister'), was serialized in the journal *Bharati* in 1907 and brought him immediate fame. It is the first of a series of explorations of the obscurantism and the cruelty of village society in late nineteenth-century Bengal, where women like the young widow Rama in *Pallisamaj* ('Village Society', 1916) are victims of oppressive social customs. Such figures are suffused in Sharatchandra's fiction with a rare tenderness and pathos, especially where individual aspirations are defeated, as in *Chandranath* (1916), *Arakshaniya* ('The Unmarried Girl', 1916), *Debdas* (1917) and *Bamuner Meye* ('The Brahman's Daughter', 1920). Poverty and economic exploitation are also searingly described in works like *Nishkriti* ('Deliverance', 1917) and *Dena-Paona* ('Debts and Dues', 1923). His revolutionary political novel, *Pather Dabi* ('Right of Way', 1926; serialized in *Bangabani* 1923–6) was condemned by the British government. Despite the conservative social mores he depicts, Sharatchandra was in fact an enthusiastic reader of Herbert Spencer's *Descriptive Sociology*, believing in the equality of the sexes and freedom of choice. Some of Sharatchandra's heroines, such as Kiranmayi in *Charitrahin* ('Unprincipled', 1917), Abhaya in *Shrikanta, Part II* (1918), Achala in *Grihadaha* ('The Burning of the Home', 1920) and Kamal in *Shesh Prashna* ('The Final Question', 1931), memorably reject tyrannical customs and assert the right of women to personal liberty. While his best-loved novel is the loosely autobiographical *Shrikanta* (four parts, 1917–33), the most unusual is the late *Shesh Prashna*, a novel of ideas depicting a radically independent woman.

Sharatchandra's fiction throws up – though it does not resolve – contemporary questions about marriage, asking how far it can be accommodated to desire or love, as to the reformed ideal of intellectual companionship. His feminism, qualified by sentiment and nostalgia, finds few followers amongst his contemporaries, who appear to be equally divided between the paths of reaction and reform. Traditional Hindu social values, celebrating Brahman orthodoxy and the chaste wife or widow, are reproduced in novels by the most popular women novelists of the time, such as *Mantrashakti* ('The Power of Incantation', 1915) and *Mahanisha* ('Eternal Night', 1919) by Anurupa Debi, and *Annapurnar Mandir* ('The Temple of Annapurna', 1913), *Didi* ('Elder Sister', 1915) and *Bidhilipi* ('Fate', 1919) by Nirupama Debi. A similar conservatism of outlook is evident in Muslim writers of the period, even if they write of the newly educated gentry, as we find in *Anowara* (1914) and *Gariber Meye* ('A Poor Man's Daughter', 1923) by Najibar Rahman, or in *Svapnadrishta* ('Seen in a Dream', 1924) by an early Muslim woman novelist, Nurunessa Khatun. On the other hand, the liberal, reformed mores of Brahmo Samaj households inspire the sentimental novels of Ramananda Chattopadhyay's daughters, Shanta Debi and Sita Debi. An unusual story of Hindu–Muslim love across class divisions is related in *Sheikh Andu* (1917) by Shailabala Ghoshjaya. The most striking female response to the woman's question, however, is in the novel *Padmarag* (composed 1903, published 1924) by the educator and essayist Begum Rokeya Sakhawat Hossain (1880–1932). This work, Rokeya's only novel, may be seen as a complement to her utopian fantasy in English, *Sultana's Dream* (1905). It is a passionate, polemical feminist satire, describing life in Tarini Bhavan, a philanthropic and nationalist institution run entirely by and for women. The narrative relates the inmates' tragic histories to the reformist project of the 'Society for Alleviation of Female Suffering', reminding us of Rokeya's own commitment to women's emancipation and nationalism.

Rural and urban

To some extent, the 'woman question' fades into the background of Bengali fiction after Sharatchandra, to be replaced by other social conflicts at a time of transition and upheaval for rural communities. The great novelists of this period, Bibhutibhushan Bandyopadhyay (1894–1950), Tarashankar Bandyopadhyay (1898–1971) and Manik Bandyopadhyay (1908–56), as well as Satinath Bhaduri (1906–65) and Advaita Mallabarman (1914–51), all focus on the Bengal countryside, but see it under the lens of change, wasted by poverty and dearth, unsettled by migration to the ruthless, all-consuming city. The project of modernity had been the principal concern of the Bengali novel from its inception in the nineteenth century, driving its search for subjects and its formal experiments. In the twentieth century, despite the hard-fought gains of the independence movement, that project loses its aura of hope. A new kind of social realism, drawing upon modernist techniques of representation as well as upon the anger, confusion and despair of the rural poor and the urban unemployed, leaves its imprint in fiction. At the same time, the lyric power of novelists like Bibhutibhushan and Advaita Mallabarman conveys the beauty of the landscapes in which their novels are set, and the dignity of their inhabitants. Bibhutibhushan's *Pather Panchali* ('Song of the Road') was published in 1929, and was followed two years later by the sequel *Aparajita* ('The Undefeated'). Immortalized by Satyajit Ray's film trilogy, the novels convey a profound, almost poetic grasp of natural and human detail, while they describe the bleak necessities that impel the priest Harihar's family to leave their village and seek a livelihood elsewhere. Apu, the hero of this *Bildungsroman*, makes the transition from village boy to urban intellectual, a movement which becomes representative of Bengali modernity. The educated estate-manager in *Aranyak* ('Book of the Forest', 1938) undertakes the reverse journey to the forests of Bihar, narrating in visionary prose the inevitable destruction of forest lands and the displacement of ancient tribal communities. Bibhutibhushan's last major novel, *Ashani Samket* ('Distant Thunder', 1959) deals with the Bengal famine of 1943, the defining event of the decade before independence, as Partition was for the decade after.

If a plangent lyricism informs Bibhutibhushan's fiction, his contemporary Tarashankar Bandyopadhyay writes in an epic vein of the grim social realities of the 1930s and 1940s in Bengal. His greatest novels deal with rural life at a time of transition, describing a decaying feudalism, the increasing impoverishment of the peasantry and a new profiteering middle class. Contemporaries attacked his reactionary nostalgia for feudal ways of life, even for traditional medicine, but his sense of history and the breadth and accuracy of his large canvases in novels like *Dhatri Debata* ('Earth Goddess', 1939), *Kalindi* (1940) and *Gana Debata* ('God of the People', 1942) are unerring. Central to his vision is a sense of place. River, land and village dominate his books, as in *Hansuli Banker Upakatha* ('The Tale of the River's Bend', 1947), capturing the inexorable decline of a poor village community struggling against economic exploitation and the depredations of war. Yet here, as in *Kabi* ('The Poet', 1944) or in the classic *Gana Debata*, Tarashankar offers no real criticism of the caste-ridden, oppressive rural society that he describes with such power and truth. Even his novel of the famine, *Manvantar* (1944), is far removed from the radical social analyses of his contemporary, the communist Manik Bandyopadhyay, whose work links the ideology of the Indian Progressive Writers' Association, in its later incarnations, with the aesthetic modernism of the Kallol group in Bengal, composed of poets who had rejected Tagore's lyrical idealism.

Manik's early reading of Freud is evident in the psychological complexities of his novels and shorter fiction, but his mature work focuses not only on the individual psyche but also on what he called 'the tragedy of land-relations'. The realism he practises exposes the repressions and anxieties of the urban middle class, as well as the changes in rural society as a consequence of peasant upheavals, political insurgency and the famine of 1943. The psychological analyses of *Dibaratrir Kabya* ('Poem of Day and Night', 1935) or *Chatushkon* ('Quadrilateral', 1948) are complemented by the broader canvases of his two greatest novels,

Padmanadir Majhi ('The Boatmen of the River Padma', 1936) and *Putulna-cher Itikatha* ('The Marionettes' Tale', 1936): intense, complex renderings of rural societies, of existences under threat, of sexual and moral adjust-ments, exploitation and hypocrisy. If *Padmanadir Majhi* is the greatest example of the 'river novel' in Bengal, in large part a deltaic plain defined more by water than by land, that genre is consolidated by Advaita Mallabarman's classic chronicle of fishermen's lives, *Titas Ekti Nadir Nam* ('Titas is the Name of a River', 1956; completed 1950), lyrically capturing the speech, rhythms and rituals of the Malo fishing commu-nity while recording the inevitability of its decline. In fact the two rivers that define Bengali identity both have novels dedicated to them, Pramathanath Bishi's *Padma* (1935) and Samaresh Basu's *Ganga* (1957).

Modernism and realism are uneasily but powerfully conjoined in the fiction of the 1940s. Its writers had already witnessed the turn to aes-thetic modernism in the reaction to Tagore in the 1920s, a movement led by the poets associated with the journal *Kallol*, some of whom, like Jibanananda Das (1899–1954) and Buddhadeb Basu (1908–1974), also wrote fiction. The former's novels *Malyaban* (1972) and *Sutirtha* (1977), which dealt frankly with marital and moral choices, were written during the 1940s, though they were only published posthumously. Buddhadeb Basu continued to write fiction from the 1930s to the 1960s, his most important novels such as *Kalo Haoa* ('Black Wind', 1942), *Tithidor* (1949) and *Rat Bhor Brishti* ('Rain through the Night', 1967) focusing on intense emotional or sexual relationships. This psychological realism is comple-mented by the social realism called for by times of famine, insurgency and unprecedented social transformation. At the same time, much fic-tion of the period is strongly experimental, like Satinath Bhaduri's *Jagari* ('The Vigil', 1946), a modernist stream-of-consciousness narrative set against the background of the Quit India movement. In his masterpiece, *Dhonrai Charit Manas* ('The Story of Dhonrai', 1949–51), chronicling society, politics and the making of identity in rural East Bihar, Satinath produced a subaltern epic, echoing the title of the medieval poet Tulsidas's classic *Ram Charit Manas*.

Modern and postmodern

For eastern India, the defining event that accompanied Independence in 1947 was Partition, drawing the new boundary of the nation-state across the heart of Bengal. The trauma of this division was prolonged by repeated waves of migration across the border into India, creating 'colonies' of refugees for whom the state did little or nothing. Peasant revolts, from the Tebhaga movement of 1946 to the Naxalbari rebellion of 1967, indicated the extent of rural unrest. There were food riots in the 1960s, and the economic recession added millions to the state's poor, dispossessed and unemployed. Bangladesh, formerly East Pakistan, fought its war of independence in 1971 with Indian help, but the 'national' recognition thus gained for the Bengali language could not ensure a single literary history. In post-Independence India, the Bengali novel took its subjects from the gap between promise and fulfilment in the new Indian republic. At the same time, print readership was closely linked to audiences for the other arts, notably theatre and film. From its inception the Bengali novel had lent itself to theatrical adaptation, and now found new life in a highly literary cinematic tradition, established not only by Satyajit Ray and Ritvik Ghatak, but also by countless 'commercial' film-makers who popularized the phrase 'watching a book'. Such adaptation may appear peripheral to the history of the genre, but in fact establishes the centrality of the novel form in modern Bengali aesthetic experience. While this may seem to lend authority to realist narrative, the novel's interaction with other genres has invited technical and formal innovations.

Despite the emergence of a cosmopolitan modernism in Bengali literature and art from the 1920s onwards, it would be a mistake to chart the history of the novel in terms of European cultural movements. Some representational tasks were made necessary by the political history of the subcontinent before and after decolonization, by the violence and suffering of Partition and by economic inequality and social unrest. A loose formal realism persists up to the third quarter of the century, though it is significantly undercut by modernist distrust of the apparent 'truths' of narrative. Urban alienation, uprootedness, exile and existentialist anguish characterize lives 'on the brink', mercilessly exposed and vulnerable. Even where realist narrative gives way to symbolic or allegorical structures, to myth, to 'stream of consciousness', to epic imperatives, or to a homegrown magical realism, it is difficult to group writers in formal categories. So strong are the compulsions of the material, the 'things themselves', that the post-colonial Bengali novel, unlike its English counterpart, is better defined by content than by form.

Nevertheless, if one novel can be seen as breaking decisively with the social realism and contemporary settings of modernist fiction a decade after Independence, it is Kamalkumar Majumdar (1915–79) in *Antarjali Jatra* ('Last Journey', 1959), an extraordinary account of Hindu death, drawing upon pre-colonial sensibilities and beliefs in a style that is at once rigorously conservative and radically new. Attacked in its own time for its rejection of a modernist idiom and its literary obscurantism, the novel now appears postmodern in its powerful, almost spectral evocation of a vanished past. But Kamalkumar's work resisted imitation, and the ideological weight of realism continued to exercise a powerful influence on writers even beyond the modernist phase. Post-Independence fiction turns its face for the most part towards the city of Calcutta: urban experience comes to define contemporary modernity. This is true of novelists such as Santosh Kumar Ghosh, Jyotirindra Nandi, Narendranath Mitra and Ramapada Choudhuri. Much of this fiction deals with the new rifts and tensions in a struggling middle class. The most subtle, deeply interiorized treatments of the psychological traumas of working lives in the city are possibly in the novels of Bimal Kar, Samaresh Basu, Shyamal Gangopadhyay and Shirshendu Mukhopadhyay. In another vein, the early work of Mati Nandi, Sunil Gangopadhyay and Shankar, popular novelists in a number of genres, focuses powerfully on urban alienation, isolation and exile.

But while international modernism appears to be inextricably linked to the city, the modern Bengali novel is certainly not exclusively urban or metropolitan. The focus on village life that we find in pre-Partition fiction is continued on the other side of the border in Syed Waliullah's *Lal Shalu* (1948), analysing the conflicts between superstitious belief and radical scepticism amongst Muslim peasants. On the Indian side, the detailed realism and epic range of the novels of Prafulla Ray, Gunamay Manna and Amiya Bhushan Majumdar deliberately present the life of rural, peasant Bengal, though in a countryside ravaged by political and social unrest, migration and resettlement. So too, Debesh Ray's *Tista Parer Brittanta* ('Tista-Side Story', 1988) continued the tradition of the 'river novel' by looking at subaltern existences on the banks of the river Tista in north Bengal, existences threatened by building of a dam, by new forms of exploitation and employment. But the most remarkable and sustained treatment of subaltern lives, especially the lives of tribal communities, is in the fiction of Mahashveta Debi, concentrating uncompromisingly on the oppressed and dispossessed of India's forests and agrarian hinterlands, as in *Aranyer Adhikar* ('Right to the Forest', 1977), which deals with the revolt of the Munda tribals in 1895. Such fiction, it could be argued, creates its own modernist or postmodernist idiom simply through the compulsions of a content that defies traditional realist practice. Mahashveta's writing is deliberately rough-edged, her narrative structures drawing both on folk tale and on contemporary politics. Different linguistic registers and dialects set up an echo chamber in the deliberately chaotic or anarchic literary space of her novels. In this, Mahashveta presents a strong contrast with other contemporary women writers, especially the much-loved Ashapurna Debi (1909–95), a unique, largely self-taught novelist of ordinary women's lives. The deceptively simple and unassuming style of Ashapurna's feminism, especially in her trilogy commencing with *Pratham Pratishruti* ('First Promise', 1965), makes an important statement for the recording of women's experience, the 'forgotten' domestic histories that lie behind public activism and politics. These two great women novelists stand at two extremes of the representational spectrum. Between them lie the forms of urban experience or historical chronicle chosen by other writers of their time, such as Bani Basu, whose sharp analyses of middle-class crises are complemented by the rich historical detail of her most ambitious work, the *Maitreya Jataka* ('The Birth of the Maitreya', 1996).

Partition, an unhealed wound in the constitution of the modern nation-state, produced searing, intense treatments in shorter fiction and in the cinema of Ritvik Ghatak, but remained a difficult subject for the novel. Jyotirmayi Debi's *Epar Ganga Opar Ganga* ('Two Sides of the Border', 1967), focusing on the stigmatization of women separated from their families during Partition violence, drew attention to history's silence about rape and abduction, though that silence is replicated in her novel. But other novels by women on both sides of the border, such as Selina Hossain's *Kanta Tare Prajapati* ('Butterfly on Barbed Wire', 1989) or Sabitri Ray's *Svaralipi* ('Notations', 1952) offer more direct and uncompromising treatments of Partition's aftermath in leftist politics and state repression. In a sense the human cost of the divide is a subtext in much fiction that does not necessarily deal with 1947, shaping histories of migration and resettlement, as in the work of Prafulla Ray. Perhaps the most sustained treatment of the individual, social, political and religious histories of Partition is to be found in two major novels, again from each side of the border: *Nilkantha Pakhir Khonje*

('In Search of the Blue Jay', 1972) by Atin Bandyopadhyay, and *Khoabnama* ('Dream-Chronicle', 1996) by the Bangladeshi novelist Akhtaruzzaman Elias (1943–97). For both of these works, but especially the second, it can be said that content creates form, impelling creative experiments that transform the genre. *Nilkantha Pakhir Khonje* is the first novel in a massive trilogy: set in pre-Partition rural East Bengal, it chronicles the gradual destruction of an entire way of life. In terms of narrative technique, however, it is less radical than Elias's *Khoabnama*, possibly the greatest modern Bengali novel. This epic work brings together subaltern experience from the Sanyasi Rebellion to the Tebhaga land movement and the political and religious pre-histories of Partition, fusing centuries of exploitation and betrayal in a single, poetic, sometimes hallucinatory narrative. Popular memory, legend, folk tale, fantasy and present experience are merged in the novel's extraordinary close, making its protagonist the representative of the hunger of generations of dispossessed peasantry. In a sense Elias's technique is magical realist, often turning reality inside-out, but it is not imitative of the Latin American masters he so admired. Rather, here as in his other great novel *Chilekothar Sepai* ('Soldier of the Attic', 1987) about the Bangladesh Liberation War of 1971, he draws on indigenous traditions of folk narrative, memory and legend, as on subaltern history.

Elias's postmodernism, at the close of the century, is not without its counterparts on the Indian side of the border. A narrative collage with magical realist elements is used in Syed Mustafa Siraj's novel of Muslim village life, *Alik Manush* ('Unreal Man', 1988), by which time the shift from modernism to a more plural, mixed narrative mode had already taken place. If the modernism of the 1940s was principally directed towards social realism, the most important departures of the later twentieth century were in the direction of fantasy, surreal farce and linguistic and narrative experiment, as in Nabarun Bhattacharya's *Herbert* (1997) or his *Kangal Malsat* (2002). This may indeed contribute to the return of the comic mode in Bengali fiction, a strain subdued (though not entirely suppressed) by a long historical experience of adversity, but marking the novel's inception with Pyarichand's *Alaler Gharer Dulal*. Formally, though, the novel has not come full circle: rather, it has developed by constantly transforming the realist terms of its initial premises, challenging the representational and referentialist illusion, yet never losing faith in the genre's commitment to 'reality'.

Notes

1 Fredric Jameson, *The Political Unconscious: Narrative as a Socially Symbolic Act* (London: Routledge, 1989), p. 152.
2 Sudipta Kaviraj, *The Unhappy Consciousness: Bankimchandra Chattopadhyay and the Formation of Nationalist Discourse in India* (New Delhi: Oxford University Press, 1995), p. 107.
3 *Ibid.*, p. 108.
4 *Ibid.*, p. 123.
5 Cited in Jnanendra Nath Gupta, *Life and Work of Romesh Chunder Dutt C.I.E.* (London: J. M. Dent & Sons, 1911), p. 189.

7

Writing in English

R. K. Narayan (1906–2001), the great stalwart of Indian English fiction, wrote over a dozen novels set in the mytho-poetic town of Malgudi; one of them, *The Vendor of Sweets* (1967), is a prescient parable for Indian writing in English. The novel is about the generation gap between a father and son, one that hinges on the differences of living in a new way as opposed to a more established one. Narayan's works are known for their subtle humour, and in this novel, it comes in the form of a story-writing machine that a young man, Mali, brings back to India after having gone to America to study creative writing. Before Mali leaves for America, his father, Jagan, questions why he has to go there to learn the art of fiction in the first place. Jagan complains to a sympathetic cousin: 'Going there to learn storytelling! He should rather go to a village granny'; and then he asks, 'Did Valmiki go to America or Germany in order to learn to write his *Ramayana?*'[1]

Here, Narayan captures the tension between two sorts of fabrications – modernity and tradition – as he invariably pits the allure of the foreign against seemingly stable home truths. But this easy East–West opposition gets much more interesting and funnier when Mali returns to Malgudi not as a writer, but as a businessman looking for investors to produce and sell an indigenous version of an American storytelling machine. What Mali has learned abroad, it turns out, is not how to write stories but how to manufacture them. He explains to his father: 'You see these four knobs ... One is for characters, one for plot situations, the other one is for climax, and the fourth is built on the basis that a story is made up of character, situations, emotion, and climax, and by the right combination ...'[2] He later continues, 'In the course of time, every home in the country will possess one and we will produce more stories than any other nation in the world … Except Ramayana and Mahabharata, those old stories, there is no modern writing, whereas in America alone every publishing season ten thousand books are published.'[3] It would appear that what India lacks is new stories to sell. Mali then explains to his father, 'Today we have to compete with advanced countries not only in economics and industry, but also in culture.'[4]

That this competition occurs in English has been vexing for some and freeing for others. To consider Indian writing in English is to consider the relationship Indians have to English and how it has changed over time. Literary questions are enmeshed with political and historical ones; and English must necessarily be seen alongside the other Indian languages, that is to say, in a dense multilingual context. It's not surprising, then, that a self-consciousness about language itself emerges in many literary texts. To write in the Indian context is perhaps firstly to be aware of which language one is writing in, even if it is not necessarily to be choosing one language over another.

The first two-thirds of this chapter offers a survey of some of the major writers from the early nineteenth century to the 1980s 'boom' in the transnational publishing of Indian novels in English. The last third focuses on the more recent, spectacular success of the novelist Chetan Bhagat; here, I attempt to understand how English and the practice of reading it across India has changed, especially for younger generations who have only ever related to the language as a global rather than a colonial or even post-colonial one.

The colonial context

Indian writing in English emerged during colonial rule and was shaped by Indians' desire and the necessity to describe their own social realities and destinies in the face of British political dominance and purported cultural superiority. English was a language that came to speak about the political and cultural issues that defined the colonial experience, and was linked with new ideas and paradigms that were part and parcel of emergent Indian modernities. From the beginning, there were certain ways of thinking and being that could only be expressed in English; conversely there were entire realms of history, experience and affect that were more difficult or even impossible to be expressed in English. The language has been marginal to the Indian experience in many respects, yet essential in others, both politically and creatively.

Most centrally, it has been the language of the educated elite, and hence linked to elite concerns, attitudes and imaginations. For most if not all Indian writers of English, one or more of the other 400 or so Indian languages have played some part in their expression in English, in terms of how they innovate in English itself or view the social worlds they are depicting. Today this linguistic diversity is represented by twenty-two languages as listed in the Indian Constitution, including Hindi, Bengali, Marathi, Telugu, Tamil, Urdu, Gujarati, Kannada, Oriya and Malayalam.

Among the first Indians to address a public in written form in the English language was the Bengali social reformer, Raja Rammohun Roy (c.1772–1833). Roy came from a high-caste Brahmin family, and his thinking was informed both by his traditional education in Arabic and Sanskrit, and through his experience of long-term employment and the friendships he made in the revenue office of the English East India Company. It is in this capacity, as a cultural negotiator between Western and Indian forms of knowledge, that Roy's use of English is significant. In response to the early nineteenth-century British 'civilizing mission', meant to justify colonial rule, Roy offered strong defences of the Hindu religion. In pamphlets such as 'The Brahmunical Magazine or the Missionary and the Brahmun, being a Vindication of the Hindoo Religion against the Attacks of Christian Missionaries' (1821), he argued against claims by Christian missionaries that Hinduism was an idolatrous and superstitious religion by highlighting its own forms of reason, which he believed had been obscured over the centuries by the indulgent practices of Brahmin priests. To prove his point, Roy translated ancient Brahminical texts such as the *Vedas* and the *Upanishads* from Sanskrit into Hindi, Bengali and English, contributed his own introductions and commentaries and, at his own cost, published these translations and distributed them widely. In addition to bringing a rationalistic interpretation to Hindu texts, Roy critiqued some of its tenets and argued with Brahmin priests about what constituted the real Hinduism, in treatises such as 'Translation of a Conference between an Advocate for and an Opponent of the Practice of Burning Widows Alive' (1818); in this regard he became known as a proponent of a British law to abolish the practice of *sati*.[5]

The role of English greatly expanded in the middle of the nineteenth century as urban, upper-class Indians gained greater access to learning the language in government-sponsored schools and colleges. This shift, which most of all served the financial interests and needs of the colonial government, is most firmly rooted in Thomas B. Macaulay's (1800–59) infamous 1835 'Minute on Education'. This document has come to represent the resolution of two competing strands in the British administration of India: the Anglicist triumph over the Orientalists. The latter believed that Indians should be educated in their own classical languages of Arabic and Sanskrit, since these languages and the cultures they represented were, at least in the ancient past, on equal footing with Western civilization. Anglicists saw no value in these languages, and perhaps more significantly, argued that Indians did not either, in the sense that they desired English education over education in Sanskrit and Arabic. Macaulay's argument has long been remembered for his pompous dismissal of Eastern cultural production in his statement that 'a single shelf of a good European library was worth the whole native literature of India and Arabia'.[6] In addition to Macaulay's denigration of non-Western cultural achievements, he argues that Indians will become more civilized (i.e., more like the English) through the acquisition of all things English (modern thought, customs and habits), and goes on to explain his reasoning for how English should be taught to Indians.[7] It is this part of his 'Minute' that is especially relevant to how English begins to become an Indian language. Macaulay was not suggesting that all Indians learn English (administratively impossible), nor was he suggesting that upper-class Indians should learn English and then teach it to the masses (financially impractical). He argued instead that the upper classes, who at that time were mostly upper-caste Hindu men living in the colonial capital of Calcutta, should learn English, serve the needs of the colonial administration and then introduce scientific vocabulary into the Indian vernaculars. Macaulay's real legacy was not his easily dismissible attempt at cultural denigration, but his conviction that Indians themselves wanted to learn English and that they saw it as a way for social mobility and access to government jobs.

In *The Discovery of India* (1946), an Indian-English epic in its own right, Jawaharlal Nehru (1889–1964) describes the legacy of Macaulay as having been both liberating and constricting:

> English education brought a widening of the Indian horizon, an admiration for English literature and institutions, a revolt against some customs and aspects of Indian life, and a growing demand for

political reform. The new professional classes took the lead in political agitation, which consisted chiefly in sending representations to Government. English-educated people in the professions and the service formed in effect a new class, which was to grow all over India, a class influenced by western thought and ways and rather cut off from the mass of the population.[8]

It was this aspect of the penetration of English in India – the creation of an English-educated class of Indians further removed from the experiences of the masses – that so rankled Mohandas Karamchand Gandhi (1869–1948). Despite the fact that English may have been one of the factors leading to the very creation of the first pan-Indian national organization, in the form of the Indian National Congress established in 1885, Gandhi saw English as another example of what divided Indians, and argued that the language obstructed real freedom or *swaraj* (self-rule). The seeming contradiction of what English allowed and prevented fitted perfectly with Gandhi's larger critique of the nationalist movement – that it was elitist and out of touch with the masses. In his polemical tract, *Hind Swaraj* (1909), written originally in Gujarati (and then translated into English by Gandhi himself) as a dialogue between a newspaper editor and reader, he writes:

> Reader: Do I then understand that you do not consider English education necessary for obtaining Home Rule?
>
> Editor: My answer is yes and no. To give millions a knowledge of English is to enslave them. The foundation that Macaulay laid of education has enslaved us. I do not suggest that he had any such intention, but that has been the result. Is it not a sad commentary that we should have to speak of Home Rule in a foreign tongue? ... Is it not a most painful thing that, if I want to go to a court of justice, I must employ the English language as a medium; that, when I become a barrister, I may not speak my mother-tongue, and that someone else should have to translate to me from my own language? Is not this absolutely absurd? Is it not a sign of slavery? Am I to blame the English for it or myself? It is we, the English-knowing men, that have enslaved India. The curse of the nation will rest not upon the English but upon us.[9]

The question of the place and role of English began to be part of serious political debate during the early twentieth-century nationalist movement; however, in the literary realm this was not the case as only a small number of Indians were creating literature in English. For instance, the classic works espousing Gandhian ideals of service to the nation, the abolishment of practices such as dowry and the valorization of peasant life were written by the Hindi-Urdu writer Munshi Premchand (1880–1936), in short stories and novels such as *Seva Sadan* (1919), *Nirmala* (1926) and *Godaan* (1936). These works were serialized in popular magazines of the time, as was the norm for *bhasha* (the term for Indian languages other than English) literatures in the various regions of the Indian subcontinent. English-language writers in this period did not have the popular appeal or local significance of Premchand and others, yet they were the progenitors of other kinds of traditions, as we will see.

For some Indian writers, English was a language to experiment with in one or more works. This was true for what is considered to be the first Indian novel in English, *Rajmohan's Wife* by Bankimchandra Chattopadhyay (1838–94). However, after writing this novel, which is not considered to be among Bankim's finest, he returned to writing in Bengali, in which he went on to be the most significant writer of his time. In the case of Rokeya Sakhawat Hossain (1880–1932), the very fact that she learned to read and write in English is part of what makes her contribution to the language remarkable for its time. Hossain had a traditional education in an orthodox Muslim home, and only with her brother's support was she able to learn Bengali and English; she was later encouraged to write by her husband, who believed strongly in women's education as 'the best cure for the evils that plagued his society'.[10] Hossain wrote 'Sultana's Dream' (1905) in English, and then translated it into Bengali, the language in which she became known as an essayist and novelist. 'Sultana's Dream' is a feminist fable in which women run a just and humane version of society. Here, the protagonist is in conversation with a guide who explains the new dream-world she has woken up to:

> 'Where are the men?' I asked her.
> 'In their proper places, where they ought to be.'
> 'Pray let me know what you mean by "their proper places".'
> 'Oh, I see my mistake, you cannot know our customs, as you were never here before. We shut our men indoors.'
> 'Just as we are kept in the zenana?'
> 'Exactly so.'
> 'How funny.' I burst into a laugh. Sister Sara laughed too.
> 'But, dear Sultana, how unfair it is to shut in the harmless women and let loose the men.'

'Why? It is not safe for us to come out of the zenana, as we are
naturally weak.'
'Yes, it is not safe so long as there are men about the streets, nor is it
so when a wild animal enters a marketplace.'[11]

In this excerpt we see how feminist issues that were already being
explored in other Indian languages (such as Tarabai Shinde's 1882
Marathi essay, 'A Comparison between Women and Men: an Essay to
Show Who's Really Wicked and Immoral, Women or Men?') make an
appearance in English, but also that dialogue itself, in all its unnatural-
ness of spoken English in the Indian context in this period, becomes a
part of literary texts and imaginations. As different writers experiment
with writing one or more of their texts in English, and translate back
and forth between English and other languages, English becomes part
of the multilingual consciousness of some Indian writers.

This new kind of sensibility is also relevant to the work of Ahmed Ali
(1910–94), who wrote in Urdu, but in his novel, *Twilight in Delhi* (1940),
employed the English language to relay an understanding of the fading
Muslim and Urdu world of Old Delhi. Here, it is the authority of the
narration that is of note, as in: 'It was the city of kings and monarchs, of
poets and story tellers, courtiers and nobles. But no king lives there
today, and the poets are feeling the lack of patronage; and the old inhabitants, though still alive, have lost their pride and grandeur under a
foreign yoke.'[12] This description is paralleled with flashbacks to the
humiliations that Muslims experienced at the hands of the British in the
1857 Sepoy Revolt. For Ali, the lament begins in 1857 and is literally
cemented when the British build a new colonial capital that will be New
Delhi. The Urdu language meanwhile represents a vanishing lifestyle
through which a cultivated Muslim sensibility is lived. Ali explains in
the preface to the novel that he wrote it in English rather than Urdu
precisely to garner an international audience, so that others beyond India's
borders would, in effect, know about his own very personal cultural loss.

In the same period, Raja Rao (1908–2006) wrote specifically of the
challenges of writing in English, which he described as a language that
was not quite his own. He became known for his novel *Kanthapura* (1938),
which is about the complexities of Gandhi's reception by the Hindu elite
in rural Karnataka. What is especially interesting about this novel is the
way in which the mostly subtle linguistic disjuncture of the text is
paralleled with the larger dissonance between urban and village life, so

central to Gandhi's politics. A contemporary of Rao's, Mulk Raj Anand (1905–2004) was a founding member of the anti-colonial All-India Progressive Writers' Association, and was also influenced by his friendships with many writers in London's Bloomsbury group, including T. S. Eliot and E. M. Forster. Anand followed Gandhian and his own socialist ideals as he wrote about the day-to-day realities and indignities of the lowest castes in *Untouchable* (1935), *Coolie* (1936) and *Two Leaves and a Bud* (1937). English was a marginal presence on the Indian scene, yet writers like Rao and Anand, as well as R. K. Narayan, were among the first to gain an international audience (albeit a small one) for their work, evidence of the early understanding of English in India as being a 'window to the world'.

After Independence

The paradigm of colonizer and colonized in the political and literary realms began to be displaced only after India gained independence in 1947; however, there continued to be much discussion, debate and political conflict over the role and place of English in post-colonial Indian society. In literary terms, the question of 'can Indians write in English' quickly turned to one of 'should Indians write in English'. Initially, in a plan proposed by Nehru, now in his role as the first Prime Minister of newly independent India, English would be phased out within fifteen years and Hindi would become the national language. However, this never happened, since there was much opposition to Hindi in southern India, especially in the state of Tamil Nadu, where Hindi was seen as being part of northern Indian cultural hegemony. In this north–south equation, English was decidedly more neutral. English was also already too entrenched in the nation's political, scientific and bureaucratic life to be easily cast aside. By 1967, English was made one of India's two 'official languages', albeit a subsidiary one to Hindi. As a result, there is no one 'national' language of India, but rather official languages of the state and regions. Significantly, English remained the language of higher education, a policy that perpetuated its elite provenance.[13]

The Indian novel on the world literary stage

The politics of language do not necessarily influence individual writers and their works, yet they do imbue the use of language with a variety of meanings that become relevant to the larger field of literary production.

In this respect, Indian literature in English in the post-colonial era became most often representative of urban, elite and often diasporic consciousness. This association was most dramatically signalled by the publication of Salman Rushdie's *Midnight's Children* (1981), an epic tale about the birth of the Indian nation that went on to win the Booker Prize. It became a watershed event for South Asian writing, as the novel created an international platform and new publishing potential for writing from or about the Indian subcontinent like no other book had before it.

It has been widely noted that Rushdie writes with great confidence and bravado as he manipulates the English language to imbibe the cadences of the Hindustani language, the most commonly spoken mix of Hindi-Urdu. And for this, Rushdie himself credits the influence of G. V. Desani's roller-coaster ride of a novel, *All About H. Hatterr*, first published in 1948. Desani's narrator proclaims, among many other things, 'I write rigmarole English, staining your goodly godly tongue … '[14] Rushdie's own language is most definitely inspired, but what is perhaps most interesting about *Midnight's Children*, beyond its style, is the way in which it was seen both as having resurrected British fiction and as having broken through the colonizer–colonized paradigm for Rushdie's own generation of English-educated, urban and diasporic Indians.[15] Rushdie himself noted that 'in the west', critics and audiences found the fantastical and surrealistic elements of the novel most notable, whereas in India, 'it was received as a history book'. In this regard, he has recounted how many Indians have said to him, 'I could have written your book, I know all that stuff.'[16] The book had put their immediate historical past and its life-changing events – such as the Partition of 1947 and Indira Gandhi's 1974–6 Emergency – into relief. The simultaneous linking, and in the process, de-bunking, of the grand narratives of Indian history to individual experiences became central to a number of novels. For instance, I. Allan Sealy's boisterous epic about Anglo-Indians, *The Trotter-Nama* (1988), composed around the same time as *Midnight's Children*, is also concerned with the specificities of historical time and the idiosyncrasies of the individual, all the while drawing attention to and playing with the concept and authority of the narrator.

Midnight's Children also made Indian writing transnational in a new way. Rabindranath Tagore (1861–1941) was internationally recognized for having won the Nobel Prize for Literature in 1913, and he had had close relationships with Irish and English writers and intellectuals. But

Tagore's relationship with them neither created nor emerged from a dense cultural and economic traffic of the sort in which Rushdie was a part in 1970s and 1980s Britain, a period which saw the emergence of a new kind of minority politics. Tagore had been the exception, whereas Rushdie was to become the rule. Rushdie was a product of the cultural struggles in Margaret Thatcher's Britain, and in his novels and essays, he made significant contributions to debates about multiculturalism in the UK.

Yet, there are also writers who straddle Rushdie's generation on either side whose work has little to do with his in terms of themes or language. Anita Desai's delicate and devastating novels, including *Clear Light of Day* (1980), *In Custody* (1984) and *Baumgartner's Bombay* (1988), are perhaps the most exalted examples. And there are younger writers, such as Amit Chaudhuri, who technically fall into the post-Rushdie generation, and who have lived and studied abroad, but who do not see Rushdie's literary voice or relationship to the East–West dialectic and its attendant notions of hybridity and post-coloniality as having much to do with their own. Chaudhuri, whose novels include *A Strange and Sublime Address* (1991) and *Afternoon Raag* (1993), explains: 'My own sensibility was formed, to a large extent, by a Bengali humanism which has its provenance in Calcutta in the nineteenth century. There is no point in either making a secret of this fact or advertising it, but understanding what it means in this instance; because one presumes that no two cases of cultural formation can be exactly alike.'[17] There are also writers, such as Shashi Deshpande and Kiran Nagarkar, who are more exclusively based in India and whose novels have not been part of the diasporic consciousness and its transnational networks, yet whose works are well known among the English-language readership in India.

Nevertheless, since *Midnight's Children*, there have been numerous South Asian-origin novelists whose work has crossed international and linguistic divides in a manner similar to Rushdie's. It is in this respect, to recall Narayan's prescience, that many South Asians have made a cultural mark in the transnational genre of the novel, news of which travels especially well because, unlike poetry or drama, it is more easily translated into other languages and has been so associated with the modern and often imperial project. More practically, and in line with the politics of decolonization and globalization, the Anglophone novel as a cultural form is supported by a number of high profile, often corporate-sponsored literary prizes. This support in turn has correlated with larger advances from multinational publishers for some of the leading novelists. A few of these novels – Arundhati Roy's *The God of Small Things* (1997), Kiran Desai's *The Inheritance of Loss* (2006) and Aravind Adiga's *The White Tiger* (2008) – have also won the Booker Prize (renamed the Man Booker in 2002 due to new corporate sponsorship), a distinction that instantly catapulted each of these authors on to the Anglophone world literary stage. Roy's novel was especially significant for the way her story of the 'small' atrocities of family life and the loss of childhood innocence captured a global readership in dozens of languages. Other novels, such as Vikram Seth's *A Suitable Boy* (1993) and Rohinton Mistry's *A Fine Balance* (1995) became international bestsellers in addition to having garnered critical acclaim and awards. Still others, such as Bapsi Sidhwa's *Ice-Candy-Man* (1988) and Amitav Ghosh's *The Shadow Lines* (1995), both of which chronicle the pain of fractured societies resulting from pre- and post-Partition violence, struck deep chords in India and abroad, and have since become staples on college syllabi in several countries. Some of these novelists have innovated linguistically and formally, and this innovation has enlivened the thematic possibilities within the genre of the novel. In the case of Vikram Chandra, his *Sacred Games* (2006) combines elements of pulp fiction and literary epic in the story of Mumbai's gangster underworld. Meanwhile, Indra Sinha's *Animal's People* (2007) parlays the deep cynicism that grew in the aftermath of the ongoing devastation caused by the Union Carbide gas tragedy in Bhopal into an affecting meditation on the notion of humanity itself.

The place of English in India

Within India there has been much debate over the fact that Indian literature outside of India (from Rushdie on, in particular) is seen as being exclusively written in English rather than in the other Indian languages (the *bhashas*), all of which have much longer histories of depicting Indian social and cultural life. But it is English-language writing by Indians that becomes recognized as being national, partly because of the globalizing power of English, and partly because of the history and place of English in India. This dynamic only fuels the question of what is deemed to be culturally authentic in the Indian context. The vast majority of Indians, including the 5 per cent who are fluent in English, mostly live their lives in one or more of the *bhashas*.

Moreover, if there was one dominant Indian language, it would be Hindi (spoken by roughly 40 per cent of all Indians as their primary language, and many more as their second or third language) rather than English. In this respect, the politics of English in India are difficult to untangle from the cultural production in the language. Shashi Deshpande, who comes from a Kannada-speaking background and has lived in various multilingual settings in India, puts it this way: 'The truth is, that while a great number of people do speak English, it is yet a language that many of the characters we write of will not only *not* be speaking, it is one they will *not be able* to speak.'

Deshpande's comment captures a central paradox of writing about India in English: the question of the linguistic authenticity of fictional characters themselves. All writing and art for that matter is a representation of reality, even when the language of the text matches the language of the street. English is certainly part of India's social reality; it has filtered in to the most common and basic level of everyday communication, often in the form of phrases, slogans, idiomatic expressions, and in advertisements. Yet, English is not a sustained presence in most people's lives; and even for those for whom it is, they are surrounded by non-English worlds. Deshpande has written about the particular challenge of forging a literary identity as an English author living in India:

> I began writing in English, not because I 'chose' to, but because it was the only language I could express myself in, the only language I really read. Yet, I had two other languages at home, languages I spoke and lived my daily life in. Living in a small town in a middle-class family, life was, in fact, lived mainly in Kannada; English came into the picture only for certain purposes and at certain times … My readers were people who read English, but lived their personal and emotional lives, like I did, in their own languages.[18]

As we see in other chapters in this volume (especially those by Supriya Chaudhuri, Sonal Khullar, Vasudha Dalmia and Amanda Weidman), the question of what is authentically Indian rears its head in the realm of cultural production, whether in terms of art, music, theatre or even within *bhasha* literatures themselves, where debates over tradition and modernity are equally strong. In the case of English, these questions are often more stark since the language has been so identified with colonialism, and the place of English in India has until recently always been marked by an upper-class and upper-caste sensibility and range of experience. These themes – about the relationship between English and other Indian languages and the attendant hierarchies among them – are also regularly explored in *bhasha* literature. For instance, in the Hindi novels *Raag Darbari* (1968) by Shrilal Shukla and *Mai* (1993) by Geetanjali Shree, English is represented in each as the placeholder for the aspiring middle class. In Shukla's satiric text, English is ridiculed by Hindi-speakers for being out of touch with local realities and yet also out of reach. In Shree's more earnest and painful tale, knowing English divides a Hindi-speaking household on gendered and generational lines as social mobility becomes an act of self-preservation. Once again, we see a self-consciousness about language that is intrinsic to what it means to exist and write in a multilingual society. In a description typical of Shukla's dark humour, the narrator describes the English advertising pervasive in small-town Uttar Pradesh of the 1960s:

> To effect a change of heart you need to command their respect, and to do that you need English. This was the native logic which led to all appeals for the extermination of mosquitoes and the eradication of malaria being generally written in English. As a result most people had accepted the advertisements not as literature but as visual art and allowed the wall-painters to write English on the walls as much as they liked. Walls were painted and mosquitoes died. Dogs barked and people went their way.[19]

The discourse on language within English and *bhasha* texts is part of the self-consciousness of language that many Indian writers have.

In the last decade one of the most significant changes in regards to English in India has come from Dalit intellectuals who have begun to demand access to English-language education for their own communities. As Debjani Ganguly's chapter in this volume shows, Dalit literature in Marathi, Hindi, Tamil and other *bhashas* has become an important presence on the literary scene in the last twenty years; but what we see now is that the question of language itself, and the social mobility that only English allows, have also become a part of Dalit political assertion. The English-language columnist Chandrabhan Prasad has been most associated with this cause in his column, 'Dalit Diary', which appears in *The Pioneer*, a national daily newspaper. His method of instilling this desire and, most crucially, what he frames as a right to the language has come in the curious form of proposing

English as a 'Dalit Goddess'. Prasad's immediate aim is not historical revisionism, but instead it is to instill the desire for English, one that he hopes will turn into a serious demand for the language among Dalits. He wonders why in the last six decades of Indian independence the demand for government-sponsored education in the language has not flourished. In line with this cause is what many see as his audacious valorization of Thomas B. Macaulay as a kind of saint for oppressed Dalits. Since 2006, Prasad has made headlines for hosting parties each year in Delhi to celebrate Macaulay's birth anniversary. What is unclear at this point is how much of an effect this kind of valorization – to what extent it is a real movement or a gimmick – will have for the actual education of Dalits or even the creation of Dalit literature in English. It is clear, however, that the idea of English education (a privilege which occurs mostly in private schools run by a variety of trusts and societies) as being the sole provenance of the elite is changing. On the one hand there is the political issue of English education and gaining wider access to it; and on the other, as detailed below there is a way in which the existence of multiple 'Englishes' within the linguistic landscape is creating a diffuse yet discernible tide of new readers with more varied class backgrounds.

A new stage for Indian writing in English

Soon after the publication of his first novel, *Five Point Someone* (2004), Chetan Bhagat was crowned 'the biggest-selling English-language novelist in India's history'.[20] Since then, that novel and his others, *One Night at the Call Centre* (2005), *The 3 Mistakes of My Life* (2008), *2 States: The Story of My Marriage* (2009), and *Revolution 2020* (2011) have collectively sold millions of copies. This kind of popularity is unusual for most Indian novels in any language and revolutionary for an English-language one. Had a product of Indian English literary production finally gone beyond its elite, urban-based readership? The Booker-winning novels by Roy, Desai and Adiga have sold between 50,000 and 100,000 copies each in India, and to be considered a 'bestseller' in English in India a book only has to sell 10,000 copies. But these numbers are not merely about a distinction between 'serious' and 'popular' literature, since before Bhagat there was no Indian-English literary text that could be considered truly popular; the only widely read English-language books were school textbooks and a few national magazines and newspapers, such as *The Times of India*. The point is that Bhagat's novels are not only sold to people who already read English novels, but to thousands upon thousands who might have never read one before. It is as if he is the first to have tapped into, or even created, a wide English readership that no one really knew was out there. It is also significant that Bhagat is not published or read transnationally, nor have his novels won any international or other awards; he is a home-grown phenomenon. The fact that his novels are not literary makes most critics dismiss them, but what can't be dismissed is that his novels represent a new kind of genre and, most significantly, a new readership whose relationship to English and to their own class identities is markedly different from before.

Five Point Someone is about the adventures, and mostly misadventures, of a B.tech student at IIT-Delhi, one of the prestigious Indian Institutes of Technology, where fewer than 1 per cent of applicants gain admission. Along with romantic trials and the antics of the main character and his friends is a gentle questioning of the Indian education system and values, the pressures it places on students and the lack of encouragement for original thought and creativity. As Bhagat has said in interviews and as evidenced by his own newspaper columns, he loves India and also wants to help change it, to see it become a real meritocracy where people can get things done and do well in life. His novels are entertaining and promote a youth-oriented, forward-thinking common culture that is less about the English language itself, and more about the kinds of aspirations expressed in that language, aspirations that may just as easily be translated back into the more commonly spoken *bhashas*. The books espouse crossing social borders and challenging traditional mores, but only for the larger goal of creating a more unified, liberal, Indian identity.

Yet, his use of English is also central to the success of his books. His own resulting stardom, in fact, signals the growth of aspiring lower and middle classes across the country that see and use English as Indian *and* global. Bhagat's works exist in a different world, a less literary one most certainly, but a world that marks a new kind of writing and sensibility in English. The sentences are short, clear and not overly expository. There are few if any novelistic passages, where people, ideas or places are described in any kind of depth. And yet, whatever is described, even if brief and mostly in the form of dialogue, is compelling enough and moves the story along. In a scene typical of the dialogue between the three friends in *Five Point Someone*, the narrator explains that colour television had just come to India, followed by satellite broadcasts, and soon he and his friends were watching the first Gulf war on CNN:

> 'Is this real? I mean is this happening?'
> Alok looked dazed.
> 'Of course, Fatso. You think this is a play?' Ryan scoffed as two American pilots hi-fived themselves after hours of pounding a perfectly real city ... Iraq was kind of anonymous then, and we unabashedly cheered on America. IIT cared about America ...
> At the same time, the war visuals become more gruesome. Americans pounded Baghdad non-stop ... I mean, the aid to IIT was fine, but how can you justify bombing kids? But then, Saddam was kind of this loser General anyway, and apparently shot his own people when he was grumpy. Oh, it was impossible to take sides in the Gulf war. And it was all pointless for us anyway.[21]

Bhagat's tone is casual, often funny, and always entertaining, but the stories involve serious topics: how to negotiate school, work, parental expectations, love, sex, desire and, as in the example above, finding one's place in the world. Bhagat has said in interviews that he aims to be socially relevant. At the same time, reading his novels could make you feel as though you were better at English than you were; simply put, they could inspire you. Bhagat keeps in character throughout; in the acknowledgments to *Five Point Someone*, he thanks Bill Gates for creating MS Word, since without this program he says he never would have been able to write a novel; similarly the dedication page to *Two States* reads, 'This may be the first time in the history of books, but here goes: Dedicated to my in-laws*' and further down the page continues, '*which does not mean I am henpecked, under her thumb or not man enough'.

It is no surprise that most of Bhagat's readers think all of his novels are factual accounts of his life rather than fictional accounts based on some of his experiences and observations. His fans, who show up in the hundreds at book readings, don't want to discuss his books so much as find out more about him and how they can be like him, either in his IIT (engineering) or IIM (business management) avatars, or better yet, as a phenomenally successful writer who was able to leave his corporate job. For many, reading him holds the promise of getting to be like him. The way his novels have caught on like wildfire and created a youth icon in Bhagat himself says something about him, but perhaps it says even more about the relationship many of his readers have to English. It is not just a language they learn, but a form of cultural expression they desire. Access and ease with the world of English are much harder to attain if you have not had an elite education and background, yet his novels offer an entrée to that world to a much larger swathe of Indian society, not to the majority of English have-nots, but to those who have some possibilities and opportunities in the language. His novels are remarkable not for putting Indian literature on the world stage in the way other novelists have, but for relating to and inspiring a vast readership within India itself.

It is interesting to consider a novel such as Upamanyu Chatterjee's *English, August* (1988) alongside *Five Point Someone* (2004), since they both involve college-aged pot-smoking youth; albeit in Chatterjee's novel the characters are situated firmly in an ironic, pre-liberalization India, caught in a bureaucratic haze, and in Bhagat's works, they exist in a comic, post-liberalization one, working at call centres or negotiating corporate salaries. *English, August* is also a serious literary achievement, and became a cult classic as compared to the easy-reading, plot pulsating, *Five Point Someone*. Not much happens in *English, August* as the protagonist, Agastya, languishes in a civil service posting in a small town far from his native Delhi. His posting in the highly prestigious Indian Administrative Service (IAS) is the most lucrative and powerful position he could hope to attain as a middle-class person in those years. Yet, his English credentials, if anything, remind him of just how out of touch he is with the rest of India. The narrator describes Agastya's journey to his posting in the small town of Madna as follows: 'Glimpses of Madna *en route*; cigarette-and-paan dhabas, disreputable food stalls, both lit by fierce kerosene lamps, cattle and clanging rickshaws on the road, and the rich sound of trucks in slush from an overflowing drain; he felt as though he was living someone else's life.'[22]

By the time we get to Bhagat, and the phenomenon of Bhagat, we realize that those towns are actually filled with lower- and middle-class aspirants, and their relationship to English has changed in the intervening fifteen to twenty years, as has their own sense of the possibilities of what the language might offer them. They represent a changing linguistic map of India, a shift that does not take census numbers away from the *bhashas*, but instead gives a strong indication of the changing role and place of English, as well as the kinds and range of writing being produced in the language.

Notes

1 R. K. Narayan, *The Vendor of Sweets* (London: The Bodley Head Ltd, 1967), p. 45.

2 *Ibid.*, p. 76.

3 *Ibid.*, p. 77.

4 *Ibid.*, p. 78.

5 See Rammohun Roy, *The English Works of Raja Rammohun Roy* (Allahabad: The Panini Office, 1906).

6 Thomas B. Macaulay, 'Minute by the Hon'ble T. B. Macaulay, dated the 2nd February 1835', Bureau of Education. Selections from Educational Records, Part I (1781–1839), ed. H. Sharp (Calcutta: Superintendent, Government Printing, 1920; reprinted New Delhi: National Archives of India, 1965), pp. 107–17. Accessed on 6 April 2010: www.columbia.edu/itc/mealac/pritchett/00generallinks/macaulay/txt_minute_education_1835.html

7 See Gauri Viswanathan's *Masks of Conquest: Literary Study and British Rule in India* (New Delhi: Oxford University Press, 1989) on the question of English education in this period.

8 Jawaharlal Nehru, *The Discovery of India* (New Delhi: Penguin Books, 2004), p. 348.

9 M. K. Gandhi, *Hind Swaraj and Other Writings*, ed. Anthony J. Parel (Cambridge University Press, 1997), pp. 103, 104.

10 Susie Tharu and K. Lalita (eds.), *Women Writing in India Volume 1: 600 B.C. to the Early Twentieth Century* (New York: The Feminist Press at CUNY, 1993), p. 341.

11 Rokeya Sakhawat Hossain, 'Sultana's Dream', in *ibid.*, p. 344.

12 Ahmed Ali, *Twilight in Delhi* (New York: New Directions, 1994), p. 3.

13 See Robert D. King's *Nehru and the Language Politics of India* (New Delhi: Oxford University Press, 1997) for more on this topic.

14 G. V. Desani, *All About H. Hatterr* (New York: McPherson & Company Publishers, 1986), p. 37.

15 For a fuller development of this argument, see Rashmi Sadana, 'Two Tales of a City: The Place of English and the Limits of Postcolonial Critique', *Interventions* 11:1 (2009), pp. 1–15.

16 Salman Rushdie, onstage interview at the Altschul Auditorium, Columbia University, Midnight's Children Humanities Festival, New York City, 22 March 2003.

17 Amit Chaudhuri, 'Introduction', in his collection of essays, *Clearing a Space: Reflections on India, Literature, and Culture* (Ranikhet: Black Kite, 2008), p. 13.

18 Shashi Deshpande, 'Where Do We Belong: Regional, National, or International?' in *Writing from the Margin and Other Essays* (New Delhi: Penguin, 2003), p. 32.

19 Shrilal Shukla, *Raag Darbari*, trans. from the Hindi by Gillian Wright (New Delhi: Penguin, 1992), p. 57.

20 Donald Greenlees, 'An Investment Banker Finds Fame Off the Books', *The New York Times*, 26 March 2008.

21 Chetan Bhagat, *Five Point Someone: What Not to Do at IIT!* (Delhi: Rupa & Co., 2004), pp. 51–2.

22 Upamanyu Chatterjee, *English, August: an Indian Story* (London: Faber and Faber, 1988), p. 5.

8
_____

Dalit life stories

Not long ago, in Khairlanji, a nondescript rural town in the western Indian state of Maharashtra's Bhandara district, often called the state's 'rice bowl', Surekha Bhotmange, a Dalit woman in a neo-Buddhist[1] household was getting ready to cook dinner for her family. Her husband, Bhaiyalal, was due to return from the paddy field on which he toiled each day. Her three teenage children, Priyanka, Sudhir and Roshan, were studying nearby, a sight that must have been a source of daily cheer for Surekha. She herself had studied up to the ninth standard and had taken to heart Dr B. R. Ambedkar's call for the Untouchable castes to educate their children. Priyanka cycled to her college in a nearby town. The previous year she had topped her class in the tenth standard. But that evening, on 29 September 2006, Surekha and Priyanka were anxious about an unspoken horror hovering on their threshold. While they had over the years grown immune to the everyday taunts of their upper-caste neighbours,[2] they found that they could not ignore the crescendo of threats that had descended upon them in recent days. At 6.30 p.m. their worst fears came true. A truck came to an ominous halt in front of their home and sixty-odd villagers including women, armed with cycle chains, knives, sticks and axes, got out. They rushed in to drag Surekha and her three children from their home. In full view of the village, the women marauders stripped the mother and daughter naked and beat them with every weapon at their disposal. Sudhir and Roshan were likewise beaten mercilessly and then commanded to rape their mother and sister. When they refused, their genitals were crushed and they were battered to death. Meanwhile, the two women were dragged further away from their home. What followed was a horrific spectacle of gang rape and mutilation with eyewitness accounts indicating that the raping continued long after the women were dead. In a culmination of this public orgy of caste Hindu rage, the four bodies were tossed into the canal that watered the meagre land of the Bhotmange family.

The attack was ostensibly carried out in the name of 'moral justice'. Surekha, the 44-year-old mother of three and a vocal Dalit woman inspired by Ambedkarite Buddhism, was alleged to have had an illicit relationship with a wealthy Dalit landowner, Siddharth Gajbhiye. Not surprisingly, investigations revealed multiple dimensions to this orgy of killing, not least a land dispute in which Surekha dared to take this issue to the court and seek, in the process, some assistance from Gajbhiye. Reasonably well educated by the literacy standards among Dalit women, Surekha was also a proud Ambedkarite and played an active role in the community of Dalit Buddhist women. Her husband owned a small plot of land on which he laboured hard and her older son was employed elsewhere in the village. While not exactly prosperous in the hand-to-mouth scheme of things that is the Dalit's lot in rural India, her family was self-sufficient. These facts, combined with her pride in her children's education, would have given her a modicum of confidence. Surekha epitomized, in short, a Dalit woman who dared to forget her place in the caste hierarchy. She had to be punished.

In the India of 2006, nearly sixty years after the nation's dramatic transformation from its state of abjection under the British in 1947 to one of the world's economic powers, one incontrovertible fact remained: the extremity of violence against the Dalits, India's 170 million ex-Untouchable castes, the detritus of subcontinental history for over two millennia. The public massacre of Surekha and her children is not an isolated event. According to what are arguably modest estimates by the National Crime Bureau, every day two Dalits are murdered, three Dalit women are raped, two Dalit houses are destroyed and eleven Dalits are beaten up.[3] Also routine is the general apathy of the state machinery to these heinous crimes, the complicity and incompetence of the medical establishment in reviewing cases of murder and rape, and the myopia of the mainstream media to these depredations.

The Khairlanji case, however, did become a catalyst for change when a major publishing house, Navayana, launched a series entitled 'Holo-caste', in which each book would be dedicated to covering a gruesome crime against a Dalit and provide a socio-cultural and historical context for it. The editorial credo is unequivocal:

Atrocities pile up, forming a landscape of tears, blood and ashes. It could be said this is not genocide. It could be argued this is not a holocaust. What is it then, this slow, everyday ritual of murder? Unreported and easily forgotten. What should we call a holocaust in installments – a 'Holocaste'? This series from Navayana chronicles dalit massacres that go almost unnoticed in the world's largest democracy.[4]

The first title in the series is *Khairlanji: A Strange and Bitter Crop* by Anand Teltumbde. Published in 2008, this book provides narrative ballast to the rape and murder of the Bhotmange family in a way that journalistic reporting in the least read sections of the national dailies and the statistics of the National Crime Bureau cannot. The gruesome scenario narrated at the start of this chapter would not have been possible but for this publication. Nor would it be possible to construct Surekha's everyday world in quite so much detail. In sum, the book seeks to restore for the average reader, desensitized by the plethora of skeletal crime reporting, the personhood of Surekha and her unfortunate family. The term 'personhood' is here used to connote not individuality and uniqueness, but the attribute of collective sameness in the eyes of the law. 'Person', as Joseph Slaughter notes, is a 'legal vehicle of human dignity, what is common to each of us as social human beings and as theoretically equal subjects.'[5]

The Navayana initiative can be seen as a high point in the evolution of a niche publishing industry for Dalit issues, an industry that has, in the last two decades, struggled to wrest the power of narrating human rights abuses against Dalits from dominant media outlets. These outlets have tended to highlight the increasingly disgruntled Indian elite's reaction to the rise of low castes in some political arenas rather than the abysmal condition of the vast majority of Dalits in rural areas.[6] Media slights and obfuscations have been countered in recent years by the proliferation of multiple genres of Dalit life writing – autobiography, memoir, *testimonio*, collective biography – that narrate the extreme violence these communities confront in their daily lives. More generally, this corpus of writing can be seen as an integral part of a continuing contest within Indian democracy about the role of caste and its visibility/invisibility in the public sphere; and of the differential relationship of caste with the temporality of Indian modernity, as both its past-in-the-present and present-in-the-past. It also brings to the fore the low-caste rejection of the civilizational claims of Indian nationalist rhetoric, while at the same time embracing its liberating potential. Most significantly, for the purposes of this chapter, such narratives herald the emergence of the Dalit as a figure of suffering, unsettling the celebratory mood of contemporary Indian democracy, even as these same narratives demand recognition, and in so doing, offer that democracy the opportunity to realize its true potential. For, the logic of absolute democracy, as philosophers such as Spinoza have reminded us, lies in the idea of the extension of personhood to *everyone*.[7]

The genre of life-writing has been an important component of Dalit literature since the publication in Marathi of Daya Pawar's *Balute* in 1978. Other landmark publications include Laxman Mane's *Upara* ('The Outsider', 1980) and Laxman Gaikwad's *Uchalya* ('Petty Thief', 1987). It is no coincidence that life-writing texts first emerged in Marathi, for Maharashtra was the site of the emergence of the post-Independence Dalit literary movement. The term 'Dalit' was first used by Ambedkar in 1928 in his publication, *Bahishkrut Bharat*. In Marathi, 'Dalit' literally means 'ground down' or 'depressed'. Ambedkar retrieved the term to counter Gandhi's appellation for Untouchables, '*harijan*' ('children of God'), a term Ambedkar found patronizing. The idea of a 'Dalit literature' emerged in the 1950s, but it was not until the founding of the Dalit Panthers in 1972 (a militant and revolutionary political formation inspired by the rise of the Black Panthers in the United States in the 1960s) that Dalit literature became a force to reckon with.[8] Many of the founders were poets and writers who had themselves struggled for decades to make an impact on the Marathi literary scene. The Dalit Panthers emerged from the slums of Mumbai and definitively proclaimed in their Manifesto that 'we don't want a little place in the Brahmin gulli, we want the rule of the whole land ... Our revolution will flash like lightning' – a sentiment reflected in the blistering register of Marathi Dalit poetry. The genealogy of Dalit life-writing can be traced even further back to the late nineteenth-century tracts of the reformer, Jyotiba Phule, the first social activist to take up the cause of India's low-caste groups, and to the early reflections of Ambedkar, the progenitor of the Dalit movement in twentieth-century India.[9] Since the 1980s, the genre has spread to other literary/linguistic clusters such as Tamil, Hindi, Gujarati, Telugu, Kannada and Punjabi, all of which have witnessed an efflorescence of Dalit literary and cultural productions in the last three decades. The dominance of life-writing over poetry and the short story in recent years is a development that reflects the incremental increase, through the 1990s, in the vocalization of low-caste aspirations in the Indian public sphere. It is a phenomenon intimately linked not just to an increased questioning, through the 1980s, of the foundations of the secular and modernizing Nehruvian state, but also to an enhanced connectivity to the discourse of human rights on the international stage. The National Campaign for Dalit Human Rights (NCDHR) and the National Federation of Dalit Women (NFDW), both established in the 1990s, are now powerful forums for the national and global articulation of Dalit rights.[10]

This chapter is a study of three such representative life-writing narratives by Dalits: *Joothan* ('Left Overs') by Omprakash Valmiki, *Akkarmashi* ('The Outcaste') by Sharan Kumar Limbale and *Sangati* ('Events') by Bama. They are all set in the post-Nehruvian era, from the 1970s to the 1990s, and come from three different regions: Uttar Pradesh, Maharashtra and Tamil Nadu.[11] While situating the three life narratives in specific regional contexts, this chapter highlights critical points of convergence in their respective modes of witnessing the ravages of Dalit existence and of articulating a vision for a Dalit future. The analysis pays close attention to the formal qualities of the texts and makes a case for why a simple categorization of these works under the rubric of *testimonio* (eyewitness accounts of collective suffering in first-person, which is how many recent studies have tended to see them[12]) is inadequate to their narrative potential to bestow 'personhood' on the suffering Dalit.

In the field of biographical studies, the term *testimonio* gained currency in the 1990s as a way to describe first-person accounts of horrific abuses suffered by minority populations around the globe. Its roots lie in the word 'testimony', which literally means testifying or bearing witness in a court of law. In 1992, John Beverley, the Latin American historian, facilitated its translation into the lexicon of literary genres, by defining *testimonio* as 'a novel or novella-length narrative in book or pamphlet ... form, told in the first person by a narrator who is also the real protagonist or witness of the events he or she recounts and whose unit of narration is usually a "life" or a significant life experience'.[13] Art becomes 'witness' to that which 'real' victims cannot, for they have been obliterated. Scholars have since made explicit the braiding implicit in such readings of the *testimonio* – of the aesthetics of witnessing with the legalities of recognition and redress.

The idea of human rights – institutionalized by the United Nations in the post-war decade following the Holocaust in the form of the 1948

'Universal Declaration of Human Rights' – has in the last two decades figured as the predominant vehicle for addressing extremes of human suffering that find no redress in the constraints of positive law frameworks of independent nation-states.[14] In the case of Dalits, constitutional law in India does prohibit discrimination on caste grounds and has explicit provisions not just to promote low-caste mobility, but also to protect Dalit life and security. But as any number of studies show, atrocities against Dalits have continued to grow in proportion with India's accelerated growth under its liberalization policy and within a dramatically globalized economic order.[15] It is hardly surprising, then, that the Dalits, much to the embarrassment and annoyance of the Indian political and social establishment, took a delegation to the 2001 United Nations Racism Conference in Durban to draw international attention to abuses against their communities. It is not far-fetched to imagine that the power of their appeal in that forum was informed by the plethora of Dalit life narratives already made available globally in English translations through the efforts of NCDHR and NFDW, working in tandem with publishers both sympathetic to the Dalit cause and acutely aware of the market potential of subaltern life stories.

However, by situating Dalit life-writing within a global conversation on human suffering, I do not mean to suggest that the human rights campaign is the antidote to the apathy of India's legal apparatus. There is enough scholarship on the limits of contemporary human rights to discourage any such optimistic reading.[16] Rather, what I hope to foreground, especially by focusing on the Dalit's 'unfulfilled' quest for personhood through a narrative of pain, is the imperative to attend to the limits that mark the language of law in literary narrative. In writing about the trauma/testimony model for analysing contemporary life narratives, Lauren Berlant perceptively notes that this model 'assumes that the law describes what a person is, and that social violence can be located the way physical injury can be traced'.[17] It also assumes that once the pain is identified, it can be made to go away. Or as Berlant puts it, 'It is … to imply that in the good life there will be no pain.'[18] In a neo-liberal world, personhood through the privacy of pain takes more forms than the language of citizenship allows.[19] One of these forms is undoubtedly a public poetics of recognition through literature and narrative, a poetics that carries a political charge primarily through its circulation and iteration in a constantly expanding discursive sphere of reciprocal respondents. Such a public is undoubtedly also a 'rhetorical space of intersubjectivity … bearing witness'[20] to unspeakable trauma. But, unlike the juridical power of testimony that aspires to render 'pain' transparent and remediable, such a public poetics keeps alive the singularity and inevitability of pain even in a 'just' world.

My argument, drawing on Berlant's critique of the trauma/ testimony paradigm, is that, in the life narratives discussed here, the Dalits no doubt articulate an aspiration to personhood through the realization of *full* citizenship, but they are also aware not just of its impossibility due to a crushing historical legacy, but also of its inadequacy – in its logic of abstract equivalence – to address the singular nature of Dalit pain. Hence, my attempt below is not only to problematize the genre of *testimonio* through my reading of Bama's *Sangati*, but also to recast at least two of the other life narratives – Valmiki's *Joothan* and Limbale's *Akkarmashi* – as variations of other literary genres, namely the *Bildungsroman* and the picaresque. Both of these prose fictional genres involve the journey of a protagonist from childhood to maturity, encountering in the process many hurdles and setbacks amidst an often intractable social ethos. But, as we shall see, there are also critical differences between the two. Importantly, for the purposes of my argument, these genres, unlike the *testimonio*, do not invest in the notion of 'witnessing the truth' of history in any transparent way, but are nevertheless apposite in attributing a form of 'personhood' to the Dalit protagonists that both resonates with and exceeds the dynamics of subject-making in liberal democracies.

A caveat to this argument will not be out of place here. I invoke the *Bildungsroman* and the picaresque in respect to what Franco Moretti calls their 'capaciousness': i.e., their capacity to provide, in a functional rather than in a strictly formal sense, a measure for all narratives of individual development and modern subject-formation. 'Even those novels that clearly are *not Bildungsroman* or novels of formation', writes Moretti, 'are perceived by us against this conceptual horizon; so we speak of "failed initiation" or of a "problematic formation".'[21] The distinction between the 'functional' and the 'formal' is crucial to my analysis lest I be open to the charge of unproblematically claiming a formal exactitude between the novel and Dalit life narratives. While I do claim some parallels in their respective modes of narrative development, I also argue for a functional equivalence in that, like the novel in the bourgeois public sphere of nineteenth-century England, these Dalit life narratives in contemporary India play a critical role in enabling the ex-Untouchable castes to imagine a coherent community of oppressed individuals, formed in the hellfire of caste persecution, and emerging, in the process, as 'persons' in their own right. Equivalence in the eyes of the law can only be posited in terms of the abstract individual, whether she is the 'citizen' in the context of national law or the 'human' in the context of international human rights law.[22] To that extent, like the *Bildungsroman* and the picaresque, *testimonios*, too, ultimately function within the conceptual horizon of individual self-making through the recovery of personhood, albeit with a focus on witnessing on behalf of a traumatized collective.

History's leftovers and destiny's deformed children

Omprakash Valmiki's *Joothan*, published in Hindi in 1997, is a powerful and graphic narrative of the life experiences of scavengers from northern India – *churhas* or *bhangis* as they are called. The narrator's last name, 'Valmiki', is a generic term for this community, a name that he consciously adopts to avow his low-caste identity, much to the embarrassment of his now upwardly mobile family. The name 'Valmiki' or 'Balmiki' was given to the scavenger community by the Arya Samaj, an influential late nineteenth-century Hindu reform movement. The Samajists were alarmed at the large-scale conversion of this community to Christianity and Islam in the 1920s. A robust Hindu cultural revivalism in the same period, of which the Arya Samaj was one manifestation, mobilized its forces to keep the *bhangi* community within the Hindu fold. The result was the conferring of the label 'Balmiki' on them, a name they adopted with pride, for in the popular Hindu consciousness, Valmiki is the Sanskrit composer of the epic *Ramayana*. In seeing themselves as descendants of such an illustrious ancestor, the scavengers recovered some of their dignity; and as Vijay Prashad has noted, closer to Independence, they preferred to be on the majoritarian side of cultural Hinduization for reasons of survival and protection: 'Balmikis experienced the strong arm of Hindutva without the illusion of protection from the state; in order to secure protection, the general feeling among the Balmikis was to yield to the new ethos. The Balmikis depended on their caste municipal officers for credit, jobs and for special treatment; for this, cultural Hinduization seemed an acceptable option.'[23] This symbolic shift, however, did not see their conditions improve after Independence. As scavengers dealing with the disposal of human dirt, garbage and excreta, the taint of 'pollution' (the single most incriminating feature of caste status) was indelibly etched on their life worlds. Consequently, even as Balmikis, they continued to languish at the bottom of the caste hierarchy. Their condition was especially abysmal in villages where they were forced to live in filthy enclaves segregated from upper-caste quarters. Omprakash Valmiki's *Joothan*, in fact, opens with an inverse tableau of the village pastoral, a dominant theme and genre in mainstream Hindi literature and a model of whole-some living in the Gandhian imaginary. The narrative begins in 1955 with the author's recollection of his days in the *churha basti*, the scavengers' hutments which were divided from the 'purer' upper-caste homes by a pond; of his family's exploitation by the landed gentry; and his segregation from upper-caste students at the village school:

> The country had become independent eight years ago. Gandhi's uplifting of the untouchables was resounding everywhere. Although the doors of the government schools had begun to open for untouchables, the mentality of the ordinary people had not changed much. I had to sit away from the others in the class, that too on the floor. The mat ran out before reaching the spot I sat on. Sometimes I would have to sit way behind everybody, right near the door. And the letters on the board from there seemed faded.[24]

In his first-person narrative voice, Valmiki plays brilliantly with the theme of purity and pollution that has, since antiquity, marked the corporeal chasm between touchability and untouchability in the caste hierarchy. The term *joothan*, which translates roughly into 'leftovers from another's plate', becomes a metaphor for the subhuman status of scavengers in Indian villages. In Valmiki's narrative, soiled food from upper-caste homes, destined for the garbage bin, makes its way to the bare and hungry kitchens of the *churhas*. The shame and degradation of eating these leftovers as a child haunts the narrator for the rest of his life, even when as an adult he has the satisfaction of feeding the grandson of his upper-caste neighbour, Surendra, in his own home. As a child he had witnessed his mother's humiliation at the hands of Surendra's grandfather, Sukhdev Singh Tyagi. While working as a cleaner at Tyagi's daughter's wedding, she had angered him by demanding more than just leftovers from the wedding feast for her children. He told her: 'You are taking a basketful of *joothan*. And on top of that you want food for your children. Don't forget your place, *Churhi*. Pick up your basket and get going.'[25] The abusive '*churhi*' hurled at her is common practice, a way of reducing the scavenger's sense of self to her destined caste, a form of recognition that doubles up as injury.[26] From that day on, not only did his mother not go back to the Tyagi house, she also instilled in her children the will to resist upper-caste leftovers, no matter how hungry they were. This one incident marks the start of the narrator's transformation from a little *churha* boy reconciled to eating upper-caste leftovers to one who fights the scourge of untouchability, a transformation that is captured in a narrative frame quite akin to the *Bildungsroman* but with some elements of the 'picaresque'.

The *Bildungsroman*, which has its antecedents in the evolution of the eighteenth-century novel in Germany, came to fruition in England during the Victorian era with the works of Charles Dickens and George Eliot. It is a genre of an individual's development from childhood to maturity within a given social order. Scholars have identified 'idealist' and 'realist' versions of the genre. The former posits a more dialectical relation between individual and society, one in which both are malleable and the individual has sufficient initiative to transform the existing social norms even as he comes to maturity. In the realist version, the protagonist has no power to change society, but achieves wholeness by adapting to existing social mores and structures.[27] The narrative takes the reader on the protagonist's often arduous and agonizing journey, both physical and psychological, as he confronts many obstacles, challenges the dominant norms of the social order he was born into and eventually learns to adapt his desires and aspirations to them. The journey ends with the hero as a fully 'socialized, normalized, and incorporated' member of his society.[28] This, at least, is the case with the *affirmative Bildungsroman* of eighteenth- and nineteenth-century Europe, in which an idealized liberal public sphere as egalitarian imaginary is one that enables the 'people' as such to 'produce and reproduce the norms and forms of themselves as "citizen-subjects"'.[29] The ideal of a 'unified' and 'developed' human nature in this literary genre is naturally suited to a liberal public sphere in which (private) 'differences are erased through the universal equivalence of citizens'.[30]

In a study of more contemporary post-colonial novels, Joseph Slaughter makes a case for a 'dissensual' *Bildungsroman*, one in which the ideals of socialization, incorporation and normalization are frustrated by a malformed and discriminatory social order, one that simultaneously asserts in principle and denies in practice the universality of rights and the abstract equivalence of citizenship. The dissensual *Bildungsroman*, thus, performs a 'double-demonstration by making a twofold rights claim that protests the protagonist's exclusion from the public realm of rights, yet articulates this protest within the normative genre of the rights claim, thereby asserting a right to make such a public narrative demonstration'.[31]

Valmiki's *Joothan* functions with precisely such a dissensual force in its narration of the painful stages of the evolution of an Untouchable *churha* boy to an educated writer, activist and professional in contemporary India. From the start, we are in the midst of a consciousness fully aware of the discrepancy between the rhetoric and reality of citizenship rights. He has the 'right' to education and avails of it at every opportunity. But he is unable to escape the disadvantages of his 'polluted' caste. He is made to sweep the school grounds while the upper-caste children are in their classrooms. His teachers cane him at the slightest provocation. He is barred from extracurricular activities for fear that his touch will pollute. During examinations, the peons refuse to let him drink water from a glass. He fails his year twelve examination due to his chemistry teacher's having refused to let him handle laboratory equipment all year. His family members are often not paid for their labour and are then mercilessly beaten by the police for asserting their 'right' to wages. 'Why', he demands, 'is it a crime to ask for the price of one's labour? Those who keep singing the glories of democracy use the government machinery to quell the blood flowing in our veins. *As though we are not citizens of this country.*'[32] The syntactical 'conditional negative' of this last phrase captures the 'double demonstration' of the 'twofold' rights claim referred to earlier: an assertion of the abstract 'right' to protest against the refusal, in practice, to extend to *all* the universality of the rights claim in normative citizenship-talk.

It is pertinent that Valmiki rejects all religious affiliations – Christian, Hindu and Buddhist – to which his community has aspired in its desperation to escape the stigma of untouchability. His eventual adoption of the name 'Valmiki' is *not* an endorsement of his community's assimilation under a majoritarian Hindu ethnos and ethos. Rather, it is a defiant and ironic gesture, daring the upper-caste citizen to take him on as a 'recognizable' Dalit, one who is not ashamed of his identity but intent on 'shaming' the privileged citizen into recognizing it as a legitimate one.

The adoption of 'Valmiki' as his last name is also a mark of his protest against his own community's desire to hide behind an upper-caste bourgeois identity on its path to upward social and professional mobility. He narrates a clash with his niece Seema, who refuses to introduce him to her college mates. 'You may be able to face it,' his niece says in defence, 'I can't. What is the point of going around with the drum of caste tied around your neck?'[33] Seema's argument epitomizes for the narrator a denial of the ravages of a fractured social order. In this context, the mark of an evolved self is the courage to confront the insularities and cruelties of the social order by wresting, on his own terms, the claims of citizenship made by the liberal democratic Indian state. Both are possible, Valmiki's life narrative avers, through a stubborn will to educate oneself and actively partake of the Ambedkarite legacy: namely, his fight for Dalit empowerment during the critical decades of the 1930s and 1940s when the Indian nation was being imagined into existence by its other, dynamic and better-known leaders, from upper-caste communities: Gandhi, Patel and Nehru. *Joothan* functions well within the generic horizon of the *Bildungsroman*, albeit in the 'dissensual' mode invoked earlier, one that exposes the limits of the generic promise of full human personality development.

By comparison, Sharan Kumar Limbale's *Akkarmashi*, while manifesting an epidermal likeness to *Joothan*, functions more as a picaresque narrative than a *Bildungsroman*. The picaresque, unlike the *Bildungsroman*, is not only unstructured by a causally related series of events that might give the journey an organic shape,[34] it is also less oriented to the end point of such a journey: the incorporation and transformation of the protagonist within a given social order and his evolution into full personhood. As opposed to the organic plot, an organically developed individual and a semblance of a restored moral order of the *Bildungsroman*, the hallmarks of the picaresque are the episodic plot movement and the protagonist's tortured consciousness, at odds with his chaotic environs and an oppressive and immutable social order. A picaro[35] remains a social outcast. His variability and capriciousness signal an abdication of organic self-determination within a social ethos he abhors and has no agency in.

If Valmiki's *Joothan* falls towards the *Bildungsroman* end of the developmental narrative spectrum, Limbale's *Akkarmashi*, a life story of a bastard child born of the seduction of a Dalit woman by her upper-class landlord, can be located at the picaresque end. Rage is the predominant mood of *Akkarmashi*, held grimly aloft by two narrative prongs: the protagonist's illegitimate, half-caste status and the constancy of hunger. In a passage of unmitigated fury, Limbale cries:

> Why didn't my mother abort me when I was a foetus? Why did she not strangle me as soon as I was born? We may be children born out of caste but does that mean we must be humiliated? What exactly is our fault? Why should a child suffer for the sin of its parents? ... Whenever I look at my mother I grow wild with anger.[36]

'Hunger' appears throughout the narrative, as in: 'I realized that God had made a mistake in endowing man with a stomach',[37] but also as stark realism: 'those were the days we starved'[38] occasionally in the figurative, 'A flock of crows fluttered in our stomach'[39] and ever so often as contemplation:

> *Bhakari* is as large as man. It is as vast as the sky and bright like the sun. Hunger is bigger than man ... A single stomach is like the whole earth. Hunger seems no bigger than your open palm, but it can swallow the whole world and let out a belch. There would have been no wars if there was no hunger.[40]

Limbale's narrative is set in the Dalit community of Mahars in the 1970s and early 1980s in Maharashtra, the home of the Dalit movement led by Ambedkar, who also came from this community. While the impact of Ambedkar does appear to temporarily dispel the protagonist's identity crisis, especially in his participation in the Marathwada agitation of 1978 when Dalits demanded the renaming of the Marathwada University after Ambedkar, the narrative as a whole has a quintessential picaresque momentum, with 'life's chaos assaulting the [picaro] in one event after another', almost in a series of accidents beyond the hero's control.[41]

To read *Akkarmashi* is to experience one traumatic confrontation after another, in this gruesome account of a life torn apart by the accident of birth and caste. As a traumatized child, the protagonist staggers between 'homes' that fail to offer the most elementary forms of nurture and nourishment. As an abandoned bastard son of an Untouchable woman, he carries the mark of his mother's rape/seduction and life-long exploitation at the hands of the upper-caste landlords of his village. He has no sense of belonging to either his Untouchable Mahar community or his unacknowledged paternal

community of upper-caste Lingayats.⁴² Unlike the protagonist of
Joothan, he never has a single roof over his head except for the few
years of his bare-bones childhood with his grandmother and her
Muslim partner, a situation tailored to make him feel even more of
an *akkarmashi* than if he had lived with his mother and her series of
lovers. Even this brief semblance of protection is marked by desper-
ate hunger. Eating baked bread that smells of dung or stealing grain
left with corpses at the crematorium seems routine to him: 'Mahar-
wada [village enclave of the untouchable Mahars] meant a heap of
jowar gathered at the resting place of a corpse. Each person was like
a grain. Why don't they too eat the jowar connected with the rites of
the dead? It too was food. Why should such jowar not be touched?'⁴³
It is hard to miss the starkness of this rationalization, and the fury at
the limitless poverty of the community. In fact, hunger and the
possibility of relieving it occupy the protagonist's mind throughout
his childhood and adolescence. If he has any sense of 'home' at all, it
is the various sites that give him some temporary relief from hunger,
whether it is his grandmother's hut, or the bus stand where he
awaits the arrival of passengers who deign to toss him a few coins
in exchange for help, or even his mother's nauseating liquor den.
The wild, anarchic nature of his experiences in a stark and amoral
world of deprivation is matched not just by the violence of his
emotions, but also by the inconsistencies and vacillation in his
narration. Was his 'father' a reasonable provider for his illegitimate
children? Which 'father' does he refer to when he uses the term
'*kaka*', all or any of his mother's lovers? Is his mother a whore *and*
a raped woman? The chaos of the protagonist's outer and inner
worlds is matched by the fragmented nature of a narrative that leaps
from incident to incident in a jagged array of tableaux, each poised
to pierce the reader's sense of comfort. Even towards the end of the
narrative, when the protagonist has moved away from his wretched
village and found employment after struggling to get educated, we
see a tortured soul attempting to reconcile the contradictions of his
inheritance with his new-found mobility as an urban, educated
Dalit. He can now afford to rent a home for his young wife and
children, but has difficulty finding one in a caste-conscious small
town. The anger surfaces once again: 'I faced the problem of finding
a house in a new town and my caste followed me like an enemy ...
Should I put this town to the torch? Such a big town – but I could

not get a single room.'[44] He settles for a home in the Dalit ghetto but feels alienated and disgusted:

> Here the houses did not have bathrooms and toilets. Women bathed openly and urinated everywhere ... Cycle-rickshaw drivers, porters and labourers were the main inhabitants of this locality. People lived in the smallest possible spaces. Each one worried only about his hunger. The stomach was the threshold of their capability.
> The locality nauseated me. I didn't want to adopt the values of such a locality. I was a Dalit who had become a Brahmin by attitude.[45]

The life story ends in a spiritual abyss, with the narrator paralysed by the aporetic nature of life and death in a cultural and moral vacuum:

> My wife Kusum had had a baby boy. I had already thought of a name for him. It was Anaarya ... At this early age of twenty-five ... I had to contend with so many responsibilities ... Who will undertake Dada's [his 'grandfather'] funeral? Will Muslims attend his cremation? How can they perform rituals after his death? What will happen to his corpse? ... Would people come for the rituals on Santamai and Masamai's [his grandmother and mother] deaths? Why this labyrinth of customs? Who has created such values of right and wrong ... ? If they consider my birth illegitimate what values am I to follow?[46]

Apart from his determination to name his son, 'Anaarya' (literally 'Un-Aryan'), a gesture firmly locating Dalit futures in opposition to the origin myth of India's Hindu civilization in Aryan culture, the narrative of his life does not culminate in the emergence of a strong and coherent self. The protagonist stands ravaged and fragmented by the singularity of his pain, a singularity that stubbornly resists translation into the lexicon of 'rights' in the 'dissensual' mode that marks *Joothan*. To that extent, *Akkarmashi* stays faithful to its picaresque narrative mode, even as it interpellates the reader as 'witness' to the protagonist's trauma in the modality of the *testimonio* which, in a 'human rights' framework could translate, in the words of Wendy Hesford, 'empathy into beneficent action'.[47]

Testimony, personhood and the collective: Bama's *Sangati*

I now turn to the life narrative of a Dalit woman from Tamil Nadu. Bama's *Sangati*, published in 1997, is her second work after *Karukku*, and records various events in the lives of the *paraiya* women in the village where she grew up. This work, more than the other two, falls squarely within the 'collectivist' credo of a *testimonio* even as it manifests features from an array of genres. It functions as prosopography (collective biography) by narrating stories of suffering and survival in the everyday life of a community of *paraiya* women in rural south India. It has picaresque elements in its episodic structure as it jumps from event to event that are not, in the final analysis, tied together into an organic plot. Finally, if one focuses on its skeletal framing by the story of a Dalit girl child growing into adulthood, it manifests some features of the *Bildungsroman*. *Sangati* signals the multiple and conflicting legacies of the history of Dalit community formation, in terms of both regional difference and gender. The setting of Bama's life story is, as we noted, Tamil Nadu, also site of the first vigorous anti-caste movement, the Self-Respect Movement (*Suyamariyadai Iyakkam*) led by E. V. Ramaswamy Periyar. Much before the emergence of Ambedkar as the redoubtable pan-Indian figurehead of the subcontinent's Dalits and the challenger of Gandhi in hegemonic narratives of Indian nation-making, in the early 1920s Periyar stormed the citadel of Brahminism in the south and broke ranks with Gandhi. From the start, his radical critique of Indian civil society incorporated the condition of women in Hindu patriarchy and led him to advocate what were then unheard-of practices, such as civil marriage with the consent of the woman.[48]

If *Joothan* and *Akkarmarshi* trace their Dalit legacies to west and north Indian low-caste reform movements, *Sangati* is anchored in the century-long tradition of low-caste mobilization in southern India even as it is acutely aware of the symbolic power of Ambedkar's name to forge a collective national identity for Dalits. As the narrator wryly notes: 'Now, in recent years, there is the whiff of Ambedkar-talk blowing right through our streets.'[49] More importantly, however, the narrative's primary focus is on the fate of Dalit women in contemporary India, a concern only obliquely represented in the other two texts through the portrayal of women – wives, mothers, sisters, lovers – hovering in the penumbra of the male protagonists' violated and violent worlds. The perpetrators are both the upper-caste establishment and the Dalit men themselves. The burden of Bama's narrative is to give voice to the magnitude and specificity of this collective pain in the face of systemic caste violence and ineffectual majoritarian attempts to address it. Neither the rituals of democracy nor the larger discourse of rights and citizenship is seen to provide the wherewithal for managing this pain, let alone alleviating it. Hence the focus is less on individual awakening through an assertion of the 'right' to education and livelihood disaggregated from traditional caste labour – though this *Bildung* theme is not wholly absent – than on a *poesis* of collective pain that avails of the open, amorphous address of public circulation. Had the narrative focused primarily on Bama's development from a timid Dalit girl in rural India to a teacher in a high school who chooses to stay single, it would have functioned as a dissensual *Bildungsroman* like Valmiki's *Joothan*. Rather than foreground her own life, Bama chooses to witness the extremities of pain and violence – domestic, community and state-sponsored – suffered by a series of women in her community: Mariamma, the victim of false accusation in the village court; Thayi, the battered wife regularly dragged through the streets by her hair; Esakki, hacked to death on the eve of her childbirth by her brothers for eloping with a man from another caste; and Raakamma, a victim of routine domestic violence who has devised her own strategies of retaliation through public abuse of her husband.

The narrator here assumes the role of the 'witness', envisioned in trauma studies as one who '[experiences] the trauma of someone else's story and [communicates] it in a way that keeps it traumatic for others'.[50] The innocuous-sounding title of Bama's work, *Sangati* (literally, 'event' or 'happening' in Tamil), belies her intent to take the reader on a traumatic journey through life after life of unimaginable cruelty. And yet the very singular, non-universal quality of the pain documented propels the reader to confront and calibrate the extremity of each painful episode against the world of the everyday *outside* the Dalit women's village. What does this mean in terms of the juridical power claimed, albeit as proxy, on behalf of the 'truth' of such a *testimonio* and its remedial logic? The dissensual force of these texts lies precisely in their embodiment through an aesthetic of suffering of the unrealizability, the 'not-yet-ness' of citizenship rights and human rights universalism.

This chapter has discussed the Dalit life narrative as a genre that has gained in prominence and popularity in the last two decades in tandem with the increasing visibility of Dalits in the public sphere and their vociferous demands for a more just political and social order. Such a phenomenon, I have argued, can be productively situated not just in the contemporary global context of the proliferation of narratives and *testimonios* of human rights violations in other parts of the world, but also in the context of an emerging conversation on the nature of 'Dalit personhood', a category infinitely more complex than legal subjectivity and abstract citizenship. The Dalit narratives analysed here are rich illustrations of this double movement, for they both witness on behalf of a suffering community and keep alive the singular, non-universal nature of Dalit pain through an aesthetic that is not wholly translatable into the lexicon of rights and justice. By invoking the historical and rhetorical force of two other prose fictional genres, the *Bildungsroman* and the picaresque, the analysis has sought to recast the *testimonio* less as a proxy for the legal witnessing and amelioration of Dalit pain than as a rich and expressive medium of Dalit personhood. Such a way of reading Dalit lives accords India's ex-Untouchables a stature beyond that of victims at the mercy of the capricious sentimentality of upper-caste solidarity with their suffering.

Notes

1 The term 'Dalit', which literally means, 'ground down' or 'depressed', refers to the ex-Untouchable castes of India. They make up approximately 12 per cent of India's population. In October 1956, one of their leaders from Maharashtra, B. R. Ambedkar, led a mass conversion of 400,000 Dalits to Buddhism. Since then, these converted Dalits are also called Neo-Buddhists.

2 The social context is complicated here. The 'upper-caste' villagers who massacre the Bhotmange family are not Brahmins, but low-caste 'Shudra' landowners in Maharashtra. In his analysis of the political economy of rural India from the 1970s to the 1990s, Anand Teltumbde notes the rise of this Shudra agricultural caste and their consolidation under a new agrarian social structure that further impoverished the Dalits. The Shudras or the Other Backward Castes (OBCs) as they are called, not only replaced the old *zamindari* system dominated by the upper castes who led India's struggle for independence, thus politically challenging the legacy of the Congress, but they also resented the rise of Dalit identity politics. The shift in the 1990s from a welfare state to a market economy exacerbated the condition of the agricultural sector as a whole which no longer had the protection of state investment and subsidies. The condition of the Dalits worsened under the state's neo-liberal policies, which no longer offered any minimum wage protection. The demand for farm labour also fell dramatically. These factors, combined with the hostility of the OBCs towards Dalits, witnessed an increase in atrocities against the ex-Untouchables.

3 'Crimes against Dalits' website at www.ambedkar.org. Downloaded on 16 February 2009. Also see Anand Teltumbde's Preface in *Khairlanji: A Strange and Bitter Crop* (Pondicherry: Navayana, 2008), p. 9.

4 These words appear on the front inside cover of *Khairlanji*.

5 Joseph Slaughter, *Human Rights Inc.* (New York: Fordham University Press, 2007), p. 17.

6 As seen recently in the vast media coverage of the phenomenal rise of Mayawati, the first Dalit Chief Minister of Uttar Pradesh, and currently an aspirant to the Prime

Ministership. No doubt, the reservation policies of successive central governments have fuelled this elite disgruntlement.

7 Benedict de Spinoza, *Political Treatise*, chapter XI, para. 1, trans. A. H Gosset (New York: Dover Publications, 1955).

8 See Lata Murugkar's *Dalit Panther Movement in Maharashtra: A Sociological Appraisal* (Bombay: Popular Prakashan, 1991).

9 See Shankarao Kharat (ed.), *Dr Babasaheb Ambedkar Yaanche Atmakatha* ('Dr Babasaheb Ambedkar's life story'), (Pune, Indrayani Sahitya, 2001); Gangadhar Pantawane (ed.), *Dalit Sahitya Charcha ani Chintan* ('Dalit Literature: Discussion and Thought'), (Aurangabad, Saket Prakashan, 1993); and Uma Chakravarti, 'Reconceptualising Gender: Phule, Brahminism and Brahminical Patriarchy', in Anupama Rao (ed.), *Gender and Caste* (New Delhi: Kali for Women, 2003), pp. 164–79.

10 Details on www.ncdhr.org.in, and in www.ambedkar.org.

11 *Joothan* by Omprakash Valmiki was originally published in Hindi in 1997. The English translation is by Arun Prabha Mukherjee, and was published from Calcutta by Samya in 2003. *Akkarmashi* by S. K. Limbale is in Marathi and was first published in 1984. The English translation by Santosh Bhoomkar for Oxford University Press (New Delhi) appeared in 2003. *Sangati* by Bama was originally published in Tamil in 1994. The English translation by Lakshmi Holmstrom was published by Oxford University Press (New Delhi) in 2005.

12 M. S. S. Pandian, 'On a Dalit Woman's Testimonio' in Rao, *Gender and Caste*, pp. 129–35; Pramod Nayar, 'Bama's *Karukku*: Dalit Autobiography as Testimonio', *Journal of Commonwealth Literature* 41:2 (2003), pp. 83–100; and Sharmila Rege's *Writing Caste/Writing Gender: Narrating Dalit Women's Testimonios* (New Delhi: Zubaan, 2006).

13 John Beverley, 'The Margin at the Centre: On *Testimonio* (Testimonial Narrative)', in Sidonie Smith and Julia Watson (eds.), *De/Colonizing the Subject: The Politics of Gender in Women's Autobiography* (Minneapolis: University of Minnesota Press, 1992), pp. 91–114, 92–3.

14 See works such as Richard Claude and Burus Weston (eds.), *Human Rights in the World Community: Issues and Action* (Philadelphia: University of Pennsylvania Press, 1992); Nicholas Owen (ed.), *Human Rights, Human Wrongs: Oxford Amnesty Lectures* 2001 (Oxford University Press, 2003); Wendy Brown, 'The Most We can Hope For: Human Rights and the Politics of Fatalism', *South Atlantic Quarterly* 103:2, 3 (2004), pp. 451–63.

15 Anand Teltumbde, 'Globalization, Civil Society and Bahujan', in *Khairlanji*, pp. 182–99; P. Sainath, 'Unmusical Chairs', and 'Head-Loads and Heartbreak', in Rao, *Gender and Caste*, pp. 336–45.

16 See Upendra Baxi, *The Future of Human Rights* (New Delhi: Oxford University Press, 2002); Costas Douzinas, *The End of Human Rights: Critical Legal Thought at the Turn of the* Century (Oxford: Hart Publishers, 2000); Jacques Ranciere, 'Who is the Subject of the Rights of Man?', *South Atlantic Quarterly* 103:2, 3 (2004), pp. 297–310.

17 Lauren Berlant, 'The Subject of True Feeling; Pain, Privacy and Politics', in Sara Ahmad *et al.* (eds.), *Transformations: Thinking Through Feminism* (New York: Routledge, 2000), p. 42.

18 *Ibid.*

19 In the Indian context, and especially in the evolution of Dalit politics beyond Ambedkar, the language of rights and citizenship (that is, the ideological power of law and its ability to confer personhood) is no longer seen as a potent medium of empowerment. Rather, what we see is the rise of cult politics in figures such as Mayawati,

who see Dalit assertion, not in terms of a rights-based discourse, but in the 'ill-liberal' register of 'muscle-power'. It is possible to argue that the life narratives discussed in this chapter keep alive the dream of a liberal politics envisaged for Dalits by Ambedkar, one that has vanished from the domain of Dalit politics altogether. I am indebted to Dipesh Chakrabarty for this insight.

20 Wendy Hesford, 'Documenting Violations: Rhetorical Witnessing and the Spectacle of Distant Suffering', *Biography* 27:1 (winter 2004), pp. 104–44, p. 105.

21 Franco Moretti, *The Way of the World: The Bildungsroman in European Culture*, trans. Albert Sbragia (London: Verso, 2000), p. 15.

22 See Winifred Brugger, 'The Image of the Person in the Human Rights Concept', *Human Rights Quarterly* 18:3 (1996), pp. 594–611; Anna Yeatman, 'Who is the Subject of Human Rights?', *American Behavioural Scientist* 43:9 (2000), pp. 1498–514.

23 Vijay Prashad, 'Untouchable Freedom; A Critique of Bourgeois-Landlord Indian State', *Subaltern Studies* x (New Delhi: Oxford University Press, 1999), p. 189. See also Prashad's 'The Killing of Bala Shah and the Birth of Valmiki: Hinduisation and the Politics of Religion', *Indian Economic and Social History Review* 32:3 (1995).

24 Valmiki, *Joothan*, pp. 2–3.

25 *Ibid.*, p. 11.

26 Judith Butler highlights this underside of 'linguistic' recognition in the performativity of personhood. See her *Excitable Speech: A Politics of the Performative* (New York: Routledge, 1997).

27 Marianne Hirsch, 'The Novel of Formation as Genre: Between Great Expectations and Lost Illusions', *Genre* 12:3 (1979), p. 298.

28 Slaughter, *Human Rights, Inc.*, p. 179.

29 *Ibid.*, p. 178.

30 Laclau and Mouffe, *Hegemony and Socialist Strategy: Towards a Radical Democratic Politics* (London: Verso, 1985), p. 181.

31 Slaughter, *Human Rights, Inc.*, pp. 181–2.

32 Valmiki, *Joothan*, p. 39; author's emphasis.

33 *Ibid.*, p. 128.

34 As René Wellek and Austin Warren in their *Theory of Literature* note, 'In the picaresque novel, the chronological sequence is all there is: this happened, then that … A more philosophic novel adds to chronology the structure of causation' (New York: Mariner Books, 1949), p. 222.

35 The term 'picaro' is Spanish in origin and literally means 'rogue' or 'rascal'. The term is used for the protagonist of the picaresque form, a subgenre of prose fiction in the first person which narrates the adventures of a low-born social outcast in an episodic manner. The origins of the picaresque form lie in Spanish literature of the sixteenth century. The genre became popular throughout Europe in the seventeenth century. Some of the precursors to the nineteenth-century realist novel in England, such as Defoe's *Moll Flanders* and Henry Fielding's *Joseph Andrews*, also drew inspiration from the picaresque form. Modern fiction from around the world continues to draw on its many features.

36 Limbale, *Akkarmashi*, p. 64.

37 *Ibid.*, p. 7.

38 *Ibid.*, p. 21.

39 *Ibid.*, p. 7.

40 *Bhakri* is bread made of jowar, a coarse grain common to Maharashtra.

41 See Stuart Miller's *The Picaresque Novel* (Cleveland, OH: Case Western Reserve), 1967, pp. 12, 36.

42 To highlight another parallel with picaresque narratives, Limbale's 'bastard child' status is found among other celebrated picaros in English fiction of the eighteenth century, such as Tom Jones, the eponymous hero of Henry Fielding's celebrated work.

43 Limbale, *Akkarmashi*, p. 12–13.

44 *Ibid.*, p. 106.

45 *Ibid.*, p. 107.

46 *Ibid.*, p. 113.

47 Hesford, 'Documenting Violations', p. 107.

48 Two recent accounts of the work of Periyar and the Self-Respect Movement with regard to the 'woman question' include S. Anandhi's 'The Women's Question in the Dravidian Movement, *c.*1925–1948', and V. Geetha's 'Periyar, Women and an Ethic of Citizenship', both in Rao, *Gender and Caste*.

49 Bama, *Sangati*, p. 103.

50 Lauren Berlant, 'Trauma and Ineloquence', *Cultural Values* 5:1 (2001), pp. 41–58, p. 45.

9

National tradition and modernist art

'Notwithstanding the fact that she has studied in and been deeply influenced by the West, Miss Sher-Gil's work must be considered as a clear sign of the artistic awakening in India', wrote the art critic Charles Fabri in 1937.[1] Fabri, an Indologist by training and a Hungarian citizen by birth, was a partisan of modern art and Gandhian nationalism.[2] His overwhelmingly positive review of the painter Amrita Sher-Gil's exhibition in Lahore indexed dominant understandings of Indian art, modern art and the relationship between India and the West in the 1930s. The idea that Sher-Gil's art heralded a national renaissance *despite* its incubation in the West reflected the way in which, by the early twentieth century, Indian art and Western art had come to be viewed as mutually exclusive cultural forms.

The idea of Indian art as decorative and fundamentally opposed to the naturalistic impulses of Western art was promoted by British colonial authorities from the middle of the nineteenth century. This opposition between Indian art and Western art was seized upon by anti-colonial nationalist artists, notably in Bengal, to produce a modern art that claimed to be 'Indian' by rejecting Western models. By the 1930s, when Sher-Gil came to practise art in India, however, there was a growing sense that this rejection could not by itself serve as the basis of what Fabri called an 'artistic awakening'. There had to be a critical engagement with the forms of Western modernity alongside those of India's pre-colonial past. Since India's link to that modernity was mediated by the experience of colonialism, its modern art could not seamlessly attach itself to the imperatives of modern art elsewhere. A link had to be forged to the art of India's past, to a 'national' tradition.

In 1936, Sher-Gil was quoted by a fellow artist, Barada Ukil, in *Modern Review*, an influential English-language journal of the nationalist elite, as saying: 'Art, it is my conviction, must be connected with the soil if it is to be vital.'[3] For Sher-Gil, this connection to the soil meant that it was insufficient to apply Western representational techniques, that is, oil painting or modernist simplification, to Indian subjects. In order to stake a claim to nationalist authenticity, Ukil reported that Sher-Gil was in the process of 'evolving a new style which is more in conformity with the indigenous art of the country'.[4]

Such a view of art was by no means unique to the artist and persisted from the late colonial into the post-colonial period. For example, Maqbool Fida Husain (1915–2011), perhaps India's most famous modernist painter, described his turn to indigenous motifs and modes of representation through the Great Exhibition of 1947–8 held in London and New Delhi on the occasion of India's independence from British rule: 'Till then I was influenced by the Expressionists. After visiting the exhibition, I combined three periods, the form of the Gupta period, the strong colors of the Basohli period and the innocence of folk art and worked on it and came out with five paintings which were shown at the Bombay Art Society in 1949.'[5]

Various critics from Govindaraj Venkatachalam, Rudi Von Leyden and Richard Bartholomew to A. S. Raman, J. Swaminathan and Geeta Kapur writing in the twentieth century, despite their divergent aesthetic and political aims, expressed the need for modern art in India to articulate its continuities with the national past and its differences from developments in Euro-American contexts. Art historian Rebecca Brown has termed this predicament as 'the paradox of being Indian and modern', whereby Indian-ness is associated with particularity and the past while modernity is equated with universality and the West.[6] For artists in India, the idea of national tradition emerged as the ground on which they could assert their belonging to modernity, and make culture and community anew in the wake of colonialism.

As several scholars have shown, the idea of national tradition has been crucial to the articulation of post-colonial modernity in South Asia. Drawing on materials from Bengal, Partha Chatterjee has argued that anti-colonial nationalists conceived a domain of national tradition, or the home, to oppose the domain of colonial modernity, or the world.[7] Whereas the nationalist 'home' was imagined as a space of femininity and spirituality, the colonial 'world' was a space of masculinity and materialism. This distinction between home and world had material effects as claims to national identity and post-colonial difference were staged in various cultural practices from theatre and film to art and music. Indeed, as Amanda Weidman has argued, in the context of classical music in South India, the categories 'tradition' and 'modernity' – and indeed their associations with India and the West – were 'produced by and through a colonial encounter.'[8] By this account, tradition is not the antithesis of modernity, it is constitutive of it. Tradition does not precede modernity, it is coeval with it. Tradition is not an unchanging essence, but a historically contingent formulation.

Each of the three artists discussed in this chapter – Amrita Sher-Gil (1913–41), K. G. Subramanyan (1924–) and Bhupen Khakhar (1934–2003) – identified a national tradition that could serve as the ground of modernism in twentieth century India. The wall paintings of Ajanta and the miniature painting of the Rajput and Mughal courts inspired Sher-Gil's oil paintings. The crafts practices and performing arts of the subcontinent sustained Subramanyan's toys, murals, terracotta reliefs and glass painting. The visual forms and print culture of the bazaar informed Khakhar's painting and poetry. Their engagements with cultural production associated with pre-colonial, folk or marginal practices and life-worlds were the hallmark of modernism in twentieth-century India. Their art exemplifies what art critic Geeta Kapur has called 'the double discourse of the national and the modern' by which nationalism and modernism hold each other in check as 'nationalism calls up the category of tradition, modernism catapults into internationalism'.[9]

The significance of a national tradition for modern art in India came to the foreground in debates on the role of art and the artist during the early decades of the twentieth century. During the nineteenth century, British colonial authorities in India promoted the idea of an essential opposition between the characters and purposes of Indian and Western art.[10] For example, in *The Two Paths* (1858), a treatise on art written in the wake of the anti-colonial rebellion of 1857, John Ruskin characterized Indian art as decorative and savage, while Western art was naturalistic and noble.[11] In the figures of the 'Indian' and the 'Highland', he found 'two national capacities distinctly and accurately opposed'; whereas the Scots were 'a race rejoicing in art', the Indians were 'a people careless of it, and apparently incapable of it'.[12]

Such distinctions between art and crafts – and by extension, East and West – were institutionalized in colonial art schools across the subcontinent, from Lahore and Bombay to Calcutta and Madras, as Indians were deemed incapable of producing fine arts and consigned to the manufacture of decorative crafts. Under the influence of the design movement based in South Kensington, these art schools offered instruction primarily in the 'applied arts', the colonialist term used to describe India's reformed national tradition of crafts. Partha Mitter has argued that the curriculum in these schools created a system by which Indians could aspire to be artisans but not artists, producing handloom and handicraft goods that were exported from colonial periphery to metropolitan centre.[13] Tapati Guha-Thakurta has suggested that the emphasis on technical and vocational skills in colonial art schools also served to produce a new class of workers to assist in the administration of empire, carrying out ethnographic surveys and construction projects.[14] Thus, under British colonial rule, India's 'tradition' of decorative crafts was redirected towards lucrative trade and efficient government.

Between 1900 and 1910, a powerful critique of colonial art education in India emerged among a group of artists and intellectuals with anti-colonial nationalist sympathies. Based in Calcutta, this group included Ernest Binfield Havell, a colonial art administrator and principal of the Government Art School in Calcutta; Sister Nivedita (Margaret E. Noble), an Irish disciple of the reformist Hindu philosopher Swami Vivekananda; Ananda Kentish Coomaraswamy, a British-educated art critic and author; and Kakuzo Okakura, a Japanese scholar and aesthete. According to Guha-Thakurta, their ideas on art represented a convergence of nationalist and Orientalist discourses, upholding many critical assumptions about the difference of East and West even as they sought to challenge colonialist thought.[15] They inverted the hierarchies of the colonial art school, proclaiming decorative Indian art to be superior to naturalistic Western art. Influenced by the contemporary *swadeshi* (of one's own country) movement, this group proposed an ideal of 'Indianness' to counter what they identified as the 'Western bias' against Indian art.[16] This Indian identity, emphasizing introspection and idealism, would form the basis of a new national art that would be the foil to Western art, which had been equated with illusionistic oil painting since the Renaissance. The dichotomy between Indian art and Western art, and their associations with spirituality and materialism respectively, corresponded to the opposition between (national) home and (colonial) world discussed by Chatterjee.[17]

These ideas of national identity and post-colonial difference laid the foundation for a movement known variously as 'Indian-style Painting', the 'Bengal School of Art' and 'Revivalism', which developed around the artist Abanindranath Tagore in the 1900s and 1910s. Abanindranath and his followers propagated a theory of art emphasizing *bhava* (emotion) over *rupa* (form) as the logical corollary of privileging Eastern spirituality over Western materialism. They rejected oil painting and naturalistic drawing as inauthentic impositions of the colonizers and forged links to pre-colonial and Pan-Asian artistic practices. Their paintings were executed on paper, deployed 'Oriental' techniques including the use of organic pigments, calligraphic brushwork and multiple washes of colour, and depicted historical or mythological themes from a glorious, pre-colonial Indian past.

Consider Abanindranath's *The Passing of Shah Jehan* (1902), in which the Mughal emperor's body forms a dematerialized heap against an architectural façade of inlaid white marble (representing the palace quarters at Agra Fort) as he gazes back at the Taj Mahal, a mausoleum commissioned in memory of his wife. In Abanindranath's painting, the disenfranchised Shah Jehan, attended by a female figure as the partly shrouded moon casts a glow over the river Yamuna, is symbolic of Indian 'tradition', now lost to British colonialism. The mysticism and melancholia of the scene had no precedent in Mughal or Rajput miniature painting. Thus, in spite of the rhetoric of revival, Indian-style painting must be understood as an utterly modern response to historical conditions of colonialism, and as an aesthetic rejoinder to the academic oil painting valued by colonial administrators.

During the 1910s, the movement initiated by Abanindranath enjoyed considerable success, as his students assumed positions across India as critics, teachers and artists. By the 1920s, however, the Bengal School came to be rejected, even by those who had initially supported it, for being insular and ineffectual. For example, the poet Rabindranath Tagore, Abanindranath's uncle and an erstwhile admirer of Indian-style painting, wrote: 'When in the name of Indian art we cultivate with deliberate aggressiveness a certain bigotry born of the habit of a past generation, we smother our soul under idiosyncrasies unearthed from buried centuries.'[18] Kanaiyalal Vakil, a critic affiliated with the Bombay Art Society, was more pointed in his criticism, summarizing the dogmas of the 'high priests of the "revival" of Indian art' for a London audience in 1934: 'Thou shalt not paint in oils – Thou shalt not paint from the life – Thou shalt not paint portraits – Thou shalt not give the shade and model thy figures – Thou shalt not paint any non-religious figures – Thou shalt not paint except in conventions and symbols – Thou shalt paint nothing except the recipes in the *sastras* [Brahminical texts].'[19] Vakil's mocking tone notwithstanding, his description of Indian-style painting reflected its status in the 1930s as simultaneously an institution and a failure. Indeed, artists in late colonial India, not least Rabindranath, who took up painting in the 1920s to much critical acclaim, actively sought a new relationship to the art of the modern West and to the art of India's past.

One of these artists, Amrita Sher-Gil, departed from her peers by insisting that Indian modernity could be rendered in oil. With the benefit of an art education in Paris and first-hand knowledge of European art, she sought a national art defined not in opposition to the modern West, but in a dialogic relationship with it. Her art was a self-conscious counter-proposal to Indian-style painting and indeed was recognized as such by a subsequent generation of artists including Maqbool Fida Husain and Francis Newton Souza, members of the avant-garde Progressive Artists' Association who came of age in Bombay during the 1940s.

Unlike the art of the Bengal School, Sher-Gil's subjects were ordinary and secular, and her treatment of them was direct and realist. Above all, her art was modernist, that is, it referenced contemporary artistic developments in Europe and was committed to a progressive social vision. Yet she did not entirely abandon the project of a national art as it had been pursued by Abanindranath and his followers. Like those artists, she believed that the art of India's post-colonial future would have to establish a critical link with the art of its pre-colonial past, specifically the traditions of miniature painting in Rajput and Mughal courts and the wall paintings of Ajanta.

Born in Budapest in 1913 to a Hungarian mother and Sikh father, Sher-Gil spent her childhood shuttling between Hungary and India. From 1929 until 1934, she trained in Paris, first with Pierre Vaillant at the Académie de la Grande Chaumière and then with Lucien Simon at the Ecole des Beaux-Arts. Her early work displayed an interest in depicting female figures and in exploring the conventions of academic painting. In December 1934, Sher-Gil returned to India, eager to build a career there as a professional painter after having 'discovered India' through the 'long stay in Europe', and specifically, 'Indian painting and sculpture' through 'Modern [Western] art'.[20] She set up a studio

Fig. 9.1 Amrita Sher-Gil, *Brahmacharis*, oil on canvas, 1937.

in an annexe of her parents' home in Simla, the summer capital of the British Raj, but she also painted in Amritsar, Lahore and Saraya, a village in Gorakhpur district of the United Provinces, where her family operated a sugar factory. From 1935 until her death in 1941, she lived and worked primarily in India, travelling extensively across the country to exhibit and sell her work and to visit archeological sites and art collections.

In her work of the 1930s, Sher-Gil was committed to representing 'the people of India', an idea that was highly unstable in the context of anti-colonial nationalist agitation and mass political mobilization under Gandhi. Her paintings of 1935 and 1936, including *Mother India* (1935), *Beggars* (1935), *Little Untouchable* (1936) and *Child Wife* (1936), rendered these people, the future citizens of the post-colonial nation-state, marginal and melancholic, as the objects of social reform and nationalist re-making. *Brahmacharis* (1937), Fig. 9.1, inspired by the artist's travels in South India and her reactions to the ancient Buddhist cave site of Ajanta, marked a break from that approach as the five *dhoti*-clad male figures, seated on the ground, formed an elegant tableau.[21]

The rhythmic postures and earthy colour of this composition cite the paintings at Ajanta, widely believed in the 1920s and 1930s to epitomize the artistic achievements of the nation's past. In this image, which Sher-Gil believed to have successfully synthesized principles of modernist art with the aesthetics of Indian painting and sculpture, 'the people of India', in the form of the young men, appear as though an ancient frieze had come to life. The semi-circular arrangement of their sensuous bodies invites the viewer into a collective space even as the *brahmacharis* appear oddly detached from each other. Indeed, they exhibit the singular mix of isolation and cohesion that characterized 'the people of India' in Sher-Gil's oeuvre even as she turned away from the grandeur and formality of the paintings at Ajanta.

In subsequent work, Sher-Gil looked to the art of the Mughal and Rajput courts and the cultural production of the village as sources of national tradition. Between 1938 and 1940, she settled in Saraya to observe and paint rural life. The village represented, for Sher-Gil as for other artists and intellectuals of her generation influenced by Gandhi, the repository of an authentic and organic national tradition that could be the model for a post-colonial future. Her oil paintings from the late 1930s engage the visual-artefactual forms of village craft – the spinning wheel, embroidered quilts and terracotta images – through the idioms of miniature painting.

Take *Red Verandah* (1938), where Sher-Gil highlights everyday labour in an elite rural home through the *phulkari* (floral) quilt and hand-knotted charpoy displayed in the foreground of the image.[22] The quilt-like patterning of colours and forms depicted in Sher-Gil's painting – the erect pillars, circular heads and geometric flowers – evoke the rhythms of labour, such as weaving, braiding and knotting, outside it. While the female figures depicted in profile and the glowing palette – the saturated yellow, bright greens and startling reds – of this picture refer to miniature painting from the Punjab Hills, its flatness and abstraction are indebted to modernist painting in Europe, specifically to the work of Gauguin and Cézanne, artists whom Sher-Gil admired. *Red Verandah* exemplifies how Sher-Gil sought a national modernism that would also be international in its affiliations and orientations.

Sher-Gil's turn to a national tradition, represented by the village and miniature painting through the medium of oil painting, was admired and emulated by many artists coming of age in the 1940s, such as Syed Haider Raza (1922–). Born and raised in Madhya Pradesh (the Central Provinces under British rule), Raza trained first at the Nagpur School of Art, and then in the 1940s at the J. J. School of Art in Bombay, an institution established in the nineteenth century and administered by the British until 1947. In 1946, Raza won the gold medal of the Bombay Art Society – an honour Sher-Gil had earned ten years earlier for her painting *Three Girls* (1935) – and became involved in the activities of the Progressive Artists' Association, a group that aspired to membership in an international community of modernists.[23] In 1950, Raza went on to study at the Ecole des Beaux-Arts in France, Sher-Gil's alma mater; he has lived and worked in France ever since, although he has remained active within the art world in India.[24]

His oil paintings of the 1950s such as *Green Fields* (1959) deploy the rich colour of Rajput painting, specifically the striking greens and browns of painting from Mewar and Malwa, and the theme of the village, which was mediated by his experience of the French country-side. Like Sher-Gil's art before it, Raza's painting also cites contemporary artistic developments in Europe, specifically mid century French responses to Abstract Expressionism as in the work of Nicolas de Staël. While the energetic brushstrokes and heavy impasto of *Green Fields* marked its affinities to an international community, the rural landscape and warm palette signalled allegiance to a national identity. Subsequently, Raza's art would set aside the village and mark its commitment to national tradition through an engagement with Hindu cosmology and iconography as he grew involved with the neo-Tantric art movement in India during the 1960s and came to an art of mystical geometries. In Raza's oeuvre as in Sher-Gil's, the national tradition in relation to which a national modernism would emerge was shifting and contingent.

A contemporary of Raza, K. G. Subramanyan, charted a rather different course to identifying and interpreting a national tradition in his practice of art. Subramanyan is best known for drawing on folk art from the nation's present, not on the elite arts of its past. He proposed that the distinctiveness of India's 'art tradition' lay in 'its hierarchical unity', which precluded 'sharp dividing lines between the major and the minor arts'.[25] To his mind, this tradition possessed 'a phenomenal linguistic breadth' with 'whispers and shouts', 'jargon and slang' and 'salty popular dialect and passages of refined poetry'.[26] Artists in India would have to emulate this sophisticated intermixing of the past in order to imagine their modern future. This view of tradition led Subramanyan, over the course of a career spanning over fifty years, to explore the intersection of the major and the minor, or art and crafts, as he experimented with drawing, oil painting, watercolour, sculpture and muralism alongside projects in set design, toy-making, book illustration and art-writing. Through these activities, he encouraged generations of artists in India to embrace a modernist practice in which diversity was privileged over purity.

Such insights into a national tradition were first developed during the 1940s when Subramanyan was a student at Kala Bhavan, Santiniketan, the art school of Rabindranath Tagore's nationalist university Visva-Bharati. The academic programme at Kala Bhavan emphasized experiential learning and indigenous image-making practices (as opposed to the academic oil painting and neo-classical sculpture encouraged in colonial art schools). In that environment, under the influence of figures such as Nandalal Bose, Benodebehari Mukherjee and Ramkinkar Baij, Subramanyan came to apprehend a continuum between art and crafts rather than their essential difference. From 1951 until 1979, Subramanyan taught art practice and art history at the Fine Arts Faculty of the Maharaja Sayajirao University in Baroda, an art school established in 1949 with a mandate to provide a post-colonial education and reject the practices of colonial art schools. In 1980, he returned to Kala Bhavan, where he had been a student some forty years before, as professor of painting until his retirement in 1989. Subramanyan's role as an educator in these settings was as significant as his model of art-making for younger artists in India, who sought to integrate materials, techniques and idioms which lay outside dominant vocabularies of modernism in their practice of art.

Subramanyan's unique perspective on art and crafts was evident in his terracotta murals of 1962–3, at the Ravindralaya building in Lucknow, a performing arts centre commemorating the centenary of Rabindranath Tagore's birth. Students from Baroda were invited to collaborate with the artist on this monumental project, which stages *The King of the Dark Chamber*, a play by Rabindranath on the relationship between truth, power, knowledge and self. At 81 feet long by 9 feet high, this artwork comprises 13,000 individual tiles, most of which were designed, fired and glazed en masse, and then fixed on to the building by improvisation on site. The processional quality of Subramanyan's Ravindralaya project recalls his mentor Benodebehari Mukherjee's 1947–8 mural, *Lives of the Medieval Saints*, at Hindi Bhavan in Santiniketan, described by Subramanyan, who assisted Mukherjee on that project, as 'a stupendous human pageant'.[27]

Yet the static repose of the Ravindralaya relief is quite unlike the riverine flow of the Hindi Bhavan murals even as they both evoke folk narrative and performative modes as sources of national tradition.

Subramanyan's use of terracotta evokes ordinary shrines and assem-blages in rural and urban India, yet his treatment produces a relatively formal frieze that conjures the ritual solemnity of stone-carved temple relief. Through these gestures towards the major and the minor, Subramanyan claimed his place within a history of national modern-ism, by way of Tagore and Mukherjee, in India and appropriated a national tradition – folk and performing arts – that would sustain and distinguish his own practice of modern art.

Alongside such large-scale public art projects, which Subramanyan pursued from the 1960s until the 1990s, he continued to paint. In the late 1970s, he revived a technique of reverse painting on glass, which had flourished in the *bazaars* (markets) of colonial India where it was likely introduced by itinerant Chinese artists, who in turn had learned it from Jesuit missionaries in the eighteenth century. In nineteenth-century India, this technique was used to make mass-produced devo-tional portraits, erotic images and theatrical scenes for new middle-class patrons. Subramanyan turned to this technique in order to generate a cultural form that was neither art-image nor commodity-object, but functioned instead as complex sign. The female subjects of Subraman-yan's reverse paintings recalled the directness and sensuality of Kalighat painting, a genre of popular pictures produced by emigrant rural *patuas* (scroll painters) in colonial Calcutta. They also cited and updated the female *bibi* of Kalighat painting, a category that encompassed a range of 'public women' including theatre actresses, courtesans, musicians, per-formers and prostitutes, whose sexuality could not be contained within the space of the home.

In *Radharani* (1981), Fig. 9.2, the artist depicts a woman and two men, perhaps a prostitute and her patrons, in a flat, abstract and brilli-antly coloured space. The title of the picture, which refers to Radha, the Hindu god Krishna's beautiful consort, appears at odds with the mun-dane and seedy action of the painting. A thick white line bisecting the image indicates a schematic division of space, not unlike that in a cinematic frame or comic strip, yet the pale blue colour of the female figure's sari leaks into the toothy cigarette-smoker's hair, suggesting an intimate traffic between male and female, proper and improper, art and commerce. The mustachioed figure with dark glasses, in the lower right corner, casts a sceptical glance in the viewer's direction, calling atten-tion to the inter-subjective nature of art-making and art-viewing in elite painting and popular pictures.

Fig. 9.2 K.G. Subramanyan, *Radharani*, oil on acrylic sheet, 1981.

Nilima Sheikh (1945–), one of Subramanyan's students at Baroda during the 1960s, has acknowledged her teacher's role as a catalyst for her explorations of image-making practices from India's past and present. Sheikh has consistently interrogated the boundary between realms of cultural practice understood as art and crafts, and their associations with masculinity and femininity, East and West, or tradition and modernity. In her recent *Firdaus* series of paintings, she initiates a dialogue with Kashmiri-American poet Agha Shahid Ali's *The Country without a Post Office* (1997). These large paintings, executed with casein tempera and Sanjhi stencils on canvas and hung vertically like *thangkas* (Buddhist devotional scrolls), depict the disputed territory of Kashmir, occupied by the nation-states of India and Pakistan. Sheikh's choice of materials – paintbrushes made of squirrel hair, like those used by artists in Mughal workshops, and paper stencils from a family of artisans in Mathura – and motifs – the crisp, golden leaves of the *chinar* (Platanus Orientalis) tree and the soft petal-like, Persianate rocks – critically engage traditions of courtly miniature painting and popular scroll painting. Her artwork recalls multiple image-making traditions and their cross-pollination in Kashmir, historically a crucial stop on the Silk Road and a place of exchange for objects and ideas.

In *Each Night Put Kashmir in Your Dreams*, Fig. 9.3, the second painting of the series, Sheikh envisions Kashmir as a land of itinerant performers and devout pilgrims, of bursting flowers and buried corpses, of shining blue clouds and fiery red earth. In other words, she conjures a mythic geography characterized by abundance and absence, stillness and movement, linear geometry and rhythmic flow. The painting's narrative and performative modes recall the *pichvais* (temple cloths) of Nathdwara, which Sheikh studied intensively in 1986–7 with the support of the National Handloom and Handicrafts Museum, New Delhi. Yet its delicate patterns and monumental scale produce a novel sensory experience – fraught, fragile and fleeting – even as it evokes familiar visual forms.

The *Firdaus* series refuses the notion of a stable or isolable cultural tradition through its complex network of associations which link painting and poetry, Hindus and Muslims, paintbrushes and stencils, modernist screens and sacred scrolls. Tradition emerges in Sheikh's work as a resource for critique and contemplation, for rethinking the world we inhabit and for remaking the present. In the viewer's encounter with her shape-shifting landscapes, tradition becomes a tool for rejecting the politics of chauvinistic nationalism by which Kashmir has been delimited as the exclusive cultural property of one group over another.

The career of Bhupen Khakhar, who, like Sheikh and Subramanyan, primarily lived and worked in Baroda, was also distinguished by a commitment to synthesizing elite and popular cultural forms, but Khakhar drew on a quite different notion of the popular than those artists. By contrast to the crafts traditions and folk art through which Subramanyan and Sheikh articulated their vision of a national modernism, Khakhar, who grew up in Bombay during the 1940s and 1950s, was drawn to marginal and ephemeral forms of cultural practice associated with the space of the bazaar: advertisements, maps, calendars, charts, cinema and photographs. Trained as an accountant, Khakhar took evening classes in painting and graphics at the J. J. School of Art in Bombay, and eventually enrolled in a two-year

Fig. 9.3 Nilima Sheikh, *Firdaus II: Each Night Put Kashmir in Your Dreams*, casein tempera with Sanjhi stencils on canvas, 2003.

programme in art criticism at the Fine Arts Faculty in Baroda, where he found a unique community of friends and mentors.[28] With their encouragement, Khakhar decided to pursue a career as a professional painter, although he continued to work part-time as an accountant until the 1980s.

During the early 1960s, Khakhar immersed himself in learning about modern and contemporary art in India and the West, becoming especially interested in Pop art and the post-Pop figuration of artists like R. B. Kitaj and David Hockney. He wrote his master's thesis on eighteenth- and nineteenth-century art in India, the mixed genres commonly referred to as Company painting and the art of Raja Ravi Varma (1848–1906), an exemplary painter and printmaker, who was famous for his sensuous images of women and Hindu deities.[29] From the beginning, Khakhar was captivated by hybrid imagery outside the bounds of good taste and proper origins.

Khakhar's exuberant collages of 1965, including *Pan Shop*, *Interior of a Temple* and *Interior of a Muslim Home*, reflected his engagement with contemporary art in the West and a fascination with sites of middle-class religiosity and sociability in India. In those works, the artist cut and pasted mechanically reproduced images, the calendar art or god posters of the bazaar, on to board, and embellished these found objects with coats of brightly coloured enamel and inscriptions in Gujarati and English. The result was a flat yet tactile surface that explored the boundary between icon and index, between cheapness and preciousness, between the mechanical and the handmade.

These collages pointed to a reservoir of images and image-practices that had been largely untapped by contemporary modernist art practice in India. For example, in the late 1950s and early 1960s, Subramanyan and Raza, despite their differences in method and materials, tended to privilege the space of the village or the figure of the craftsman in order to mark their affiliation to a national tradition. By contrast, Khakhar was an enthusiast of an urban life-world that was widely regarded by his peers not only as vulgar but also as inauthentic. In mid century India, the art of the bazaar did not fall into either of the two categories, the classical or the folk, which had been used to encapsulate the artistic traditions of India's past. Khakhar's funny and fantastical reclamation of the bazaar and its cultural forms redrew the proper boundaries of 'tradition' and also of modernism in India.

Consider this excerpt from a list of 'visual sources' for his art, published in the inaugural issue of *Vrishchik*, a short-lived yet influential journal Khakhar came to edit with the artist Gulam Mohammed Sheikh in 1969:

> Dark green leaves with a film of rich Prussian Blue on the corners – dark brown branches extending all over the tree – luscious orange fruit hanging on the branches.

Calendars with Meerabai's face. She resembles Meena Kumari wearing a white sari with cymbals in hands and with full and sensuous breasts and a vacant smile.

Advertisement of Badshai Soap with clean armpits (What magic!).

Angels flying in the sky, well fed cherubims licking the feet of the King Jehangir who is sitting on the throne talking with old fakirs.

Eternal grin on the trio's face (Gandhiji, Jawaharlal, LalBahadur) only their busts seen in light grey color against the blue sky. Farmer tilling the land with a tractor giving an even broader smile, as if stating that the Five Year plans have been successful and he owes his happiness to them.

Film strips on the use of Sapotex which aids gradual growth of whiteness, white – whiter – whitest.

Geographical charts of Haji Malang. The chart shows the main shrine. Sideways reaching the Shrine are railway bridges, high mountain cliffs, railways stations, and the main road to the high summit, people giving alms, sitting near the tree shades, climbing the mountain.

High plaster relief in Jain Temples depicting the Palitana mountain range with every Tirthankara staring at you with glassy eyes.

Photographs of a family group near Taj Mahal, newly married couple in a cinema pose near Chamba dam.[30]

As art critic Geeta Kapur argued in a subsequent issue of *Vrishchik*, this archive of images and image practices represented sensibilities that were dismissed by artistic elites of the period as cheap, ugly, imitative and common.[31]

Yet the ordinary rituals of the western Indian middle classes were rendered quite extraordinary in Khakhar's paintings of the late 1960s and early 1970s, such as *Parsee Family* (1968) and *Portraits of My Mother and Father Going to Yatra* (1971), which charted an intimate cultural geography and mined a rich aesthetic economy. While the lurid colour of these pictures cited Raja Ravi Varma-inspired chromolithographs of the bazaar, the flat yet dynamic conception of space updated the strange perspective of nineteenth-century painting from the courts of Kishangarh and Avadh. In Khakhar's art, a motley group of popular visual-cultural traditions – colonial photographs, Hindi cinema, contemporary advertisements, Jain *tirthankars* (ascetics), Vaishnavite temples and Irani teashops – and their sensory impact were reinvested with value and wonder. With great wit and verve, the artist reminded his viewers: 'Advertisement of Badshai Soap with clean armpits (What magic!).'

Fig. 9.4 Bhupen Khakhar, *Man with Bouquet of Plastic Flowers*, oil on canvas, 1976.

In the 1970s and 1980s, Khakhar's interest in the popular and marginal coalesced around the figure of the common man, an individual belonging to the middle class whom the artist deployed as an instrument of social critique. Khakhar portrayed this common man participating in everyday tasks, as he minded a shop in *Janata Watch Repairing* (1972) or got a haircut in *Barber's Shop* (1972), as he enjoyed a syrupy dessert in *Man Eating a Jalebee* (1974) or surveyed the street from his balcony in *You Can't Please All* (1981). Take the *Man with a Bouquet of Plastic Flowers*, Fig. 9.4, where the sad and sensitive subject of the painting embodies a peculiar mix of inner reserve and outward extension, as he gazes at the viewer cradling a bunch of precious – yet plastic – roses in his arms.

The domestic scenes flanking this Man along the frame of the image recall the composition of a calendar art genre in which events from the lives of 'national leaders', such as Khakhar's beloved trio of 'Gandhiji, Jawaharlal, and LalBahadur', are shown in sequential frames around the portrait of a heroic, central figure. In Khakhar's painting, however, it is unclear whether the events unfolding around his male subject are fantasies or memories occurring in a dreamed future or distant past. These ambiguities are highlighted by the garish pinks and orange tones, reminiscent of 'Hindi film with their perverse absurdity'[32] and 'Calendars with Meerabai's face' that Khakhar admired, which lend *Man with a Bouquet of*

Fig. 9.5 Atul Dodiya, *The Bombay Buccaneer*, oil, acrylic and wood on canvas, 1994.

Plastic Flowers a hyper-real quality. The national traditions of the cinema and the street became, in this artist's hands, the means to mapping emergent constellations of sexuality, sociability and subjectivity.

Atul Dodiya (1959–), raised in Ghatkopar, a suburban *chawl* (tenement area) of Bombay, and trained at the J. J. School of Art in the 1980s, has built a career that continues Khakhar's legacy of inventive bricolage from avant-garde art and commodity kitsch.[33] Dodiya's admiration for Khakhar is visualized in his autobiographical portrait, *The Bombay Buccaneer* (1994), Fig. 9.5, modelled after a contemporary Bollywood film poster of the actor Shahrukh Khan as the consummate anti-hero in *Baazigar* ('Gambler') (1993). The sleek handgun brandished by the male subject of Dodiya's painting is juxtaposed with his combed-back hair and proudly displayed watch, suggesting an elaborate performance through which masculinity is produced on film sets and under street lamps. Dodiya presents his artistic heroes, David Hockney, on the left, and Bhupen Khakhar, on the right, in the reflection of the large sunglasses, a strangely reverent gesture in an image about striking out on one's own and being a risk-taker in a glitzy, gritty metropolis. This tension between original and copy, between mastery and masquerade, and between serious gesture and silly joke, visible in the image of the young Buccaneer, animates much of Dodiya's oeuvre, extending to his installation of cabinets, *Broken Branches* (2001), and his series of paintings, *Saptapadi: Scenes from Marriage (Regardless)* (2003–6). In these works, the mechanically reproduced image is juxtaposed with masters and masterworks of the twentieth century in order to relate urban life and social relations to lived subjectivity and non-normative sexuality. It is no surprise that Mohandas Karamchand Gandhi's autobiography, *The Story of My Experiments with Truth*, was a touchstone for Dodiya's practice of art as it was for Khakhar before him.[34]

Truth, as Gandhi suggested in that work, did not refer to pre-ordained knowledge about the nature of the world, but was the product of sustained effort and examination. It was both a mode of political action and the basis of human subjectivity. Indeed Gandhi's ethical quest for self and community in the wake of colonialism, and especially his emphasis on experimentation, resonates with the artistic projects surveyed here. Truth, in his sense, can be likened to the national tradition that inspired the modernism of Amrita Sher-Gil, K. G. Subramanyan, Bhupen Khakhar and generations of artists that followed them.

Their national traditions, spanning artistic practices from the wall painting of Ajanta and the *pichvais* of Nathdwara to *phulkari* quilts and popular Hindi cinema, was the result of critical inquiry and individual exploration. It was the means to imagine belonging to community, country and culture in modernity. Sher-Gil's oil paintings integrated traditions designated as the classical and the folk through her engagements with miniature painting and village craft. Subramanyan's turn to India's folk and performing arts traditions stressed process over product, suggesting the possibilities for a symbiotic relationship between art and crafts in post-colonial India. Khakhar's embrace of marginal forms and practices outside the established spectrum of the classical and the folk yielded an art that celebrated everyday life and urban space. The discovery of these traditions and their transformation in modern art was a process marked by trial and error, creating multiple pathways to being an Indian artist and world citizen.

Notes

1 Charles Fabri, 'Miss Amrita Sher-Gil: "One-man" Art Exhibition in Lahore', *The Tribune*, Lahore, 2 November 1937. Reprinted in Gyula Wotjilla, *Amrita Sher-Gil and Hungary* (New Delhi: Allied Publishers, 1981), p. 71.

2 Fabri joined the archeologist Aurel Stein in preparing annual reports of the Archeological Survey of India from 1930 to 1934. During the 1930s, Fabri was active in nationalist circles, reviewed art exhibitions for newspapers, directed excavations in Punjab and acted as curator of the Central Museum in Lahore in 1936–7. In 1937, he became a British citizen, and upon India's independence from the British in 1947, became a naturalized Indian citizen. Based in New Delhi, he had a successful career as a writer and critic until his death in 1968. See Geza Bethlenfalvy (ed.), *Charles Louis Fabri: His Life and Works* (New Delhi: Sterling Publishers, 1980).

3 Barada Ukil, 'Amrita Sher-Gil and Her Art', *Modern Review* (September 1936), pp. 266–8, p. 267.

4 *Ibid.*, p. 268.

5 Yashodhara Dalmia, *The Making of Modern Indian Art: The Progressives* (New Delhi: Oxford University Press, 2001), pp. 50–1.

6 Rebecca M. Brown, *Art for a Modern India, 1947–1980* (Durham, NC: Duke University Press, 2009), p. 5.

7 Partha Chatterjee, *The Nation and Its Fragments: Colonial and Postcolonial Histories* (Delhi and New York: Oxford University Press, 1993), pp. 6–9.

8 Amanda Weidman, *Singing the Classical, Voicing the Modern: The Postcolonial Politics of Music in South India* (Durham, NC: Duke University Press, 2006), p. 9.

9 Geeta Kapur, 'National/Modern: Preliminaries', in *When was Modernism: Essays on Contemporary Cultural Practice in India* (New Delhi: Tulika, 2000), p. 288.

10 Partha Mitter offers an intellectual history of these developments in *Much Maligned Monsters: European Reactions to Indian Art* (Oxford: Clarendon Press, 1977).

11 John Ruskin, *The Two Paths, Being Lectures on Art and its Application to Decoration and Manufacture* (New York: John Wiley, 1859), p. 14.

12 *Ibid.*, p. 14.

13 Partha Mitter, *Art and Nationalism in Colonial India, 1850–1922: Occidental Orientations* (Cambridge University Press, 1994), 52.

14 Tapati Guha-Thakurta, *The Making of An 'Indian' Art: Artists, Aesthetics and Nationalism in Bengal, c. 1850–1920* (New York: Cambridge University Press, 1992), p. 64.

15 *Ibid.*, p. 184.

16 In the wake of the 1905 partition of Bengal, *swadeshi* nationalists asserted economic and political self-sufficiency by promoting Indian handmade goods and boycotting British manufactured goods. The rhetoric of self-expression which sustained these efforts likely inspired the Nationalist-Orientalist ideologues. *Ibid.*, pp. 258–60.

17 Indeed, Chatterjee cites the artists and ideologues of the Bengal School as the best example of his theory of an 'inner domain of national culture' that would be modern, but not Western. Chatterjee, *The Nation and its Fragments*, p. 8.

18 Rabindranath Tagore quoted in W. G. Archer, *India and Modern Art* (London: Allen and Unwin, 1959), p. 54.

19 Kanaiyalal Vakil, *Modern Art in Western India* (Bombay: Kitab Mahal, 1939), p. 13.

20 Amrita Sher-Gil to Marie-Antoinette Gottesman and Umrao Singh Sher-Gil, September 1934, reprinted in Vivan Sundaram (ed.), *Amrita Sher-Gil: Essays* (Bombay: Marg, 1972), p. 92.

21 The Hindu *dharmasatras* (texts devoted to law and ethics) specify four idealized *ashramas* (life stages) for male human development among the three 'twice-born' *varnas* (castes): *brahmacharya* (education and celibacy), *grihasta* (marriage and household), *vanaprastha* (forest-dwelling) and *sanyasa* (asceticism). In the 1930s, the notion of *brahmacharya* was given new and politicized inflections by Gandhi's practice of celibacy and frugality, and its association with bodily techniques aimed at greater self-government and self-awareness. The cause of *brahmacharya* increasingly preoccupied Gandhi towards the end of his life, and coincided with his period of residence at Sevagram (1936–42), a remote village in Maharashtra, where he established a model community.

22 *Phulkari*, which literally means flowering, is a form of embroidery native to Punjab typically executed on garments and quilts with brightly coloured silk thread called *pat*. A closely and densely worked-over design, such as the one featured in Sher-Gil's painting, is called *bagh* (flower garden), symbolizing a confluence of natural and material wealth. Gifts of *phulkari* mark births, marriages and other auspicious occasions.

23 For a history of the Progressive Artists' Association, see Dalmia, *The Making of Modern Indian Art*.

24 For a detailed account of Raza's career, see Ashok Vajpeyi, *A Life in Art: S. H. Raza* (New Delhi: Art Alive, 2007).

25 K. G. Subramanyan, 'The Image in the Indian Art Tradition', in Gulam Mohammed Sheikh (ed.), *Moving Focus: Essays on Indian Art* (1978; repr. New Delhi: Lalit Kala Akademi, 2006), p. 95.

26 *Ibid.*

27 K. G. Subramanyan, 'Benodebehari Mukherjee', in Sheikh, *Moving Focus*, p. 75.

28 Timothy Hyman, *Bhupen Khakhar* (Bombay: Chemould, 1998), p. 11.

29 Geeta Kapur, 'The Uncommon Universe of Bhupen Khakhar', in Kobena Mercer (ed.), *Pop Art and Vernacular Cultures* (Cambridge, MA and London: MIT and Iniva, 2007), p. 133, n.6.

30 Bhupen Khakhar, 'Notes on the Visual Sources of My Painting', *Lalit Kala Contemporary* 10 (1969), pp. 24–6.

31 Geeta Kapur, 'In Quest of Identity: Art and Indigenism in Post-Colonial Culture with Special Reference to Contemporary Indian Painting', serialized in *Vrischik* (1971–2): no page numbers.

32 Khakhar, 'Notes on the Visual Sources of My Painting', pp. 24–6.

33 For the biographical and art historical contexts of Dodiya's career, see Gayatri Sinha, 'Artist/Arranger', in Atul Dodiya, *Broken Branches* (Bombay: National Centre for the Performing Arts, 2003).

34 See Mohandas K. Gandhi, *An Autobiography: The Story of My Experiments with Truth*, trans. Mahadev Desai (Boston: Beacon, 1957).

10

Mass reproduction and the art of the bazaar

The visual field in India underwent rapid transformation from the middle of the nineteenth century onward. This was due to an increased circulation of pictorial techniques and images from Europe and elsewhere, and to the introduction of technologies of mass-reproduction such as lithographic printing, photography and eventually cinema. New pictorial forms developed through a relay of three distinct elements: existing iconographic and artistic traditions, modern practices of fine art introduced in the colonial era and – in the twentieth century – elements of both local and global popular cultures. These forms were enthusiastically taken up as part of a growing Indian culture industry, particularly in the vernacular business arena that emerged from the trading communities of what historians have called the 'bazaar'.[1] Mass reproduction and commodification allowed images to become more mobile and thus circulate in an arena delinked from the territorial and symbolic control of temples and courts. As naturalism and realist techniques provided an alternative to strict iconographic codes, and access to images no longer depended exclusively on the intercession of priests or membership of a particular caste or class, commercially available images came to address – and indeed to constitute – differently composed audiences. These newly commercialized images then became available to the various projects of identity formation that have come to characterize Indian modernity – projects of nation, region, sect, caste and language, as well as the political and ideological projects of the nascent nation-state. The new iconographies, figural schemes and modes of perception enabled by new image-making techniques thus became sites for reformulating structures of symbolic power that both reflected and enacted changes in social relations.

Following an initial reflection on analysing mass culture in the Indian as against the European context, this chapter will examine these processes by tracing four phases of the ubiquitous mass-produced icons known as 'calendar art' or 'bazaar art'. I begin with a genealogy of these images' emergence in proto-mass-mediated devotional forms. Next, I turn to their role as one of the earliest mass-manufactured 'Indian' commodities in the context of anti-colonial nationalism. In the third phase, I explore the role these images maintained in consolidating a post-Independence pan-national culture. Finally, I turn to their deployment in the service of a resurgent Hindu nationalism within the context of political upheaval and neo-liberal market reforms towards the end of the twentieth century. At each of these four moments, new technologies for creating and disseminating images have held out the promise of a reconfigured social order: equitable access to the divine, independent nationhood and political representation for all. However, the marketplace has also subjected the inherent democratic potential of these images to its own generic recodifications through the culture industry's predictably risk-averse, conservative imagining of audience composition and preferences.

The context for mass culture in India

This suggestion of tensions between the liberating potentials and conservative deployments of new image-making technologies would seem to echo accounts of mass culture's early twentieth-century emergence in Western Europe, particularly those written by Frankfurt School theorists such as Walter Benjamin, Theodor Adorno and Max Horkheimer – and at this level of generality it does. But, precisely because of the influential nature of these accounts, it is important to keep in mind the significant differences between the contexts of mass culture in modern Europe and modern India; these differences devolve primarily from the post-colonial character of India's modernity.

Approaching mass culture from India

First, Benjamin and Adorno understood the era of mass culture as challenging a liberal-bourgeois cultural formation that privileged 'high' or 'fine' art.[2] The bourgeois conception of art assumed that the individual's cultic relationship to the image had been sublimated into aesthetic reflection, a process that began in the Renaissance. This conception thus valorized artistic 'genius', authorial originality and authenticity as vehicles of quasi-spiritual efficacy – though for Benjamin, both artistic and cultic images are imbued with an 'aura' associated with their unique locations in time and space. Versions of this liberal-bourgeois cultural formation were introduced into India by travelling artists, paintings and prints, and by a colonial administration that instituted art schools and organized exhibitions as elements in the apparatus of colonial domination. However, given the many forms of feudal and colonial power at work in India, it could not achieve the hegemonic status here that it had in the European context. In India, the primary site of mass culture's challenge was not, at least initially, the values and modes of reception associated with bourgeois high art; indeed, one might argue that in the colonies, fine art was not so much threatened by reproductive technologies as it was dependent on them for its dissemination.

We might begin to understand the impact of visual mass reproduction in India by way of a second important distinction from the European context, i.e. the colonial character of the Indian commercial sphere. It was in this 'native' sector of the economy, or 'bazaar' as colonial administrators and later historians have termed it, that the vernacular culture industries first emerged. The bazaar, in its technical sense, refers to a peculiarly colonial formation indexing the imperial regime's reconfiguration of Indian mercantile trade, banking and credit networks. These networks had once been powerful and extensive, but by the mid nineteenth century their scope had been drastically reduced. In the new colonial economy, their primary function was to link foreign traders and colonial industrialists in the great port cities of Bombay and Calcutta to the credit pools, markets and rural producers of the interior. Mercantile and money-lending communities such as the Banias and Marwaris from northern and western India thus came to constitute a highly mobile comprador class, serving both as middlemen and translators. These bazaar traders channelled the handsome profits they realized in the colonial economy into manufacturing consumer goods for the Indian market, including vernacular cultural goods: 'bazaar' prints, calendars, magazines and ultimately popular cinema.

The bazaar: informality
Three features of the bazaar have been particularly influential in determining the nature of India's culture industries, whether prior to

Independence or since. The first of these features is its informality. The bazaar's trading communities relied heavily on family, community and personal networks for the circulation of credit and goods, and wealth was kept within the family. Performance of social and religious duties was inseparable from the conduct of business, as reputation and moral standing were crucial elements of an economy in which credit depended on social relations rather than formal legal institutions. Informality served to distinguish the bazaar from the official colonial economy, even as the bazaar was in fact integral to the latter's operation; indeed, the Indian Companies Act of 1882 excluded indigenous commercial firms from its statutes, characterizing them as 'Hindu Undivided Families' (and therefore as domestic, implicitly patriarchal and explicitly religious) and regulating them instead under Hindu personal law.[3] This perpetuation of difference facilitated colonial trade by allowing local structures of exploitation to persist. What resulted was the development of a parallel business ethos that did not – and was not obliged to – follow the same rules as the European 'market'.

In the post-Independence era of Nehruvian socialism, indigenous manufacturers were highly regulated, resulting in the development of a robust black economy. The vernacular culture industries emanating from this parallel business culture tended to operate on a semi-formal basis, at least until the economic reforms of the 1990s. The popular print industry has depended on casual labour and informal distribution networks, while the Indian film industry – the largest in the world – has had a notorious history of informal if not illegal finance involving both 'Hindu Undivided Families' and major crime syndicates (it finally obtained official industry status in 1998). In other words, the mass culture industries, in tandem with the 'bazaar', have functioned under legal and epistemological conditions of exclusion or semi-exclusion from the formally legitimate 'market'. They have therefore developed in an arena supplementary to the secular modernist separation between religion, culture, society and political economy. The mass culture that has developed in this arena, in its form, production and circulation, has admitted little salience to the distinctions between these realms. Crucially, however, while the 'porous legality' of this commercial arena articulates with 'traditional' structures of kinship and power, it has also enabled the introduction of new technologies that reconfigure traditional occupations and social hierarchies, often enabling significant social mobility.[4]

Imbrication of religion and commerce

The second feature of the 'bazaar' to influence India's culture industries has been its imbrication of commerce and religion. Colonizer and colonized alike perpetuated the use of religious imagery in the bazaar; European and American manufacturers in particular used images of Hindu deities to advertise goods aimed at Indian consumers. Thus, trade labels or 'tickets', bearing colourful illustrations of deities, mythological episodes and other 'native' subjects, were affixed to bales of cloth entering India from British mills, and were often the chief selling point for otherwise indistinguishable goods (Fig. 10.1). Post-Independence domestic capitalists enthusiastically adopted the practice of giving illustrated calendars as annual gifts to their customers, associates and contacts, such that popular prints in general have come to be known on the subcontinent as 'calendar art' or 'bazaar art' (see the section on Sivakasi below). The explicitly religious or implicitly auspicious subject matter of these calendars has served to reinforce the central role of social and ethical relations within the bazaar economy, while the annual act of gift-giving actively performs these relationships and lubricates the bazaar's social–commercial networks. This intimacy of commerce and religion is encapsulated in the twinning of the Hindi words *shubh* (auspicious) and *labh* (profit) that still appear on many calendars (Fig. 10.2).

The Frankfurt school's account of mass culture assumed a largely post-sacred universe mediated by the aesthetic. Because of its location within the bazaar, however, Indian mass culture has been an extraordinarily prolific arena for the production of icons and a primary site for the configuration and reconfiguration of modern religious practices. New media and technologies have had a crucial role in this process, enabling new forms and sites of iconography and iconopraxis. The proscenium stage, naturalist painting techniques, printing, photography and cinema in the nineteenth century, along with audiocassettes, video, cable, satellite television and digital media in the twentieth century have all contributed to the process. Most of these new media and techniques made their initial appearances with religious or mythological themes – indeed, one might argue that in India, religion has been the most responsive arena for new technologies of all kinds.

Dominant and subaltern, marginal and majoritarian

A third important feature of the bazaar and its culture industries is that, because of their vernacular and religiously marked character, they are

Fig. 10.1 Cloth label or 'ticket' from William Stirling and Sons depicting Krishna as Shrinathji (the primary form worshipped by the Pushtimarg sect). The textile printing and dyeing firm of William Stirling was one of the three major companies from Scotland's Vale of Leven that came together in 1897 to form the United Turkey Red Company (Turkey Red was a popular colour-fast dye).

neither straightforwardly dominant nor entirely subaltern in status. The religiosity perpetuated by the culture industries in the late colonial period enjoyed sanction in the vernacular arena, even as the idioms of popular devotion and mythology were being reformulated as part of a civilizational narrative harnessed to the anti-colonial movement (as in the work of Raja Ravi Varma, discussed below). However, there was little scope for explicit religiosity to register in the secular modernist political and civic institutions of the independent state – or in the officially patronized cultural forms of modernist painting, civic architecture, public sculpture and the like. In these institutions, religion was

Fig. 10.2 2004 calendar for Dabur Agencies, Lucknow, dealers in herbal products. It depicts the deities Ganesh, Lakshmi and Saraswati; above them is the motto '*shubh labh*' (holiness/auspiciousness and prosperity).

reformulated in terms of culture and identity, rather than recognized as an ongoing presence in public life.

So while mass-cultural forms such as calendar art flourished with the growth of domestic capitalism, they also grew aligned with a semi-official, religious and vernacular constituency, distinguished from the secular modernist, leftist, cosmopolitan and English-educated elite (though the boundaries between the two communities have never been entirely distinct). When compared to the culture of the elite, the mass-culture industries seemed to address a marginalized, subaltern constituency. And yet these culture industries aligned with the interests of specific constituencies who were asserting their own hegemony within the vernacular arena. The mercantile communities of the bazaar established themselves as indigenous capitalists in the early decades of the twentieth century and became the primary players in the picture publishing industry. While local variations and niche markets certainly remained, the mobility and expansive networks of these communities enabled them to reach a pan-national audience and thus formulate a hegemonic version of Indianness.[5] In the visual register, the Indianness they formulated was dominated by Hindu sects advocating the use of icons (Vaishnava or Vishnu-worshipping sects in particular) and was therefore constructed along specifically Hindu lines. Thus, even as the more centralized, pan-Indian culture industries (such as the Bombay cinema or the Sivakasi calendar industry) addressed the market for Muslim, Christian and 'lower' caste themes, this was often done in a figurative idiom inflected with Hindu tropes (see Fig. 10.3).[6]

The Hindu majoritarian tendency could flourish in the vernacular culture industries precisely because of their marginalization by the sanctioned cultural forms of official state nationalism; when Hindu nationalist political parties re-emerged in the late 1980s, they turned immediately to the visual idioms of calendar art for their propaganda posters, processions and videos. The concurrent marginality and majoritarianism of the vernacular culture industries have made them a highly productive, responsive and volatile site for mediating political currents and social transformations. In securing the scandalous contemporaneity of religion, they have been able to confound the political and aesthetic protocols of civil society and the officially sanctioned secular public sphere.

In large part, then, the story of mass reproduction and bazaar art in India is the story of the shifting compact between religion and

Design No. 552   MUSLIM HOLY PLACES

THE IDEAL COLOUR CRAFTS
POST BOX No. 320,
Ideal Complex,   Solai Colony.   SIVAKASI-626 123 (S.I.)

OUR SOLE SELLING AGENTS:-
M/s. KHURANA CALENDAR COMPANY
2685, Roshanpura,   DELHI-110 006

Fig. 10.3 Muslim calendar from the 1992 catalogue or 'file' of Ideal Products, Sivakasi. Hindu and Muslim themes in the mainstream Sivakasi calendars have been painted by artists from both communities interchangeably and often in collaboration, but they tend to adopt a few stereotypical images of Muslim shrines and worshippers, unlike the Muslim niche market images which make a much more sophisticated use of calligraphy.

modernity. Walter Benjamin glimpsed the radical potential of European mechanical reproduction in its de-auraticization of bourgeois art, but in India, what mass reproduction threatens is priestly control over the icon's aura. This control has depended on textually codified iconographic canons and liturgical practices that form the basis of Brahminical caste privilege. The mass reproduction of icons poses a fundamental challenge to these sources of power. The following sections focus on four moments in the articulation of images and symbolic power on the subcontinent as reconfigured by mass reproduction.

Bhakti and the desire for mass reproduction

Woodblock illustrations first appeared in vernacular Bengali books and almanacs around 1816. These were largely produced by artists from the metal-working communities who had already been carving typefaces for English missionary presses. To understand the further development of printed bazaar images from the mid nineteenth century, we need to place these images within a longer genealogy of demotic devotion and serial image production. These devotional traditions provided a ready framework, both for the individual possession of images via mass replication and for a humanized, 'realist' depiction of deities.

The *bhakti* movements

Image-based temple worship mediated by priests became prevalent in South Asia around the eighth century CE, and a number of popular devotional movements emerged shortly thereafter – first in the south, then sweeping northward in the fifteenth and sixteenth centuries. Led by charismatic teachers and poet-saints, many from the artisanal classes, these movements privileged *bhakti* or devotion as an alternative to priestly or Brahmanic intercession with the divine. The *bhakti* movements espoused direct, personal forms of devotion and a deeply affective, often ecstatic, relationship to a benevolent, loving god. The cultural forms generated by such demotic devotional movements tended to operate in the more abstract registers of poetry, song and dance, either advocating the formlessness of the divine or communicating poetic visions of intimacy that did not pose the problems of access attendant on temple icons. This informal, individualized, demotic devotion prefigured – in a sense *demanded* – inexpensive, universally available, mass-produced icons in which the figured deities are 'humanized' through naturalist means.[7] The proto-mass-reproductive impulse can be located, for instance, in the famous *ras-lila* episode from the Bhagavata Purana. Here the youthful god Krishna responds to the desires of his beloved *gopis* (cowherd women) by replicating himself as many times as there are women; he then dances with each simultaneously and stretches the night of revelry to cosmic length.[8]

Given the preponderance of devotional cults whose ultimate aim is to behold a personalized vision of the divine (personal in both senses:

addressed to the individual worshipper and manifesting a human form), it is hardly surprising that as soon as affordable image-making technologies appeared, they were taken up to produce just such icons. Demotic icons catering to highly localized 'folk' and household worship were already available in the form of clay statuettes and wall or floor paintings used in domestic rituals, as well as roadside shrines sanctifying certain stones and trees. However, the novelty and unique appeal of mass-produced images, which found their first major market as souvenirs at important pilgrimage sites, lay in their ability to mediate between the aura of the great, sanctified temple icons and the everyday ritual practices of ordinary devotees. This was certainly the case for several early forms of commoditized icons, including those associated with the Shrinathji (Krishna) temple in Nathdwara, near Udaipur in Rajasthan. While such souvenir icons catered to varying constituencies – whether Marwari traders migrating eastwards or rural householders and recent city-dwellers at Calcutta's Kalighat temple – they are significant as new forms catering to new social configurations, and as commodities forging a market for the later chromolithographs.

Nathdwara and photography

The Shrinathji temple at Nathdwara is a major pilgrimage centre of the Vallabha or Pushtimarg sect of Krishna worshippers, whose primary constituency has been the Vaishya-caste trading communities of the bazaar working the northern and western trade routes; these communities include many who grew wealthy as middlemen under the colonial administration. Patronage for Pushtimarg temples and images came from these mercantile pilgrims, as well as from local rulers who profited from the pilgrim economy.[9] In this respect the cult represents the re-institutionalization or reterritorialization of the radical, liberating impulses of the *bhakti* movements. Images have come to play a central role in Pushtimarg: Shrinathji and other local idols are seen as living embodiments (*svarupa*) of the god Krishna, and service towards them (*seva*) is the means by which devotees attract the *pushti* or grace of God. In keeping with the materialist preoccupations and plentiful means of his devotees, the rituals of Shrinathji are highly sensual, with an emphasis on painting, textiles, music and fine food. The icon has eight daily *darshan*, or public viewings, for which he is specially dressed. What is more, the priests or *gosains* have been patrons of portraiture, using portraits to establish legitimacy by recording and displaying their

Fig. 10.4 Painted cloth *pichhvais* (votive backdrops) for sale alongside printed framing pictures, Shailesh Art Studio, Nathdwara, 1995. Many of the paintings for sale depict the *ras-lila* episode, while others depict the Shrinathji icon.

descent from the sect's founder. By the nineteenth century, therefore, the temple had attracted a community of miniature painters displaced from the neighbouring princely states – then suffering political turmoil – and had instated its own chief painter. Engaged to paint murals, *pichhvais* (decorative cloth backdrops for the idol), portraits, manuscript illustrations and paintings, temple artists also began to produce souvenirs depicting Shrinathji and scenes from Krishna's life; a particular favourite even today is the depiction of the *ras-lila* (Fig. 10.4).

In keeping with the emphasis on images, Vallabha priests enthusiastically embraced photography. By the end of the nineteenth century the *gosains* of Nathdwara and Kankroli (a Pushtimarg centre nearby) employed their own photographers to document functions, fairs and festivities, and to take portraits of themselves and their patrons. Ghasiram Hardev Sharma (1868–1930) for example, was both chief painter and head of photography for the temple at Nathdwara, doing his own developing and printing.[10] This combination of artistic techniques in a single figure indicates how photography was adopted as a part of the image-making process on a continuum with painting. Many artists used a combination of photography and painting in their work, painting on photographs or pasting photographic faces into painted compositions. This was particularly the case for votive images of priests or patrons' families worshipping a central icon in which it was important to establish the identity of particular individuals. In this instance, photography was used primarily for its ability to provide an accurate likeness rather than its ability to deliver multiple copies. However, naturalism also formed the basis of photography's use as a technique of mass reproduction, where young boys posed for a photograph dressed as Krishna. Such images were replicated and sold, paving the way for chromolithographic replication of Nathdwara images beginning in the 1920s: a similar photographic Krishna was one of the first printed images from Nathdwara.[11]

These photographs provided immediacy in apprehending a humanized form of the divine – an important tenet of *bhakti*-style devotion – that the earlier, more stylized Nathdwara paintings could not match. In the twentieth century, the popular print industry took up the work of Nathdwara's post-photographic artists, characterized by a treatment of deities' faces and skin that replicated the tones of black and white photography. In this new mutation, the photographic naturalism desired by *bhakti*-style devotion combined with the frontal imperative of the icon, ensuring an unimpeded flow of benevolence to the worshipper/viewer. The expanded circulation of these prints again rendered icons nomadic, unmooring them from their particular temples. As the Nathdwara icons set off on their travels alongside an increasingly mobile and pan-national network of trader and middlemen worshippers, their backdrops changed from the decorative cloth *pichhvais* to lush pastoral landscapes borrowed from European prints circulating at the time – landscapes which now stood in both for the mythic landscapes inhabited by the gods and for the mythic or 'messianic' imagined space of an emerging nation.[12]

Representing and enacting the nation

The second half of the nineteenth century saw the rise of many, often competing, articulations of Indian cultural identity, whether in the English- and vernacular-language public spheres or in the domain of image-production. While the Nathdwara images were associated with devotion and ritual as such, these identity projects introduced a new register of meaning, emphasizing the representation of an essential Indian culture as exemplified in the canons of 'classical' aesthetics. In signifying civilizational identity rather than embodying the divine, these newly mobile icons became reterritorialized once again, this time figuring forth the nation. The iconography of Mother India or Bharat Mata demonstrates the importance of the nation to these identity projects, although subnational, transnational, regional, linguistic, sectarian, caste- and community-based formations were also in evidence.[13] The new formulations of identity often deployed categories, ideas and idioms derived from colonial administration, missionary activity, Orientalist scholarship and European cultural forms (although, as in the case of Nathdwara photography, the translation of these ideas and forms often made for significant and productive differences).

Raja Ravi Varma

A case in point is that of Raja Ravi Varma (1848–1906), a self-taught artist from an aristocratic family of Kerala, celebrated by the colonial administration and elite Indian nationalists alike for his mastery of the newly introduced medium of oil painting and its naturalist techniques. Starting out with portraiture and genre painting, he achieved national fame through his explicit project of figuring 'Indianness' through reinterpretations of the epic narratives of the Ramayana and Mahabharata, and the mythological stories of the Puranas. These texts were currently enjoying a literary and theatrical revival through translations into English and thence into the vernaculars. One of Varma's most celebrated works, 'Shakuntala Patralekhan', took up a theme from *Abhijnana Shakuntalam* by the Sanskrit playwright Kalidasa, which had been translated into English by William Jones in 1789 and much later into Malayalam by Varma's brother-in-law. These literary texts provided pan-national 'Indian' counterparts to the Greco-Roman subjects of European academic neo-classicism, and Ravi Varma visualized them in the same European idiom, albeit with evident traces of the highly decorative Tanjore painting tradition, Kathakali dance-drama and Parsi theatre (Fig. 10.5). Varma was thus able to give tangible form to the 'classic' mythical Hindu past that anti-colonial nationalists sought to inscribe as the origin of India's national history.

Ravi Varma's work was wildly popular, and he was one of the first artists discussed within the emerging field of Indian art criticism. Thus for Balendranath Tagore, writing in 1894, the ability of Raja Ravi Varma's works to express *bhava* or emotion, understood as an essential component of 'Indian' (that is, classical Sanskrit) aesthetics, made them far superior to competing naturalist images. Ravi Varma painted several

Fig. 10.5 Raja Ravi Varma, 'Shakuntala Patralekhan', lithograph.

versions of 'Shakuntala Patralekhan', some of which were also initially reproduced photographically, and his admirers and patrons urged him to have his work lithographed as a 'service to the country'.[14] In 1894, at the height of his artistic success, Varma set up the Ravi Varma Fine Art Lithographic Press, which reproduced his academicist mythological paintings as well as an expanding repertoire of devotional images rendered frontally in the fashion of the Nathdwara images, but stylistically drawing on the Tanjore tradition.

Varma embodies a brief moment, before the advent of full-blown modernism, when fine art and mass reproduction could overlap, and mechanical reproduction could amplify rather than diminish the value of the artwork as an authentic repository of a national cultural essence. 'Authenticity', as it was invoked in the growing critical discourse on art in the vernacular press, referred not to modernist autonomy but to this homegrown 'genius'-artist's expression of 'Indianness' as embodied in the 'classical' texts. Shortly after his death, however, Varma was pushed to the margins of Indian art history (until the critic Geeta Kapur reinstated him as 'the indisputable father-figure of modern Indian art').[15] Calcutta critics pounced on the contradictions between Varma's nationalist undertaking and derivative formal means, mounting a series of polemics against him and propounding in his place the 'Indian style' in art and the neo-traditionalist experiments of Abanindranath Tagore that spearheaded the 'Bengal School'.

But in the commercial arena of the bazaar, the 'Ravi Varma' brand had become synonymous with his prints, which continued to be bought, plagiarized, imitated and recycled. Ravi Varma's role in mapping the Indian national public as a political-cultural entity on to a pan-national arena of consumption has often been overlooked, yet Varma was the manufacturer of a commodity that helped to define 'Indian' consumers. His prints made available multiple ways of performing Indianness to a wide audience, which did not need to be literate, wealthy or male to participate in a nationalist arena. These prints – from Varma's press as well as others in the early decades of the twentieth century – spoke to a range of engagements with images that did not necessarily map on to the aesthetic terms of fine art, or even on to an explicit, self-reflexive assertion of cultural identity. They continued to cater to devotional and ritual relationships with deities as well as to the melodramatic enjoyment of mythic narratives, they embarked on explicit caricatures and allegorical critiques of the colonial regime and they cultivated the emergent pleasures of figuring woman as an object of the gaze. Finally, they provided the visual idiom adopted by vernacular capitalists in the growing arena of manufacturing for a pan-Indian market – the idiom of corporate advertising calendars as well as commodity packaging and labelling.

The Sivakasi calendar industry

In the first half of the twentieth century, the culture industries – prints, cinema and magazines – were important sites for indigenous entrepreneurship and the formation of a pan-national market; after Independence in 1947, a range of domestic commodity manufactures and services came into their own. While larger domestic corporations and majority Indian-owned multinationals employed advertising agencies, smaller businesses and entrepreneurs who kept one foot in the informal trading, money-lending and speculative activities of the bazaar forged a parallel arena of vernacular commodity aesthetics based on the mythological and devotional idioms of the chromolithographs. Companies gave out illustrated calendars and advertising posters on Diwali (the start of the Hindu financial year) and on the secular New Year, and these became a new ethical index of the 'informal' kinship- and community-based networks of the bazaar. Calendar art and popular cinema became the pre-eminent visual forms of a vernacular, non-secular public from the 1950s up until the market reforms of the early 1990s.

The development of the new form was aided by the Indian economy's relative insulation under the Nehruvian socialist regime, and by the affordable printing machinery made available by Eastern bloc countries like the German Democratic Republic which accepted Indian rupee payments. High-volume colour offset printing allowed trading and manufacturing firms with widely dispersed small dealerships to use calendars as gifts-cum-advertisements aimed at pan-national, vernacular mass markets. By 1960, pre-printed colour images were being issued with blank areas at the bottom so that older letterpress technology could be used to add customized text and images, including details about particular companies.[16] Although most of the larger towns and cities acquired offset presses, by the 1970s, lower-end printing jobs were increasingly sent to Sivakasi, a tiny town in Tamil Nadu. Due to a combination of factors including climate and the availability of cheap labour, Sivakasi claimed to house 40 per cent of India's entire offset printing capacity by 1980 (a 2001 estimate put the figure at 60 per cent).

Sivakasi was already well known as a centre for producing fireworks and matches, as well as some lithographed product labels and posters; however, with the introduction of offset presses it also became the hub of the pan-national calendar and print industry, servicing publishers in the major cities. Touring agents carried full-colour catalogues of ready-made designs to local businesses, which would often specify their orders in terms of the number of 'Hindu', 'Muslim', or other (depending on the client's constituency) calendars required. Agents then liaised with calendar publishers in the larger towns to fill their orders from Sivakasi and arrange for printing the required text on one-colour letterpresses. Sivakasi also became the major production centre for extremely cheap 'framing pictures': variously sized prints, mostly religious icons, consisting only of an image (without the calendar portion). These continue to be sold at framing shops, pavement markets and pilgrimage sites all over the country.

Sivakasi not only wove together an extensive web of agents, publishers, businesspeople, consumers, printers and workers, but its presses also brought together the work of commercial artists from all over the country. Most of these artists were from more vernacular backgrounds; while some were self-taught, others received art school training in Western realist techniques, but turned away from the modernism that had become increasingly important from the 1940s onwards. Some combined their work for the popular print industry with work in cinema and vernacular-language illustrated magazines. S. M. Pandit (1916–91), for example, started out in a Gulbarga (Karnataka) goldsmith family, then moved to Madras and finally Bombay. After attending three art schools and honing his naturalist techniques, he worked for several years in advertising and film publicity, producing, for example, showcards for Hollywood films in MGM's characteristic style. The influence of this style is evident in Pandit's later mythological illustrations for prints and magazines, and in the work of his student Raghubir Mulgaonkar (1922–76), who used the airbrush technique to photo-realist effect.

In Pandit and Mulgaonkar, we see how the new forms of mythic imagery inaugurated by Raja Ravi Varma and the Nathdwara artists remained receptive to technical innovations. The very novelty of these forms, particularly their realist departures from canonical iconography, enabled them to address and configure the expanded markets made possible by mass reproduction. Heterogeneous social constituencies were thus brought into an arena of common address, even as they grew to be defined along broadly regional and religious/secular axes within a pan-national frame (as reflected in the Sivakasi 'files'). And to the extent that the vernacular, non-secular publics addressed by the calendar industry, the popular cinema and illustrated magazines did not coincide with the liberal, secular-modernist, English-educated elite, these culture industries paved the way for the emergence of what Arvind Rajagopal has called the 'split public' that would become instrumental in the resurgence of Hindu nationalism from the late 1980s onwards.[17]

Hindutva, neo-liberalism and the reconfiguration of 'culture'

In the late 1980s and early 1990s, neo-liberal economic reforms combined with increasingly powerful Hindu nationalist political organizations to transform the country politically, economically and culturally. Articulating with the erosion of the Congress-led Nehruvian regime following the undemocratic suppression of political opposition during Indira Gandhi's Emergency of 1975–7, these processes had significant consequences for the art of the bazaar and its retooling of religiosity. Market reforms provided opportunities for economic and social mobility that pushed erstwhile bazaar traders and industrialists into the arena of multinational collaborations and global business protocols;

they also enabled the entry of new players into the market through the continuing informal and semi-formal economies. Given that the vernacular trader-industrialists of the bazaar have been the primary constituency of India's Hindu nationalist parties, their ascendancy has further consolidated and naturalized the hegemony of the discourse and visual vocabulary of Hindutva – that is, the idioms of an aggressively majoritarian Hindu nationalism – over the space of national culture. Not surprisingly, these idioms have also been reconfigured by the changing economic and political environment.

For one, the speed, scale and style of business growth and social mobility meant that for many players in the new economy, inexpensive and reiterative forms like the calendar were no longer appropriate to the conduct of business, particularly as entrepreneurs from bazaar-style backgrounds entered into collaboration with multinationals (and multinationals in turn began to woo vernacular consumers). Though calendar art did not disappear, the devotional address of its printed images was no longer tied to the same extent with the maintenance of business networks. As part of the same process, the calendar printers of Sivakasi diversified or went up-market. For the overseas market, they began to print books and stationery, while for the domestic market they developed products that were more Hallmark than Puranic, more Disney and *manga* than *Amar Chitra Katha*.[18]

In the domain of popular religion, printed bazaar icons have been supplemented by new forms drawing on global visual and aural idioms as well as a range of new technologies: video, internet, cell phones, animatronics, IMAX, and the non-canonical sculptural materials of cement and fibreglass that enable the emergence of spectacular religious monuments and theme parks. This process is entirely consistent with the genealogies traced above. Just as the vernacular culture industries of the late-colonial period adopted the formal idioms of the colonizer to forge national and other identities, the post-liberalization Indian culture industries (particularly Bollywood) have reformulated Indianness as lying within a global marketplace of consumption and production.[19] However, while the colonial regime demarcated 'culture' – and with it the bazaar – as a category separate from the formal market, culture in the post-reform era is increasingly delinked from the social-cum-commercial ethos of the bazaar. Instead, following the metropolitan model of multiculturalism, visible, portable forms of cultural identity (religious rituals, festivals, myths, languages, dress, food and music) are separated into an arena of leisure and consumption cloistered from the increasingly homogeneous, secular and more selectively vernacular realm of work and economy.

Secondly, Hinduism's forms of visual expression have changed dramatically in the era of liberalization, indexing more than just the adoption of new technologies or the globalization of cultural identities. For instance, the Hindu Right's initial rallying point in the late 1980s, the Ramjanmabhoomi campaign (an ultimately successful effort to destroy the Babri mosque in Ayodhya, which Hindutva campaigners claimed had been built atop the birthplace of the god Ram), used calendar art idioms in its propaganda, but made significant changes to the iconography of the god Ram, depicting him as muscular and aggressive rather than in the more traditional style as benign and loving, with a smooth, almost flabby body.[20] The change spoke to the Hindutva project's violence, as well as to the ascendancy of a global (that is, Euro-American) aesthetic of the male body, but it also signalled a shift in the symbolic complex around masculinity and power. More specifically, this new iconography indexed a shift in the value attributed to muscularity and bodily strength. The new male figure no longer derived its power from a divine source, but from the work of his body. Bodily labour had earlier been denigrated in the symbolic terms of caste, which is why, even after the introduction of Western methods for depicting anatomy, there was resistance to rendering the gods as muscular. Arguably then, these violent images unwittingly enacted a reconfiguration of social power's symbolic basis in caste society – an acknowledgment of and response to the political assertions of the trade unions, and to the successful organization of lower-caste and Dalit (Untouchable) groups in the 1970s and 1980s.[21]

With the growing assertion of Dalit and Backward-caste political parties at the national level since the 1990s and the palpable threat this has posed to caste privilege, the stakes attached to such images have been raised yet again. A massive reterritorialization seems to be underway in this post-reform era, as gigantic malls, highways, temples, monumental icons and new spiritual complexes are constructed all over India. The identity-claims expressed through the shifting, mobile domain of circulating images have thus been reconverted into material claims on space and territory. As I have argued throughout, then, the social and political stakes of mass reproduction in India are not mapped on to bourgeois notions of high art, but rather on to the symbolic and territorial significations of caste and feudal privilege in the visual domain of modern religion. I have also tried to demonstrate that the culture industries are a moving target, lending themselves to different projects at different moments. The forms taken by the 'art of the bazaar', whether understood in reference to religion or high art, cannot be read off from any given ontology of particular media, technology of mass reproduction or global history of capitalism; indeed, part of the productivity of these images lies in the challenges they pose to the very terms in which we understand them.

Notes

1 C. A. Bayly, *Rulers, Townsmen and Bazaars: North Indian Society in the Age of British Expansion, 1770–1870* (Cambridge University Press, 1983); Rajat Kanta Ray, 'Introduction', in Rajat K. Ray (ed.), *Entrepreneurship and Industry in India 1800–1947* (New Delhi: Oxford University Press, 1992); Anand A. Yang, *Bazaar India: Markets, Society, and the Colonial State in Bihar* (Berkeley: University of California Press, 1999).

2 Theodor Adorno and Max Horkheimer, *The Dialectic of Enlightenment* (New York: Continuum, 1972); Theodor Adorno, 'Culture Industry Reconsidered', in J. M. Bernstein (ed.), *The Culture Industry: Selected Essays on Mass Culture* (London: Routledge, 1991, pp. 85–92); Walter Benjamin, 'The Work of Art in the Age of Mechanical Reproduction', in *Illuminations*, ed. Hannah Arendt, trans. Harry Zohn (New York, Schoken Books, 1969).

3 Ritu Birla, 'Capitalist Subjects in Transition', in Dipesh Chakrabarty, Rochona Majumdar and Andrew Sartori (eds.), *From the Colonial to the Postcolonial: India and Pakistan in Transition* (New Delhi: Oxford University Press, 2007).

4 On this aspect of 'porous legality' see Lawrence Liang, 'Porous Legalities and Avenues of Participation', in *Sarai Reader 05: Bare Acts* (New Delhi: Sarai/CSDS, 2005).

5 On the Muslim 'niche market', for instance, see Sandria B. Freitag, 'South Asian Ways of Seeing, Muslim Ways of Knowing: The Indian Muslim Niche Market in Posters', *Indian Economic & Social History Review* 44:3 (2007), pp. 297–331.

6 See Patricia Uberoi, 'Feminine Identity and National Ethos in Calendar Art', in Patricia Uberoi (ed.), *Freedom and Destiny: Gender, Family, and Popular Culture in India* (New Delhi: Oxford University Press, 2006), pp. 48–68.

7 The theology of icons and icon-worship in India is beyond the scope of this chapter; for a detailed discussion see Kajri Jain, *Gods in the Bazaar: The Economies of Indian Calendar Art* (Durham, NC: Duke University Press, 2007).

8 Dating from around 1300–1400 CE, the *Bhagavata Purana*, also known as the *Shrimad Bhagavata*, recounts the life of the Hindu god Krishna. It is the most recent and most popular of the *Puranas*, a collection of mythological stories written in the form of Sanskrit verses elucidating aspects of the *Vedas* to the laity.

9 Norbert Peabody, 'In Whose Turban Does the Lord Reside?: The Objectification of Charisma and the Fetishism of Objects in the Hindu Kingdom of Kota', *Comparative Studies in Society and History* 33:4 (1991), pp. 726–54. On Pushtimarg and its image-cult see also Amit Ambalal, *Krishna as Shrinathji: Rajasthani Paintings from Nathdwara*

(Ahmedabad: Mapin, 1987) and Tryna Lyons, *The Artists of Nathdwara: The Practice of Painting in Rajasthan* (Bloomington: Indiana University Press and Ahmedabad: Mapin, 2004).

10 Ambalal, *Krishna as Shrinathji*, pp. 85–90; interview with Ramchandra Paliwal (Parasram's grandson) and his father Kanhaiyalalji, Geeta Studio, Nathdwara, 1995.

11 See Christopher Pinney, *'Photos of the Gods': The Printed Image and Political Struggle in India* (London: Reaktion Books, 2004), p. 86, illus. 61.

12 On the 'messianic' aspect of the Nathdwara landscapes see *ibid*. While 'messianism' is the term used by Benedict Anderson to denote the sacral regimes preceding the modern nation-state, its Judaeo-Christian connotations need to be further interrogated in this context.

13 On Mother India and other mother goddesses such as Tamilttay (a symbol of Tamil linguistic nationalism) see Sumathi Ramaswamy, *The Goddess and the Nation: Mapping Mother India* (Durham, NC: Duke University Press, 2010).

14 Ashish Rajadhyaksha, 'The Phalke Era: Conflict of Traditional Form and New Technology', *Journal of Arts & Ideas* 14–15 (July–December 1987), pp. 47–78.

15 Geeta Kapur, 'Ravi Varma: Representational Dilemmas of a Nineteenth Century Indian Painter', in *When Was Modernism: Essays on Contemporary Cultural Practice in India* (New Delhi: Tulika, 2001), p. 147.

16 Offset printing is the most common mass-scale printing technology in use today. Here the matter to be printed is photographically transferred to a flat metal or plastic plate and then to a rubber-blanketed cylinder before being impressed on paper. Letterpress is an older technology, using smaller and less expensive machines. Here lead types and photographic 'blocks' are manually set in a tray, which is then inked and impressed on paper. The calendar industry's system cleverly uses economies of scale, as offset printing is only economical for runs of a thousand and above, while letterpress printing is only suited to runs of a few hundred.

17 Arvind Rajagopal, *Politics after Television* (Cambridge University Press, 2001).

18 *Amar Chitra Katha* is a mythological comic book series started in 1967, its style in turn influenced by the Tarzan and Phantom comics.

19 On 'Bollywood' as a phenomenon extending beyond the cinema to include a range of consumer products (websites, tapes, DVDs, ringtones, theatrical performances, festivals and so on) selling a particular version of Indianness, see Ashish Rajadhyaksha, 'The "Bollywoodization" of the Indian Cinema: Cultural Nationalism in a Global Arena', in Preben Kaarsholm (ed.), *City Flicks: Indian Cinema and the Urban Experience* (Calcutta: Seagull, 2004), pp. 113–39.

20 See Anuradha Kapur, 'Deity to Crusader: The Changing Iconography of Ram', in Gyanendra Pandey (ed.), *Hindus and Others* (New Delhi: Viking, 1993).

21 I make this argument in some detail through a series of images in 'Flexing the Canon', in *Gods in the Bazaar: The Economies of Indian Calendar Art* (Durham, NC: Duke University Press, 2007).

11

Urban theatre and the turn towards 'folk'

The theatre of the new cities

The culture of the great metropolises of nineteenth-century India, foremost amongst them the colonial harbour cities of Calcutta and Bombay, produced a new kind of theatre which played itself out on a stage meant to replicate real life, as it claimed to present real situations, real history and even real gods. It catered to the middle classes, themselves in a formational stage, and was clearly a configuration of parts that had heterogeneous origins. But to the progenitors of this new culture, playwrights, actor-managers and critics no less than audiences, operating under colonial rule in constant interaction with a dominant, still very foreign culture with which it was also essential to establish equivalences, it was of vital importance to stress the indigenous origins of this new theatre and the classical tradition to which it declared itself heir. And if Western orientalists were most often quoted as authorities as to what constituted this classical tradition, their views were adapted by Indians to suit increasingly nationalist purposes.

William Jones, the first high-standing civil servant to write at any length on such matters, in the preface to his translation of Kalidasa's fifth-century Sanskrit drama *Shakuntala* (1789), had also been the first to announce the sensational new discovery of the national drama of the Hindus to the Occident. 'Dramatic poetry must have been immemorially ancient in the Indian empire', he had speculated.

> The play of Sacontala must have been very popular when it was first represented; for the Indian empire was then in full vigour, and the national vanity must have been highly flattered by the magnificent introduction of those kings and heroes in whom the Hindus gloried;

the scenery must have been splendid and beautiful; and there is good reason to believe, that the court in Avanti was equal in brilliancy during the reign of Vikramaditya, to that of any monarch in any age or country.

Jones had also been the first to identify the genius of Kalidasa with that of Shakespeare, and while drawing up a list of the dramatist's available works, he had expressed immense regret 'that he has left only two dramatick poems, especially as the stories of his *Raghuvamsa* (a long narrative poem chronicling the history of the Raghu clan) would have supplied him with a number of excellent subjects'.[1]

Jones's deductions were to have manifold and far-reaching implications. First, Jones maintained that the Hindus had a national theatre, an Indian drama, which bore testimony to the glory of the old Indian empire, to whole genealogies of kings who had reigned of old, 'before the conquest of it by the Savages of the North'.[2] This drama was then related intimately to the collective national history of the Hindus. It had suffered a decline when the Muslims reached the subcontinent. Jones equated Hindu and Indian without second thought, though he was himself trained as a Persianist and it was his linguistic skills which had initially been seen as his special qualification for being sent to India. Second, Kalidasa was for Jones both the poet and chronicler of kings; also the representative of the people's national pride in their kings.

The comparison with Shakespeare served at once to elevate Kalidasa to national status, as well as provide key critical concepts in matters of playwriting and appreciation: that dramatic characterization be consistent, a coherent whole, as well as that it fulfil a moral purpose. If it was the historical grandeur of a thus concretized past which proved to be most significant, as with Shakespeare, the depiction of the 'meaner' characters of Sanskrit plays acquired a renewed significance. The intimate association between the national theatre of India and Shakespeare was a major driving force in the creation of urban literary theatre in the nineteenth century, as the histories of the period testify. After the first stiff translations and adaptations from Sanskrit and Shakespeare into the major print languages of the day, Indian drama as envisaged by the modernizers did indeed proceed to make creative use of the traditions thus canonized. For the need of the day, as felt by contemporary Indian patrons and theatre enthusiasts, was to establish links with a collective *present*. In addition to the historical and mythological plots which would come to dominate the stage in the last decades of the nineteenth century, more ostensibly contemporary themes could be addressed in social and later also political satire.

Theatre production developed so rapidly in Calcutta that in 1872 it became commercially viable to establish a 'national' theatre in the city. The process of creating modern drama in Bengali, as unfolding from the preoccupation with the classic, is best documented by a contemporary observer, Babu Kissory Chand Mittra, in a long article for the *Calcutta Review*.[3] Mittra had obviously witnessed the performance of Bengali translations from the Sanskrit in the private theatres where this new drama was first performed until at least the mid nineteenth century; he provides a vivid account of the successive productions. He is aware that this modern theatre was indebted to the West for its presentational mode, but he also stresses the affiliations with the Indian past: 'The age of Kalidasa opens a new era in the annals of the dramatic literature of the Hindus. He has been justly called the Shakespeare of India, and his marvellous knowledge of human nature in all its varied and profound phases is almost Shakespearian.' Yet, while reporting the opening of a public national theatre in Calcutta, he hopes that

> the modern Hindu theatre will, in the words of an intelligent critic, become to the spectators as it ought to be, not merely the pastime of an idle hour, but a place of study, a whetstone of the imagination and the sympathies, a revealer of secret springs of character and emotion, and the subtler beauties of our finest poetry. They would learn at the same time to appreciate the niceties and the difficulties of histrionic art; and by their knowledge be enabled to stimulate merit and rebuke defects of the careless, instead of encouraging (as audiences too often do at present) whatever is most false in conception and meretricious in style.[4]

Playwrights and theatre-goers had in fact responded to the needs of the day and explicitly political plays had already excited much public comment. After the publication of Dinabandhu Mitra's *Nildarpan* ('The Indigo-Planters Mirror'), in 1860 there had been a spate of plays which used *Darpan* in their titles which held up the mirror to expose, in one way or another, the exploitation practised by the British, whether as a class or as government servants, or simply in their capacity as white traders and planters. From 1875 onwards, there had been increasing agitation in official circles in Calcutta regarding the political tone of the plays printed and produced there. In 1876 the Dramatic Performances Bill was passed, prohibiting drama 'likely to excite feelings of disaffection to the Government established by law in British India' and promising penalty to all those participating in the performance, including the spectators, if a prohibited play continued to be staged. Though there was protest, and the critical-political theatre of the Presidency towns suffered a setback, drama continued to flourish.

There was an equally lively scene in the western part of the country. Poona, the old Peshwa capital, evolved a style more musical and histrionic, with entirely new scripts in Marathi, while Bombay had a somewhat different history. The hugely popular Parsi or Company theatre concocted a heady new commercial mix which drew liberally from Western drama and staging practices but equally from Indian narrative traditions and regional popular forms. Beginning with plays scripted in Gujarati, it soon switched almost entirely to productions in Hindustani, establishing itself not only in the city but as a presence on the subcontinent. The many touring companies that sprang up in response to the eager audience response toured the length and breadth of the country.

But in all the writing and thinking that accompanied this process, a third and vital source of the new configurations, the lively popular performance modes of the respective region, seldom found mention. They were regarded as vulgar, low and rustic. If at all they were invoked, it was in order to serve as reminders of all that was to be left behind and transcended.

The disapproval of popular theatre forms, rural or urban, and the elite attempt to marginalize them, did not mean that they disappeared. On the contrary, they flourished in towns and cities through the nineteenth until well into the twentieth century, and modern urban productions continued to borrow heavily from them, though without express acknowledgment. But however vital their mode of expression and whatever their entertainment value, in the early decades of the twentieth century it would have been hard to imagine that these rural and urban popular forms could ever come to be regarded as repositories of tradition.

It is this creative tension with popular forms, most of which eventually came to be subsumed under the umbrella term 'folk', that this chapter will explore as a window into the evolution of theatre in modern India. It will trace and chart the winding trajectory of folk forms, spanning a whole century of transmutations, from the first emergence and consolidation of the category 'folk' in the late nineteenth century to its transformation into the veritable storehouse of indigenous values and essences in the late twentieth. The attempt will be to trace broad patterns and shifts rather than undertake detailed analyses of plays and productions.

The discovery of 'folk' theatre

J. G. Herder in the late eighteenth century, and following him the European romantic poets through the first half of the nineteenth century, had seen the culture of the 'Volk' or people as mirroring the soul and epitomizing the spirit of the nation. Documenting and understanding folk culture amounted to tracing the past roots of a given culture. As Raymond Williams has pointed out, this practice often served to 'backdate' culture.[5] This backdating would remain a persistent tendency. Folklore as a field and as part and parcel of colonial anthropology, with its dynamic connection to Indian source material, cut a network of inroads into British India. A cluster of enthusiastic British scholar-administrators and missionaries embarked upon extensive research in the folklore of the region in which they were posted. This was an endeavour in which the Indian intelligentsia would soon begin to participate.

The towering presence in the field, for creative writing and for drama, was none other than Rabindranath Tagore (1861–1941). He wrote an essay seeking to draw the attention of the Bengali intelligentsia to the importance of folklore as early as 1895. As a modernist who was drawn to the culture of the people as an endlessly rich resource of poetry and philosophy, Tagore inspired and drew many to work in folklore. Dineshchandra Sen (1866–1936), one of the many thinkers and artists who clustered around Tagore, became a major presence in the field of folklore. Sen turned to 'high' and folk culture at the same time, writing the history of Bengali literature even as he collected the folk songs of the region, the one seeming to come into sharper relief when offset against the other. But it was Gurusaday Dutt (1882–1941), a scholar-administrator turned folk enthusiast, who was responsible for the significant theoretical and practical breakthrough in creating wider public awareness of the contemporary potential of folk forms. Dutt grew up in an East Bengal village, surrounded by the very forms in folk art, crafts, music and dance that he was to study and propagate later in life as an antidote to the ills of modern civilization. He was aware that much needed to be done in order to create an archive for folk forms. He organized the Rural Heritage Preservation Society of Bengal in 1932, with the express object of undertaking research and taking steps for the conservation and furtherance of the folk dances, songs and art of Bengal. He organized training camps for schoolteachers on folk dances and rural sports; he founded the All-India Folk Song and Dance Society in 1932 in Delhi and he published widely on folk art and dance; his last work, the *Folk Dances of Bengal,* was edited and published posthumously.

'Folk' is a relational category, as Roma Chatterjee has pointed out. It comes into use as against or in contrast with more elite formations.[6] By the 1930s, the 'classical' dances of India, most prominently Bharat Natyam and Kathakali, had begun to be codified and integrated in the nationalist genealogy of art. 'Folk' dance could now be offset against these classical forms, not only as feeding into them, but for Dutt and others, as being far more vital as the live expression of the people's spirit. The classicizing of tradition and the turn to the common 'folk' were in a sense interdependent processes.

By this time, a certain kind of theatrical performance was coming to be seen as belonging firmly in the realm of 'folk'. It included forms so vast and so varied, their performance styles often so fluid as to defy neat definitions, that there was no serious attempt to set up a comprehensive genealogy of these forms. Nor is it possible to do so in retrospect. What came to be seen as folk theatre ranged from storytelling by one or more narrators to elaborate performances by troupes of varying sizes, lasting several nights. Sometimes the term used for them was 'traditional', and they were categorized along with the forms now considered classical. However, there continued to be lines of distinction, though they were never formally defined. Classical was nearly always associated with the temple or royal court; its performative language was often so heavily coded as to need specialized knowledge to understand it. 'Folk' played itself out in larger arenas, such as fairs in villages and towns. It had larger audiences who were familiar with and quick to understand and respond to the given performance code, in its specific verbal and vocal, spatial and visual patterns.

The linguistic, cultural and religious diversity of these forms confined them to the regions in which they had evolved; many had first taken shape only in the eighteenth and nineteenth centuries. The elements they had in common were music, song and more often than not, dance. And they drew their narratives, at times elaborately, at other times sketchily, from mythology, legend, romance and current tales of social or political interest. Some ritual-religious plays could conceivably also fall under this heading, some of them relatively modern and also catering to mass audiences, such as the nineteenth-century Ramlila of Ramnagar, its performance stretching for a whole month on the banks of the Ganges at Benares. But generally, the performance context was one of entertainment alone. To cite just a few of the well-known forms: there was *Jatra* in Bengal, *Tamasha* in Maharashtra, *Yakshagana* in Konkan and Karnataka, *Burrakatha* in Andhra, *Nautanki* in Uttar Pradesh and Bihar, with variants in Haryana and Rajasthan. Realizing the immense vitality and potential of these forms, urban theatre practitioners would soon begin to use them to carry a new political and social message.

A people's theatre movement

Organizationally, the people's theatre movement of the 1940s grew out of the frame established by writers and intellectuals connected to the progressive writers' movement, which initially came together in England in the mid 1930s, when Mulk Raj Anand and S. Sajjad Zaheer, two of the founder-members of the Progressive Writers' Association of India (PWA) called the Association's first meeting in November 1935 in London.[7] The immediate forerunner for this act was the Conference of World Writers in Paris in June 1935, which led to the formation of the International Association of Writers for the Defence of Culture against Fascism. The PWA was part, then, of an international movement, which turned to local popular culture with explicitly social and political aims.

The PWA programme declared explicitly that the writer was first and foremost a socially and politically responsible member of his society. It asked the writer to take cognizance of the specific Indian situation, to participate in the struggle for political and economic emancipation, to take culture to the 'masses' and finally, to develop regional languages and literatures. The PWA of India opened branches in 1936 in Lahore, Delhi, Allahabad and Aligarh, and an All-India gathering of writers was organized in the same year in Lucknow. Out of this frame grew the Indian People's Theatre Association (IPTA), which held its first meeting in Bombay in 1943. The unifying forces, as the draft resolution of the

All India People's Theatre Conference, drawn up in May 1943 made clear, were anti-fascism and anti-imperialism.

As the First Bulletin of the Association, entitled *Historical Background* and issued in July 1943 specified, this theatre movement took up currents of renewal and reinvigoration which had already begun to manifest themselves in the arts, though it did so with a new agenda, that of social communication and commitment. There was a new emphasis on Indianness, a new enthusiasm for the culture of the people coupled with a fervent post-1942 patriotism which condemned alien rule in its entirety. There was close cooperation with trade unions and Kisan Sabhas (peasant associations). The organizers realized the importance of traditional folk forms for the purpose of direct communication with, as well as creative participation by, the people. New was the publicly proclaimed need to turn to folk forms if the people themselves were to be reached. IPTA branches sprang up all over India. If the original impulse had radiated from large metropolitan centres such as Calcutta and Bombay, it was now being taken up across the country.[8]

IPTA's Central Cultural Squad was formed in 1943; it attracted dancers, singers, musicians and theatre people. IPTA remained loosely organized, however, and it produced a heterogeneous corpus of plays and performances. Three strands can be distinguished in the theatre activity and vigorous experimentation of the period. The first strand consisted of traditional folk theatre forms which were remoulded for contemporary purposes. In Gujarat, Dina Gandhi, a Bombay member of IPTA, worked with *Bhavai*, the traditional dance-drama form of Gujarat, weaving a stronger narrative line into the music and dance, which had predominated until then. She combined a collection of *veshas,* the short narrative skits which comprised the form, with a topical content which was politically oriented. This was the first creation of a scripted play in this form. To the *rangla* or the narrator, Dina Gandhi added the female companion *rangli,* inaugurating thereby the participation of women in Bhavai. Mulk Raj Anand recalled the effect of this kind of remoulding in Andhra Pradesh, which attempted a similar recasting of the *Burrakatha,* a musical narrative enacted by three men:

> I have had occasion to see how the groups of the Indian People's Theatre Association in Andhra have rescued this form from the ignorant, who practised it as a formula and how, by composing new ballads with fresh social content, they have combined with the natural vigour of the old form a new urgency of conscience, without

> diminishing any of the gaiety and joy which is inherent in the
> form itself. I shall never forget how three peasant boys held an
> audience of thirty thousand citizens of Guntur spell-bound up to
> the early hours of the morning with their recitation of the *Ballad of
> Venkataramani*, the bad boy who ate his mother's ears.[9]

Thus there was also the use of the art of the various itinerant folk performers for new purposes, such as the singing mendicant, 'dressed in strange garb, wandering through the land, fortune telling, selling medicines, diagnosing diseases and generally exhorting people to be good and charitable'. The IPTA retained the old style, but changed the content: 'Instead of diagnosing bodily ills, the mendicants now diagnose social diseases.'[10]

In spite of all the rhetoric to the contrary, the urban approach to folk theatre was inevitably patronizing. But the difference from the older folklore archivist was also evident in that the intentions of IPTA activists went beyond mere conservation or revival. And behind the sometimes heavy-handed attempt to remould the contents while leaving the form more or less intact, the patent concern was to reach out to and communicate with rural audiences rather than remould for urban use alone. In addition, there was the unsentimental awareness that folk forms also needed to change with the times.

The second strand of IPTA's agenda could be said to consist of plays which made no explicit attempt to use folk forms, but focused instead on the widest possible outreach. The most famous attempt to use urban theatre for new purposes was *Nabanna* (New Harvest) by Bijon Bhattacharya, a production performed by members of the Bengal wing of IPTA in Calcutta, as well as in the surrounding district towns. The central character, Pradhan Samaddar, was a peasant caught in the devastating Bengal famine of 1942–3, a man-made catastrophe created by the British, who used the harvest of those years to feed the troops fighting in Europe and Japan.

The third and final form generated by IPTA could be viewed almost as the beginning of a modern 'epic' theatre in India. In the ballet *Immortal India*, the narrator was a worker, but there was no effort to establish or unfold the personal history of his character, strive for psychological verisimilitude or create suspense. And it was he who held together the episodes of the play rather than the narrative itself:

> The latest ballad by the troupe gives a picture of India from the
> earliest times to the present days, touching momentous events that

form the landmarks in the cultural history of India. It starts from the early worship of the Himalayas and passes through past impacts of culture to modern times.

A worker sleeping in a factory through exhaustion falls asleep, but is kicked and awakened. He grumbles but relates to his lamenting associates the wonderful dream he had of poverty, and of exploitation and hoarding, but also with the darker side; he saw the people happy and contented. In his dream the people finally unite together in the determination to become free, to mould their own destiny.[11]

IPTA was a largely spontaneous movement of groups, held together by a common cause, and one with a utopian bent; not surprisingly, perhaps, its activities were to disintegrate after the passing of the British Raj.

With the coming of Independence, the burden of organizing cultural activity became a state concern. The last All-India Conference of IPTA was held in Delhi in 1957–8. It recognized the leading role that the Sangeet Natak Akademi (National Academy for Music, Dance and Drama) was supposed to play in the future and offered cooperation and help to it. However, though the activities which were inaugurated by the newly created institutions in the capital of the new nation-state set the tone, it is important to bear in mind that, in fact, there was much that happened outside the institutional sphere, and one could almost say, in spite of it. Though the newly formed central institutions would come to exercise much directive power, many a writer and theatre person was to continue to invoke IPTA as the formative influence for future work.

The state as patron

The Sangeet Natak Akademi was established in Delhi in 1953 as the national academy for the performing arts. The primary object of the Akademi, as seen initially, was to provide patronage and conserve tradition. This made for radically different dimensions in cultural activity. Firstly, artists and performers came under the direct patronage of the state, exercised by the cultural bureaucracy set up exclusively for the purpose in the capital of the new nation. Secondly, the regional was subsumed firmly within the national. Folk forms were thus seen as rural derivations and deviations of the all-encompassing Sanskritic tradition from which they had emanated and into which they could, under the new dispensation, flow again. It is in this connection, as against the former IPTA aims and attitude, that 'folk' practice was now to be researched and conserved. Thus, Article XII of the 'Powers and Functions of the Sangeet Natak Akademi' saw it to be the task of the institution to revive, preserve and encourage folk forms. However, theatre was specially privileged. It was extracted from within the larger frame of music and dance and given its own institutional base. The idea of establishing a national drama institute had long been in the air, Nehru himself being one of the instigators of it.[12] A steering committee of forty distinguished scholars, educationists, journalists and theatre persons from all over the country met for a seminar in March 1958. It was V. Raghavan's paper on 'Sanskrit Drama and Performance' which elicited the most discussion, for Sanskrit drama had become a matter of state concern, not only as the fountainhead of all past forms but also as providing orientation for all further development. By and large the preoccupation with finding an indigenous theatrical idiom showed little concern for reaching out to the 'masses'. The focus now was much more on integrating the artistic forms of the people into mainstream national culture.

A year later, in 1959, the Sangeet Natak Akademi established the National School of Drama (NSD) in Delhi. Under the able directorship of Ebrahim Alkazi, who came into office in 1962, the School established a reputation for disciplined training in methods of acting, directing and stagecraft. NSD was an attempt at the centralization of theatre with all its advantages and drawbacks. The advantages in these early years of Independence were clear: NSD provided and sustained a forum for the mediation of the many regional forms and plays, and it offered an institutional base for visiting directors. Though Alkazi was to remain cautious in his approach to traditional theatre, folk forms were to exercise much fascination in the decade to come. In a statement typical of the early 1960s, Mohan Upreti was to urge that an effort be made to discover and understand folk theatre and with that the 'the entire heritage' of the country, in the interest of creating a truly national theatre, taking from 'the theatre of the West only that which is of real value to us'.[13]

However, the search for the theatrical idioms for these new times was by no means confined to the discussions spawned by the Sangeet Natak Akademi alone. The impulses generated by IPTA had been taken up by writers and playwrights working in very different regional cultures. *Lok natak*, folk theatre, had indeed become a part of the theatre vocabulary and could inspire a play such as Dharamvir Bharati's *Andha yug* (1954); the 'masses' could also occupy the stage, as in Habib Tanvir's *Agra Bazar* (produced first in 1954 and published in 1979) and later in Tanvir's production of Sanskrit plays, such as *Mitti ki gari*, a Hindi adaptation of Shudraka's *Mricchakatikam* ('The Little Claycart', 1958). In Karnataka, Adya Rangacharya had written a new kind of play in Kannada, *Suno Janmayjaya* ('Listen, Janamejaya', 1960), the novelty of which he himself placed in a nationwide context. Here, he was combining conventions from the Sanskrit play and the folk play in Kannada, but in doing so, he stressed that the combination should not be seen as only being indigenous. It was also embedded in the live contact with and knowledge of European stagecraft.

The theatre of these early decades after Independence was propelled by a belief, not yet totally shattered, in the idea of India, while groping for a culture which could be defined as Indian. It made the 1960s and 1970s the most productive age in playwriting, to which Delhi in general, and the National School of Drama and the Sangeet Natak Akademi in particular, could and did indeed, provide a forum. The playwrights and theatre practitioners present at the Akademi's 1971 'Roundtable on the Contemporary Relevance of Folk Theatre' were already part of a process which was reconfiguring playwriting; the search for a new idiom was seen as a genuine need and the recourse to folk forms a spontaneous, un-engineered act. In the decade to come, many of them would go on to become key figures in the national theatre scene. The major question at this stage was about the 'use' of folk forms for the urban stage, use in the sense of deployment as well as utility; no one seemed to be asking about the use of urban forms for rural audiences.

Directors and playwrights turn to folk

The 1960s and 1970s brought a new political consciousness on many fronts, as it became increasingly clear that the benefits of Independence were restricted to a small urban and rural middle class. Unemployment, food shortages and high inflation led to countrywide unrest. The failure on the part of the government to implement land reforms led to armed agrarian resistance in several parts of the country. Even groups conventionally regarded as quietist, such as engineers, teachers, doctors and civil servants, were led to protest. The enemy was not so easy to identify on the national level as it had been in the heyday of IPTA, and it was not so easy to forge solidarity; yet there was an upsurge in theatre activity during this time. A great many experiments were made with folk forms which were used in a variety of ways. Of those that used folk devices, and many of the best known did so, there were four broad types.

First, there were plays in which both form and narrative were taken from the folk repertoire and moulded thematically. The most typical and popular example of this would be Shanta Gandhi's version of the traditional *Bhavai vesha*, *Jasma Odan* (1982). Shanta Gandhi had been a member of IPTA in its heyday and had vast experience with *Bhavai veshas*. In her new production of the play, the thematic emphasis was no longer on Jasma's heroic act of committing *sati*, with which the play culminated. Instead, the 'personality of Jasma as a working woman' was given importance. At the end of the play, when Jasma was asked to come back to heaven, from which she had fallen to earth, she 'prefers to stay and struggle here on earth, rather than go back to a heaven, which is still too unchanging for her'.[14] The other characters underwent similar changes of dimension.

Second, there were plays which were outside the folk repertoire but were adopted into folk forms. This included Sanskrit and canonical Western plays. An example of the former was Habib Tanvir's 1958 adaptation of Shudraka's *Mricchakatikam* into the *Chhatisgarhi nacha* style. Tanvir emphasized the political uprising in the play, which had formed one of the subplots in the original Sanskrit play. Tanvir would go on to become the pre-eminent practitioner of folk theatre, founding a company of folk actors who would retain the connection to, and continue to perform for, rural audiences.

Of the plays which adapted Western plays into traditional folk forms, B. V. Karanth's 1980 production of Shakespeare's '*Macbeth*' as *Barnam Vana* for the NSD Repertory in the Kannada dance-drama form *Yakshagana* was the most spectacular attempt in the direction of such creative transformations. Karanth's influence as propagator of folk theatre, aesthetically and thematically, was far-reaching and enduring. He succeeded Alkazi as director of the NSD and created an infrastructure for exposure to folk forms in the training imparted by the school; but most of all, he set up models based on his own brilliant work.

Third, the folk form was left more or less intact but was used primarily to carry an explicitly political message. In Bengal, Utpal Dutt had used the traditional *Jatra* most consistently for this purpose. In Hindi, Sarveshwardayal Saxena's *Bakri* 'Goat' (1974), is the most characteristic and successful example of this kind of theatre. Saxena used the *nautanki* structure to satirize and expose political hypocrisy and corruption, and show how they increased before elections; the goat symbolized a decrepit Gandhianism. The play was produced most often by the street theatre group, Jan Natya Manch, an active presence on the Delhi theatre scene.

Whereas all of the three above-mentioned types of plays attempted to keep the original folk form intact, the fourth and largest group was composed of playwrights who borrowed elements from different regional folk forms in order to widen the dramatic technique and presentation of their plays. Here a kind of spontaneous formal synthesis was attempted, whereby the playwright presented his individual compositional formula, which remained unique to his play. The best-known examples are Dharmvir Bharati's *Andha Yug*, Vijay Tendulkar's *Ghasiram Kotwal* and Girish Karnad's *Hayavadan*. These plays have become classics of modern Indian theatre and a great deal of critical literature has sprung up around them. For our purposes here, a bare mention of their relationship to 'folk' theatre conventions will have to suffice. Dharmavir Bharati's *Andha Yug* ('The Blind Age') written in 1954, inspired by the post-war situation in Europe, treated the epic battle at the centre of the *Mahabharata* in a contemporary moral and political frame. Bharati used an epic narrator to establish links in time and space, for the narrative is partly episodic in character, and features chorus-like characters to comment on the action, especially the horror and devastation of war conveyed in free verse rhythms. The play's dramatic devices draw upon classical Greek theatre, possibly mediated through the poetic plays of T. S. Eliot and Indian folk theatre devices such as the epic narrator.

Tendulkar's *Ghasiram Kotwal* (1972) treated a semi-historical theme from a contemporary socio-political perspective, using the devices offered by the folk theatre of Maharashtra. It is the story of Ghasiram, a Brahman who rises to power under the ruthless Nana Phadnavis, only to end up a pawn in the political machinations of the callous Nana, who does away with him once he has fulfilled his function. The play relentlessly exposes the unscrupulous and self-serving Brahmanical orthodoxy which ruled in Pune. The folk frame turned out to be more than a convenience, for in spite of its historical matter, it allowed Tendulkar to insist on the universality and agelessness of the social phenomenon presented in the play. However, Tendulkar was more of a

Fig. 11.1 Chorus of Brahmans in *Ghasiram Kotwal*, directed by Jabbar Patel for Theatre Academy Pune 1989.

historian than he himself laid claim to, for he recorded and thus anticipated, even if only inadvertently, the future course of Maratha history, and the passing of the feudal into the capitalist mode, by twice showing an Englishman as an observer of the scene. The folk framework allowed, then, for vaster historical and political generalization than would have been possible in a more realistic mode of play composition and presentation. (Fig. 11.1)

Girish Karnad's *Hayavadan* (1970) used elements of the *Kannada Yaksagana* and a frame-story, as in traditional Sanskrit narrative compendia. The central narrative, itself almost like a folk tale with its focus on the solution of a dilemma posed as a riddle, also came from a Sanskrit collections of tales. The Sanskrit tale had been given a psychological emphasis in an interpretation by Heinrich Zimmer and in a short story by Thomas Mann; it was now further transformed by Karnad. The frame-story presents the theme symbolically, in the shape of a mythologized half-horse-half-man who seeks to become whole. The actual drama of the situation, between two men and a woman, is played out in the main narrative. This subtly wrought configuration of Sanskrit tale, modern psychology and the layering of meaning offered by masks and half curtain, as well as the interpretations made possible by

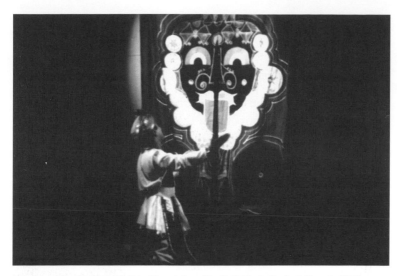

Fig. 11.2 The Goddess Kali in *Hayavadan*, dir. B. V. Karanth, for Mitravindi Theatre, Mysore, 1989.

narration and song, makes for an extremely complex treatment of the story, which operates on several levels: myth, dream, fantasy and a tale within a tale. Karnad was to go on to make several highly successful experiments in this direction in the next decades (Fig. 11.2).

The richness of folk forms still prevailing in most parts of India, and as produced on a modern urban stage seeking new means to articulate the new, made for a heady mix. The plays produced in this period have become staples of the modern theatrical canon. They are performed again and again in state and national theatre festivals.

This particular process, however, seemed to have run its course as the political and cultural environment changed once again in the last years of the first term of Indira Gandhi's prime ministership. The years of the internal emergency declared by her government, which lasted from 1975 to 1977, put an abrupt end to freedom of expression; there was also a marked change in playwriting and production. A process similar to that which set in after the Dramatic Performances Bill was passed in 1876 seems to have taken place again. The tide was to turn thereafter. The coalition government that came to power in the general election which followed also included a large segment belonging to the right wing. This turn towards the right would remain in place even when Indira Gandhi's Congress Party came back to power. Contemporary observers noted this turn and what it meant for the politics of theatre: folk theatre would henceforth become decorative and conformist.

The theatre of roots

The theatre-makers of the late 1960s and 1970s had seen their experiments with folk forms as rooted in the concerns of the urban middle class and thus rooted in a modern sensibility. At the rate that the medium was now being exploited, folk theatre was being increasingly drained as a source of vitality for the urban stage. The festivals celebrating Indian culture, of which a good part was covered by folk performers, sponsored by the Indian government and launched from the early 1980s, cemented this very tendency. The first Festival of India, held in Britain, took place in 1982, to be followed by similar festivals in the USA, France and the Soviet Union. Folk art and folk performances were here being used as export items which safely backdated culture rather than contemporizing it. The international cultural festivals propagating the image of a timeless India had begun to draw upon the arts in a way which once again sought to bring together the classical and the folk as static categories.

What, then, were the uses to which folk theatre, would be put during this period? Several schemes were under way. The Sangeet Natak Akademi stepped forward to take the lead and instituted the Scheme of Assistance to Young Theatre Workers. The Akademi would support the efforts of directors engaged in exploring and developing a theatre idiom indigenous in character, inspired by the traditional folk theatres of the country. The activity at the regional or zonal level would flow into a grand show in Delhi. The number of zonal centres grew to five in 1985–6; two more were to be added in 1986–7. They were to have a powerful impact on the cultural landscape of the country. The modern, seen as messy, conflict-ridden, culturally hybrid, socially restless and possibly politically unstable, would necessarily be sidelined as far as official patronage was concerned.

In order to propagate these ideas and surely also in a genuine attempt to thrash out the issues related to this massive new surge of interest in traditional theatre, the Sangeet Natak Alademi organized a National Seminar on Perspectives of Contemporary Indian Theatre in December 1984. The views presented could be broadly said to be those of three main groups. The first group was composed of those, and it included the organizers, who were enthusiastic and more or less uncritical proponents of indigenous theatre, which they now no longer called 'folk' theatre or even 'traditional'. The new nomenclature employed for it was 'theatre of roots' and classical Sanskrit theatre was at its unapologetic origin. Western or realist theatre, and the theatre productions in India which followed in its footsteps, were seen as the polar opposites of the theatre of roots. The second group, by far the smallest, consisted of those who proceeded more cautiously, who weighed the pros and cons of turning in such an absolutist manner in the direction of an unquestioned tradition. Finally, there was the group which regarded this attitude to the indigenous as anti-modernist and as politically questionable.

It was important, as playwright and critic G. P. Deshpande emphasized in an article written several years later, to recognize the plurality of the linguistic and theatrical idioms currently at work in the subcontinent: 'Each mode is uniquely important. There are several, equally valid and legitimate Indian theatres.'[15] To reduce these to three – folk, Sanskrit and modern Western – was to take unproductive short cuts, and most of all, it was to deny the very history of modern Indian theatre. Thus, experiments with folk theatre, borrowings, adaptations and transformations of folk forms for the urban stage, would only be meaningful, if, as theatre director and scholar Anuradha Kapur put it, there was 'not a disenchantment with today's world but a stake in it'.[16] It would also mean creating space for the folk performers themselves, who needed more than ever to find ways to survive in the modern world. Urban audiences could take occasional delight in performances by folk performers. However, once folk forms were considered socially acceptable, they were literally taken over by urban performers, who then proceeded to represent folk traditions not only to each other, but most of all, on the international arena; there was little or no space left for the traditional performer. Was form to be saved at the expense of the performer? There could then be nothing inherently good or bad about borrowing, changing or remaking a given form. As we have seen, modern urban practitioners of 'folk' theatre can do what they do for diametrically opposed political and aesthetic purposes. They can question established truths, they can subvert them, they can open up new avenues and while doing so they can address both elite and popular audiences. But such folk enthusiasts can equally be backward-looking and conformist, and serve to freeze and exclude, while also setting out to address elite or popular audiences.

Beyond 'folk'

The beginning of the twenty-first century has seen the dissolution of these dichotomies, though the rhetoric about traditional and modern, classical and folk continues to flourish. But in the meantime, small towns and regions once regarded as entirely peripheral, such as the northeast, have responded with their own peculiar mix of plays and presentation, formally and thematically, as the annual theatre festivals orchestrated by the National School of Drama in January of each year in Delhi have shown. Cable TV and the cell phone have brought about vast changes in communication. One such change is that there is remarkably little self-consciousness about the provenance of any given play, whether from West or East; whether ancient or modern; whether the Sanskrit dramatists Bhasa and Bhavabhuti, Tamil Sangam poetry, or modern Indian playwrights such as Vijay Tendulkar, Dharmavir Bharati or Mahesh Elkunchawar; whether Euripides, Shakespeare, Ibsen, Chekhov, Pinter, Ionesco, Giradoux or Sartre; whether featuring the lives of the great men and women of the past or everyday issues in the lives of ordinary men and women today. What is noteworthy about these productions is their experimental nature, the emphasis often being on the visual as opposed to the verbal alone, on music, movement and dance, rather than on clearly worked out plots. Most noteworthy of all, the sophistication of these explorations and experiments is by no means confined to the big metropolitan centres. They can turn up equally in bigger and smaller towns, and even in relatively remote regions. It seems to depend almost entirely on the talent at hand, the performance traditions of the region, the dynamism of a given group of individuals and their exposure to new impulses – theatrical, social and political. In the strife-torn regions far from the political centre, such narrative content engages the social and political violence of everyday life. The activities of the National School of Drama in the past decades have contributed in no small measure to this dynamism by producing talented and motivated alumni, by holding workshops and outreach activities in schools and universities.

Today, there is a much wider notion of the classic, which includes more than it excludes. And there is no question of straight recourse to any given script. The classics have indeed become a shared idiom to a large extent; their storylines and the words only need to be suggested. The modern theatre today is experimental at many levels. Traditionalists could see it as a turning back to long familiar conventions of dance-drama, though it seems much more fruitful to regard this experimentation as a new licence to explore, to risk, to disregard and rearrange the accepted hierarchies of classic, folk and popular, and to allow audiences to encroach into performance space. The advantage of working with known vocabularies, be they classical dance, the stock characters of the Bombay film of any given period, or long familiar tales from the *Mahabharata*, known not only from childhood retellings and from TV serials, but as danced and enacted in *Chhau* from Purulia and Pandavani from Chattisgarh, is to be able to recharge them with new energy, new relevance. Today, there is more freedom to work across these divides, to take stock characters and play with them, to address issues such as communalism. This experimentation with scripts holds true for work across the metropolitan and small-town divide, engaging insistently with social and political issues, leading often to the scripting of new plays. International festivals may continue to present folk theatre but in the meantime the folk seem to have moved on.

Notes

1 William Jones, *The Works of William Jones. With the Life of the Author by Lord Teignmouth. In Thirteen Volumes*, vol. IX (New Delhi: Agam Prakashan, 1979), pp. 367, 370 and 369.

2 *Ibid.*

3 Kissory Chand Mittra, 'The Modern Hindu Drama', *The Calcutta Review* 57 (1873), pp. 245–73.

4 *Ibid.*, pp. 249, 273.

5 Raymond Williams, *Keywords* (London: Flamingo, 1983), pp. 136–7.

6 Roma Chatterjee, 'The Category of Folk', in Veena Das (ed.), *The Oxford Companion to Sociology and Social Anthropology* (New Delhi: Oxford University Press, 2003), pp. 567–97.

7 The following account is based on Sudhi Pradhan (ed.) *Marxist Cultural Movement in India. Chronicles and Documents (1936–47)*, vol. I (Calcutta: Mrs Santi Pradhan, 1979).

8 Bombay, Bengal, Punjab, Delhi, Uttar Pradesh, Malabar, Mysore, Mangalore, Hyderabad, Andhra, Central Provinces and Berar, and Madras were represented on the All-India Committee, and there were Organizing Provincial Committees in Bengal, Punjab, Delhi, Uttar Pradesh, Malabar, Mysore, Andhra and Madras. *Ibid.*, pp. 132–4.

9 Mulk Raj Anand, *The Indian Theatre* (London: Dobson, 1951), p. 29.

10 *Ibid.*, p. 31.

11 Pradhan, *Marxist Cultural Movement*, p. 386.

12 In the account that follows, I am indebted to Reeta Sondhi for her article 'History' in the National School of Drama Special Issue of *Enact*, January–March 1981.

13 Mohan Upreti, 'Foundations of a National Theatre', *Indian Express,* 6 May 1962.

14 From the unpaginated programme brochure.

15 G. P. Deshpande, 'History, Politics and the Modern Playwright', *Theatre India* (May 1999), p. 93.

16 Kapur, Anuradha, 'Notions of the Authentic', *Journal of Arts and Ideas* (20/21 March 1991), p. 12.

12

Aesthetics and politics in popular cinema

Recent discussions of cinema and national identity in the 'third world' context have tended, by and large, to cluster around the concept of a 'third cinema'. Here the focus is on recovering or reinventing local aesthetic and narrative traditions against the homogenizing impulses of Hollywood in its domination over markets and normative standards. One of the hallmarks of third-cinema theory has been its firmly unchauvinist approach to the 'national'. In its references to wider international aesthetic practices third cinema asserts but also problematizes the boundaries between nation and other. In the process, it also explores the ways in which the suppressed internal others of the nation, whether of class, sub- or counter-nationality, ethnic group or gender, can find a voice.

A substantial lacuna in this project has been any sustained understanding of the domestic commercial cinema in the 'third world'. This is important because in countries such as India the commercial film has, since the dawn of the 'talkies', successfully marginalized Hollywood's weight in the domestic market. This is not to claim that it has functioned within an entirely self-referential autarchy. The Indian popular cinema stylistically integrated aspects of the world 'standard', and has also been influential in certain foreign markets. But it constitutes something like a 'nation-space' against the dominant norms of Hollywood, and so ironically fulfils aspects of the role which the avant-garde third cinema proclaims as its own.

Clearly, the difference in verbal, as opposed to narrative and cinematic, language cannot be the major explanation for this autonomy, for other national cinemas have succumbed to the rule of the Hollywood film. Instead, it is in the peculiarities of the Indian commercial film as an entertainment form that we may find the explanation for its ascendancy over the home market. In the Indian case the theoretical silence around the specificity of the commercial cinema is due not so much to third-cinema discourse but to the discourses and institutions of art cinema in the 1950s, which refused to seriously consider the commercial film as a focus of critical discussion.

Indian commercial cinema has exerted an international presence in areas of the world where there has been substantial Indian migration, such as in East Africa, Mauritius, the Middle East and South East Asia, but also in a significant swathe of Northern Africa. On one hand, this cinema has often been regarded by the local intelligentsia and film industry in as resentful and suspicious a way as the Hollywood cinema in Europe. On the other hand there are instances when the Bombay film's penetration of certain markets is not viewed as a threat. The popularity of the Hindi cinema in the former Soviet Union is a case in point. Such phenomena make one think of a certain arc of narrative form separate from, if overlapping at points, with the larger hegemony exercised by Hollywood. The diegetic world of this cinema is primarily governed by the logic of kinship relations, and its plot driven by family conflict. The system of dramaturgy is a melodramatic one, displaying the characteristic ensemble of Manichaeism, bipolarity, the privileging of the moral over the psychological and the deployment of coincidence in plot structures. And the relationship between narrative, performance sequence and action spectacle is loosely structured in the fashion of a cinema of attractions.[1] In addition to these features, the system of narration incorporates Hollywood codes of continuity editing in a fitful, unsystematic fashion, relies heavily on visual forms such as the tableau and inducts cultural codes of looking of a more archaic sort.

At issue, then, is how traditions of identity, aesthetic form and cultural address are deployed for a politics of creative adaptation and interrogation of social transformation in a colonial and post-colonial world. To examine this process, I will take examples primarily from the Bombay cinema, but will also refer to films from other regional film cultures in the period from the 1930s through to the first decade after independence was won, in 1947.

In exploring these issues, I want to analyse the various types of cultural adaptation involved without losing sight of certain larger political frames. For the problem of Indian popular cinema lies not only at the interface between the local and the global in the constitution of a politics of cultural difference, but must also be seen in terms of the internal hierarchies that are involved in the constitution of a national culture. The formation of a national market is a crucial aspect of these multi-layered relations of domination and subordination. Bombay became ascendant in the home market only in the 1950s. Earlier, Pune in Maharashtra and Calcutta in Bengal were important centres of film production, catering to the Marathi- and Bengali-speaking 'regional' audience as well as to the Hindi audience, the largest linguistic market in the country. While these regional markets continued to exist, Bombay became the main focus of national film production. This ascendancy was curtailed by the emergence of important industries in Tamil Nadu, Andhra Pradesh and Kerala, producing films in Tamil, Telugu and Malayalam. From the 1980s these centres produced as many and often more films than Bombay.[2] There has been a certain equivalence in the narrative form of these cinemas, but each region contributed its distinct features to the commercial film. In the Tamil and Telugu cases the cinema also has a strong linkage with the politics of regional and ethnic identity. In recent times the cinemas of the south have also made a greater effort to diversify their products than the Bombay industry.

The domestic hegemony achieved by the commercial cinema has had ambivalent implications for the social and political constitution of its spectator. All of India's cinemas were involved in constructing a certain abstraction of national identity; by national identity I mean here not only the pan-Indian one, but also regional constructions of national identity. This process of abstraction suppresses other identities, either through stereotyping or through absence. The Bombay cinema has a special position here, because it positions other national/ethnic/socio-religious identities in stereotypical ways under an overarching north Indian, majoritarian Hindu identity. The stereotypes of the 'southerner' (or 'Madrasi', a term which dismissively collapses the entire southern region), the Bengali, the Parsi, the Muslim, the Sikh and the Christian occupy the subordinate positions in this universe. Bombay crystallized as the key centre for the production of national fictions just at the moment that the new state came into existence, so its construction of the national narrative carries a particular force.

Indian popular cinema genres and discourses of transformation

Arguments for cultural transformation have defined Indian cinema from very early on in its history. The key theme in these discussions was the social and cultural implications of film genres. In the initial phase, Indian cinema was dominated by the mythological film, which used Hindu myths as their major resource. Very soon, other genres developed, including the social, which addressed issues of modern-day life, the costume film or the 'historical', the spectacular stunt or action-dominated film, and the devotional film, which recounted tales of popular saintly figures who criticized religious orthodoxy and hierarchy.

The film industry understood the devotional and social films, with their emphasis on social criticism, to be the favoured genres of the middle class. A running theme in social films was the need to maintain indigenous identities against the fascination with Western cultural behaviour. While this has become part of the armature of films dedicated to contemporary society down to the present day, a substantial vein of social films was dedicated to making a critique of Indian society and setting up an agenda for change. Recent discussions of Tamil film of the 1930s and 1940s argue that there were repressive and disciplinary elements to the agenda for a modern social grounding of film narratives. The agenda here was for the social film to displace the mythological and the superstitious and irrational culture it founded. In the 1930s, a host of studios emerged who employed scriptwriters to develop reformist narrative, and an alliance emerged in these decades between literature and cinema, with films adapting important novels as their source material.

However, by the 1950s, the industry reformulated genre and audience appeal. After the collapse of the major studios, Bombay Talkies, Prabhat, New Theatres, the new, speculative climate of the industry encouraged an eye for the quick profit and therefore the drive for a larger audience. This encouraged the induction of the sensational attractions of action, spectacle and dance into the social film, a process explained by industry observers as a lure for the mass audience. Industry observers clearly believed the genre label to be quite superficial, and, indeed, there is something inflationary about a large number of films released in the 1950s being called 'socials'. The label of the 'social' film perhaps gave the cinematic entertainment that cobbled sensational attractions together in a slapdash way a certain legitimacy. However, arguably, the mass audiences earlier conceived of as being attracted only by sensation and themes of moral affirmation were now being solicited by an omnibus form which also included a rationalist discourse as part of its 'attractions'.

The reasons for the restructuring of the 'social' film are complex. Artists associated with the Indian People's Theatre Association (IPTA), which had ties with the Communist Party of India, had started working in the film industry from the 1940s. Amongst these were the actor Balraj Sahni, the director Bimal Roy and the script-writer K. A. Abbas. The latter was involved in *Awara* ('The Vagabond', dir. Raj Kapoor, 1951), a film representative of the new drive to combine a social reform perspective with ornate spectacle. However, the years after Independence were characterized by a broader ideological investment in discourses of social justice associated with the image of the new state and the personality of its first prime minister, Jawaharlal Nehru.

We will observe a replaying of these discussions in more recent paradigms of the Indian popular cinema. One of my arguments will be that, rather than oppose different types of audience disposition on the ground of genre and subject matter, one needs to explore how forms of address may set up certain similar problems in constituting spectatorial subjectivity, whether this is played out within the domain of the mythological or the social. Especially important here is an agenda of moving beyond the deployment in Indian cinema of a rhetoric of traditional morality and identity to a focus on how cinematic address, the way spectators are positioned in terms of vision, auditory address and narrative intelligibility, may complicate and rework the overt terms of narrative coherence.

In terms of narrative form, the popular imperative engages in a series of transactions, both with methods and idioms marked as traditional or culturally distinctive as well as those defined as modern. Here, I would like to consider the location of the spectator's position around three issues: (1) how is the ideology of the traditional constituted in cinematic narration; (2) what are the function of cinematic techniques of subjectivity in the construction of narrative space; (3) how does the overall attraction-based, presentational rather than re-presentational field of the popular film system address the spectator. These questions amount to an engagement with a history of the methods of film narration, film-style, as well as a history of the relationship between screen practices and audience reception.

Iconicity, frontality and the tableau frame

The question of mode of address concerns how objects and figures are located with respect to the look of the spectator within the spatial and temporal coordinates of scenic construction. Central here is the aesthetics of frontality and iconicity noted for Indian films in certain phases and genres by Ashish Rajadhyaksha[3] and Geeta Kapur.[4] The iconic mode is not used by these writers in its precise semiotic sense, to identify a relation of resemblance, but to identify a meaningful condensation of image. The term has been used to situate the articulation of the mythic within painting, theatre and cinema, and could be conceived of as cultural work which seeks to bind a multiply layered dynamic into a unitary image. In Geeta Kapur's definition the iconic is 'an image into which symbolic meanings converge and in which moreover they achieve stasis'.[5] This concept of the iconic needs to be grounded within a conception of *mise-en-scene*, and it is here that the question of frontal address surfaces. At one level frontality would mean placing the camera at a 180° plane to the figures and objects constitutive of filmic space. These may display attributes of direct address, as in the look of characters into the camera, but a frontal, direct address is relayed in other ways, as in the way the knowledge of the spectator is drawn upon in constructing the scene, through the stylized performance, ritual motifs and auditory address that arise from a host of Indian aesthetic and performance traditions.[6] This position of knowledge is not one which relays the spectator through a hermeneutic play, the enigma of what is to come, but through existing paradigms of narrative knowledge, although these may be subject to reworking. In genres such as the mythological film, the narrative process assumes audience knowledge of the narrative totality it refers to, so that a fragmentary, episodic structure can be deployed. The film song displays this function of 'frontal' address across genres, reaching over and beyond the space of the scene, locking the spectator into a direct auditory relay.

Frontal planes in cinematic composition are used to relay this work of iconic condensation and also to group characters and objects in the space of the tableau. In the course of this argument, I will show that the temporality of the tableau can be deployed cinematically, its shape setting the geometrical terms of the temporal construction of the scene as it extends over a series of shots. The tableau also displays interruptive, interventionist functions in the flow of scenic construction. In my argument, the function of this spatial figure is to encode a socially and communally defined address to the spectator.

The reconstruction of the icon

I will illustrate the dynamic employment of the frontal, iconic mode and of tableau framing in a sequence from Mehboob Khan's saga of peasant life, *Mother India* (1957). This segment presents, and then upsets, a pair of relatively stable iconic instances. The mother-in-law, Sundar Chachi, is centred through a number of tableau shots taken from different angles to highlight her authority in the village just after she has staged a spectacular wedding for her son. This representation of Sundar Chachi takes place in the courtyard of her house. The other instance is of the newly wedded daughter-in-law, Radha, shown inside the house, as she massages her husband's feet. It is a classic image of the devout Hindu wife.

The two instances are destabilized because of the information that the wedding has forced Sundar Chachi to mortgage the family land. The information diminishes her standing, causing her to leave the gathering and enter her house. Simultaneously, it also undermines Radha's iconic placement as submissive, devout wife. As the larger space of the scene, the actual relationship between the inside and the outside, remains unspecified, the relationship is suggested when Radha, hearing the conversation, looks up and away towards off-screen left. The likelihood of this positioning is further strengthened when Sundar Chachi enters the house, and, looking in the direction of off-screen right, confesses that she has indeed mortgaged her land (Figs. 12.1 and 12.2). There is the use here of a Hollywood eyeline match, where the direction of looks cast is consistent with the convention that characters separated into successive shots face each other in space. The women are narrativized out of their static, iconic position through narrative processes of knowledge circulation and character movement, and by the deployment of Hollywood codes of off-screen sound and eyeline match.

The mobilization of Radha out of one convention of iconic representation is completed when she assumes maternal functions extending beyond her family, and over the domain of village community and nation. In turn, she becomes the focal point of community norms, and her gaze acquires punitive functions in delineating the limits of permissible action. A process of the narrative dispersal of one iconic figure is thus finally brought to a close by instituting a new iconic figure to ground subjectivity. Central here is a particular reinscription in the cinema of a discourse of the image and the look in indigenous conventions.

Fig. 12.1 Iconic transfer in *Mother India*, dir. Mehboob Khan, 1957.

Fig. 12.2 Still from *Mother India*, dir. Mehboob Khan, 1957.

Darsana

I refer here to *darsana*, the power exercised by the authoritative image in Hindu religious culture. In this practice, the devotee is permitted to behold the image of the deity, and is privileged and benefited by this permission, in contrast to a concept of looking that assigns power to the beholder by reducing the image to an object of the look.[7] *Darsana* has a wider purchase, being invoked in discourses of social and political authority as well. In a certain rendering of the category of *darsana* as an authoritarian form, social status derives from the degree of access which social groups and individuals have to a central icon of authority, whether of kingship, divine authority or the extended patriarchal family and its representatives. This eligibility then rests on very hierarchically coded criteria of social rank. There is a task here of identifying how the *darsanic* locates characters and is responded to by them within cinematic narration. One hypothesis would be that an authoritative figure, symbol or space (temple, landlord's house, court of law), is mobilized to order the place of characters within a scene and over the time of the narrative. But if such a diegetic instance is located, it is not necessary that characters abide by the positions they are assigned by it, nor that filmic techniques subordinate the spectator to the sway of *darsanic* authority.

Indeed, to assume otherwise could lead to the conclusion that the cinema is merely the vehicle of an archaic way of inscribing power on the visual field. Instead of seeing the discourse of *darsana* framing cinematic narration, we need to think of *darsana* as being enframed and reconstructed by it. Here, the localized deployment of filmic techniques in the micro-narration of a scene – editing, shot-distance and angle, camera movement, lighting, sound elements – alert us to how characters and spectators are being cinematically positioned in relation to the *darsanic*. The *darsanic* is not static, and generates new sources of authority from it, and in ways not entirely comprehensible in terms of established conventions. Thus, while much of the moral authority of Radha in *Mother India* derives from the preservation of her chastity, and thereby the assertion of her devotion to her absent husband, this patriarchal rhetoric is condensed along with other features, including a solidarity with other women, and an insistence on the maintenance of community norms.

The cinematic process of iconic reconstruction may in fact deploy and subordinate modern methods of subject construction modelled on Hollywood narration. By convention, the continuity system, and especially its point of view editing, is associated with the drives and perception of individuated characters. However, it is quite common in popular Hindi cinema to observe the yoking of such views to the bearer of *darsanic* authority. But the emergence of such enshrining views is tied to the dynamic of reconstruction, and is mobilized to the end of a patriarchal transformation.

To suggest the transactional basis on which popular cinema inducts those methods of narration marked as modern, I will cite an example from *Devdas* (Bimal Roy, 1955), a film based on a well-known Bengali novel by Sarat Chandra Chatterjee. Devdas, the son of a powerful landed family, is prohibited from marrying the girl he desires, Parvati, because of status differences. He is a classic renouncer figure of the type favoured in Indian storytelling, a figure who is unable or refuses to conform to the demands of society, and wastes away in the contemplation of that which he could never gain. I want to refer to a scene which employs continuity conventions to the highly 'traditional' end of deifying the male as object of desire. The sequence deals with Devdas's visit to Parvati's house, and indicates a strategy of narration whereby Parvati's point of view is used to underline the desirability and the authority exercised by Devdas's image. In this sequence, Parvati returns to her house to find her grandmother and mother discussing Devdas's arrival from the city, and the fact that he has not yet called upon them. Devdas, off-screen, calls from outside the door. From this moment, Parvati's auditory and visual attention dominates the narration. Before we can see Devdas entering the house, we withdraw with Parvati to her room upstairs, and listen to the conversation taking place below along with her. Devdas announces that he will go to see Parvati himself. In anticipation of Devdas's arrival Parvati hurriedly starts lighting a diya, devotional lamp, and the melody of a kirtan, a traditional devotional song expressing Radha's longing for Krishna, is played. We hear the sound of Devdas's footfalls on the stairs, and Parvati's anxiety to light the lamp before Devdas enters her room is caught by a suspenseful intercutting between her lighting of the lamp and shots of the empty doorway. The door-frame in this sequence suggests the shrine in which the divine idol is housed. Devdas's entry is shown in a highly deifying way; first his feet are shown in the doorway, followed by a cut to the lighted lamp. Finally his face is revealed. There follows a cut to Parvati, suggesting that this is the order through which she has seen Devdas's arrival. As she looks at him, conch shells, traditional accompaniment to the act of worship, are sounded. The future husband as deity, object of the worshipful gaze, is established by the narration's deployment of Parvati's point of view. Her lighting of the devotional lamp and the extra-diegetic sound of the kirtan and conch shells underline the devotional nature of the woman's relationship to the male image (Figs. 12.3 and 12.4).

Fig. 12.3 *Devdas*, dir. Bimal Roy, 1955: Devdas.

Fig. 12.4 *Devdas*, dir. Bimal Roy, 1955: Parvati.

Here we can see how the cinema reinscribes *darsana*, locating it within a new figure, that of the emergent if ultimately ineffectual patriarchal figure of Devdas, who cannot be assimilated to the reigning feudal order. And it does this in such a way as to both enable and limit the conditions of subjectivity. For, while the film mobilizes point of view codes to represent the subjectivity of the woman, this is done in such a way as to constrain the field of her look by focusing the beloved within a discourse of divinity. This setting of certain limiting coordinates for the woman's look also significantly institutes a division between the incipient formation of a new domesticity and the wider external world: Devdas's enshrinement in the doorway converts the public space beyond the door into his domain, restricting the woman to domestic space.

Tableau, time and subjectivity

A more complicated version of this pattern of looking is observable in Guru Dutt's *Pyasa* (Craving, 1957), a film which refers to but in many ways controverts the narrative of Devdas. In the pertinent scene, the poet-hero Vijay refers to the prostitute, Gulab, as his wife in order to protect her from a policeman who is pursuing her. The prostitute is unaccustomed to such a respectful address, especially one suggestive of intimate ties to a man she loves, and is thrown into a sensual haze. Vijay ascends a stairway to the terrace of a building where he will pass the night. Gulab sees a troupe of devotional folk-singers, performing a Vaishnavite song, 'Aaj sajan mohe ang laga lo' (Take me in your arms today, O beloved) and follows Vijay up the stairs. The scene is structured by Gulab's desire for Vijay, expressed in the song, and these relations of desire are simultaneously relations of distance, as the woman follows, looks at and almost touches the man she loves (who is entirely unaware of all this) but finally withdraws and flees as she believes herself unworthy of him.

The relation between devotional voice, devotee and object of devotion determines the space of this scene, providing the coordinates for the extension and constraining of space. The relationship between characters is not one of the iconic frontality of traditional worship. The desired one is not framed in this way, for continuity codes dominate the scenic construction. Even in the scene I have cited from *Devdas*, continuity codes construct space and it is a shot–reverse shot relationship which defines the ultimate moment of looking. The spectator is offered a rather complicated position. If we think of the male icon as a 'traditional' marker of authority and desire which anchors the view of the female devotee, as in *Devdas*, then the scene conforms to the logic of *darsana*.

However, within the *bhakti* or devotional tradition, while the female devotee's energy is channelled directly into the worship of the deity, without the mediation of the priest, the Lord still remains a remote figure. The devotional act thus becomes a somewhat excessive one, concentrating greater attention on the devotee than the devotional object, and this is only underlined in the maintenance of Gulab's distance from Vijay, and his failure to see her. This rather complicated

Fig. 12.5 *Pyasa*, dir. Guru Dutt, 1957. 'Keertan and female subjectivity'.

structure of spectatorship needs to be framed within the address relayed by the devotional voice. The space assigned this voice emerges from Gulab's look off-screen, but it remains autonomous, never sharing her space. The narration periodically cuts back to the singer, and cutting and camera movement closely follow the rhythms of the song. The soundtrack maintains a steady pitch to the singing, irrespective of how far the action moves away from the singer's (imaginary) space, and places it thereby at an extra-diegetic location (Figs. 12.5, 12.6, and 12.7).[8] The relatively stable articulation of these three points in the narrative construction – devotional voice, desiring woman and her object – effects a dynamic, temporal deployment to the essentially spatial category of the tableau. The result for the spectator is neither the subordination of subjectivity to *darsanic* authority, whose circuit is left incomplete by withholding Vijay's authorizing *darsanic* look, nor the unmediated identification with the desiring woman, but a framing of these elements of scenic composition within the narrative community solicited by the kirtan. Here the audience is invited to participate in a culturally familiar idiom that reinvents itself by providing a supportive frame to the cultivation of new techniques for the representation of an individuated feminine subjectivity. However, the supportive frame of narrative community, while inducting a new view through the deployment of modern perceptual codes, cannot, it would seem, abjure the anchorage given by the authoritative object. In this instance, where the *darsanic* circuit is not completed, the woman ultimately lies outside

Fig. 12.6 Still from *Pyasa*, dir. Guru Dutt, 1957.

Fig. 12.7 Still from *Pyasa*, dir. Guru Dutt, 1957.

the sanction provided by the man returning her look. Later, however, the *darsanic* circuit is completed, instituting a new paternalist form in the conclusion of the film. Gulab's view enshrines Vijay, as travelling point of view shots punctuate her running down towards the beloved as he appears at the doorway of her dwelling, and his return of her look acknowledges her eligibility to reside within the orbit of his gaze.

How the cinema deploys these discourses of visual and auditory authority, how it hierarchizes them into its levels of narration is the issue at stake: who authorizes a view, locates a figure in narrative space, who speaks, who sees, who listens. Where these relations are organized to highlight the compact between the narrating instance and the spectator's attention, the place of the third look of the character is subordinated to the spectator's knowledge that it is s/he who looks and listens.

However, while these community-grounded and socially coded modes of direct address constitute a fundamental aspect of cinematic narration for the popular cinema, the character-driven codes of subjectivity and narration associated with Hollywood may stand quite independently of such an address, inducting another set of subjectivities or storytelling conventions into the architecture of filmic narrative. *Andaz* ('Style', dir. Mehboob Khan, 1949) drew upon Hollywood narrative conventions in order to highlight the enigmatic dimensions of its female character's desires, and especially the conventions of hallucinations and dream to define her in terms of an ambivalent psychology and a transgressive if involuntary sexuality. Such conventions were drawn upon to be contained and disavowed. A nationalist modernizing imperative had to symbolically contain those ideologically fraught aspects of modernity that derived from transformations in the social position and subjectivity of women. The result was a fascinatingly perverse and incoherent text, one whose ideological drives are complicated by the subjectivities it draws upon.

I would suggest that these examples indicate that for the popular Indian cinema the categories of public and private, and of feudal and modern scopic regimes may not adequately comprehend the subjectivity offered the spectator, and that this would in turn have implications for the culture of citizenship. The rupturing of an integral, self-referential narrative space via direct address suggests a circuit of imaginary communication, indeed, a making of audience into imaginary community. The authorizing voice of narrative community is not fixed, however. While speech may be pre-interpreted in the sense that characters do not speak in the register of everyday, naturalist conversation, but are vehicles of existing language systems, cinematic narration subjects these to a reconstitution which enables an inventive, dynamic address to contemporary issues. As I have suggested, the solicitation of the cinema audience into a familiar community of meaning via direct address may afford a certain movement, an outlining of new forms of

subjectivity on to the grid of the culturally recognizable. We have seen
how this works in terms of a transgressive rendering of romance. An
overt political address, bearing directly on questions of citizenship and
state legitimacy, also emerges in new languages of direct address. The
development of a new linguistic nationalist community in the direct
address of the Dravida Munnetra Kazhagam-influenced Tamil cinema
would be an obvious example.[9] In fact, Indian popular cinema has,
throughout its history, deployed such modes of address to constitute
imaginary political communities, around issues of social reform and
nationalist mobilization. Here, direct address may argue for change on
somewhat different grounds than the protocols of narrative continuity,
realism and individual characterization.

Community authorization then rests alongside, and complicates
'feudal' and 'modern' ways of organizing narrative. Song sequences
deployed from a host of musical traditions have often worked in this
way, and in cases such as the one I have cited from *Pyasa*, have assumed
the role of a narrational authority external to the main story. This is
enacted by a source other than any of the fictional characters, and
sometimes in a space separated out from theirs. In this sense the narrational song can be identified with the properties of extra-diegetic music.
They both inhabit a location outside the fiction and shape a cultural
space for the representation of characters. We are both inside and
outside the story, tied at one moment to the seamless flow of a charac-
ter-based narration from within, in the next attuned to a culturally
familiar stance from without.

Not only does this narrating instance function to outline new types
of subjectivity that in a sense emerge from within the community
of meaning; it may be deployed to offer a critical view on narrative
development. In *Awara* ('Vagabond', dir. Raj Kapoor, 1951), the judge,
Raghunath, expels his wife, Leela, on suspicion of bearing another
man's child. The event is framed through a song critically invoking
the mythical King Rama's expulsion of his wife Seeta, and performed by
a troupe located separately from the main action. The critical stance
offered by the song renders the iconic figure of the judge as an oppressive one, subjecting the *darsanic* to censure.

The comic, deriving from earlier theatrical traditions of the *vidushak*
(jester), also left his mark as one of the staple figures of the commercial
cinema. Here he sometimes plays the role of a narrator external to the
main narrative and is often engaged in a relationship of direct address

to the audience. There is a certain didacticism involved in his functions, but this is a didacticism gone wrong, relaying authoritarian discourses voiced elsewhere through a figure entirely lacking the status and integrity carried by a *darsanic* rendering of such discourses. For example, in *Andaz*, V. H. Desai, as the charlatan and free-loading Professor Dharmadas Devdas Trivedi or DDT (the assigning of a Brahmin name to the comic sends up the pretensions and parasitical features of upper-caste status claims), is a spokesman and even a narrative agent of what he claims to be authentic indigenous attitudes to marriage. Such attitudes are similar to those voiced by the film's patriarchal figure and his delegates, but when the comic is made their vehicle they are subjected to a lampooning idiom. In a more commonplace function, it is the very absurdity of the comic figure, quite obviously opposed to the larger-than-life attraction of the hero, which invites a less flattering point of identification for the audience, and thereby a certain narratorial distance towards the story. Further, in the very superfluousness of his functions, we could say that the comic was the spokesman within the story for a different order of storytelling, one which celebrates the disaggregative relationship to narrative and, indeed, makes coherent meaning within the world of the narrative a problematic agenda.

This would imply that, instead of only looking to the overall work of ideology that 'officially' organizes the text, perhaps one should also attend to the fissiparous qualities of cinematic form to focus on the importance of non-continuity in evaluating the narrative worlds offered the spectator. In terms of sensory experience, non-continuity would suggest a characteristic modern culture of distraction, where the spectator's world is governed by a multiplicity of focuses and not by a carefully calibrated, goal-oriented channelling of her investment in the narrative process. At issue here is the subjectivity arising from the development of this particular type of cinematic modernity.

The political terms of spectatorial subjectivity

The terms of cinematic narration I have sketched here are rather different from the notions of spectatorship which have emerged from that model of the successful commodity cinema, Hollywood. Historians and theoreticians of the American cinema have underlined the importance of continuity editing in binding or suturing the spectator into the space of the fiction. The undercutting of direct address and the binding of the spectator into a hermetic universe onscreen heightens the individual psychic address and sidelines the space of the auditorium as a social and collective viewing space.

The mixed address of the Hindi cinema, along with the spaces which open up within the commercial film, the song and dance sequences and comic skits, might suggest a rather different relationship of reception. Something rather more complicated than the idea of a cinema of attractions is happening here. For the direct address of popular Indian cinema, while inviting immersion in fragmentary ocular sensation and exhibitionist performance in the manner of an attraction-based rather than narratively integrative form, does more than this by founding elaborate scenic construction. The address, whether voiced directly by characters or relayed through song ensures a mediated relationship to processes of identification. At one level, this form of spectatorial subjectivity can deny the atomizing modernity associated with the construction of individuation and a privatized sphere for the couple. The comedian, for example, often disrupts a scenic construction that verges on an intimate moment or kiss, and thereby brings the couple back within the purview of a public view, but one which entirely lacks the disciplinary drives of an authoritarian gaze. Instead, the intervention could be said to draw the couple away from a hermetic space and back into a more expansive communitas. On the other hand, this non-atomistic form of spectatorship may also be harnessed to cultivate an aesthetic of the private. This constitutes a narration of desire in which the relationship between zones of intimacy and socio-political arrangements need not follow a model of opposition and separation of public and private experience. As I have suggested, narrative communities, both relayed and produced afresh by the cinema, may provide sanction to privatized storytelling codes such as character point of view.

One needs to think this through in terms of the relationship between socially symbolic narrative forms and their political resonances. I would suggest that fictional processes parallel, interrogate and question the authoritative functions communities have exercised under the colonial and post-colonial Indian states. While espousing the standard repertoire of democratic principles – civil liberties, universal suffrage – the nationalist movement also mobilized people in terms of community appeals, and this inevitably left its stamp on state and civil institutions after Independence. Governments have regarded the rights of minority groups over their civil and familial laws, such as those of the Muslim community, as an area to be regarded with caution, apprehending that arguments for universal codes would take on an oppressive dimension. This has often meant the state shoring up the most retrograde patriarchal community authority in the field of women's rights to property and maintenance.[10] And the historical backwardness of ritually lower groups in the Hindu hierarchy – lower castes, and those outside the caste hierarchy – have given rise to state policies of affirmative legislation on their behalf. The assertion of the rights of such groups in government service and educational institutions has generated multi-community strategies in larger political formations, as well as distinct political parties catering to particular swathes of the socially deprived. The category of community has thus become central, even when contesting oppressive community practices. In this paradigm, rather than entirely vacate the discourse of community in favour of that of the individual citizen, other dissenting traditions of community need to be mobilized to develop a consensus for change.[11]

In terms of how this broader frame impinges on cultural practices, I would suggest that rather than regard the pre-modern or the traditional merely as a repressive construction engaged in by the state and ruling elites we need to see it as a source of creativity, where traditions are reinvented in accord with the dynamics of social and political transformation. In this context, I would like to draw attention to how the cinema deploys traditions such as *darsana* to enable the redefinition of collective rather than individual identity. As I have pointed out, *bhakti* constituted a form of worship which sought to circumvent the traditional mediation of the divine by the priest. As represented in saintly devotional figures of low-caste origin, the *bhakt* or devotee was dedicated to the worship of the deity through popular language rather than sacred texts monopolized by a priestly class. The establishment of direct links between worshipper and the sacred thus subverted ritual hierarchies and afforded a new sense of self. The devotional genre of the 1930s and 1940s is a case in point: critiquing brahmanical orthodoxy, films such as *Sant Tukaram* (Fatehlal and Damle, Marathi, 1937), have the reformist saint of the seventeenth century invoking the deity to provide an alternative vision of social conditions and political self-determination for the character/spectator. In a key sequence of the film, the saint, Tukaram, is involved in expounding a discourse of duty to the Maratha king Shivaji, and this extends into a more general address, as the film frames Tukaram in relation to other segments of the general public who have assembled in the shrine of Tukaram's deity, Pandurang. Tukaram's discourse of duty is designed to persuade Shivaji not to abjure his kingly role for a life of devotion, and it would appear to have conservative dimensions, fixing people to the roles they are assigned. But Tukaram's message emphasizes that all will find their path to the divine, and the film then goes on to replay this message of ultimate, transcendent equality in terms of an earthly political equivalent. Shivaji's enemies, taking advantage of his absorption in the religious dialogue, descend on the shrine, and at this point Tukaram appeals to Pandurang to save his devotee. Cuts from Tukaram to Pandurang ultimately culminate in a series of phantom images of Shivaji being released from the deity and coming to repose in the assembled public; wherever the invaders look, they see Shivaji, but when they grasp the figure, he turns into a startled member of the public. This dissemination of kingship amongst the public, an image of popular sovereignty that undermines political hierarchy, is rendered through a transfer of looks: the spectator looks at the saint, who beseeches the deity, who then looks back, releasing images of the king which transform the identity of characters and spectators. In this instance the transfer is affected via a cinematic materialization of the miraculous. But redefinitions of subjecthood through image practices are more widely observable across genres. Indeed, one may observe a plurality of cinematically constructed *darsanic* motifs within a film, setting up a conflicting political force field of images and image-constituencies.

Notes

1 The term comes from Tom Gunning, 'The Cinema of Attraction: Early Film, Its Spectator and the Avant-garde', *Wide Angle* 8:3–4 (1986), pp. 63–70.

2 For the standard account, E. Barnouw and S. Krishnaswamy, *Indian Film* (London and New York: Oxford University Press, 1980).

3 Ashish Rajadhyaksha, 'The Phalke Era: Conflict of Traditional Form and Modern Technology', *Journal of Arts and Ideas* 14–15 (1987), pp. 47–78, reprinted in T. Niranjana *et al.*, *Interrogating Modernity: Culture and Colonialism in India* (Calcutta: Seagull Books, 1993), pp. 47–82.

4 Geeta Kapur, 'Mythic Material in Indian Cinema', *Journal of Arts and Ideas* 14–15 (1987), pp. 79–107, reprinted as 'Revelation and Doubt: *Sant Tukaram* and *Devi*', in Niranjana *et al.*, *Interrogating Modernity*, pp. 19–46.

5 *Ibid.*, p. 23.

6 Kapur defines the formal category of frontality as arising from

> the word, the image, the design, the performative act ... This means, for example,
> flat, diagrammatic and simply contoured figures (as in Kalighat *pat* painting) ...
> It means, in dramatic terms, the repetition of motifs within ritual 'play', as in
> the *lila*; it means a space deliberately evacuated to foreground actor-image
> performance, as in the *tamasha*. Frontality is also established in an adaptation
> of traditional acting conventions to the proscenium stage, as when stylized
> audience address is mounted on an elaborate *mise-en-scène*, as in Parsi theatre.
>
> *Ibid.*, p. 20.

7 For *darsana*, see Lawrence A. Babb, 'Glancing: Visual Interaction in Hinduism',
Journal of Anthropological Research 37:4 (1981), pp. 387–401; Diana Eck, *Seeing the Divine
Image in India* (Chambersburg, PA: Anima Books, 1981).

8 I owe this observation to Jim Cook.

9 See M. S. S. Pandian, 'Parashakthi: the Life and Times of a DMK Film', in Ravi
Vasudevan (ed.), *Making Meaning in Indian Cinema* (New Delhi: Oxford University Press,
2000).

10 For an outline of the complexity of these issues, see Nivedita Menon, 'State/Gender/
Community: Citizenship in Contemporary India', *Economic and Political Weekly*, 31 January
1998, PE3–PE10.

11 Sudipta Kaviraj, 'Democracy and Development in India', in Amiya Bagchi (ed.),
Democracy and Development (London: St Martin's Press, 1995), and 'Dilemmas of
Democratic Development in India', in Adrian Leftwich (ed.), *Democracy and Development:
Theory and Practice* (Oxford: Polity Press, 1996); Veena Das, 'Communities as Political
Actors: the Question of Cultural Rights', in *Critical Events* (New Delhi: Oxford University
Press, 1996).

13

Musical genres and national identity

In the film *Shankarabharnam* (Telugu, 1979), a drama about a south Indian classical singer and a young prostitute's devotion to him, there is a scene which epitomizes the way 'classical' music and 'film' music came to be opposed to each other in post-colonial south India. The larger theme of the film, the backdrop against which its events take place, is the destruction of south Indian, or Karnatic, classical music at the hands of charlatan gurus and hypocritical concert organizers, and through the steady encroachment of Westernized musical tastes. In this particular scene, the hero, Shankara Sastri, is fast asleep one night in his house when he is suddenly awakened by the strains of electric guitars being played Western-style. He opens his door to find a band of ruffians mocking his devotion to Karnatic music. 'Our music is an ocean', they sneer, parodying what is often said about Karnatic music to invoke its depth and complexity. Shankara Sastri challenges them to a musical contest. The ruffians sing their song, and Shankara Sastri proceeds, to their utter astonishment, to convert it into the syllables used to sing Karnatic music and sing it back to them. Then, improvising a short piece of Karnatic music, he challenges them to reproduce it, leaving them completely at a loss. Shankara Sastri scolds them: 'While so many foreigners recognize the greatness of Indian music, how can you mock it? It is like making fun of your own mother.' To make his point, apparently too important to be uttered merely in Telugu, he switches into English: 'Music is divine, whether it is Indian or Western.'

This scene thematizes the relationship between classical music and film music in India, an opposition that is usually framed as a battle between 'high' and 'low' culture. With Shankara Sastri's English statement, the contest is transposed; it is no longer a battle between Indian music and Western music, but between classical music (that which is 'divine, whether Indian or Western') and its assumed profane opposite, popular music. At the time of its release in 1979, *Shankarabharnam* was a tremendous hit in the south Indian states of Andhra Pradesh and Tamil Nadu; it is said to have popularized Karnatic classical music among people who had never listened to it before. Ironically, however, the voice of Shankara Sastri – a subject of much controversy during the making of the film – was, in the end, provided not by a classical Karnatic vocalist, but by the famous film singer S. P. Balasubramaniam. It seems that at the time *Shankarabharnam* was made it was not acceptable to have a classical voice provided by a classical singer; instead, the voice had to be translated into the medium of film music, with its own distinct vocal aesthetic.

Music has been an integral part of Indian cinema since sound films were first produced in 1931. Interspersed with the filmic narrative, song sequences relate to the plot and characterization in a film in multiple ways but also move beyond them. The music circulates independently of the films, and was until the 1980s the only form of popular music in India produced, distributed and consumed on a mass scale.[1] The film music world and the classical music world in India have always been deeply intertwined, musically, socially and economically, with musicians and composers crossing between them in multiple ways. Since 'film music' emerged as a distinct category in the 1940s, however, the two genres became progressively separated in ideological and aesthetic terms, a legacy which both the content and the making of the film *Shankarabharnam* clearly demonstrate. How did this distinction come about?

The creation of classical and film music as two distinct and ideologically opposed genres has much to do with the dynamics of Indian nationalism. In *The Nation and Its Fragments*, Partha Chatterjee has argued that Indian nationalism operated by dividing the world of social institutions into two distinct realms, the inner, or spiritual, realm of a supposedly pristine, uncolonized Indian culture, exemplified by its 'classical' arts, its religion, its families and women, and the outer, or material, realm, the realm of economics, technology and politics, in which India mixed with and had to emulate the West.[2] The realms had to be kept strictly separate, since the legitimacy of the inner realm, indeed, its very existence, depended on its non-contamination by the outer realm. One of the ways this distinction was made real and brought into being in south India was through music. It was not simply that music was relegated to the inner realm, but that classical music could occupy the inner realm precisely because another category, film music, came to occupy the outer realm, the realm in which things Indian mixed with the West, in which music was impure because it mixed with money and technology.

Focusing mainly on south India, this chapter will discuss the discourses that emerged around classical and film music in the 1940s, 1950s and 1960s, considering the importance of both of these genres, with their competing notions of authenticity, to the consolidation of Indian national identity. In some imaginings, classical music was seen as an authentically Indian realm, while film music came to be seen and heard as hybrid, illegitimate and imitative of the West. In other imaginings, classical music was seen as outdated and overly conservative, while film music was valued positively as a kind of music that could keep pace with and represent India as a modern nation. The first part of this chapter briefly examines how, out of diverse existing traditions, a genre called Karnatic classical music was established through the standardization of repertoire and concert format, and dissemination on All India Radio. The second part of the chapter examines the place that film music came to occupy within this hierarchized musical field. It addresses debates surrounding the emergence of film music as an independent category of music, as well as the new kinds of performers, personae and sounds it introduced. More broadly, this chapter is concerned with the ways public discourse about music became a means for debating other issues: modernity, the definition of 'art' and 'music', and the status of national culture.

Making music classical

Towards the end of the nineteenth century, when older temple- and court-based forms of patronage ceased to be viable in the late colonial economy of south India, musicians moved in large numbers to the colonial city of Madras (now Chennai). There, music organizations, concert halls and music academies were established by an upper-caste, largely Brahmin elite interested in what they called the 'revival' of Karnatic music and its transformation into the classical music of south India. This 'revival' consisted in large part of selecting particular sounds, performance conventions and repertoire from different existing musical traditions, including the *pallavi* tradition, which was practised in courtly contexts, and the *periya* and *cinna melam* traditions, which were practised by hereditary musicians and dancers in primarily ritual contexts.[3] In the early decades of the twentieth century, the emerging urban middle class in Madras became the primary sponsors of musical concerts through their participation in *sabhas*, neighbourhood organizations that raised money through donations and ticket sales to pay for the presentation of musical concerts. In controlling the musical institutions of the city, this elite influenced how classical music came to be defined, and how its place in modern India came to be imagined. The Madras Music Academy, established in 1928, served as an institution that would define the standards for the teaching and performance of classical music.[4]

What came to be known as Karnatic music was a genre of music based on the principles of *raga* and *tala*, with particular instrumentation and conventions of presentation. *Ragas* are melodic material, somewhere between a scale and a tune in their specificity, which provide a guide for making a melody, either in composition or in improvisation; compositions are thus set in a particular *raga*. *Talas* are repeating time cycles within which a composition or improvisation can be set. In concert, a solo voice or instrument imitating vocal sound and style (common instruments are the violin, flute and veena) would be accompanied by percussion, most often provided by a double-headed drum called mridangam. Short compositions, words set to a melody in a particular *raga* and a particular *tala* cycle which could be elaborated on and improvised upon at length in performance, became the basis of the musical tradition.

As the concert, rather than the royal court or the temple, became the predominant forum for hearing Karnatic music, certain hierarchies emerged. While improvisation was still a prized element of the music, it was subordinated to composition, and certain composers were ranked over others as being more classically oriented. In the eighteenth and nineteenth centuries, musicians composed lyrics in praise of their human patrons, as well as lyrics in devotion to particular Hindu deities. In the first few decades of the twentieth century, however, the works of a group of three composers were selected as the canonical repertoire. All three composed solely devotional lyrics. This meant a shift from compositions tied to the context of their performance towards compositions that stood free of such social contexts and instead were perceived to

have their origins in a kind of timeless devotion to God. The canoniza-
tion of these composers functioned ideologically to mark Karnatic
music off as a realm apart from history, politics and money.[5]

Under the influence of the Madras Music Academy, melody, and particularly the voice, was emphasized over rhythm and percussion accompaniment, which were now described as 'interfering' with the melodic aspects of
the music. In 1933, for example, E. Krishna Iyer, a prominent member of
the Madras Music Academy, wrote that too much attention to rhythm and
percussion accompaniment led to excessive showiness on stage, bringing
the level of the music down to that of popular entertainments.

> One mridangam is sufficient accompaniment for any concert. Add to
> this ... kanjeera, dolak, morsing, and konnakole [other percussion
> accompaniments], and you have a regular circus performance of the
> lion, tiger, bear, wolf, and all other animals vociferously brawling
> and fighting with each other and the poor lamb of a vocalist
> quivering in their midst and the heart and soul of Indian music ...
> dished up beyond redemption.[6]

Sabha concerts also acquired a standard format. The first part would be
given over to compositions of middling weight and difficulty, followed
by a 'main' composition involving several kinds of improvisation. The
concert would end with 'lighter' pieces: *javalis* or *padams* from the dance
repertoire, north Indian (Hindustani) pieces, 'Western notes' based on
European songs, or film tunes: in short, anything that fell outside the
boundaries of strictly classical music. By including such pieces but
relegating them to a position of lesser status, the new concert format
was set up to repeatedly perform, and thus maintain, the boundary
between 'classical' music and other genres.[7]

With this new concert context and format there emerged what
William Weber has called a 'moral ideology of taste': an ideology that
connected the recognition of a musical canon with the assumption of an
elite class of educated listeners, a hierarchy of genres and the demand
that audiences be serious and quiet.[8] P. Sambamoorthy (1901–73), one
of the most prominent modernizers of Karnatic music, wrote several
essays in the 1940s and 1950s in which he laid out the principles of
'concert etiquette' for performers and audience alike. While
improvisation could remain, the spirit of spontaneity and competition
between musicians performing together had to be tightly contained.
Performers on the classical stage, suggested Sambamoorthy, needed to

maintain absolute professionalism, never letting their weaknesses show, taking unnecessary risks or drawing attention to the lapses of their accompanists. Audiences, similarly, were enjoined not to talk, become restless, or enter and exit during the concert.[9]

But it was All India Radio (AIR), established in 1938, which really took on the role of enforcing this moral ideology of taste. From its inception, AIR, as a national institution, had a reforming and purifying mission. While gramophone records had flooded the market with all kinds of music produced for commercial gain, radio was conceived as a didactic medium which would train and elevate the tastes of the listening masses. In the early 1950s, under the leadership of Minister of Information and Broadcasting B. V. Keskar, AIR introduced strict audition standards for musicians. Envisioning radio as an important patron and popularizer of Indian classical music, Keskar instituted regular programmes featuring classical musicians and instituted a standardized audition and grading system to rank musicians. Narayana Menon, the director general of AIR, wrote in 1957 that

> broadcasting ... will turn out to be the biggest single instrument of music education in our country ... It has given our musicians the qualities of precision and economy of statement. The red light on the studio door is a stern disciplinarian. Broadcasting has also ... given many of our leading musicians a better sense of proportion and a clear definition of values that matter in music.[10]

Most importantly, in 1952 Keskar banned the broadcasting of film songs, trying instead to meet the demand for popular music by commissioning classical musicians employed by AIR to create 'high standard light music' based on Indian classical music and folk songs.[11] 'Light music' was a term coined to cover what Keskar saw as a middle ground between classical music and film songs: an alternative popular music that used some of the melodic material associated with *ragas*, combined with simple harmony and orchestrated for an ensemble of Indian instruments. When AIR's light music programmes failed to attract sufficient numbers of listeners, Keskar compromised and created a special service called Vividh Bharati, which broadcast mostly film songs, but on separate channels from the main AIR programs, so as not to compromise the purity of the classical programming.[12]

The object of these standardizing and purifying moves was to create a musical tradition that could be considered both 'classical' and unmistakably Indian: modelled on the classical music of Europe, with its composers, compositions, conservatories and concerts, and yet with a distinctive practice and aesthetic that could claim roots in Indian antiquity. Karnatic music was imagined to be classical in this sense because it was oriented to the past, not the present; its standardized pedagogy, repertoire and concert format constructed it as an 'art' form removed from the modern world and 'modern' genres such as light music or film music.

The emergence of film music as a genre

A number of developments, technological, musical and social, led to the emergence of film music as a recognized genre in the 1940s. In the earliest years of sound film production, singing actors and actresses were drawn from several sources: the theatre companies, women of the courtesan and *devadasi* communities who were trained singers and dancers, and classical vocalists. The picture and soundtrack were recorded simultaneously, with accompanying musicians pulled along near the actor but just out of the camera's sight. In the mid 1930s, the technology to record visuals and sound separately became available, giving actors more freedom and music directors more opportunity to concentrate on the music and quality of recording. At this time, Indian film-makers adopted the pre-recording, or playback technique, in which the songs were pre-recorded in the studio before the action, enabling the actor to concentrate solely on his or her singing.[13] The recorded song would then be 'played back' on the set, to be lip-synched by the actor. In the early 1940s, music directors began to employ separate singers, termed 'ghost singers', to record the songs. Although the emphasis was still on matching the singer's voice as accurately as possible to the actor's voice in the 1940s, this ideal gave way in the 1950s to a different situation in which the singers were no longer anonymous 'ghost' singers, but were now called 'playback singers', credited and recognized as celebrities in their own right.[14]

This mode of producing film music produced new kinds of public musical personae as well as new musical ideals. The advent of pre-recording and playback singing elevated the role of the music director, who became a new kind of celebrity. Unlike classical musicians, who proudly traced their musical lineages back through generations of gurus whose style they claimed to emulate closely, film music directors presented themselves as self-taught, one-of-a-kind composers who flouted tradition. Having command of more than one musical tradition, they became known for their ability to produce novel hybrid forms of music. Playback singers, likewise, were new kinds of musicians who adhered to different notions of authenticity than classical singers. While classical singers were judged less on their voice quality than on their rendition of compositions and their ability to improvise in perform- ance, playback singers emphasized the cultivation of the voice and their duplication, in performance, of the recorded 'original' song. Playback singers, both male and female, now singing into microphones in the studio, also cultivated a voice very different from classical singers: one that tended to be smoother and lighter, capable of brisk ornamentation and with a relatively wider vocal range.[15] In the 1950s, the female film voice in particular became standardized in a sound embodied by north Indian playback singer Lata Mangeshkar and widely emulated by her south Indian contemporaries. High pitched and dependent on the microphone, this voice had no precedent in classical or other existing female singing styles in India, and thus could be claimed as suitably 'modern'.[16]

Imagining film music

As film music emerged as a distinct genre, its potential was imagined very differently from that of classical music. *Circa* 1938, the Tamil journal *Bharata Mani* published a short piece entitled 'Cinema: Is It An Art?' The author, Ve. Su. Ramakrishnan, wrote that 'if cinema is truly an art, then we can use it as a tool to spread our Indian culture/ civilization, just as the West is spreading its own culture'. Ramakrishnan claimed that cinema was superior to drama in its portrayal of human life, its ability to start a revolution, its ability to touch the human soul; it was a medium begging to be exploited.[17]

Some years later, in 1946, a Telugu writer, Garimella Satyanarayana, similarly suggested the revolutionary potential of film music to repre- sent India as it really was. South Indian music directors had already broken free of the hold of classical music; now they needed to escape the hegemony of north Indian film music. In his piece entitled 'There Cannot Be a Telugu Film without Telugu Music!', he wrote that 'cinema is the most effective medium for the promotion of a love towards our indigenous art forms ... The film world has the duty to depict not an imaginary world but that which people ought to see and hear, that which they ought to feel proud about and that which they should learn about.' Satyanarayana wrote with outrage about how the use of 'Hindustani' tunes in films had completely wiped out Telugu songs, to the point that only Hindustani tunes were considered to be music. 'Music is the spirit not only of the cinema field but of the nation as a whole', he wrote. 'If we manage to reform the field of music [in cinema] all the other associated fields will automatically change to suit the music. Or else all the arts will lose their national characteristics and become foreign.' Thus it was the responsibility of cinema music directors to create a recognizably Telugu music, neither classical nor folk, and definitely not foreign, but new:

> Therefore from now on, our directors should neither import . . . music directors from the north, nor should they send their technicians to be trained under them. Instead they should send their talented singers into the interior parts of their own region. These singers should mingle with the common folk, not with reputed artistes. These singers should be able to drink deep from the fount of the people's music, absorb its tunes and its style and music be able to adapt it to the cinema in a new style.[18]

In recommending that film singers learn folk music and adapt it, Satyanarayana was calling for a film music that would be equally 'national' as Karnatic classical music, but popular. The idea was to reflect the life and music of the common folk through the medium of film, back to those very masses. Film music had to be popular not just in the sense that Hindustani tunes were popular, but in the sense that they had come from, and thus represented, the people.

In 1955, an article appeared in the newspaper *Telugu Swatantra* claiming that film music was the most 'highly evolved' form of music. Tracing a path from the recitation of the Vedas right down to the emergence of film music, the author claimed that film music represented a new synthesis of poetry and music, a better synthesis than Karnatic music had achieved.

> Though there is a mingling of poetry and music in the kritis, there is not always a match between the emotion of the poetry and the emotion of the music. For instance, if the kriti 'sobhillu sapta sundarula bhajimpave manasa' were to be played on the violin, those who do not know its words will mistake it for a compassionate

song. The stage music is a little more evolved than this form;
though the music and poetry are quite bad, at least their synthesis is
done in a much better manner. It is in this aspect that film music
has progressed even further.

Indeed, the author suggested, the very fact that film music was *not*
classical was what made it more sophisticated. Precisely because film
music was outside the frame of Karnatic classical music, it was endowed
with a greater power of representation.

> The film music reflects the situation or context of the song and the
> characters in the film, at least it ought to do so. The scope of the
> cinema allows us to include the most classical of music as well as the
> songs of the bullock cart drivers. Moreover there is no need for the
> hero in the film and an ordinary beggar to sing in the same style
> and with the same musical accompaniments, like they do on stage.
> This is indeed a truly considerable development in the field of
> music.[19]

What is important to note here is the new notion of authenticity being
promoted by the idea that film music can accurately represent different
kinds of people. Defending himself against attacks from patrons of
classical music in the late 1950s, the north Indian film music director
Salil Chowdhury wrote:

> We must realise that the modern Indian composer has around him a
> way of life, sights and sounds, aims and ideas entirely different
> from what his ancestors had. He tries to express in his music these
> values and ideals. Exploring the entire range of ancient Indian music
> … it is possible he may find it inadequate to express his feelings.[20]

Film music, as a genre, was authentic not because it adhered to the
sound or grammar of one musical tradition, but because it encompassed
many different sounds and traditions, making it, in the words of
Bombay film music director Madan Mohan, 'the first really national
music we ever had'.[21]

Is it music?

Keskar's 1952 ban on film songs came in the midst of ongoing public
debate about the relative merits of film music and classical music. For
example, a series of vehement exchanges about film music took place in
the Tamil journal *Kalki* over several issues published between 1949 and

1952. Kalki Krishnamurthy, the editor, himself a Brahmin and connoisseur of Karnatic music, railed against film music in his columns. 'There is a difference between producing a film and running a radio station', wrote Kalki. The goal of radio, he stated, was to form the tastes of the people through useful and educational programmes. Playing cinema songs endlessly did not contribute to this goal, but actively went against it.[22] In 1951, opening the annual conference of the Madras Music Academy, T. R. Venkatarama Sastri remarked that 'now more than ever, people are getting to hear music through the gramophone, cinema, and radio'. This was a good thing, but at the same time it was contributing to the lowering of musical standards, since 'the common people are attracted to mixed-up cinema tunes which do not belong to any tradition'. The danger was not that Karnatic music would be destroyed, but that people would begin to think of cinema songs as good music.[23]

The novelist R. K. Narayan wrote in to Kalki's column in 1949 that AIR should completely stop broadcasting film songs, which he referred to disparagingly as 'talkie music'. 'Let them instead play gramophone records of high-standard Karnatic music', he wrote, urging that AIR should emulate the BBC's high standards in music. Kalki echoed Narayan's sentiments, suggesting that while it was not practical to ban film music entirely, measures could be taken to stop its complete dominance of the airwaves. There could be a rule, he suggested, that no song could be played more than three times; in addition, radio magazines like *Vanoli* and *Indian Listener* could stop publishing long lists of the latest film songs released on record.[24]

While film music directors presented themselves as composers with an eclectic musical background and unique ability to combine musical traditions, patrons of classical music criticized the mass production of film music as overly industrialized, resulting in thousands of songs that all sounded the same. 'Tappa', a word used to describe songs with a dance beat, became the term for film music in general among its critics. The satirical portrayal of music directors as callous, unfeeling types only interested in recycling already popular tunes even surfaced in the films themselves. *Munru Pillaikal*, a Tamil film released in 1952, featured a scene in which a Bombay music director comes to set to music a sad song that the main character must sing. The music director, without heeding the song's words, sets it to a 'tappa' melody. The singer beseeches him: 'What is this, sir?! This tune is not suitable for sadness. The audience will all want to get up and dance! Can't you think up another tune?' The music director promptly selects a European tune, and the singer is equally dissatisfied. 'Can't you listen to what I'm singing?' he asks the music director in comic despair.[25]

In a piece entitled 'Music Makes Money', Kalki marvelled at the way film songs were the part of the film that directors and audiences alike considered to be the most important; the songs were the money-makers. In fact, money and music had become so interchangeable in the film world that, Kalki remarked, the title of his article could be reversed – 'Money Makes Music' – without changing the meaning. Cine music directors borrowed indiscriminately from gramophone records of all kinds of music to make a fearful mixture, a music without any form or shape. Formerly this method was reserved for background music, but, Kalki noted with horror, it was now becoming common practice for songs to be 'composed' by taking bits and pieces from gramophone records. Kalki referred to this kind of music as a 'westernized, mixed-up formless mass of flesh'. Such film songs could hardly be dignified with the label 'music' at all; much less could they be called 'Indian'. He quoted the Hindi playback singer Shanta Apte to underscore his point: 'The reason for the degraded state of Indian music today is precisely this entrance of foreign music into our films.'[26]

Film music was portrayed by those on both sides of the debate as having a natural, almost instinctual, appeal to children and common folk. Kalki used the Tamil word *vacikara*, meaning attractive or alluring, with distinct sexual connotations, to describe the female film voice. A sympathetic reader wrote in that the problem was that film songs attracted children before they knew the difference between good music and bad: 'This dirty and unwholesome music does more harm than good to the children. If anything is done so that this music is not heard in India, every parent will be grateful to the authorities.' Several readers, however, disagreed. One responded with the following tirade:

> Music, music, you say, what is music? Is it music when a vidwan [classical singer] with the voice of a buffalo sings sa and ga so you can hardly tell the difference? Tomorrow take your crying child on your lap and see if you can comfort him with Karnatic music. See if hearing 'sarasiruha' [a Karnatic composition] has any effect on him.

'What is music, anyway?' another asked in a letter to Kalki. 'Is it not that which truly attracts the ordinary people, something which they can enjoy? ... Seventy percent of radio owners have radios not to listen to

Karnatic music, but to enjoy film songs in their free time. If AIR bans film music, these people will simply tune in to Radio Ceylon and Radio Goa.' Indeed, Keskar's ban on film music cost All India Radio a large number of its south Indian listeners, who tuned in instead to Radio Ceylon's broadcasts of Tamil and Hindi film songs.[27]

These debates settled on the voice, particularly the female voice, to distinguish Karnatic music from film music. In the passage quoted above, the writer used the Tamil terms *erumai* (buffalo; by extension, heavy, lethargic) and *kuccal* (loud, confused noise or hubbub) to describe the Karnatic singer's voice. In contrast, film voices were described as *inimai* (sweet). For fans of film music, this 'sweetness' was exemplified by the light clarity of Lata Mangeshkar's voice, unencumbered by the grammar of Karnatic music and the weight of tradition. But for Kalki and others who disapproved of film music, that quality of 'sweetness' was insipid and deceptive. 'Our readers have been writing in ecstatic terms about the sweetness of Lata Mangeshkar's voice', Kalki wrote in his column in 1951.

> If the sweetness they speak of were really in her voice, she and other playback singers could just as well sing high-standard Hindustani music. No, this supposed sweetness is not in her voice at all, it is in the artificially sweet-sounding songs like 'Panjabi tune'. Even a person with an ordinary voice would sound sweet singing such songs.[28]

This quality of sweetness was thus artificial, deceptive: almost mechanical. In contrast, Kalki used the Tamil word *utainta*, meaning broken, split, or giving way with emotion, to describe the authentic Karnatic voice. The sweet cinema voice was insipid compared with this kind of Karnatic voice, which showed the emotional involvement of the singer in what he was singing.[29] What distinguished Karnatic music from film music was that in Karnatic music listeners were not deceived or led astray by the mere sound of the voice, considered to be a superficial charm; they were able to hear past the voice to the musical ideas being elaborated.

As the ideological opposition between film music and Karnatic music became more entrenched, their respective voices became more differentiated as signifiers of the 'classical' or the 'popular'. We find the legacy of this opposition in another film, *Sindhubhairavi* (1984). As in *Shankarabharnam*, the classical Karnatic voice is used as a foil for the creation of the film voice, but here the value judgment is reversed. Film music, rather than being imagined as an artificially assembled hybrid of other musical genres, is valued positively as 'natural' and unpretentious. The film tells the story of a love affair between a Karnatic singer and a young, uneducated woman who eventually persuades him that it is important to sing Tamil songs on stage 'that the people can understand', as well as songs in Telugu and Sanskrit considered to be more 'classical'. Near the beginning of the film, there is a scene in which the Karnatic singer is giving a concert. Sitting in the audience, the young woman, Sindhu, becomes increasingly angered by the audience's lack of respect for the singer, and by the fact that he is singing in Telugu instead of Tamil. When he has finished, she strides up to the stage to complain, and he challenges her to sing. Unlike his classical singing, she begins with no accompaniment, just a simple snap of the fingers, as if she is making up the song as she goes along. The words of the song further contribute to the image of the film voice as natural and unschooled, unlike the overly schooled voice of Karnatic music:

Patariyen patippariyen
Pallikkutam tan ariyen
Etariyen eluttariyen
Eluttu vakai nan ariyen
Ettula elutavillai
Eluti vaiccu palakkavillai
Ilakkanam patikkavillai
Talaikkanamum enakku illai

I don't know singing, don't know reading
I don't have schooling
I don't know writing, don't know the letters
I don't even know how to write . . .
I've never written anything down
I've never read literature
and I have no arrogance

This song scene is ostensibly about the movement to have more classical songs in the Tamil language, a movement begun in the 1940s that continues to resonate through the present in south India.[30] But it also uses this more outwardly political message to make a claim about the authenticity of film music as a kind of music that comes directly from the heart, unencumbered by classical rules or structures.

Conclusion

The emergence of both classical Karnatic music and film music as recognized genres is contemporaneous with the height of the Indian nationalist movement and the first decades of India's independence, a period when the explicit negotiation of India's identity as a modern nation was at its height. Classical music and film music, imagined as 'high' and 'low' culture respectively, presented competing notions of what it meant to represent the nation. In one, authenticity was imagined to lie in what was constructed as India's history, the classical roots of its civilization, while in the other, representing the nation was imagined to lie in incorporating different musical styles into a hybrid genre that represented the diversity of contemporary India. In a basic sense, the strategy that south Indian elites employed to consolidate and standardize a 'classical' south Indian musical tradition was one of exclusion: picking out certain sounds, practices and composers as exemplary of a new canon. The creators of film music, by contrast, employed not only a strategy, but also a rhetoric of encompassment; film music was imagined to have an endless ability to incorporate other genres and to use them in the portrayal of different kinds of people.

Musical genres are created by a combination of discourse, practice and ideology, and these elements mutually reinforce each other. That is, a genre consists not only of musical sounds and practices, but also of the ways those sounds and practices are ideologically framed through discourse. For example, the framing of Karnatic classical music as a genre growing out of a tradition of Hindu religious devotion affected the kinds of repertoire that became canonized. In a similar way, the framing of film music as 'modern' rather than 'traditional' enabled the emergence of such self-taught musicians as film music directors and playback singers, whose musical practices and sound had little precedent in other existing genres. Examining the different ways that these two genres were discursively constructed provides a sense of the ideological forces that shaped musical practice and sound in the decades just before and after India's independence.

At the beginning of the twenty-first century, different ideological and economic forces are at work. As major sites of patronage for classical music have shifted from institutions within India to the diaspora and the West, south Indian classical musicians have engaged with the world music industry and have participated in a new genre called 'fusion', which self-consciously seeks to mix Indian and non-Indian (usually Western classical or jazz) musical elements. With the arrival of non-government-run satellite television and FM radio in the 1990s, film music has gained much more airtime in India; there are now multiple television and radio channels devoted to playing films and film song sequences, as well as websites devoted to film song history. Film music has, in the decades since it first emerged as a recognized genre, acquired its own canon. It has become the object of academic study both in India and in the West and has gained the status of authentically Indian popular music, but has also been discovered as music outside of its film setting in the context of the rise of 'Indo-chic' in the United States. Meanwhile, south Indian film music directors such as Illayaraja and A. R. Rahman have gained international recognition through their work beyond the context of Indian popular cinema. Thus, while classical and film music in South India came into being as genres through their imagined relationship to the nation, they are now being reimagined in relation to a transnational imaginary, one in which prestige is not based on claims to purity and antiquity, but rather on the ability to mix with other genres and to participate in transnational circuits of appropriation and borrowing. In this new context, old hierarchies of 'high' and 'low' musical culture are giving way to different standards of determining cultural value.

Notes

1 Allison Arnold, *Hindi Filmgit: On the History of Commercial Indian Popular Music*. Ph.D. dissertation, University of Illinois, 1991, pp. 236–7.
2 Partha Chatterjee, *The Nation and Its Fragments: Colonial and Postcolonial Histories* (Princeton University Press, 1993), pp. 6–13.
3 Yoshitaka Terada, 'Temple Music Traditions in Hindu South India: Periya Melam and its Performance Practice', *Asian Music* 39:2 (2008), pp. 108–51.
4 Amanda Weidman, *Singing the Classical, Voicing the Modern: The Postcolonial Politics of Music in South India* (Durham, NC: Duke University Press, 2006), pp. 78–82; Lakshmi Subramanian, *From the Tanjore Court to the Madras Music Academy: A Social History of Music in South India* (New Delhi: Oxford University Press, 2006), pp. 84–114.
5 Weidman, *Singing the Classical*, pp. 99–104.
6 E. Krishna Iyer, *Personalities in Present Day Music* (Madras: Rochehouse and Sons, 1933), p. 53.
7 Weidman, *Singing the Classical*, p. 98.
8 William Weber, *The Rise of Musical Classics in Eighteenth-Century England: A Study in Canon, Ritual, and Ideology* (Oxford: Clarendon Press, 1992), p. 21.
9 Weidman, *Singing the Classical*, p. 83.

10 Narayana Menon, 'The Impact of Western Technology on Indian Music', *Bulletin of the Institute of Traditional Cultures* (1957), p. 75.

11 Erik Barnouw and S. Krishnaswamy, *Indian Film* (New York: Oxford University Press, 1980), pp. 207–14.

12 David Lelyveld, 'Upon the Subdominant: Administering Music on All-India Radio', in Carol Breckenridge (ed.), *Consuming Modernity: Public Culture in a South Asian World* (Minneapolis: University of Minnesota Press, 1995), pp. 59–60.

13 Arnold, *Hindi Filmgit*, pp. 102–5.

14 Neepa Majumdar, 'The Embodied Voice: Song Sequences and Stardom in Popular Hindi Cinema', in A. Knight and P. Wojcik (eds.), *Soundtrack Available: Essays on Film and Popular Music* (Durham, NC: Duke University Press, 2001), pp. 161–81.

15 Arnold, *Hindi Filmgit*, pp. 106–7.

16 Sanjay Srivastava, 'The Voice of the Nation and the Five-Year Plan Hero', in *Fingerprinting Popular Culture: The Mythic and the Iconic in Indian Cinema* (New Delhi: Oxford University Press, 2006), pp. 125–6.

17 Ve. Su. Ramakrishnan, 'Cinema: Oru Kalaiya? ('Cinema: Is It An Art?')'. *Bharata Mani*, c.1938, pp. 141–2.

18 Garimella Satyanarayana, 'There Cannot Be a Telugu Film without Telugu Music!' *Roopavani*, October 1946. Translated by Uma Maheswari.

19 'Of Film Music', *Telugu Swatantra*, 12 August 1955. Translated by Uma Maheswari.

20 *Filmfare*, 27 February 1959. Quoted in Sumita Chakravarty, *National Identity in Indian Popular Cinema, 1947–1987* (New Delhi: Oxford University Press, 1996), p. 77.

21 *Filmfare*, 19 July 1957. *Ibid.*

22 *Kalki* magazine, 27 July 1952, p. 8.

23 *Kalki* magazine, 30 December 1951, p. 15.

24 *Kalki* magazine, 23 January 1949, pp. 27–8.

25 Described in '*Tappa Cankitatukkuc Cappaik Kattu!*,' *Kalki* magazine, 27 July 1952, pp. 6–7.

26 *Kalki* magazine, 26 October 1951.

27 Barnouw and Krishnaswamy, *Indian Film*, p. 211; V. S. Sambandam, 'For That Old Magic', *Frontline* 23:1 (14–27 January 2006).

28 *Kalki* magazine, 26 October 1951.

29 *Ibid.*

30 Weidman, *Singing the Classical*, pp. 150–91; Lakshmi Subramanian, 'A Language for Music: Revisiting the Tamil Isai Iyakkam', *Indian Economic and Social History Review* 44:1 (2007), pp. 19–40.

14

Voyeurism and the family on television

In an interview on a leading Hindi news channel in 2009, Congress Member of Parliament Ambika Soni remarked that she had never watched as much television in her life as she had in the five months since taking office as the Minister of Information and Broadcasting.[1] 'You never know when an NGO or fellow MP might raise a complaint about a programme being unsuitable for broadcast.' Her remark referred in part to complaints against specific shows that had been aired on private television channels in 2009; their content had been criticized as being unsuitable for Indian audiences. Soni went on to say that most of the complaints related to the depictions of women or children, and the publicization of issues that Indians consider 'extremely private'. 'There are things,' she said, 'that Indians are not mentally prepared to publicise in front of everybody ... even if we don't do it ourselves, seeing somebody else do it is hurtful.'[2] The complaints addressed two reality shows that were aired in July and October 2009, both adaptations of foreign reality shows: *Sach Ka Samna* ('Facing the Truth'; hereafter *SKS*) was the Indian version of US television giant Fox's *The Moment of Truth* and *Pati, Patni, aur Woh* (*Husband, Wife, and the Other*; hereafter *PPW*) was the Indian version of the BBC 3 reality show *Baby Borrowers*. In *SKS*, contestants answered twenty-one increasingly personal and embarrassing questions before an audience including their friends and family to win a large cash prize. In *PPW*, five celebrity couples took on the task of parenting children (toddlers to teenagers) chosen from an audition for a period of a month while being filmed 24/7. *SKS* came under fire from politicians for the 'obscene' nature of questions that opened discussions on pre- or extra-marital sex, practices considered contrary to Indian culture and values.[3] *PPW* was brought to the attention of the Ministry of Women and Child Development by a local Delhi NGO concerned that the children on the show were being 'exploited' by the channel for monetary gain.

Complaints over content in entertainment and news coverage on private television channels have been a concern among women's groups and popular discussion since the early 1990s. Since the arrival of cable and foreign satellite channels in India after 1991, media scholars have focused on the debates over television content as the 'culture wars'. Studies of Doordarshan (the state broadcasting network) have shown how its monopoly over content during the 1980s cultivated gendered and religious forms of nationalism through soaps and mythological serials, and promoted a pan-Indian identity through documentaries and cultural programming. The advent of economic liberalization from 1991 onwards, however, is usually seen as having forced a break from this homogenized narrative of 'Indianness'. The growth of private television channels has diversified content for audiences, in recent times bringing them reality shows and talent hunts, which draw them into a complex relationship with global consumerism and local identification. Concerns over televisual content and cultural integrity, however, have been part of the narrative of television's expansion since the 1960s and 1970s. Central in this narrative is the Indian family, which is seen as the basic viewing and consuming unit, rather than the individual. Most importantly, it is the family as a moral unit and value – both as depicted on screen and as the viewing audience addressed by it – that animates the discussions on television programming, as well as the place of television in Indian private, and impact on public, life. This chapter explores how the family as cultural and moral value has been thematized on a recent Hindi reality show; the reality show being a relatively recent format on privately owned entertainment channels in India.

Contrary to the argument that private cable and satellite channels have been responsible for unprecedented cultural change, which is usually accompanied by an anxiety that it will engender a loosening of ties to what it means to be 'Indian', programming on private channels in India participates in strengthening particular aspects of a cultural grammar of Indianness that has its roots in popular culture. This trend has been shown in the case of recent Hindi soap operas, which since the early 2000s have been the mainstay of Hindi general entertainment channels. In the marriage reality show, *Rakhi Ka Swayamvar* ('Rakhi Chooses a Husband'), for instance, the production team drew on diverse genres including popular Hindi film, television soap operas, north Indian wedding ritual traditions and kinship symbolism to engage viewers. I attempt to show the creative process through which new genres of programming are generated, while drawing on other familiar genres for their appeal. By using the notion of genre as dialogic – that is, an act of communication linked to other moments, places and persons who came before it as well as to potential future acts – I show that private television production is not only the product of global formats adapted to local tastes, but that it is a process of citation from familiar genres and cultural artefacts that make up the rich field of popular and public culture in India.

Early beginnings and the formation of the middle-class television family

From its experimental beginnings in 1959, the public service broadcaster Doordarshan (literally, seeing from afar) grew in fits and starts, supported by a UNESCO proposal to the Indian government to promote the use of television as an educational medium. Early programming aimed at spreading education and information by focusing on issues like health, family planning, gender equality and improving agricultural productivity. Vikram Sarabhai, one of the early advocates of television as a developmental technology, visualized India 'leapfrog[ging]' over decades of backwardness thanks to educational programming on television. Images would communicate instantly where print would require the investment of time and learning; farmers could be provided adequate information on weather and farming techniques; and isolated rural communities could be integrated with the rest of the country. This hypodermic model of development communication would address 'all sections of the population, the young and the old, men and women, the literate and the illiterate, the privileged and the under-privileged'.[4]

By the early 1970s, the state had invested in a model of community television viewing; televisions were set up in community centres and schools in villages and towns, where viewers could watch educational programmes beamed from their local regional broadcasting centre. This initiative was known as SITE (Satellite Instructional Television Experiment); transmission was in black and white, and volunteers who would act as educators, at least in principle, appeared alongside the broadcasts. In practice, however, broadcasting initiatives were often not backed up by other institutional amenities that would have been necessary to supplement community broadcasting in its developmental aims. Villages that had television sets often did not have proper electrification or community centres that could house transmission equipment. Even if one were to grant that the hypodermic model of development might have had some successes, government services were not equipped to sustain it. The state thought of television as an instrument of modernity, development and progress but lacked sufficient or engaging means – both in terms of 'hardware' (equipment) and 'software' (content) – to reach and engage an audience. In 1982, long after Sarabhai's initial push for a National Programme, which he saw as being supplemented by regional programming, New Delhi hosted the Asian Games and acquired satellite equipment to broadcast the event across Asia. The first National Programme went on air on 15 August 1982 and Doordarshan entered the phase of colour television and national programmes. Gradually, central control over programming became more total and the local broadcasting centres lost a great deal of their early innovation and identity.

The emphasis on education and information remained a concern for state broadcasting policy. Entertaining the audience was, at least initially, a secondary concern. However, the airing of the first national soap opera, *Hum Log* ('We People', 1984) made it clear to officials at Doordarshan that pedagogic sermons thinly disguised as entertainment were not popular with audiences. The soap was far more successful once the show's producers pared down the initial tone of moral edification. By the end of the 1980s, Doordarshan was approving shows for broadcast that catered more to the audience's need for entertainment. Shows like Ramanand Sagar's *Ramayana*, for instance, earned Doordarshan good advertising revenues, determinedly shifting the balance in favour of television as a commercial enterprise, rather than a developmental medium. Between 1984–5 and 1992–3 its annual advertising revenues rose from Rs. 60 million to Rs. 360 million as advertisers made the most of Doordarshan's increased reach into the middle-class home.[5]

During the late 1970s, state subsidized television sets had also entered the market, targeting not so much communities as collective beneficiaries but rather individual households as owners. With the fruits of advertising revenue quite clearly visible, the government eliminated the licensing fees on television and radio ownership, further consolidating the sale of television sets as a durable consumer good rather than as community development infrastructure. The move to encourage sponsorship of programmes on television via advertisers made Doordarshan a mediator that facilitated the exchange between the advertisers and a growing middle class by selling airtime. The television itself became a product that was indicative of a particular class and lifestyle. The state had become the arbiter of aspirational consumer fantasies, rather than promoter of community-based programming. Television soon thrived on the image of the on-screen nuclear family in advertisements and serials, addressing itself increasingly to the urban middle-class family.

By the early 1980s, even before the era of national programming, critics of the state's broadcasting policy and politely dissident insiders were expressing dismay that the developmental focus of television was deliberately being led astray. In the P. C. Joshi Report on Doordarshan in 1985, concerns regarding the growing emphasis on consumerism were being expressed in terms of the influences that television could have on the family. From the optimism about television as a relatively transparent medium of communication that could instruct, inform and entertain, there now came the voices of concern expressing ambivalence over the nature of the technology. What kind of object was the television? What kind of space did it occupy in everyday life? Television was rapidly becoming one of the first consumer durables that a family would invest in, before others like a fridge, a two-wheeler or a mixer, like 'a tool, a bargaining chip or status symbol people could wield in their lives'.[6] While the growing middle class was buying televisions as a marker of class belonging or social capital, there was a growing concern among policy-makers about the nature of television as a domestic object.

For P. S. Deodhar, adviser to Prime Minister Rajiv Gandhi on electronic media in the mid 1980s, television was distinguishable from the cinema because it was watched at home. Most homes in the 1980s (and even today) had only one television set that the whole family watched together, making the issue of appropriate television content rather significant.

> Every home follows a code of behaviour ... everyone is bound by it, although outside their homes, some may plead for entirely revolutionary ideas on behavioural conduct and ethics ... The television cohabits with the family in their living rooms and bedrooms ... Television is a guest in a home and like a decent, well-behaved and honourable guest, it must follow the codes of

conduct and ethical standards of an average Indian family consisting of a mixed audience of children and adults in varying age groups.[7]

Arvind Rajagopal also suggests that, apart from being a means of communication, television is an 'object entering the life-world, taking its place among other things'.[8] However, where Rajagopal examines how viewers of television seek to nullify its novelty, or domesticate its aura into the routines of everyday life, what Deodhar seems to be concerned with relates more to television as an intrusive being, which itself has to be careful about how it enters the domestic space as a cultural product. By the mid 1980s, how television as a form of cultural production might influence change within the home was becoming not a small source of anxiety for some policy-makers. The Joshi report had made significant suggestions on 'software', i.e., content, which would keep Doordarshan true to the initial educational and informational aims of television. This included a cap on the amount of foreign-produced serials for both children and adults, encouragement of positive representation of women and gender relations, and controlling the flow of information from 'the affluent world' to prevent 'the transfer of the high consumption attitudes, values and styles from the affluent world to the poverty-stricken world'.[9] The medium of television was still seen as a powerful technology for change, but controlling the medium to direct the goals of development and progress began to seem more urgent. Television was like a knife; 'depending on who holds it, it could become a killer's weapon or a surgeon's healing knife'.[10] Allowing Doordarshan to become more dependent on advertising revenue could tip the balance towards a 'self-invited cultural invasion',[11] one that could be righted by showing more programmes that showcased Indian culture and history. At the end of the day, Doordarshan was 'not in the business of television for raking in the maximum revenue from commercials; advertisements [were] incidental to its essentially educative role as a publicly owned mass medium'.[12]

The move towards regulation

Doordarshan might not have been in the business of growing revenue, but private channels clearly were. With the coming of cable and foreign satellite channels in the 1990s, scholars have argued that the media landscape underwent a radical change. There was increased choice of programming. Initially only in English (STAR Network), by the mid 1990s it had begun to diversify into Hindi (with Zee TV) and regional languages (with Sun TV and Eenadu TV). There had only been one state-run channel until 1990; by the end of the 1990s there were over 100. Today there are an estimated 700 national and local channels – terrestrial, cable and satellite combined – in major urban centres, backed by diverse business and political interests. The terms used in scholarly writing as well as popular commentary to describe the coming of foreign channels indicate some of the early distaste for their content: an invasion, influx or assault, which could potentially threaten India's cultural sovereignty. Although Doordarshan had been airing foreign content, these shows, like all others, were highly controlled and cleared by internal censors before going on air. Shows like *Baywatch*, *The Bold and the Beautiful* and unrated Hollywood movies were new fare in the domestic space and, most importantly, they were shown at prime time, prompting critics to speak of a severe assault by foreign content on the senses, morality and relations within the family. Particularly sensitive issues were the 'derogatory and disrespectful'[13] representation of women and the impact of sex and violence on young children. NGOs and media watchdogs raised demands for the state to regulate cable and satellite channels strictly and formulate a content code for television. Given this disquiet over culturally 'inappropriate' television content, legislation over cable and satellite broadcasting in India has been a long time in the making. In 1995, the Cable Television Networks (Regulation) Act was passed, in which guidelines for cable operations, registration and a programme code were laid down. The Act was to be a placeholder until the more detailed Broadcasting Bill could be put in place; however, despite being introduced as a bill in Parliament in 1997, the lack of consensus among broadcasters as well as between them and legislators means that it has not yet been formalized as law. As a result, the Cable Act and the Cinematograph Act of 1952 are invoked in any complaint or grievance regarding content on private television channels. These acts prohibit the broadcasting of programmes or advertisements that, among other things, offend against good taste or decency, exploit women through derogatory or submissive roles in family or society, or endanger the safety of children.

Localization and adaptation

Part of the challenge for foreign satellite networks like STAR when it first began broadcasting in India was how to woo non-English speaking, mass audiences. The success of Hindi-language programming on

Zee TV prompted STAR to gradually switch from primarily foreign content in the early 1990s to first Hindi, then Marathi- and Bengali-language programming on separate channels by the 2000s. STAR's successful policy of 'localization' – producing specific content for their Indian market – opened up the industry for locally produced serials, talent shows and also news channels. Reality shows in India are a recent genre of entertainment, which borrow from successful international formats and change them to Indian contexts. Channel heads refer to this process of adaptation as catering to local tastes and sensitivities. In 2008–9, several international reality show formats were adapted for Indian television – *Fear Factor* as *Khatron ka Khiladi*, *Big Brother* as *Bigg Boss*, *So You Think You Can Dance* as *Jhalak Dikhla Ja*, *I'm a Celebrity, Get Me Out of Here!* as *Iss Jungle Se Mujhe Bachao*, and *Moment of Truth* as *Sach Ka Samna*, among others. Most of these were in the genre of adventure sports and talent hunts, with the exception of *Bigg Boss* and *Sach ka Samna*, mentioned above as the centre of a controversy over its content. The reality show *Rakhi ka Swayamvar* ('Rakhi Chooses a Husband', hereafter *RKS*), which I will discuss in detail here was the first of its kind – a marriage reality show – on Indian television. The inspiration for the show might have come from international shows like *Who Wants to Marry a Millionaire* or *The Bachelorette*, but through their narrative and aesthetic choices, the producers of *RKS* drew profusely on local per-formative traditions and popular culture. Localization of international television formats in this case was a process of adaptation that drew on and modified motifs from much-loved Hindi films, soap operas and popular narratives around marriage and family to appeal to audiences. The key to the show's success lay in turning a controversial, overtly sexual, Hindi film star into a respectable bride-to-be, making her 'marriage' a family affair, suitable for all ages.

In April 2009, NDTV Imagine, a less than moderately successful Hindi language general entertainment channel, announced a new reality show that would be the first of its kind in the country. Inviting viewers to the 'marriage of the season', Imagine was to showcase the 'journey of a bride-to-be; from selecting her groom to the marriage ceremony'.[14] Produced by Sol Productions for NDTV Imagine, *RKS* would feature controversial Bollywood dancer and actress, Rakhi Sawant, as the bride-to-be, in a marriage reality show. In this form of marriage (*swayam* (self) *var* (husband)), which features in the *Ramayana* and *Mahabharata* epics, the princess chooses her husband from a group of princes or is won in a competition by the most worthy. Sixteen contestants drawn mainly from the Hindi-speaking demographic targeted by the show would live together for over a month and perform tasks of physical and mental endurance to win Rakhi's affections. Each episode would see Rakhi eliminate a contestant and eventually choose the winner from the final three, after which the two would be married in a never-before televised event. At the press launch, bride-to-be Rakhi Sawant told the print and television news that she felt ready to choose a life partner (*jeevansaathi*) and that she had approached NDTV Imagine to realize her search for true love and marriage. Although the show was arranged like a reality show, its promotion and narrative structure deliberately blurred the lines between fantasy and realism, drawing on iconic cinematic and televisual images of love, family and marriage.

As a celebrity, Rakhi Sawant is a product of the medium of television more than any other media. Although her first Bollywood breaks came in dancing roles, making her known as an 'item girl', she shot to prominence in gossip columns in print and on TV entertainment news for her brash and outspoken behaviour on the reality show *Bigg Boss* and then the talent hunt show *Nach Baliye* ('Dance, Dance!'). Rakhi is able to exploit television's need for strong visuals that can be caught on camera for constant replay on news shows and provides sound bites that serve the format of short but punchy stories that grab viewers' attention. In other words, she has learned how to work the medium in her favour. Her advice for television fame is simple: 'before you do anything, it's important to check where the camera's gaze is directed'.[15] Her outspoken and carefree behaviour and overtly sexual image have made her a controversial feminine icon, seen as the object of male desire and (some) feminist affirmation on the one hand, and as a dangerous form of female assertion and drama queen on the other. Nevertheless, 'Brand Rakhi' has understood the basics of the television business, which is that no matter what she does, most people will not change the channel she is on.

RKS highlighted like never before the mastery with which Rakhi orchestrated her on- and off-screen life. During the press launch, Imagine's executive vice-president Shailja Kejriwal said, 'Reality has never been so real on TV before.' Along with Rakhi's insistence that she would prove through the *swayamvar* how authentic (*sachhi*) she is, the channel's emphasis on reality, rather than simply reality television, marked their promotional campaign. In the press launch, Rakhi fielded questions from journalists and news reporters dressed in complete bridal finery, seated on a decorated chair like those used in Indian wedding receptions, demurely holding out a box of *sindoor*[16] as she invited contestants: 'If you have that special something in you, then come and claim my hand.'[17] She said that she had always been 'bold' and 'honest' since childhood, and everything she had done had been with full disclosure: 'I am full of confidence and have the right to live freely which is why I am conducting a *swayamvar*.'[18] Citing Sita's *swayamvar* from the beloved Indian epic, *Ramayana*, as her inspiration, Rakhi explicitly brought herself together with one of the most sacred icons of female fidelity and chastity in Indian mythology. She claimed to be revitalizing a mythic Hindu custom, which had always given women the freedom of choosing their own partners. On being asked why she was conducting such a private and significant moment of her life on national television, Rakhi responded, 'I have always been a public property. Whatever I am today is because of reality TV.'[19] She adopted NDTV as her '*maika*' (natal kin) because '*main media ki beti hun*' (I am the media's daughter), and she planned to invite all of the country to her wedding via a reality show.[20]

The news of this show was received in predictable ways – mostly as part of Rakhi's continued desire to be on television in whatever way possible. Also, the dissonance between Rakhi's image as an item girl and the demure image she was casting herself in irked her critics. Rakhi's depiction of herself was as 'a cultured Indian woman with good values', inspired by Sita, one of India's most sacred icons of feminine purity.[21] This was too much for some viewers and commentators to bear. Rakhi was seen as being far from pure, leave alone possessing either the characteristics of a good wife or those of a good daughter-in-law: 'Everyone likes to watch Rakhi dance, but no one wants to set up a home [*ghar basana*] with her.'[22] The significance of *ghar basana* extends to more than simply setting up house together: it initiates a new phase of life, sanctified by marriage and resulting in procreation. This line of criticism displays the central axis of the patriarchal double standard towards female sexuality – disarticulating sex for pleasure from sex for procreation. The disbelief that Rakhi could in fact inhabit a docile, submissive image has its roots in the popular discourses of femininity in India, which separate the virgin as gift in Hindu marriage from the courtesan (or the 'anti-heroine'), who is an object of desire but never suitable for marriage. In fact, it is by drawing on the simultaneous tension and dependence between these extremely potent female icons in Indian popular culture – particularly in cinema – that Rakhi's 'wedding' became a spectacle worth watching. Her image, sanctified for family viewing, became both the voyeuristic pull of the show, as well as a figure around which the disquiet around television content in relation to the family could be articulated.

The figure of the courtesan has a long history in South Asian performative and narrative traditions, but Rakhi's story as she told it is best understood as an ode to the Hindi film courtesan. The main protagonist of this genre is a young woman who has been forced by circumstances into a life of the brothel (*kotha*) and who sings and dances for the pleasure of men. She is diametrically opposed to the lady of the house, who is kept veiled from all but the man who might see her, her husband. The figure of the courtesan is the voyeuristic object par excellence in film, created both as an object of the male gaze within the narrative of the film as well as for the spectators.[23] Building on Laura Mulvey's formulation of how the male gaze operates in narrative cinema, Steve Derné and Lisa Jadwin have shown that for Indian male spectators, not all women are open to the gaze in a sexually objectifying way.[24] The courtesan and in later iterations, the anti-heroine, is opposed to the figure of the wife or legitimate female companion through a series of conflicting articulations of what it means to be Indian and modern at the same time. Central to these articulations are the sartorial choices of film actresses; those who 'expose' and are 'Western' in how they reveal their bodies, like Rakhi, are legitimately open to the sexualized gaze, whereas those who dress modestly and conduct themselves as obedient and family-minded are incorporated within a domesticated desire. Nevertheless, both these figures became objects of voyeuristic pleasure, particularly so in the way that they were brought together in the show; the tensions between the two being fought out in a single figure, Rakhi Sawant.

The courtesan as imagined in the cinematic mode is pure of heart if not of body; her story oscillates between defiance in the face of her circumstances and yearning for love and the respectability of marriage, which she might never be able to realize. As Ira Bhaskar and Richard Allen show in their work on the courtesan film genre, 'the courtesan is presented as essentially pure at heart but one whose upbringing and lifestyle condemn her to a condition of permanent self-alienation'.[25] The courtesan genre is almost always a tragic love story, where choice and individual desire are thwarted to maintain the patriarchal status quo.

Rakhi's own self-presentation echoes many elements of this genre, less with the pathos that so epitomizes the characters that have made them immortal in Hindi film, and more in keeping with her outspoken nature. The autobiographical narrative occasioned by the show served to construct Rakhi as a moral self, refashioning her in an appropriate televisual image. Rakhi chose to give her own voice to her very public life, presenting a person that was very different from the image of her that gossip magazines and television shows had created. In the first episode of *RKS*, during an intimate chat with the host, Rakhi addressed her critics by saying, 'They should not believe the image of me that they see on the news. One should not judge someone so hastily.' In the same vein, Rakhi said she didn't want an actor, but a husband and true love. In response to the gathering scepticism over whether she would actually choose a groom and settle down, Rakhi repeatedly told newspapers that she was conducting this *swayamvar* in good faith and that it was not a 'publicity stunt'.[26] During the show, too, she repeatedly made reference to her family and personal life. Her parents' separation had deprived her of a father's love; she had to dance to make enough money for her brother to go to college, to marry off her sister and pay for her mother's medical bills. These trials themselves recall motifs from hugely popular Hindi family melodramas from the 1970s, further suggesting that the mode of Rakhi's self-presentation was itself a citation of popular narrative and affective devices. She had danced at 'private bachelor parties' and struggled to find her place in the Bombay film industry without a reputed family name or patronage of a 'godfather'. Today she thought of herself as successful in the entertainment business, but her lifestyle had become the cause of a permanent and very public rift between her family and her. No member of her family was present during any part of the show, nor invited at the end for the grand finale when she chose her groom. In the past Rakhi has lauded her mother's support during her early dancing career, but during the show this was not how she chose to describe her mother's role in her life. Whether truth or embellishment, Rakhi comes across to viewers as a young woman deprived of a loving family life, forced to use her charms and body to achieve success in a cut-throat and corrupt entertainment industry.

If Rakhi's back-story was rendered through the motif of the pure-hearted yet misjudged courtesan, the affirmative narrative for the future came through another cinematic genre, that of the romantic family drama. In the courtesan genre, marriage, which is the only way that the fallen woman can be redeemed and rehabilitated in mainstream social life, rarely occurs. Illicit love, individual choice and the expression of unrestrained desire are highly disruptive of familial and community bonds and social values. The courtesan genre relies on a woman's trangressive desire to create pathos. It can only end as a tragic love story. The family drama, on the other hand, focuses on a woman's desire as encompassed within and expressed through her roles of procreation and nurture, foregrounding the ideal joint family as the object of the audiences' gaze. The romantic family film is 'quintessentially ... classed in popular parlance as a "family" film – "family" understood in the double sense of (i) for a family audience, and (ii) about family relationships, inclusive of, but much broader than, the true romance that provides its basic storyline'.[27] For *RKS* to be a success with a television – read family – audience, the courtesan's story had to be sanitized and made into a family saga, much like the tele-serials with which it was competing for viewership. Two moves made this possible – drawing on popular iconic families from the cinematic world on the one hand and from the domestic object par excellence – television – on the other.

Realizing the fictional family

Exemplary hit films of the family drama genre are Sooraj Barjatya's *Hum Apke Hain ... Kaun!* ('What Am I to You!' 1994, *HAHK*) and Aditya Chopra's *Dilwale Dulhania Le Jayenge* ('Those With Heart Will Win the Bride', 1995, *DDLJ*). These films have had some of the longest runs in Hindi cinema and continue to be iconic films of and soundtracks for the ideal marriage in north India. In *RKS*, some of the most beloved songs from these films were used repeatedly at moments to create affective intensity: *Pehla Pehla Pyar Hai* ('It's First Love') from *HAHK* and *Mehendi Laga ke Rakhna, Doli Saja ke Rakhna* ('Decorate Your Hands, Keep the Palanquin Ready') from *DDLJ*, as well as from other films known for their extravagant sets, costumes and melodramatic scenes. Film songs also played a key role in underscoring certain ritual moments on the show, as when Rakhi played pre-wedding games with each of the contestants, or when she performed *karvachauth* (fast for the husband's long life) for her potential grooms. Popular songs also provided the soundtrack to some of the tasks that the contestants had to perform as part of the competitive aspect of the reality show. Music was used as an extra-narrative element that helped to suture together ritual, festive and cinematic moments on television, intensifying the viewing experience. It is testimony to the success of the show that these ritual and intimate moments were the main focus of news reports on television and in print with the competition between the 'grooms' relegated to secondary consideration.

The richness of the visual experience also evoked (now all too familiar in both the family film and television soaps) themes of opulence and festivity around the ideal bourgeois north Indian wedding. *RKS* was filmed for the most part in Fatehgarh fort palace in the state of Rajasthan, known for tales of love and valour associated with the Rajputs and a popular wedding and honeymoon destination. In keeping with Rakhi's desire to marry like a princess, her clothing and jewellery exceeded $200,000 in the making. Through the extravagant sets, clothes and accessories, the show nurtured a form of pleasure that arises from the desire to consume; what Patricia Uberoi has called 'being witness to a spectacle of unlimited consumption'.[28] The voyeuristic fantasy of the great Indian wedding was translated on to the television screen through romantic architecture and contemporary fashion. The palace was captured in daylight as well as at night to highlight the charm of the location as a marriage and honeymoon destination, and famous designers made Rakhi's wedding outfits and jewellery, discussions on which constituted whole episodes during the show. *RKS* was about 'nurturing the social and material aspirations of one class, while providing wholesome fantasy of married bliss for all',[29] coming together simultaneously as a product (the destination wedding), fantasy (the princess in the myth) and value (the ideal of the Indian family).

RKS drew on the rich televisual world of soap operas to create a fictive kinship network around Rakhi, emulating the relationships that provide the structure of north Indian kinship necessary for a wedding. In keeping with Rakhi's claim that she was 'the media's daughter', iconic characters were drawn from some of the most popular soap operas since 2000, particularly *Kyunki Saas Bhi Kabhi Bahu Thi* ('Because a Mother-in-Law Was Once a Daughter-in-Law'), *Ghar Ek Mandir* ('The Home is a Temple'), *Kasautii Zindagi Kay* ('The Challenges of Life'), and *Kahani Ghar Ghar Ki* ('The Story of Every Home'). The production house behind the success of these shows, Balaji Telefilms, and their creative director, Ekta Kapoor, became synonymous with the *saas-bahu* (mother-in-law/

daughter-in-law) soap operas in the early 2000s, and their success spawned a number of others on rival channels eager to cash in on the success.

Relying on the intimate relationship that had grown between the serials and their audiences, NDTV Imagine brought some of the more enduring characters to perform the roles of Rakhi's natal kin. The host of the *swayamvar*, Ram Kapoor, had become a household face in the tele-serial *Ghar Ek Mandir*, and was referred to by the potential grooms as *bhai* (older brother). In episode 4, Kapoor's 'reel life' co-star and 'real-life' wife, Gautami, came on as Rakhi's *bhabi* (older brother's wife) to meet all the grooms and gently interrogate them as to their intentions of marriage. The importance of the *bhabi* relationship in north Indian kinship is a well-explored theme in traditional songs as well as in Hindi films and was underscored by its repeated evocation in subsequent episodes of the show. In episode 8, Sudha Shivpuri, Sakshi Tanwar, Rakshanda Khan and child actor Swini Khara – all of whom had been well-loved actors in Ekta Kapoor's soap operas – made appearances as members of Rakhi's *maika* (bride's natal kin). They represented three generations of the Indian joint family – father's mother/*dadi*, older brother's wife/*bhabi* and sister/friend of the bride. Swini, as the youngest, was seen in the role of the potential *saali* (wife's younger sister) to the grooms. Although all were known by their real or off-screen names, the character of Ba (mother) from *Kyunki Saas Bhi Kabhi Bahu Thi* had the same name in *RKS*. Their presence as Rakhi's natal kin was to help her take one of the most important decisions in a girl's life. As one of the potential grooms said when the grooms were told who the special guests on the episode were, 'It looks as though there will be a family function today.'[30] All of these characters, along with other serial stars, were prominent in the penultimate pre-wedding episode. This was dedicated to numerous pre-wedding rituals drawn from practices of the north Indian wedding made popular in films, such as *haldi* (purifying the bride with a turmeric paste), *mehendi* (decorative henna patterns on the bride's hands and feet) and the *sangeet* (wedding songs and dances by the bride's female kin and friends).

Significantly, Rakhi's fictive natal kin did not include a father. How-ever, the role of the bride-giver – the father, or in his absence, a brother – is crucial in Indian marriage and was not overlooked by NDTV Imagine. The Bhojpuri film star Ravi Kishen, who is also a close friend of Rakhi's and a fellow reality show star, played the role of father-brother.

His appearance on the show never coincided with or overlapped with any of Rakhi's female kin until the 'marriage day', a move which indicates that the creative heads of the channel might not have wanted to take the fictive nature of the kinship so far as to make it unbelievable. However, genre might be another way to think about this separation as well. The episodes with female 'kin' were rather light-hearted and full of games, foregrounding gossip, teasing and flirtatious interaction. With Rakhi's female kin the grooms discussed issues around relationships, trust and mutual emotional support. However, episodes with Ravi Kishen struck a serious, almost apprehensive note among the contestants and Rakhi. Kishen asked all the grooms questions that a father or older brother would ask about financial status, job security and age, as well as consulting an astrologer on the show to ascertain which of the potential grooms was the right match for Rakhi. He claimed that his questioning was necessary to obtain facts about the contestants. Even though Rakhi repeatedly said that she wasn't looking for a rich husband, since she was a 'self-made woman', the appropriateness of age, income and status of her future partner were concerns that were raised by the patriarch, so to speak. As far as gossip, storytelling and singing are considered women's genres, one might suggest that the ritual roles of Rakhi's fictive male and female kin were also divided on the basis of genres of performance.

Aside from being surrounded by her fictive kin, Rakhi herself espoused the virtues of the joint family fantasy more as the show progressed. In keeping with the international format of the wedding reality show, Rakhi visited the families of the last five 'grooms' before she made her shortlist of the final three. It was her aim to prove herself to be an ideal wife, daughter-in-law and mother, and she repeatedly told the mothers of the grooms that she saw herself as being the glue that kept the family together. Rakhi self-consciously modelled herself on the image of the same soap opera heroines that had been part of family viewing since 2000, shedding her filmic skin for an iconic, domestic image. While *RKS* followed the reality show format, it was produced more like a soap opera. Sharing certain elements from the recent soap genre on private television, the characters, the costumes and sets, the lavish locations and use of stirring music to detail key dramatic moments in the narrative, *RKS* nevertheless managed to appear novel to some viewers. As one viewer who was quoted in a newspaper poll on the show said, 'After being bored watching the same old stories on our serials over and over again, everything about this seems new.'[31] Most of

all, the success of the show rested on its family appeal. Through her
swayamvar, Rakhi had achieved a new high in her career, what one
commentator called a kind of 'mythical reality'.[32] At the same time,
this transformation of Rakhi's character was not a complete one – not
only did she end up not marrying the winner of the show, but starred in
Pati, Patni, aur Woh with her chosen groom/partner, during which she
orchestrated their break-up. She retained the outspoken aspects of her
personality that have always made her good television material. She
promoted herself as the image of the an ideal wife, daughter-in-law and
mother while remaining unapologetic about her background in the
entertainment industry or the fact that she planned to continue as a
dancer, attempting the merging of an idealized domestic fantasy with
the image of a modern and self-made working woman. In her first
interview after the show had been telecast, she claimed that she had
wanted to orchestrate a new history, where girls would be able to choose
their own partners.[33] She did not apologize for her image as a sex
symbol, but attempted to merge it with an image of televised domesticity; therein lay the draw of the show. This gamble was precisely what
made the show so popular among viewers and thus a success for NDTV
Imagine, giving them their highest television ratings since their launch
in 2008. The success of the show depended on the audacity of the
merging of the sex symbol with the *ghar ki lakshmi* (treasure of the
home), not the sublimation of the former in the latter, nor any complete
realization of this merge. Its very attempt offered a spectacle on television that could be counted as novel.

The aim of this chapter was to show how a controversial film actress
sought to be remade in the image of respectability for television in a
newly emerging genre – the marriage reality show. This respectability
was cultivated by drawing on iconic images of the family from popular
culture and ritual contexts, which would immediately resonate with
audiences. But at the same time, the incommensurate nature of the two
images that Rakhi was cast in, by her own cultivation, her critics, or
both, rendered this respectability somewhat duplicitous, which itself
became the draw for its audience. By drawing on other familiar genres
of storytelling and performance, Rakhi's 'wedding' should not be
understood as merely the representation of the family as a value, but
as an intensely multi-sensory experience of an intimate, emotional and
family-oriented affair. Precisely this 'realness' of the show was what
produced discomfort for critics who could not reconcile her sexuality

with the image of wholesome family entertainment. Seen alongside *Sach Ka Samna* and *Pati, Patni, aur Woh*, which had become controversial for bringing the intimacies of the family into the format of the reality show, *RKS* produced the 'real' family itself as the object of voyeurism.

Notes

1 Fieldwork for this project has been made possible by a generous doctoral dissertation grant from the Wenner-Gren Foundation.

2 Ambika Soni with Deepak Chaurasiya on *Jo Bhi Kahunga Sach Kahunga* ('I Will Speak The Truth'), Star News, 8 November 2009.

3 Kamal Akhtar (MP) during Rajya Sabha Proceedings, 22 July 2009.

4 P. C. Joshi, *An Indian Personality for Television. Report of the Working Group on Software for Doordarshan* (New Delhi: Publications Division, Ministry of Information and Broadcasting, 1985), p. 16.

5 Sevanti Ninan, *Through the Magic Window: Television and Change in India* (New Delhi: Penguin Books, 1995), p. 147.

6 Arvind Rajagopal, *Politics after Television: Hindu Nationalism and the Reshaping of the Public in India* (Cambridge University Press, 2001), p. 124.

7 P. S. Deodhar, *The Third Parent: Growth and Development of Indian Electronics Media* (New Delhi: Vikas Publishing House, 1976), pp. 91–3.

8 Rajagopal, *Politics after Television*, p. 128.

9 Joshi, *An Indian Personality*, pp. 108–9.

10 Deodhar, *The Third Parent*, p. 93.

11 Joshi, *An Indian Personality*, p. 165.

12 *Ibid.*, p. 179.

13 Centre for Advocacy and Research (CFAR) website www.cfar.org.in/mediaadvocacy.aspx accessed 15 November 2009 and CFAR, 'Contemporary Woman in Television Fiction: Deconstructing the Role of "Commerce" and "Tradition"', *Economic and Political Weekly*, 26 April 2003, pp. 1684–90.

14 NDTV Imagine press release for *Rakhi ka Swayamvar*, www.ndtvimagine.com/about/mediacenter/pressroom/allpresscontent.php?press_id=160 accessed August 2009.

15 Saurabh Dwivedi, '*Bala ki Baalaa*' ('Burden or Beauty'), *Navbharat Times*, 5 July 2009.

16 *Sindoor* is the red powder that the groom puts on the bride's forehead. It is a potent symbol of marriage in visual representations of the Hindu wife.

17 NDTV Imagine television promo for *RKS*.

18 Rashtriya Sahara, '*Swayamvar mein Kohinoor Chunengi Rakhi Sawant*' ('Rakhi Sawant Will Choose Her Gem Through a *Swayamvar*'), 12 April 2009.

19 Haribhoomi, '*Rakhi Rachengi Swayamvar*' ('Rakhi Conducts Her Search for a Groom'), 9 April 2009.

20 Dainik Bhaskar, '*Mein Media Ki Beti Hun*' ('I Am the Media's Daughter'), 18 April 2009.

21 NDTV Imagine press release.

22 *Navbharat Times*, '*Na Patni Ke Lakshan, Na Bahu Ke*' ('Neither Wifely Characteristics, Nor Those Of A Daughter-in-Law'), 16 May 2009.

23 Laura Mulvey, 'Visual Pleasure and Narrative Cinema', in Constance Penley (ed.), *Feminism and Film Theory* (New York: Routledge, 1988), pp. 67–8.

24 Steve Derné and Lisa Jadwin, 'Male Hindi Filmgoers' Gaze: An Ethnographic Interpretation', *Contributions to Indian Sociology* 34 (2000), pp. 243–69.

25 Ira Bhaskar and Richard Allen, *The Islamicate Culture of Bombay Cinema* (New Delhi: Tulika Books, 2009), p. 48.

26 Punjab Kesri, '*Imandari se Jeevansaathi Talash Rahi Hun: Rakhi Sawant*' ('Rakhi Sawant Says She Is Sincerely Looking For Her Life Partner'), 2 July 2009.

27 Patricia Uberoi, 'Imagining the Family: An Ethnography of Viewing *Hum Apke Hain Kaun ...!*', in *Freedom and Destiny: Gender, Family, and Popular Culture in India* (New Delhi: Oxford University Press, 2006), p. 140.

28 *Ibid.*, p. 164.

29 P. Uberoi, 'Aspirational Weddings: The Bridal Magazine and Canons of "Decent Marriage"', in Christophe Jaffrelot and Peter van der Veer (eds.), *Patterns of Middle Class Consumption in India and China* (New Delhi: Sage, 2008), p. 255.

30 Episode 8, *RKS*, 8 July 2009.

31 Dainik Bhaksar, 12 July 2009.

32 Saurabh Dwivedi, *Navbharat Times*, 5 July 2009.

33 Rakhi Sawant with Prabhu Chawla on 'Seedhi Baat' ('Straight Talk'), *Aaj Tak*, 3 August 2009.

Further reading

Introduction

Breckenridge, Carol (ed.), *Consuming Modernity: Public Culture in a South Asian World*. Minneapolis: University of Minnesota Press, 1995.

Chakrabarty, Dipesh, *Provincializing Europe: Postcolonial Thought and Historical Difference*. Princeton University Press, 2000.

Deshpande, Satish, *Contemporary India: a Sociological View*. New Delhi: Penguin Books, 2003.

Guha, Ranajit, 'Dominance without Hegemony: History and Power in Colonial India', *Subaltern Studies*, vol. VIII, ed. David Arnold and David Hardiman. Oxford University Press, 1994.

Kaviraj, Sudipta, *The Imaginary Institution of India: Politics and Ideas*. New York: Columbia University Press, 2010.

Khilnani, Sunil, *The Idea of India*. London: Hamish Hamilton, 1997.

Nandy, Ashis, *The Intimate Enemy: Loss and Recovery of Self Under Colonialism*. New York: Oxford University Press, 1983.

Rao, Velcheru Narayana, David Shulman and Sanjay Subrahmanyam, *Textures of Time: Writing History in South India 1600–1800*. New York: Other Press, 2003.

Chapter 1: Scenes of rural change

Deshpande, Satish, 'Modernization', in Veena Das (ed.), *The Oxford India Companion to Sociology and Social Anthropology*. New Delhi: Oxford University Press, 2003, vol. I, pp. 63–98.

Gold, Ann Grodzins, 'Tasteless Profits and Vexed Moralities: Assessments of the Present in Rural Rajasthan', *Journal of the Royal Anthropological Institute* 15 (2009), pp. 365–85.

Gupta, Akhil, *Postcolonial Developments: Agriculture in the Making of Modern India*. Durham, NC: Duke University Press, 1998.

Harriss-White, Barbara and S. Janakarajan (eds.), *Rural India Facing the 21st Century: Essays on Long Term Village Change and Recent Development Policy*. London: Anthem Press, 2004.

Mines, Diane and Nicolas Yazgi (eds.), *Village Matters: Relocating Villages in the Contemporary Anthropology of India*. Delhi: Oxford University Press, 2010.

Roy, Ramashray and R. K. Srivastava, *Dialogues on Development: the Individual, Society, and the Political Order*. New Delhi: Sage Publications, 1986.

Sivaramakrishnan, K. and Arun Agrawal (eds.), *Regional Modernities: The Cultural Politics of Development in India*. Stanford University Press, 2003.

Srinivas, M. N., 'Modernisation', in Romesh Thapar (ed.), *Change and Conflict in India*. New Delhi: Macmillan Company of India, 1978, pp. 119–29.

Vasavi, A. R., *Harbingers of Rain: Land and Life in South India*. New Delhi: Oxford University Press, 1999.

Wadley, Susan S., 'The Village in 1998', *Behind Mud Walls: Seventy-five Years in a North Indian Village*. Berkeley: University of California Press, 2000, pp. 319–38.

Chapter 2: The formation of tribal identities

Abbi, Anvita, *Languages of Tribal and Indigenous Peoples of India: The Ethnic Space*. New Delhi: Motilal Banarsidass, 1997.

Baruah, Sanjib, 'The Nationalisation of Space: Cosmetic Federalism and the Politics of Development in Northeast India', *Development and Culture* 34:5 (2003), pp. 915–39.

Béteille, André, 'The Concept of Tribe with Special Reference to India', *Society and Politics in India*. London: Athlone Press, 1991 (1986), pp. 57–78.

Fürer-Haimendorf, Christoph von, *Tribal Populations and Cultures of the Indian Subcontinent*. Cologne: Brill, 1985.

Singh, K. S., *Tribal Society in India: An Anthropo-historical Perspective*. New Delhi, Manohar, 1985.

Triosi, J., *Tribal Religion: Religious Beliefs and Practices among the Santals*. New Delhi, Manohar, 2000.

Xaxa, Virginius, 'Tribes in India', in Veena Das (ed.), *The Oxford India Companion to Sociology and Social Anthropology*. New Delhi: Oxford Univesity Press, 2002, pp. 373–408.

Chapter 3: Food and agriculture

Achaya, K. T., *Indian Food: A Historical Companion*. New Delhi: Oxford University Press, 1994.

A Historical Dictionary of Indian Food. New Delhi: Oxford University Press, 1998.

Alter, Joseph S., *Gandhi's Body: Sex, Diet, and the Politics of Nationalism*. Philadelphia: University of Pennsylvania Press, 2000.

Appadurai, Arjun, 'How to Make a National Cuisine: Cookbooks in Contemporary India'. *Comparative Studies in Society and History* 30:1 (1981), pp. 3–24.

'Gastro-politics in Hindu South Asia', *American Ethnologist* 8:3 (1981), pp. 494–511.

Banerji, Chitrita, *Feeding the Gods: Memories of Food and Culture in Bengal*. Calcutta: Seagull Books, 2006.

Caplan, Pat, 'Food in Middle-Class Madras Households from the 1970s to 1990s', in Kataryza Cwiertka with Boudewijn Walraven (eds.), *Asian Food: The Global and the Local*. Richmond: Curzon, 2002, pp. 46–62.

Khare, R. S. (ed.), *The Eternal Food: Gastronomic Ideas and Experiences of Hindus and Buddhists*. Albany: State University of New York Press, 1992.

Khare, R. S. and M. S. A. Rao (eds.), *Food, Society and Culture: Aspects in South Asian Food Systems*. Durham, NC: Carolina Academic Press, 1986.

Osella, Caroline and Filippo Osella (eds.), *Food: Memory, Pleasure and Politics*, special issue of *South Asia: Journal of South Asian Studies* n. s., 31:1 (2008).

Zimmerman, Francis, *The Jungle and the Aroma of Meats: An Ecological Theme in Hindu Medicine*. Berkeley: University of California Press, 1987.

Chapter 4: Urban forms of religious practice

Flueckiger, J. B., *In Amma's Healing Room: Gender & Vernacular Islam in South India*. Bloomington: Indiana University Press, 2006.

Hancock, M. and S. Srinivas, 'Spaces of Modernity: Religion and the Urban in Asia and Africa', *International Journal of Urban and Regional Research* 32:3 (2008), pp. 617–30.

Heitzman, J., *The City in South Asia*. London and New York: Routledge, 2008.

Heitzman, J. and S. Srinivas, 'Warrior Goddess Versus Bipedal Cow: Sport, Space, Performance and Planning in an Indian City', in James Mills (ed.), *Subaltern Sports: Politics and Sport in South Asia*. London: Anthem Press, 2005, pp. 139–71.

Kumar, N., *The Artisans of Banaras: Popular Culture and Identity, 1880–1986*. Princeton University Press, 1988.

Ring, L., *Zenana: Everyday Peace in a Karachi Apartment Building*. Bloomington: Indiana University Press, 2006.

Srinivas, S., *Landscapes of Urban Memory: The Sacred and the Civic in India's High-Tech City*. Minneapolis: University of Minnesota Press, 2001.

'Cities of the Past and Cities of the Future: Theorizing the Indian Metropolis of Bangalore', in J. Eade and C. Mele (eds.), *Understanding the City: Contemporary and Future Perspectives*. Oxford: Blackwell, 2002, pp. 247–77.

In the Presence of Sai Baba: Body, City, and Memory in a Global Religious Movement. Leiden and Boston: Brill and Hyderabad: Orient Longman, 2008.

Waghorne, J. P., *Diaspora of the Gods: Modern Hindu Temples in an Urban Middle-Class World*. New York: Oxford University Press, 2004.

Werbner, P., *Pilgrims of Love: The Anthropology of a Global Sufi Cult*. Bloomington and Indianapolis: Indiana University Press, 2003.

Chapter 5: The politics of caste identities

Bayly, S., *The New Cambridge History of India, IV. 3, Caste, Society and Politics in India from the Eighteenth Century to the Modern Age*. Cambridge University Press, 1999.

Dirks, Nicholas, *Castes of Mind. Colonialism and the Making of Modern India*. Princeton University Press, 2001.

Galanter, M., *Competing Equalities – Law and the Backward Classes in India*. New Delhi: Oxford University Press (1984), 1991.

Geetha V. and S. V. Rajadurai, *Towards a Non-Brahmin Millennium. From Iyothee Thass to Periyar*. Calcutta: Samya, 1998.

Gore, M. S., *Non-Brahman Movement in Maharashtra*. New Delhi: Segment Books, 1989.

Jaffrelot, C., *India's Silent Revolution. The Rise of the Lower Castes in North Indian Politics*. New York: Columbia University Press, 2003.

Shah, G., *Caste Association and Political Process in Gujarat*. Bombay: Popular Prakashan, 1975.
Srinivas, M. N., *Social Change in Modern India*. New Delhi: Orient Longman, 1995.

Chapter 6: The Bengali novel

Blackburn, Stuart and Vasudha Dalmia, *India's Literary History: Essays on the Nineteenth Century*. New Delhi: Permanent Black, 2004.
Chakrabarty, Dipesh, *Provincializing Europe: Postcolonial Thought and Historical Difference*. Princeton University Press, 2007.
Clark, T. W., ed., *The Novel in India: Its Birth and Development*. Berkeley: University of California Press, 1970.
Das, Sisir Kumar. *A History of Indian Literature. Vol. VIII. 1800–1910. Western Impact: Indian Response*. New Delhi: Sahitya Akademi, 1991.
    A History of Indian Literature. Vol. IX. 1911–1956. Struggle for Freedom: Triumph and Tragedy. New Delhi: Sahitya Akademi, 1995.
Jameson, Fredric, *The Political Unconscious: Narrative as a Socially Symbolic Act*. London: Routledge, 1989.
Kaviraj, Sudipta, *The Unhappy Consciousness: Bankimchandra Chattopadhyay and the Formation of Nationalist Discourse in India*. New Delhi: Oxford University Press, 1995.
Mukherjee, Meenakshi, *Realism and Reality: The Novel and Society in India*. New Delhi: Oxford University Press, 1985.
    ed., *Early Novels in India*. New Delhi: Sahitya Akademi, 2002.
Pollock, Sheldon, ed., *Literary Cultures in History: Reconstructions from South Asia*. New Delhi: Oxford University Press, 2004.
Rajan, P. K., ed., *The Growth of the Novel in India, 1950–1980*. New Delhi: Abhinav Publications, 1989.

Chapter 7: Writing in English

Ahmad, Aijaz, *In Theory: Nations, Classes, Literatures*. London: Verso, 1991.
Chaudhuri, Amit, ed., *The Picador Book of Modern Indian Literature*. London: Picador, 2001.
Devy, G. N., *In Another Tongue: Essays on Indian English Literature*. London: Peter Lang Publishing, 1993.
Dharwadkher, Vinay, 'The Historical Formation of Indian-English Literature', in Sheldon Pollock (ed.), *Literary Cultures in History: Reconstructions from South Asia*. Berkeley: University of California Press, 2003.
Gandhi, Leela, *Postcolonial Theory: A Critical Introduction*. New York: Columbia University Press, 1998.
Iyengar, K. R. Srinivasa, *Indian Writing in English*. London: Sterling Publishers, 1994.
Joshi, Svati, ed., *Rethinking English: Essays in Literature, Language, History*. New Delhi: Trianka, 1991.
Khair, Tabish, *Babu Fictions: Alienation in Contemporary Indian English Novels*. New Delhi: Oxford University Press, 2001.
Mehrotra, Arvind Krishna, ed., *A Concise History of Indian English Literature*. Ranikhet: Permanent Black, 2008/Palgrave Macmillan, 2009.

Mukherjee, Meenakshi, *The Perishable Empire: Essays on Indian Writing in English*. New Delhi: Oxford University Press, 2000.

Rushdie, Salman and Elizabeth West, eds., *The Vintage Book of Indian Writing, 1947–1997*. London: Vintage, 1997.

Sadana, Rashmi, *English Heart, Hindi Heartland: The Political Life of Literature in India*. Berkeley: University of California Press, 2012.

Sunder Rajan, Rajeswari, *The Lie of the Land: English Literary Studies in India*. New Delhi: Oxford University Press, 1992.

Chapter 8: Dalit life stories

Bhave, Sumitra, 'Pan on Fire: Eight Dalit Women Tell their Stories', in Anupama Rao (ed.), *Gender and Caste*. New Delhi: Kali for Women, 2003, pp. 114–28.

Das, Sisir Kumar, 'Narratives of Suffering: Caste and the Underprivileged', in Tapan Basu (ed.), *Translating Caste*. New Delhi: Katha, 2002, pp. 150–80.

Deo, Veena, 'Dalit Literature in Marathi', in Nalini Natarajan (ed.), *The Handbook of Twentieth Century Literatures in India*. London: Greenwood Press, 1996, pp. 363–81.

Ganguly, Debjani, 'Of Urban Dystopias and New Gods: Readings from Marathi Dalit Literature', *Caste, Colonialism and Counter-Modernity*. London, Routledge, 2005.

Limbale, Sharan Kumar, *Towards an Aesthetic of Dalit Literature: Histories, Controversies, Considerations*, trans. Alok Mukherjee. New Delhi: Orient Longman, 2004.

Nayar, Pramod, 'Bama's *Karukku*: Dalit Autobiography as Testimonio', *Journal of Commonwealth Literature* 41:2 (2003), pp. 83–100.

Pandian, M. S. S., 'On a Dalit Woman's Testimonio', in Anupama Rao (ed.), *Gender and Caste*. New Delhi: Kali for Women, 2003, pp. 129–35.

Punalekar, S. P., 'Dalit Literature and Identity', in Ghanshyam Shah (ed.), *Dalit Identity and Politics*. New Delhi: Sage Publications, 2001, pp. 214–41.

Racine, Jean-Luc and Josiane, 'Dalit Identities and the Dialectic of Oppression and Emancipation in a Changing India: The Tamil Case and Beyond', *Comparative Studies in South Asia, Africa and the Middle East* 18:1 (1998), pp. 5–19.

Rege, Sharmila, *Writing Caste/Writing Gender: Narrating Dalit Women's Testimonios*. New Delhi: Zubaan, 2006.

Chapter 9: National tradition and modernist art

Brown, Rebecca M., *Art for a Modern India, 1947–1980*. Durham, NC: Duke University Press, 2009.

Dalmia, Yashodhara, *The Making of Modern Indian Art: the Progressives*. New Delhi and New York: Oxford University Press, 2001.

   Amrita Sher-Gil: A Life. New Delhi: Penguin Viking, 2006.

Guha-Thakurta, Tapati, *The Making of an 'Indian' Art: Artists, Aesthetics and Nationalism in Bengal, c. 1850–1920*. Cambridge University Press, 1992.

Hyman, Timothy, *Bhupen Khakhar*. Bombay: Chemould, 1998.

Kapur, Geeta, *Contemporary Indian Artists*. New Delhi: Vikas, 1978.

When was Modernism: Essays on Contemporary Cultural Practice in India. New Delhi: Tulika, 2000.

Mitter, Partha, *Art and Nationalism in Colonial India, 1850–1922: Occidental Orientations*. Cambridge University Press, 1994.

The Triumph of Modernism: Indian Artists and the Avant-Garde, 1922–1947. London: Reaktion, 2007.

Panikkar, Shivji, *et al.* (eds.), *Towards a New Art History: Studies in Indian Art*. New Delhi: D. K. Printworld, 2003.

Siva Kumar, R., *K. G. Subramanyan: A Retrospective*. New Delhi: National Gallery of Modern Art, 2003.

Subramanyan, K. G., *The Living Tradition: Perspectives on Modern Indian Art*. Calcutta: Seagull, 1987.

'The Image in the Indian Art Tradition', in Gulam Mohammed Sheikh (ed.), *Moving Focus: Essays on Indian Art*. First edn 1978. New Delhi: Lalit Kala Akademi, 2006.

Sundaram, Vivan (ed.), *Amrita Sher-gil: Essays*. Bombay: Marg, 1972.

Tuli, Nevile, *The Flamed Mosaic: Indian Contemporary Painting*. Middletown, NJ and Ahmedabad: Heart and Mapin, 1997.

Chapter 10: Mass reproduction and the art of the bazaar

Davis, Richard (ed.), *Picturing the Nation: Iconographies of Modern India*. New Delhi: Orient Longman, 2007.

Guha-Thakurta, Tapati, *The Making of a New 'Indian' Art: Artists, Aesthetics and Nationalism in Bengal, c. 1850–1920*. Cambridge University Press, 1992.

Jain, Jyotindra, *Indian Popular Culture: The Conquest of the World as Picture*. New Delhi: National Gallery of Modern Art, 2004.

Jain, Kajri, *Gods in the Bazaar: The Economies of Indian Calendar Art*. Durham, NC: Duke University Press, 2007.

Kapur, Geeta, 'Ravi Varma: Representational Dilemmas of a Nineteenth Century Indian Painter' and 'Revelation and Doubt: Sant Tukaram and Devi' in *When Was Modernism: Essays on Contemporary Cultural Practice in India*. New Delhi: Tulika, 2001, pp. 145–78 and 233–64.

Pinney, Christopher, *Camera Indica: The Social Lives of Indian Images*. London: Reaktion Books, 1997.

'Photos of the Gods': The Printed Image and Political Struggle in India. London: Reaktion Books, 2004.

Rajadhyaksha, Ashish, 'The Phalke Era: Conflict of Traditional Form and Modern Technology', in Tejaswini Niranjana, P. Sudhir, Vivek Dhareshwar (eds.), *Interrogating Modernity: Culture and Colonialism in India*. Calcutta: Seagull Books, 1993, pp. 47–82.

Ramaswamy, Sumathi, *The Goddess and the Nation: Mapping Mother India*. Durham, NC: Duke University Press, 2010.

(ed.), *Beyond Appearances: Visual Practices and Ideologies in Modern India*. New Delhi: Sage, 2003.

Uberoi, Patricia, 'Feminine Identity and National Ethos in Calendar Art', in Patricia Uberoi (ed.), *Freedom and Destiny: Gender, Family, and Popular Culture in India*. New Delhi: Oxford University Press, 2006, pp. 48–68.

Chapter 11: Urban theatre and the turn towards 'folk'

Bharucha, Rustom, *Rehearsals of Revolution: The Political Theater of Bengal*. Honolulu: University of Hawaii Press, 1983.

Bhatia, Nandi, ed., *Modern Indian Theatre: A Reader*. New Delhi: Oxford University Press, 2009.

Dalmia, Vasudha, *Poetics, Plays, and Performances: The Politics of Modern Indian Theatre*. New Delhi: Oxford University Press, 2006.

Dharwadker, Aparna Bhargava, *Theatres of Independence: Drama, Theory, and Urban Performance in India since 1947*. Iowa City: University of Iowa Press, 2005.

Gokhala, Shanta, *Playwright at the Centre: Marathi Drama from 1843 to the Present*. Calcutta: Seagull Books, 2000.

Gupt, Somnath, *The Parsi Theatre; Its Origins and Development*, trans. and ed. Kathryn Hansen. Calcutta: Seagull Books, 2005.

Hansen, Kathryn, *Grounds for Play: The Nautanki Theatre of North India*. Berkeley: University of California Press, 1992.

Kapur, Anuradha, *Actors, Pilgrims, Kings and Gods: The Ramlila at Ramnagar*. Calcutta: Seagull Books, 1990.

Lal, Ananda, ed., *The Oxford Companion to Indian Theatre*. New Delhi: Oxford University Press, 2004.

Richmond, Farley, P., Darius L. Swann and Phillip B. Zarrilli, eds., *Indian Theatre: Traditions of Performance*. New Delhi: Motilal Banarasidass, 1993 (University of Hawaii Press, 1990).

Chapter 12: Aesthetics and politics in popular cinema

Kapur, Geeta, 'Mythic Material in Indian Cinema', *Journal of Arts and Ideas* 14–15 (1987), pp. 79–108; reprinted as 'Revelation and Doubt: Sant Tukaram and Devi', in Tejaswini Niranjana, *et al.* (eds.), *Interrogating Modernity*. Calcutta: Seagull Books, 1993, pp. 19–46.

Majumdar, Neepa, *Wanted Cultural Ladies Only: Female Stardom in India 1930s–1940s*. Chicago: University of Illinois Press, 2009.

Mazumdar, Ranjani, *Bombay Cinema: An Archive of the City*. Minneapolis: University of Minnesota Press, 2007.

Pines, Jim and Paul Willemen, *Questions of Third Cinema*. London: British Film Institute, 1989.

Prasad, Madhava, *Ideology of the Hindi Film: A Historical Reconstruction*. London and New York: Oxford University Press, 2001.

Rajadhyaksha, Ashish, 'The Phalke Era: Conflict of Traditional Form and Modern Technology', *Journal of Art and Ideas* 14–15 (1987), reprinted in Tejaswini Niranjana *et al.*, eds., *Interrogating Modernity*. Calcutta: Seagull, 1993, pp. 47–82.

Indian Cinema in the Time of Celluloid: From Bollywood to the Emergency. Bloomington: Indiana University Press, 2009.

Vasudevan, Ravi, 'Andaz', in Lalitha Gopalan (ed.), *Cinema of India*. London: Wallflower Press, 2009, pp. 56–65.

The Melodramatic Public. New York: Palgrave Macmillan, 2011.

ed., *Making Meaning in Indian Cinema*, New Delhi: Oxford University Press, 2000.

Chapter 13: Musical genres and national identity

Bakhle, Janaki, *Two Men and Music: Nationalism in the Making of an Indian Classical Tradition*. New York: Oxford University Press, 2005.

Booth, Greg, 'That Bollywood Sound', in Mark Slobin (ed.), *Global Soundtracks: Worlds of Film Music*. Middletown, CT: Wesleyan University Press, 2008, pp. 85–113.

Getter, Joseph and B. Balasubramaniyan, 'Tamil Film Music: Sound and Significance', in Mark Slobin (ed.), *Global Soundtracks: Worlds of Film Music*. Middletown, CT: Wesleyan University Press, 2008, pp. 114–51.

Gopal, Sangita and Sujata Moorti, eds., *Global Bollywood: Travels of Hindi Song and Dance*. Minneapolis: University of Minnesota Press, 2008.

Guy, Randor, *Starlight, Starbright: The Early Tamil Cinema*. Chennai: Amra Publishers, 1997.

Lelyveld, David, 'Upon the Subdominant: Administering Music on All-India Radio', in Carol Breckenridge (ed.), *Consuming Modernity: Public Culture in a South Asian World*. Minneapolis: University of Minnesota Press, 1995, pp. 49–65.

Srivastava, Sanjay, 'The Voice of the Nation and the Five-Year Plan Hero'. *Fingerprinting Popular Culture: The Mythic and the Iconic in Indian Cinema*. New Delhi: Oxford University Press, 2006, pp. 122–55.

Subramanian, Lakshmi, *From the Tanjore Court to the Madras Music Academy: A Social History of Music in South India*. New Delhi: Oxford University Press, 2006.

Weidman, Amanda, *Singing the Classical, Voicing the Modern: The Postcolonial Politics of Music in South India*. Durham, NC: Duke University Press, 2006.

Chapter 14: Voyeurism and the family on television

Butcher, Melissa, *Transnational Identity, Cultural Identity and Change: When Star Came to India*. New Delhi: Sage Publications, 2003.

Das, Veena, 'On Soap Opera: What Kind Of Anthropological Object Is It?' in D. Miller (ed.), *Worlds Apart: Modernity Through the Prism of the Local*. New York: Routledge, 1995, pp. 169–89.

Derné, Steve, *Globalisation on the Ground: Media and the Transformation of Culture, Class, and Gender in India*. New Delhi: Sage Publications, 2008.

Mankekar, Purnima, *Screening Culture, Viewing Politics: An Ethnography of Television, Womanhood, and Nation in Postcolonial India*. Durham, NC: Duke University Press, 1999.

Mazzarella, William, *Shoveling Smoke: Advertising and Globalization in Contemporary India*. Durham, NC: Duke University Press, 2003.

Mehta, Nalin, *India on Television: How Satellite News Channels Have Changed the Way We Think and Act*. New Delhi: Harper Collins, 2008.

  ed., *Television in India: Satellites, Politics, and Cultural Change*. New York: Routledge, 2008.

Munshi, Shoma, *Prime Time Soaps on Indian Television*. New Delhi: Taylor and Francis, 2009.

Page, David and William Crawley, *Satellites over South Asia: Broadcasting Culture and the Public Interest*. New Delhi: Sage Publications, 2001.

Singhal, Arvind and Everett Rogers, *Entertainment-Education: A Communication Strategy for Social Change*. Mahwah, NJ: Lawrence Erlbaum Associates, 1999.

  India's Communication Revolution: From Bullock Carts to Cyber Marts. New Delhi: Sage Publications, 2001.

Index

Cambridge Companions to Culture

The Cambridge Companion to Modern American Culture
Edited by CHRISTOPHER BIGSBY

The Cambridge Companion to Modern British Culture
Edited by MICHAEL HIGGINS, CLARISSA SMITH *and* JOHN STOREY

The Cambridge Companion to Modern Indian Culture
Edited by VASUDHA DALMIA *and* RASHMI SADANA

The Cambridge Companion to Modern Irish Culture
Edited by JOE CLEARY *and* CLAIRE CONNOLLY

The Cambridge Companion to Modern Latin American Culture
Edited by JOHN KING

The Cambridge Companion to Modern French Culture
Edited by NICHOLAS HEWITT

The Cambridge Companion to Modern Italian Culture
Edited by ZYGMUNT G. BARANSKI *and* REBECCA J. WEST

The Cambridge Companion to Modern German Culture
Edited by EVA KOLINSKY *and* WILFRIED VAN DER WILL

The Cambridge Companion to Modern Russian Culture
Edited by NICHOLAS RZHEVSKY

The Cambridge Companion to Modern Spanish Culture
Edited by DAVID GIES

The Cambridge Companion to Victorian Culture
Edited by FRANCIS O'GORMAN